MEDIEVAL ENGLISH POETRY

The Non-Chaucerian Tradition

by the same author

★

CHAUCER THE MAKER

THE SCOTS LITERARY TRADITION

POETRY TOWARDS NOVEL

MEDIEVAL ENGLISH POETRY

The Non-Chaucerian Tradition

by

JOHN SPEIRS

Sesonnez schal yow never sese of sede ne of hervest,
Ne hete, ne no harde forst, umbre ne droghte,
Ne the swetnesse of somer, ne the sadde wynter,
Ne the nyght, ne the day, ne the newe yerez,
Bot ever renne restlez.

CLEANNESS

FABER AND FABER

3 Queen Square

London

First published in 1957
by Faber and Faber Limited
3 Queen Square London W.C.1
Second impression 1966
First published in this edition 1971
Printed in Great Britain by
Latimer Trend & Co Ltd Whitstable

ISBN 0 571 06738 7 (Hard Bound Edition)
ISBN 0 571 09617 4 (Faber Paper Covered Edition)

For

RUTH and LOGAN

ACKNOWLEDGEMENTS

A considerable part of the substance of what was to form this book appeared first in *Scrutiny*—the essays on *Sir Gawayne and the Grene Knight* (1949), on *Wynnere and Wastoure* and the *Parlement of the Thre Ages* (1950) and on *The Mystery Cycle* (1951–52). *Scrutiny* itself has now passed into history, though its achievement stands. But it is a pleasure to be able to take this chance to acknowledge again my debt to F. R. Leavis, the great critic to whom my generation has owed so much. I have at the same time had the privilege of a stimulating correspondence with Q. D. Leavis on my specific subject-matter. My students at what is now the University of Exeter—and, indeed, a number of Cambridge and Oxford students—have also had some considerable part in the making of this book through their responsive interest. I have also had valued support from individual American scholars and critics, notably Stanley Hyman. Finally, I wish to acknowledge my debt to my wife for her understanding help; every change which she has suggested to me has been clear improvement. All the many faults that remain in the book are entirely my own.

JOHN SPEIRS

March 1957

CONTENTS

Contents

I

INTRODUCTION

I. INTRODUCTION

§ 1

This book was intended to carry on from *Chaucer the Maker*, the supposition being that one would wish to inquire whether Chaucer was, as might seem improbable, alone as an English poet and, if he was not, what the English poetry contemporary with his was like. It is evident from his poetry itself that he had French and Italian predecessors and contemporaries and that in some ways they formed the community of poets to which he belonged and knew himself to belong. But it does not appear to have been so much a matter for his conscious consideration that there was a contemporary poetry in English.

There *was*, however, an English poetry other than the Chaucerian; a portion of it has survived. What is surprising is the extent to which it is *not* like Chaucer's. But this non-Chaucerian poetry is not simply to be defined as exhibiting an absence of the Chaucerian qualities. It has positive qualities of its own; it constitutes a positive achievement comparable to, though different from, Chaucer's.

In order to form an idea of the nature and the value of this poetry the familiar—the too familiar—contrast between *Piers Plowman* and the *Canterbury Tales* needs to be extended into a larger, detailed comparison between the non-Chaucerian poetry as a whole and Chaucer. A knowledge of the one will sharpen one's sense of the other. Such a comparison can, however, be no simple one, if only because the non-Chaucerian poetry turns out to be not all of a piece but to be a diversity of individualities. Generalization—so often falsifying in its effect when brought to bear on literature, as on life—can be peculiarly unsafe and uncritical in relation to poems so different from one another. The task of defining the characteristics of the non-Chaucerian poetry as a whole can only be begun when a number of these poems are examined together. The present book can attempt only to be such a beginning and can offer in the end only a partial account. What has to be attempted is the *relevant* kind of beginning; and for medieval poetry, just as much as for the poetry of any other time, that can only be by way of some detailed criticism of individual poems.

If the greater part of the English poetry contemporary, or near-contemporary, with Chaucer proves to be non-Chaucerian that does not mean that there are no affinities and no connexions between the two. One of the things to discover is what these relations are—and what, if any, are the relations of the non-Chaucerian poetry with Chaucer's *great* successors, not the fifteenth-century Chaucerians, but Shakespeare and the later masters of English. Chaucer's poetry, though as English as the non-Chaucerian, stands out from it as in some ways belonging more with the contemporary European—French and Italian—poetry. Even when Chaucer's poetry is most English, as in the *Canterbury Tales*, when it has developed its maximum freedom from the French and Italian poetry, it is still different in important respects from the English poetry that preceded or was contemporary with it. It is different from both the Continental poetry and the other English poetry; in some ways it goes far beyond either.

The comparison between the non-Chaucerian poetry and Chaucer brings out the uniqueness of both, the remarkable originality of Chaucer and the distinctive features of the non-Chaucerian tradition. The two are in some ways complementary, and a knowledge of both is needed for any true sense of the total variety and range of medieval English poetry. Even if we subtract Chaucer there was still an English tradition—non-Chaucerian—which achieved some great things. It was, perhaps, as important a development towards the Shakespearian achievement and consequently towards later literature in English as was Chaucer's poetry.

Introduction

§ 2

The titles of poems are the chapter headings of this book because the poems themselves are the subject, the facts with which criticism is concerned. The study of literature has its appropriate discipline, that of literary criticism, which is therefore also the discipline appropriate to the study of medieval English poetry. It is essential to get it recognized and established as such, because 'medieval studies' have, as a consequence of its not being, suffered from a critical vagueness and slackness. They have too rarely been studies of poetry as such but nearly always of something else. The word 'medievalist' has acquired, not without some reason, a limiting suggestion as indicating one who is not *widely* read and, partly as a consequence, one whose judgement in literature would be likely to be naïve and unreliable, one who would not be able to know which are the best poems, and one who is remote from modern literature—and from life. To overcome these limitations the student of medieval literature would have to be essentially interested in literature itself and be widely read in literature other than medieval. No one is in a position to judge a work of literature who has not read (fully to have read means in such a case to have profoundly experienced) *Lear* or *Macbeth*. These things are our standards of greatness in literature. No one is in a position to judge a novel who has not read, for example, *Anna Karenina*. He could not otherwise know what a great novel is, what a novel is capable of. *Anna Karenina* is our standard, or one of our standards, of greatness in the novel. The judgement of one who has never experienced these and other greatest things in literature could not be trusted among medieval works either. Abstract standards, principles or criteria of judgement, however philosophically worked out, are of no practical utility in the realm of literary judgement; in relation to the actual experiencing of literature they are illusory. In such a realm *Lear* is our standard, *Anna Karenina* is our standard. One work of literature finds its place in relation to other works. It is a commonplace of criticism that when a new, a truly original work of literature appears it alters the whole standard, the standard

15

established by all the works of literature of the past. For that reason our standards can only be ours and not those of another century. No one who has not responded to modern literature, who has not found his bearings in the present, can be trusted therefore to find his way about with any certainty in medieval or any other litera~ ture of the past; it is correspondingly true that no one who has not responded to the best literature of the past, a wide range of that literature, can find his way with any certainty in modern literature. The best in medieval literature is an important part of the literature of the past, and we cannot therefore afford to be unacquainted with it, if for no other reason than that it is relevant to our sense of the present. The best contemporary standards—and no others, not those of any other century, can be active and actual in the present —are those formed by what the best contemporary readers have experienced of the accumulated literature of many centuries past and present.

The breaking~up of 'English studies' into a heterogeneity of specialisms therefore positively imperils the best standards. To try to take as wide and inclusive a view as is humanly possible when considering any one author or the authors of any one century should, on the contrary, be the ideal. The tendency, for example, to set as research in English some minor authors of a single decade or some matter of 'background', and to confine the reading to that, is bad for the researcher, if not stultifying also in its effect on his research, and bad for the whole study of English because it actually *prevents* the student from reading as widely as he might otherwise have done and from consorting to the extent he could otherwise have done with the best authors; at the end of his time he is as a consequence actually less well read than he could otherwise have been, and his experience of great literature less profound. The medievalist appears to be peculiarly prone to shutting himself in and cutting himself off from the main currents of literature as a whole, and medieval literary studies have undoubtedly suffered as a result of this kind of exclusiveness. Medievalists at present are, judging from the evidence, still too anxious and preoccupied to keep their studies safe from the literary critic. I cannot think that they do either themselves or their studies any real good by doing so. To insist that the scholar should be a critic, and the critic a scholar, seems rather what is needed. This book was therefore partly, or at least incidentally, conceived as a deliberate attempt (perhaps quixotic) to lift medieval English poetry out from the professional 'Middle English' specialism. Only by working on the assumption that there is still, potentially at least, an appeal open to a critical reading public interested in literature can any⁄thing be done to assist humane culture. Medieval literature cannot actually matter, cannot be made operative at the present time except—with the aid of literary criticism—to a critical reading public, a public for literature, however small; it could no longer be a reality if such a public should be extinct.

§ 3

The phrase 'non⁄Chaucerian tradition' is here intended to in⁄dicate a body of poetry—songs, plays, alliterative poems, romances —that was flourishing in the England of Chaucer. Every poet, of course, works in a tradition, Chaucer not least. If we are to describe this non⁄Chaucerian poetry as 'traditional' in that more limited sense in which the word is sometimes associated with 'anonymous' and 'oral', it should be recalled that the Homeric poems, as well as folk⁄songs and ballads, are also traditional in this same sense; it was not by any means simply a folk poetry. The whole of this poetry and also Chaucer's came at the end of long traditions of verse⁄making and story⁄telling in various languages, Northern and Mediterranean, and was the outcome of a collabora⁄tion between the poets, their predecessors and their audiences. The anonymous makers were also, in their way, artists even when engaged in no more than reshaping the poems—the songs, plays and romances—of their predecessors.

There is a sense in which the non⁄Chaucerian poetry may be set over against the Chaucerian as being at that time already an old⁄fashioned type of poetry. Though a Chaucer had appeared whose poetry, English and European, is a remarkable individual development, the age of minstrelsy was not yet entirely over. There was still a poetry intended for recital, for chanting or singing or semi-dramatic performance on festal or social occasions.[1]

Though Chaucer's poems, too, appear to have been designed to be listened to in a company, they are quite evidently written poetry, not simply written down, and the work of a lettered poet whose reading of poetry was in French, Italian and Latin. It is poetry designed to be read, whether or not read *aloud*. A further, perhaps consequent, difference is that a more personal note has entered; we are listening to a personal voice. The poet occasionally even presents himself, as a character, in his own poetry. Though Chaucer and a great part of the non-Chaucerian poetry have in common an energy of dramatic and objective presentation, we are aware also, in Chaucer's poetry, of the poet's presence as a subtly comic observer of the people and society he presents. It is one of the respects in which Chaucer strikes one as being already, in medieval English, a new, a more 'modern' type of author, although there had been, in this same respect, such poets before in earlier European civilization. Chaucer, for this reason, sometimes appears closer to the Latin Augustan and later poets, to Petrarch and Boccaccio, and to some of his French contemporaries than to the greater part of the English poetry contemporary with himself. He has in common with the English poetry, on the other hand, all that is implied in the fact that he is an English poet.

The error of endeavouring to regard the author of the *Canterbury Tales* as a member of a narrow, exclusive courtly circle with a rigid code, instead of as in the fullest sense an English poet, should not need correction. There could certainly be nothing exclusive about the author of that most comprehensive poem. If Chaucer belonged to such a circle he has transcended its exclusiveness. He had already done so (if indeed he ever needed to) in *Troilus and Criseyde*.

[1] Poetry of an earlier phase may exist contemporaneously with that of a later or new phase, as civilizations belonging to earlier and later phases may exist side by side. There have been social and cultural conditions in various places at various times when not only short poems but poems of epic length, and even longer, could be composed, carried in the memory and recited by professional minstrels (many of whom must have been makers as well as reciters) without the aid of writing. Professor Chadwick, in a note 'On the Heroic Poetry of the Slavonic Peoples' in *The Heroic Age*, describes such conditions as still existing in the Balkans in the early years of the present century.

For, although Criseyde and Pandarus, as well as Troilus, are certainly members of the courtly society, the poet penetrates to the living woman and the living man. But there is no evidence in Chaucer's poetry to lead us to suppose that his contemporary courtly society was itself narrowly exclusive. Certainly Chaucer's Canterbury pilgrims, though men and women of diverse social classes and professions, easily form a company—'a felawshipe'—united not simply in a transient common purpose but in an easy intimacy as they ride together talking, quarrelling and sharing one another's tales. This breadth and depth of humanity that shows itself in Chaucer's poetry as it develops into the *Canterbury Tales* is clearly related to the poet's increasingly full use of the resources of the spoken English of his time.

The greatest of the English poems contemporary with Chaucer's is, if not *Piers Plowman*, certainly *Sir Gawayne and the Grene Knight*. It is unmistakably a complete work of art, as *Piers Plowman* hardly is. It may not unreasonably be regarded as a poem of much the same traditional kind in English as the Homeric poems are in Greek. There must, one feels, have been an individual artist of genius, a single mind at work to have re-created his traditional material into so complete a masterpiece. But it is equally apparent that he has worked in a tradition that had been, at least until not long before his time, of the oral kind in which inherited material was shaped and re-shaped for successive recitals. The same may be said of the nature of most of the alliterative poetry which we may associate with this poem.

It is hard to see why a French romance (or group of romances) need be assumed to have existed in order to provide a French original for this particular English poem, or why effort should have to be expended on constructing a conjectural pedigree for it instead of concentrating on the poem we do have. There are of course very many French words in the vocabulary, as there were by that time in the spoken English, at least of the gentlefolk. But though some of the words may seem to have been taken directly from French poetry and are evidence that French romances were familiar, an argument from vocabulary need not by itself be conclusive. From the vocabulary of the poem, which is also full of

Norse words, we might equally well argue for an Old Norse original, possibly alliterative, as for a French original. The Norse words may well have also belonged to the spoken dialect of the region, where there had been Norse settlements. Some at least of the words may, on the other hand, have been carried down in the alliterative tradition itself from the earlier heroic poetry. The poem may have had French, Norse and Celtic ancestors.

The poet has, of course, had his sources. He has had, as the poem seems to me to show, a body of myth and ritual, tales and ceremonies that still meant something, was still an active feature of the life of his English community, in addition to his specifically English tradition of alliterative verse-making with its Old Norse as well as Anglo-Saxon connexions. This is not to deny that, being clearly a poet belonging to the 'noble' order, he could and did draw on the chivalric and courtly tradition embodied in the French romances and in the life of the noble order itself. Finally, it is not to deny that his whole poem has been modified by medieval Christianity, its theology, its feeling, morality, vision and symbolism. But he has used his sources as Shakespeare used his, as a great original artist. The poem does not look as though it was composed by a poet who sat down with an MS of a French romance in front of him which he then proceeded to translate, in writing, into English alliterative verse. He has obviously handled his various sources and materials with the largest freedom, with Shakespearian creativeness.[1]

[1] Incidentally, some lines near the beginning of the poem appear explicitly to refer to oral tradition and to live recital.

> I schal telle hit astit,* as I in toun herde, with tonge,
> As hit is stad and stoken
> In stori stif and stronge,
> With lel letteres loken,†
> In londe so hatz ben longe.

    * straightway.   † linked (i.e. alliterated).

'I shall recite it, as I heard it', he says, not 'as I read it'. On looking up Tolkien and Gordon's glossary, I note that 'stad' is explained as 'put down (in writing)' and 'stoken' as 'set down (in writing)'. It is true that 'in writing' is bracketed. But I can see no reason for the implication. All that the phrase 'stad and stoken' may be taken to mean is 'as it has been put together or composed'. Nor would the 'letteres' of two lines later necessarily mean written or visible letters rather than audible letters in an alliterative poetry that 'has long been the custum in the land'.

Nevertheless, the alliterative poet, comparable though he is to the Homeric or heroic poet of a noble order, differs (like the humble balladist) from the more modern kind of poet in that he worked in a highly conventionalized medium in which so many elements, both subject-matter and formal or stylistic elements, were 'given', were there before him, formulated, ready to hand. Yet the hand of the master when it shows, as it does pre-eminently in the finished achievement of *Sir Gawayne and the Grene Knight*, is instantly distinguishable from merely competent workmanship. Professor E. W. Tristram, in his *English Wall-Painting of the Fourteenth Century*, brings this out clearly in describing the traditional painting which he spent a lifetime in examining (if the analogy between the two arts of poetry and painting of the same period may be allowed). 'So uniform are the resulting formulae that through observation of large numbers of examples and constant practice in copying them, one may have the experience of "completing" a half-visible fragment, in the imagination, and then, on further search of the wall-surface and removal of obliterating lime-wash, of finding the remainder in the expected position. Conventions such as those we have just been discussing, when they were used by a painter who was merely competent, were helpful to him in practice; but the brush of a master informed them with a degree of life and expression that lies beyond the compass of all formulae in themselves.'[1]

Most of the English rhymed or stanzaic romances, though on the whole inferior to the alliterative poems, may also be described as art of this kind—to be distinguished, however, from traditional folk art, the art of the folk-ballads—the greater part of it little better than competent re-handlings of traditional material apparently for recital rather than for private reading. About half of the extant English medieval songs and lyrics, notably the carols, may also be described as traditional art in this sense, though only a very few can possibly be regarded as folk-songs. Most of them, including many of those that are specifically Christian, are in a humane—perhaps what may even be called a 'humanist'—tradition that in its modes of expression descends from some of the

[1] *English Wall-Painting of the Fourteenth Century*, I, p. 9.

early medieval Latin lyrics (such as the *Cambridge Songs*, which have been dated as early as the tenth century, and the *Carmina Burana*) and from the troubadour and early French lyrics of the twelfth century. In that respect they are closer to Chaucer's poetry than is the rest of the non-Chaucerian poetry. Finally, the Mystery Cycle is a huge collaborative work of several generations. But this is not to deny that in the Cycle, too, the work of an individual may stand out from that of his collaborators. The Wakefield Master, like the poet of *Sir Gawayne and the Grene Knight*, though anonymous and working in a more conventionalized medium than Chaucer, is none the less an innovator, remarkably original in his way and a master of colloquial English in intricate verse.

§ 4

The non-Chaucerian poetry is rich in material that not only could interest, but has interested anthropologists. The anthropologists as such are not critics of literature. But it does not follow that their findings might not prove of use to a literary critic, provided he uses these findings not as an anthropologist but as a critic. What concerns the critic is what the poets have made of the traditional subject-matter which they did not invent but inherited from the past.

The question at issue, then, is whether a critic can properly and profitably make use of the results—or tentative results—of anthropological researches without turning himself into something other than a critic, without becoming an amateur anthropologist. How far is the anthropological evidence, in regard to the medieval romances, relevant to the reading of them as poems? The romances —or rather the traditional material embodied or embedded in them—have evidently been found to be a suitable subject for anthropological studies, as Chaucer and more modern literature have not been; and, though the anthropologists are not (as I said) critics of poetry, they have in the romances abundantly found the kind of evidence that concerns them as anthropologists. It may therefore seem that what has been extracted from the poetry, no matter by whom, may be restored to it by the critic and may thus help to promote a more conscious, more complete reading of the poetry.

The test, for the critic, is not to what extent these things that concern the anthropologist were there in the life of the time—that, as a critic of poetry, he cannot judge—but whether or not these things are there in a particular poem. Nor is he limited to what may have been the conscious intention of the poet—what the poet would have said he supposed himself to be doing if we could have asked him—nor to what may have been in the conscious mind of the audiences, what they would have said they supposed them-selves to be listening to. The critic is concerned with nothing less than the totality of the poem.

A remarkable number of anthropological 'facts', assembled by different workers in different fields but having a bearing on the subject-matter of this traditional poetry, do seem—to an outside observer—to fit together so impressively that the obvious con-clusion might well be that they confirm one another. Different anthropological scholars have constructed different theories to try to account for the 'facts'. The critic, however, in making use of these 'facts' is not called upon to propound any theory of his own to account for them. To do so would be to write quite a different book from his own, an anthropological book and not a book of literary criticism. The critic is not called upon to prove or dis-prove, defend or find support for, accept or reject, on the evidence of the poems, any theory, anthropological or other. The facts with which he is concerned are (as I have said) the poems. The anthro-pologist may legitimately use the poems, as he may use any other piece of evidence, to assist him in establishing his facts or to con-firm or invalidate a theory. The critic must not do so.

But it still remains a possibility that the critic might make use of the anthropological facts—or even the surmises and guesses of anthropologists—in relation to *his* facts, the poems. If these anthro-pological facts, or even guesses, have the effect of making the critic—the reader of the poems—alert to things in the poems which he might not otherwise have noticed and which he, nevertheless, now sees to be actually there, in the poems, this is surely a positive gain for the reading of them. If, on the other hand, these things cannot be discovered to be actually in the poems, no theories or guesses could put them there. For the critic the words are always the test, the final check—the words in their context, and that is neither more nor less than the whole text. His object, the poem, is the structure of meaning which these particular words, arranged as they are arranged, compose.

There are, of course, risks. If the critic is safely to take account of the views of anthropological scholars in his reading of the poetry—and he may be in danger of missing things in the poems if he does *not* do so—he would probably be wise to treat these views *as if* they were guesses rather than the well-authenticated conclusions, based upon impressive accumulations of evidence, that some of them appear to be. But there is a positive use for 'guessing', or imagination, in the process of critically apprehending poetry. If one guesses that there might be something in a certain place and then, to one's critical satisfaction, actually finds it there, the guess is justified. It has served a useful purpose; it has led one to look for some particular thing where it was to be found. On the other hand, one cannot find what is not there; one only has to avoid fancying it to be so, reading something into the poem that is not there. The critic's task is to arrive at the fullest possible reading which is at the same time an accurate reading. But in reading 'early' poetry, such as medieval poetry is, the modern reader must (I think) deliberately allow for a much wider margin of doubt than in reading more modern literature. It is important for him to indicate clearly the meanings that are possible or probable but not certain. There is not only a place, in the criticism of this traditional poetry, for words such as 'perhaps' and 'possibly', but a positive obligation occasionally not to avoid them. It has also to be kept in mind that some possibilities may be more possible than others.

When reading, then, the critical reader is not applying a theory, anthropological or other, or even a body of knowledge to the poem. He is applying his sensibility to it—and, together with his sensibility, his intelligence, everything he *is*, in short. His judgements—and the quality of his judgements—of literature, as of life, will ideally be those arrived at by the whole of himself and his whole experience both of literature and of life. Nothing less is committed and engaged in the critical reading of any work of literature.

This book is therefore not intended to be an argument, but rather to avoid argument because it has something else to do—to try to promote appreciation of the poetry. The intention is not to try out any imaginary 'anthropological approach', but to try to get the poems read and more fully apprehended. There is only one 'approach' to poetry, and that is to begin to read it—in the fullest sense of 'read'.

One of the first things we apprehend about any poem, as about any other work of art, is that it has a pattern or structure. Unless we believe in 'pure art'—which I take to mean believing that this pattern may somehow exist in and by itself for admiration—we shall believe that it is a pattern or structure *of* something; that it is a structure of meanings—the unique structure of specifically *those* meanings and no others; and that, if it is not so, it has no meaning and there can be no reason to occupy oneself with it. Beliefs, of one kind or another, are an important part of what gives meaning to life, and consequently to art. But beliefs are of various kinds and are not necessarily confined to those of which one is most conscious or which one might formulate to oneself. There are inherited beliefs and there are beliefs which (as one imagines) one 'arrives at' for oneself by rational or other processes. We cannot, of course, know what the maker of *Sir Gawayne and the Grene Knight* would have said he believed in, if asked. But such a poem could not have arisen except out of the fundamental beliefs, as well as experience, of the author. Some of a poet's deepest beliefs may be those traditional beliefs which he, in his own more sophisticated way, shares not uncritically with his people. A sophisticated mind may consciously accord the *personae* of traditional belief—the Green Knight or Gawain—the kind of belief that the vividly imagined symbols of a deeply and freshly apprehended truth appear to demand. There is, as it happens, evidence enough for those who need to have evidence external to the poem, that ceremonies and fragments of dramatic ritual such as those to which the story of the contest between the Green Knight and the

Gawain of the poem unmistakably relates were by no means things of the past in the poet's own time; that they were, on the contrary, still being practised among the people, both high and low, for whatever conscious reason; and that, therefore, such a poet could count on his audience's familiarity with these things. To deny that this was so is as much as to deny that there was ever such a thing as the Maypole or Christmas mummeries. Even Chaucer's poems have their references to the May rites.[1]

It is inadequate to think of the poet of *Sir Gawayne and the Grene Knight* as simply a story-teller, at least in the ordinary limited sense, as inadequate as to think of a great novelist as such. The coherent whole of what Tolstoy, for example, thought, felt and believed about life—life very completely responded to and presented—went into the creative process which gave us *Anna Karenina* and *War and Peace* and is responsible for their structures. The art of 'telling a story' involves in the Gawain poet's case, as in Tolstoy's, much more than is generally allowed. W. P. Ker's conclusions, in *Epic and Romance*, about the Dutch Gawain romance *Walewein* are worth looking at in this connexion.[2] He finds that the author 'has all the mechanical business of romance', and more: 'In *Walewein* there appears quite plainly what is lost in Gaelic and the German stories, the character of the strange land in which the quests are carried out.' Nevertheless Ker finds the romance a failure: 'But if this may be supposed to belong to an older form of the story not evident in the popular version, a story of adventure in the Land of the Dead, on the other hand the romance has no conception of the meaning of these passages, and gets no poetical result from the chances here offered it.' It is worth pondering the implications of 'meaning' here—'meaning' in its relation to 'poetical result'.

Mr. M. J. C. Hodgart in an essay wittily entitled 'In the Shade

---

[1] Remnants of these or such-like ritual practices were still there as late as the seventeenth century when an enlightened Church and State took certain of them so seriously as not to shrink from destroying hundreds of village women as witches. Hawthorne's imaginative sense of how this element was present still in the life of Puritan New England is an important part of his sense of the past, as shown in his tales, *The May-Pole of Merry Mount*, *Young Goodman Brown* and *My Kinsman, Major Molineux*.

[2] *Epic and Romance*, V, p. 341.

of the Golden Bough'[1] has said apropos of my criticism of *Sir Gawayne and the Grene Knight*: 'This is not the place to show why Mr. Speirs's theories cannot be accepted by Arthurian scholars, but it is worth noting his basic critical assumption, since it is shared by other "mythological" critics. If a poem can be shown to be based consciously on primitive myth and ritual (or even unconsciously) is it thereby a better poem than one which is not so based? Mr. Speirs seems to answer with an unqualified yes.' Theories are, as I have explained, exactly what I have tried not to put forward in my criticism. But, even supposing I had done so, I cannot well discuss the reasons why theories attributed to me cannot be accepted by unspecified Arthurian scholars since I have not been shown, in this or any other place, what these reasons are. Where I might meet the Arthurian scholars, in agreement or disagreement, might be in some detailed critical discussion of the poems themselves, which is what I am offering. But I am here told by Mr. Hodgart that my 'basic critical assumption', which I share with other 'mythological critics',[2] is that a poem 'based on primitive myth and ritual' is thereby 'a better poem than one which is not'. It is a pity if I am supposed to have suggested that it is necessarily thereby a better poem. What I do suggest is that it is certainly a *different* poem. As to value, there may be poems based on myth and ritual (why does Mr. Hodgart say 'primitive'?) that have little value and others that have great value. Of the poems discussed in this book, for example, some are of less value than others, as I hope will appear. But in each case the nature, and therefore the value, of the poem will surely have been affected in one way or another, for better or for worse, if it has a myth-and-ritual element. It is what has been made of the myth-and-ritual element that is, of course, decisive in each case.

[1] *The Twentieth Century*. Cambridge Number, February 1955.
[2] What is a 'mythological critic'? Literary criticism is literary criticism. It cannot be something else.

Introduction

§ 5

One has to avoid turning a book intended to be literary criticism into an anthropological argument. One has also to avoid turning it into a metaphysical or ethical argument by questioning, at the point where literary criticism itself should begin, the assumptions on which the activity of literary criticism is based. Every activity of the mind is necessarily based on some assumptions or beliefs. It may be that the question whether or not these assumptions were justified can only be settled by judging the fruits of the activity that was based on them. There is no limit to scepticism; and scepticism, too, has its place and uses. But to set out to try to justify beforehand an activity such as literary criticism would be like trying to justify art beforehand. Doubtless it would be worth trying to do so. But it would leave little time for the exercise of literary criticism itself. The result might be a book of metaphysics, ethics, psychology or social philosophy; it would not be literary criticism. One has to occupy one's time either with the one thing or the other. It has been suggested to me, for example, that I ought to justify my 'apparent assumption'—an assumption on which a great deal of literary criticism seems to be based—that the 'richest reading of a poem is the right one'. But even if the richest reading is not the right one—and it would be harder to prove that an impoverished reading is—it would surely still be a service done to point to as many as possible of the various meanings or effects in a poem. It would be a beginning. The total structure, which is the poem, is the structure or hierarchy of all its various meanings and elements of meaning, some more important than others, some subordinate. The whole cannot be fully apprehended apart from a detailed apprehension of all these, its constituent parts.

The critic as such is, then, not called upon to enter into an argument outside literary criticism. He is called upon wholly to use what sensibility and judgement he has in the practice of criticism itself and to try to decide which are the best poems. In the process he will quote—his quotations are his evidences—and will necessarily have to make up his mind which passages and episodes in a poem are more significant than others. This process of selecting things that are most significant in a poem, as of selecting the most significant poems, is again part of this activity in which sensibility and intelligence are inseparable. The reader as critic seizes on (or selects) whatever he feels to be most significant in the poem he is discussing, in the hope that the 'common reader' —if there is a twentieth-century 'common reader'—will concur.

§ 6

The purpose of any criticism of the non-Chaucerian poetry should be to assist to get it read and apprehended. But we may well ask why we should wish to bring it into circulation. Why devote time to medieval English poetry apart from Chaucer's, time that might perhaps more profitably be devoted to other literature? Is it not, perhaps, better that this particular body of poetry should remain neglected? It is true that a great deal of the literature of the past is nowadays being kept somewhat artificially alive in the universities, and that some of it might indeed be better forgotten, at least for the time being. The literature that matters is that which really does matter to the reader personally in the present, which bears some felt significant relation to his life, and such literature appears always to have differed somewhat from one generation to another. We cannot, therefore, afford to allow even the good critics of a generation previous to our own to settle for us which authors really matter to us, though we may benefit from carefully re-considering their reasons for their judgements.

The body of poetry with which the present book is concerned, more especially the alliterative poetry, seems to me the most important part, the core, of English medieval poetry other than Chaucer's and, for that reason, an important element in the tradition that the *whole* of the literature in English, in its chronological order, constitutes. The poets, mostly anonymous, who composed this non-Chaucerian poetry are as recognizably, in the way they use the English language, the predecessors of Shakespeare, Ben

Jonson and Donne, as is Chaucer.[1] The characteristics that show themselves in their work do so again and again throughout the whole of English literature. The characteristics of the alliterative poetry, for example, crop up in the later poetry though English poetry is never again formally alliterative. They reappear in the dramatic verse of the later and greater plays of Shakespeare, in that of Ben Jonson at its most vigorously English and in the gnarled and knotted and incredibly subtle verse of Donne. They reappear in unexpected places—even within the formal couplet verse of Dryden and Pope, Johnson and Crabbe. They reappear even in the nineteenth-century poetry, in Keats (for example, in the *Ode to Autumn*) and in Hopkins, notably in his last sonnets in which tragic inner conflict is expressed in poetry that has characteristics corresponding to those of the soliloquies of the Shakespearian tragedies. They reappear in Yeats's later, as distinct from his early, poetry; and, while Eliot's verse has a conversational quality from the beginning, in *Gerontion* his verse, too, first assumes a comparable dramatic strength.

The alliterative poetry of the fourteenth century—along with Chaucer's poetry to which it is in some respects complementary—already develops these dramatic characteristics of English. At its best it conveys sensations of bodily action and movement through effects of rhythm and types of imagery not confined to the purely visual or auditory. It thus helps to prepare the language for the Shakespearian dramatic representation of inner perplexities and conflicts, the bodying forth of complex states of soul. In rendering external action, it is already (at its best) using 'the body of the language' in a way that could later be used to render the movements and turnings of the mind.

At the same time as it prepares the language for the later tragic poetry, it does the same for the later comic and satiric literature. It already shows a tendency, by way of a kind of drastically selective and vigorously exaggerative process, to caricature and to the

[1] A notable poem intermediate between Chaucer and Donne and late Elizabethan dramatic verse is Gavin Douglas's *Aeneid*. Although this poem is in rhymed couplets, its heavy, clogged, charged movement, suggestive of huge and powerful struggle, is quite different from the limpid flow and ease of Chaucer and is more like the movement of the alliterative poetry.

grotesque that re-emerges in Jonsonian comedy, in the satiric poetry even of the 'polite' Augustan line that was often anything but polite, and in the novelists from Fielding to Dickens.

Finally, the massive effects and build-up of the alliterative poems remind us—as do *Troilus and Criseyde* and the *Canterbury Tales* in their different, delicate and subtle ways—of the potentialities of the large-scale poem, the dramatic poem, or the novel. These large-scale poems are created, as Shakespeare creates, out of a staple of spoken, often homely colloquial English in which both the occasional survivors of Anglo-Saxon or Norse 'heroic diction' and the new French words have been assimilated and play their parts. They do not exhibit a fabricated, artificially elevated 'grand style'. In that respect they are achievements not of the artificial but of the natural use of language. But they are art. They have mistakenly been regarded as naïve and crude, and as rhythmically rugged and harsh, for much the same reasons as Donne once was. The same large claim cannot be made for the greater part of the rhymed or stanzaic romances or of the Mystery Cycle; but the alliterative poems on the whole and the plays of the Wakefield Master turn out, when examined, to be accomplished art, as many of the carols and other lyrics should more immediately be recognized as being.

It is therefore possible for modern readers to feel that more modern English literature has intimate connexions with the medieval. At the same time, the comparison between the two may help to bring out what have been the modern losses as well as the gains. It reveals more sharply the limitations as well as the positive achivements *both* of the earlier and of the later literature, and helps the reader to form a more adequate idea of the literature in the English language.

The paradox about such of the literature of the past as really matters to us is its likeness and unlikeness, its similarity to and difference from our own experience, our own ways of feeling and thinking. The authors of the past who matter to us establish an understanding, a communication as immediate as if they were our own contemporaries speaking. But they communicate the differences between themselves and us, together with the similarities; the differences are part of what is communicated. The value for us is as much in our perception of these differences as of the ways in which we recognize that they are like ourselves. Here in medieval English poetry is a civilization in many respects very different from our own, though it is a civilization from which our own has evolved; and the value, for us, is partly in the shock of this recognized difference.

The value of such literature as really matters is in its relation to our own lives. Poetry entirely dissociated from living—if such could be imagined—would be poetry that could not matter; both life and art, though never to be confused with one another, suffer impoverishment as soon as the connexions between them become tenuous. Such part of medieval poetry as can matter will do so because it may, in the present, have some bearing on our lives. But, further, for the very reason that it is different, in certain respects, from more modern literature it can help to break down our modern limitations, prejudices and assumptions, release locked-up energies of mind and spirit. A more complete consciousness of medieval English poetry can mean a more complete consciousness of English literature as a whole and, therefore, of what we ourselves are.

§ 7

I said that we could not know what greatness is in drama or in the novel if we did not know, let us say, *Lear* or *Anna Karenina*. We would not know what literature is capable of. Here, too, is the importance—or one important aspect of the importance—of the living literature of the past in relation to the present and to the prospects of contemporary literature. It establishes not models for mere imitation but standards. A modern poet (or novelist) would be quite unlike, for example, any medieval poet. But the living literature of the past can perpetually remind us of the potentialities of literature, the powers which may have been neglected, may have lain dormant for a time and may be recovered and released again in quite new and different creation. In some such way it is possible that English medieval literature can have relevance not only for readers but for literature at the present time. It may be worth indicating here two of the ways in which it might have such relevance.

(1) There is a great deal that is of the nature of drama in English medieval poetry. This dramatic element is more developed in the alliterative poetry and in Chaucer than in the Cycle Plays themselves. One or two of these latter—notably the Towneley Shepherds' Plays—do stand out, as already dramatic poems, from the Mystery Cycle in which they have their setting. But these little plays ought not to be dissociated from the alliterative poetry and from Chaucer which point forward together to the Shakespearian dramatic poetry. This whole body of English medieval verse, in which we hear not only the poets themselves but characters talking, is much more dramatic in nature than most nineteenth-century verse is—and most twentieth-century verse also, if we except some of the early poems of Eliot and some of the later poems of Yeats in which poetry seems to come closer again, momentarily, to drama and to the novel.

Perhaps, indeed, it is another way of saying the same thing if we say that the medieval verse-makers have more of the qualities of the novelist than have the English poets of the nineteenth century, when the strength of English literature seemed to pass out of poetry into the novel. (*Middlemarch* is surely greater literature than Tennyson's poetry, exquisite though some of that is.) English medieval poetry, both the alliterative poetry and Chaucer's, transcends the division between prose and verse. Prose fiction never developed in English medieval literature. It might be said that it did not need to. Some of the kind of interest that was later developed in the novel as well as the drama was already provided for, to varying extents, in the verse. Medieval poetry can therefore be a reminder of these particular possibilities in poetry. It can help to break down limiting conceptions of poetry.

(2) There is a considerable element of the comic and satiric in English medieval poetry. To put it at its simplest, it could be jolly. If we accept the view that the comic and satiric cannot be poetic, then we must not only deny (as Arnold did) that Pope is a poet, we must assert that Chaucer is less of a poet in the *Canterbury Tales*

as a whole than he is in his earlier and lesser poems—and we must deny that a considerable part of English medieval verse is poetry. It seems wiser to accept the view that the comic and satiric *may* be poetry, that there can be not simply satire but satiric poetry, not simply comedy but comic poetry. For, in comic or satiric poetry there is no such thing as the comedy or the satire apart from the poetry—and apart from the language out of which the poetry is made, the copiousness and fertility of surprising phrase and image. The comedy and satire are inherent in the whole imaginative, creative process and the result is comic or satiric creation. Chaucer remains in this as in other respects the supreme master of medieval English. The nearest to him in his own time and immediately after, as masters of medieval English are not the so-called Chaucerians (I do not include the Scots masters, Henryson and Dunbar, among these) but the alliterative poets, the makers of some of the carols and the Wakefield Master.

§ 8

One of the ways in which the traditional literature that was contemporary with Chaucer may be felt to be different, different more especially from modern literature since Chaucer and Shakespeare, is that it is closer to social activities and pastimes, closer to 'holidays' in the old sense, to ritual and dance and song; and that it is designed for minstrel recital, for dramatic and near-dramatic performance on festive and other occasions. It must at the present time, however, be appreciated mostly through private and silent reading, as we are accustomed to appreciate literature. Yet its particular powers are such that the modern reader can to some extent share even in private reading, in the theatre of the mind, the effect of its public performance. As it is a poetry shaped directly out of the spoken language, the effect of most of the poems is that of English being spoken with the difference that it is heightened rhythmically to accord with the actions it represents and the kind of dramatic recital on great occasions for which it was designed.

Although the alliterative poetry, the romances, the carols and

the plays of the Wakefield Master are themselves rational and conscious art, they do take rather more account than Chaucer does of
the irrational borderland of experience, the supernatural and what
we should call 'the unconscious'. This may be one of the reasons
why the medieval romances, as well as the folk-ballads, interested
some members of the 'romantic' generation in their dissatisfaction
with the limitations of eighteenth-century rationalism. The
modern interest in these things cannot but be affected by anthropology and psycho-analysis. There is the more reason to insist that
literary criticism has its part to play, that the reader's responses to
these poems should be controlled critically.

Many of these poems (*Piers Plowman*, *Sir Gawayne and the Grene
Knight*, *Pearl* and the carols, in particular) presuppose audiences
accustomed to symbolism and its interpretation.[1] The paintings

---

[1] The combination of realism and symbolism characteristic of much medieval
poetry may be illustrated already from the Prologue to *Piers Plowman*. It may, for
example, be guessed that it is more than a physical weariness which, already in the
opening lines, afflicts the wanderer. The refreshing stream that lulls him asleep
preludes the spiritual refreshment which his dream, as if magically, provides.

> *Ac on a May mornynge on Malverne hulles*
> *Me byfel a ferly of fairy me thoughte;*
> *I was wery forwandred and went me to reste*
> *Under a brode banke bi a bornes side,*
> *And as I lay and lened and loked in the wateres,*
> *I slombred in a slepyng it sweyved so merye.*
> *Thanne gan I to meten a merveilouse sweuene,*
> *That I was in a wildernesse wist I never where . . .*

While there is certainly a relation between the wilderness in which he finds himself and that in which, in the romances, the knights journey and meet with wonders
and magical events, it is unambiguously in this religious allegory a wilderness of the
spirit. The 'faire felde ful of folke' between the tower on the hill and the 'dongeon'
in the deep dale is almost certainly not simply 'faire' in the sense of lovely but a fair-
ground (cf. Chaucer's 'al nis but a fayre This world, that passeth sone as floures
fayre'). The crowd of all sorts and conditions of people is of course mankind in the
world, suspended between Heaven and Hell, as on the stage of the Miracle Plays.
At the end of the Prologue it becomes momentarily the poet's contemporary London crowd; the street cries of his London are heard. It is no 'Unreal City' ('Under
the brown fog of a winter dawn'). It is real and substantial, though seen *sub specie
aeternitatis*, with judgement suspended over it. Haukyn the Waferman (Passus XIII
and XIV) is one of those who might have been met in that city, a familiar figure
of the London streets, selling his wafers. But he is also a figure charged with
symbolical significances.

and sculptures in the churches were in fact mostly symbolical and, in conjunction with the sermons and church ritual, must have played a large part in accustoming the audiences of the poetry to look for more than the literal meaning, to expect a tale not to be 'simply a tale'. The modern reader is not so likely to be deceiving himself, therefore, when he thinks he perceives symbolical meanings in some of the poetry in addition to the literal ones. It is indeed surprising that symbolism, at least of the overt kind, is very much less evident in Chaucer's poetry than in the alliterative poems and the carols. It is perhaps another sign of his comparative modernity. Yet it happens that the contemporary reader is perhaps more sympathetic and alert to symbolism of one kind or another than eighteenth- and nineteenth-century readers. There have been Yeats and Eliot, the French poets since Baudelaire, and Rilke. The element of symbolism in medieval literature should therefore not only be a reminder of one of the ways in which it is different but should present less initial difficulty than it did.[1]

We should not, of course, necessarily or always identify this element of symbolism in medieval literature with the irrational or even the mystical. The rational mind may be very much concerned with symbolism and may express itself through certain types of symbolism. The moral symbolism of medieval literature, as of medieval art, has obviously been worked out often in the greatest and most complicated detail by the rationalizing mind. The Middle Ages, at least one side of them, have almost as much right to be called an Age of Reason as the eighteenth century.

The great mistake, it seems, would be to regard this poem as if it were an argument, to suppose that it is enough to try to extract by paraphrase its 'sense', to rationalize it in one's elucidation, to seek for a logical progression of ideas in it, to treat it as though it were philosophical prose, to ignore the fact that it is, at least at its best, a use of language that is essentially poetic—an exploratory-creative use of language, not formulation of preconceived meanings but new formations.

[1] Of course, to read simply as realism *Anna Karenina*, *La Chartreuse de Parme*, *Middlemarch*, *A Portrait of a Lady*, *Nostromo*, *Women in Love*, *Hard Times*, *The Europeans*, *St. Mawr*, *Heart of Darkness*, *The Shadow Line* (to name a few of the greater longer and shorter novels almost at random) would be to miss nearly as much as Bradley misses in Shakespeare. Such things are complex poems, as F. R. Leavis shows in *The Great Tradition* and *D. H. Lawrence: Novelist*. The extent of the 'symbolism' in Dickens, in *Bleak House*, *Little Dorrit*, etc. is made clear by Edmund Wilson in his essay in *The Wound and the Bow*.

Introduction

Paradoxically it is the pre-eminently reasonable and humane Chaucer who is freest from this type of rationalizing. It is an instance of his ultimate freedom or final disengagement from moral, allegorical, social or other *schemata*, such as the medieval mind was apt and accustomed to impose on experience, that the characters in the great Prologue are deliberately—it must have been deliberate—*not* arranged in any single order, *not* arranged according to any single one of the *schemata* into which they could (and might have been expected to) have been fitted. In this way the poet achieves not only a truer impression of the rich disorder of human life but of its multiplicity of aspects. It is true that Chaucer's earlier poems make considerable use of allegory and that he never quite abandoned this resource even when he became more directly and largely an observer of man and society. In this respect Chaucer's earlier poems are his most medieval, those that most closely associate him with the literature of his age.

§ 9

The poems which form the subject of this book are necessarily a selection. But the selection is itself intended to be an act of criti-cism and to indicate a body of English medieval poetry that seems to me the most important other than Chaucer's—and other than *Piers Plowman* and *Pearl*. *Pearl* is here reluctantly omitted because it seems to me that this fine poem, being more personal or private, does not quite belong with the traditional poetry and that it there-fore requires separate treatment.[1] *Piers Plowman*, on the other hand,

---

[1] A parallel between Eliot's lovely poem *Marina* and *Pearl* was once suggested to me—the image of the daughter lost and found (but hardly restored), the longing for the farther shore (*tendebantque manus ripae ulterioris amore*), the sense of a movement or progression (in *Marina* a voyage in a home-made, leaky boat) towards a reality beyond appearance. The differences are, of course, equally striking. Eliot's poem seems to work more by means of half-formed suggestions, delicate hints and in-tuitions, whereas *Pearl*, without discarding the reticence of allegory and symbolism, is much more elaborated. The theology, too, of the dialogue in *Pearl* between father and child—in which the now heavenly child instructs her earthly father—is quite explicit. The elaborate art of the *Pearl* poem is, perhaps, itself a part of the dis-ciplining of the rebellious will towards its ultimate acceptance of the divine will (once again, *E'n la sua volontade è nostra pace*).

belongs more to the present context. But to have treated it in detail proportionate to that of the poems in this book would have needed another book, a book devoted entirely to that immense work.

It is impossible to consider in a useful degree of detail more than relatively few poems in any one book, especially if the reader cannot be presumed to be already familiar with some of them. Since the useful thing in criticism seems to be to consider a few poems in detail rather than a great many generally, the usefulness of a book of criticism would seem partly to depend on the number of poems it manages to leave out. One's initial task, therefore, is a task of rather drastic selection. If it appears presumptuous to make one's choice on the grounds of personal interest (or taste), it may appear even more presumptuous to try to interest other readers in what has not (in the first instance) interested oneself. Critical discussion can only begin from what has interested *someone* at least. It may be that criticism is the endeavour to erect one's personal impressions into law; but the process must begin from personal impressions even if it must not end there. It is as true to say that, in the reading of poetry, understanding follows from enjoyment as it is to say that enjoyment follows from understanding. The enjoyment is the indication that something has been experienced, that something is already there to be understood. The poems selected for discussion in this book are therefore those which have particularly interested me as poems. There was no intention to select poems that might be used as evidence to prove or disprove any theory, anthropological or other, or to conduct any argument.

Once the poems had been selected they had to be arranged. Since the poems are what the book is about, the arrangement of the book is that of the poems which are discussed in it. In the case of an individual poet, dramatist or novelist the most satisfactory critical arrangement of his works is the chronological. Such an arrangement will inevitably exhibit the progression or development of the author's mind and art, a recognition of which is necessary for the fuller understanding and appreciation of his work. The same is true for the whole succession of works which constitutes a literature. But one of the peculiarities of the particular body of poetry with which the present book is concerned—

traditional poetry—is that few of the poems constituting it can be dated exactly or with any certainty. The chronology of the romances, the carols or the Cycle plays is as difficult to determine as is that of the folk-ballads. The nearest fairly exact date that we can associate with many of these pieces is that of the earliest MS on which the extant copy is found; and that date—when the extant version was written down—may be very misleading if we are trying to determine when the poem itself was originally com-posed. The 'original' may indeed have been composed in quite a different place as well as time from that in which the extant version was copied; even its language or at least dialect may have been changed.

It was therefore not practicable to allow the poems with which this book is concerned to arrange themselves chronologically, and so to arrange the book. In the end the arrangement, like the choice, has had to be a personal (but responsible) one, an arrangement according to felt affinities, to how individual poems seem to go together or make critically interesting contrasts, an arrangement such as seemed on the whole to be the least unsatisfying to a critical viewing.

The selection of such a number of the romances as could be described in detail within a reasonable amount of space in this book has had to be an absolutely minimal one.[1] It has again seemed more useful, a better way of conveying some particular idea of the nature of the English romances, to give a detailed account of a few of them rather than merely to express general opinions about a great number of them with most of which most readers are un-likely to be familiar. It is here in the book that I am most conscious

---

[1] Among the romances omitted with most reluctance are three Kentish romances of about the end of the thirteenth century, *Arthur and Merlin*, *King Alisaunder* and *Richard Coer de Lion*, which are possibly the work of a single author. Sections of these romances are introduced by delightful, gay lyrical passages that might well find their place in an anthology of medieval English lyrics—for example:

> *In tyme of hervest mery it is ynough;*
> *Peres and apples hongeth on bough.*
> *The hayward bloweth mery his horne;*
> *In everyche felde ripe is corne;*
> *The grapes hongen on the vyne:*
> *Swete is trewe love and fyne.* (King Alisaunder.)

of having departed, to some extent, from a criterion of value, from the 'best poems', or at least from those which I have judged to be such. On the whole, even here I have chosen to discuss what seem to me the best, or among the best, examples. But the much battered and garbled versions of Gawain romances in the Percy Folio MS of *c.* 1650 cannot be claimed as fine specimens of English medieval poetry. They have been included not only as specimens of the tradition of the English romances in its final stage but as re-handlings of the ancient Gawain material that help towards a less incomplete view of a tradition that has great gaps in it, a tradition that includes *Sir Gawayne and the Grene Knight*, *The Awntyrs of Arthure*, *Sir Percevelle of Galles*.

In presenting the individual romances of my small selection I have had (or it seems to me that I have had) to employ a rather elementary method. My descriptions have had to include a good deal that is preliminary to literary criticism, a necessary first stage in the process. It could not be assumed, as it could in discussing more modern works of literature, that the reader who might be interested is already familiar with them. It has therefore seemed necessary to follow through the 'story', together with substantial quotations, if some initial idea of each of these romances is to be conveyed. But the method differs (I hope) from that of simply 're-telling the story' in that it is intended at the same time to suggest and bring out the particular significances of each and so to initiate a critical discussion of them. If my concern had been to present an argument or theory, anthropological or other, instead of the poems, I should have extracted evidence from here and there in this, that or the other romance as suited such a purpose. Instead, my concern has been to convey some initial impression of particular romances, each as one whole. I have, for example, ventured to describe at some length *Sir Percevelle of Galles*, one of the longer and finer of the English romances, in order to trace the convolutions of its intricate pattern. Similar episodes and themes recur not only in this romance but throughout the romances. To follow through in detail the 'story' of a few of the romances is, therefore, a way of illustrating the whole body of them. Since the romances themselves are repetitive, as patterns are, a certain amount of repetition can scarcely be avoided in using such a method of describing them. The method at least serves the purpose of reflecting these patterns. Repetition is not necessarily or in every romance an artistic fault; the repetition of figures or motifs is itself what constitutes a pattern, and the recognition of the pattern may at the same time be a recognition of significance.

II

CAROLS AND OTHER SONGS AND LYRICS

II. CAROLS AND OTHER
SONGS AND LYRICS

§ 1

In his introduction to *Secular Lyrics of the XIV and XV Centuries*
R. H. Robbins refers to a 'metrical analysis' of 1,211 lyrics of the
fifteenth century. Miss Geary, who made the analysis, found 527
lyrics of what she calls 'the polite Chaucer type' (ballades, roundels,
lyrics in rhyme royal, and similar forms); but 641 lyrics of what she
calls 'the indigenous song verse type' (carols and similar songs).
She concludes: 'Now this, considering that the formal verse, being
of greater acknowledged importance at the time of its being written,
would have better chances of survival in manuscript, points con-
clusively to a strong body of indigenous song verse, stronger even
than the polite Chaucer type which is generally taken as representative of the period.' In this chapter I propose to consider chiefly the
'indigenous song verse'—carols and similar traditional song-lyrics
that are not so far removed from their origins in dance or ritual
games as are the more 'literary' lyrics. But even if the more literary
lyrics are excluded, there are still a considerable number of the
other kind. Not many English lyrics of any kind have chanced to
survive from the thirteenth century; but a good many have survived from the fourteenth and many more from the fifteenth.

Yet all that has been preserved may be regarded as a fragment of
all there must have been. We owe most of the finest lyrics that we
do have to a few windfalls, about half a dozen outstanding MSS
collections. The losses in the 'indigenous song verse' must certainly have been the heaviest. The more elaborate lyrics composed
by men of letters from Chaucer onwards for reading privately or

to a select company would be more esteemed than the traditional songs by the kind of persons who could read and write. They would have been written when composed, and once written would be the more likely to be copied. The traditional songs, besides being more lightly regarded by lettered persons, would in any case be more easily remembered and would therefore be less likely to be written down. What was being sung by many people—and had long been sung—might also be more easily taken for granted. The more traditional of the songs and lyrics that have happily been preserved may therefore be regarded more especially as stray survivors.

Among the lyrics that have been preserved there is a numerical preponderance of Christian religious lyrics. This may not mean that among the medieval communities as a whole there was such a preponderance of Christian religious singing and meditating. But, as has often been remarked, a large proportion of medieval lyrics owe their preservation to having been copied and kept in religious houses. The ecclesiastical authorities, upon whom preservation in MSS must largely have depended up to the end of the fourteenth century, would not have been particularly concerned to preserve profane songs—unless these had been first sanctified, transformed into Christian songs. That may be the reason why so many Christian religious lyrics have been preserved. There is little doubt that the medieval communities as a whole were more pagan than appears from the written evidence. There are, indeed, a sufficient number of records of ecclesiastical denunciations and prohibitions which indicate active opposition on the part of the Church to profane song and dance. It is clear from these records alone that profane song was associated with old Paganism, its rites and dances. On the other hand, we may regard it as certain that we owe the preservation of so many of the traditional Christian carols to the fact that they were traditional carols that had been *made* Christian. Their structure is still based on that of the traditional dance-song which accompanied the *carole* (ring-dance or processional dance), as R. L. Greene has shown in his valuable introduction to his *Early English Carols*.[1] (Greene, as well as

[1] Introduction, II, The Carol as Dance-Song.

Chambers and Robbins, has also indicated the part that the Franciscans may well have played in this whole movement of transforming profane songs into Christian.)[1]

This distinction between 'religious' and 'secular' lyrics is apt, however, only to get in the way of criticism. The main question for the critic is whether or not the poem is a *good poem*. In imagery, metrical patterns and other essential characteristics, the religious and secular songs will be found to have, as English medieval songs, virtually everything in common. The distinction between them would appear to be a surface one, a difference in the intended application of the thing rather than in the thing itself.

If, therefore, the critic will seek his good poems impartially from both the secular and religious lyrics that have survived he will still be confronted with a great many to choose from. Though it may seem almost outrageous to say so, not everything that has been preserved from the Middle Ages has been equally worth preserving. We may believe that there are a number of quite unusually fine poems among the English medieval lyrics. But it is necessary to distinguish which they are. In other words, we ought to try to see which of them still work, are still effective. We ought to ask ourselves whether anything happens when we read them and, if so, what. If nothing happens, there is nothing there to discuss; we cannot begin to discuss what is not there, as something experienced. But if a medieval lyric *is* there, as something experienced, it has become contemporary with the reader; it now exists in the present. In this sense the poems of past ages may be contemporary with one another, i.e. contemporary with the reader.

A considerable proportion of the best Early English lyrics are conveniently to be found in Chambers and Sidgwick's admirable little selection, first published in 1907. It should, of course, be supplemented by R. L. Greene's *Early English Carols*, R. H. Robbins's *Secular Lyrics of the XIV and XV Centuries* and Carleton Brown's collections.[2] The cultivated 'general reader' is not likely,

---

[1] Introduction, V, 2, The Franciscans and the Carol, cf. E. K. Chambers, 'Some Aspects of Mediaeval Lyric' in *Early English Lyrics*, p. 288, and R. H. Robbins, *Secular Lyrics*, Introduction, 1.

[2] *English Lyrics of the Thirteenth Century, Religious Lyrics of the Fourteenth Century, Religious Lyrics of the Fifteenth Century.*

however, to be interested in the medieval lyrics as edited by Carleton Brown or his successors in the modern academic school of editing. The ideal of editing of Middle English texts established in the universities since the nineteenth century appears to be that an editor should do *no* editing. He should simply exert himself to see that the spelling of the fourteenth- or fifteenth-century copyist— as if that particular spelling, which is not even the author's spelling, were sacrosanct—should be transferred exactly as it is on the MS to the printed page (with the interpolation, rather inconsequently, of twentieth-century punctuation). But to risk some editing should not mean that the editing would necessarily be badly done, that the poem itself would be injured. It is surely not too much to expect that editing should be done intelligently, sensitively and tactfully; that an editor of poetry should be a critic.

Equally discouraging is the idea—it may have derived from the idea that lay behind the not very successful historical fiction of the nineteenth century—that before the modern reader can properly appreciate a medieval poem he must first have somehow put himself back into the fifteenth or fourteenth century; he must reconstruct what the poem meant to its first audience. Thus a shift occurs from the idea of discovering what the poem *means* to that of discovering what it once meant. The reader, before he is aware, becomes concerned less with reading and responding to a poem than with reading and researching outside it with a view to arriving ultimately at some conclusion as to how some audience in the past might have responded to it.

The English medieval songs and lyrics were once responded to —some of them sung, some of them read—in the fifteenth century and earlier; they are now read, if at all, in the twentieth century— not by fifteenth-century but twentieth-century people. The modern reader should not suppose that he is a better reader than those for whom the medieval songs and lyrics were originally composed; but he is necessarily a different kind of person with a very different viewpoint. For one thing, he may be well read in the literature composed since the fifteenth century; his mind and sensibility will have been shaped at least as much by the literature that has come into being since that century as by the literature there was before.

He must now in his turn respond to the medieval songs and lyrics in his own way, which will necessarily be different from the way the medieval people who made them may be supposed or fancied to have done.

The songs and lyrics must, of course, have been composed in particular places at particular times and for particular companies and occasions. These circumstances may be considered to account for the songs and lyrics being the kinds of things they are; it may therefore be useful to know something of these circumstances. On the other hand, it is not the role of the reader as critic to account for the poetry, even supposing that to be entirely possible, but to respond to it and value it truly, as what in fact it is. The medieval communities no longer exist. Yet the songs and lyrics—or at least some of them—still exist, as poems that may be responded to. The poems are therefore independent of the vanished communities in which they originated; in that sense, they transcend time.

But if we concern ourselves with discovering which of the medieval songs and lyrics still mean, or do, something significant we shall find ourselves, it may be argued, left with only a few poems; that these will be quite exceptional poems; and that therefore there will result a misleading impression of the characteristics and quality of the English medieval lyrics as a whole. The best is of course exceptional in comparison with the ordinary. Yet to be concerned with the best makes it unnecessary to go on frequently re-reading the ordinary. One re-reads what one has judged to be ordinary merely to make sure that it really is only ordinary. The best is felt to have done (or much more nearly) what the ordinary has failed to do or has not even attempted. Furthermore, the best of the songs and lyrics are not less characteristic—not less characteristically English medieval songs and lyrics—than are the ordinary ones. They have gathered up into themselves all that is in the ordinary ones and have also in one respect or another reached beyond them.

§ 2

The earliest surviving English songs and lyrics are of the thirteenth century. The best of them imply a craft of song-making
that must have been long practised before it could have attained
that degree of accomplishment. 'Lenten is come with love to
toune' and 'Bytuene Mersh ant Averil' (in the Harley 2253 MS
of the early fourteenth century, and therefore probably thirteenth-
century lyrics) are at the opposite end of the scale from rudimen-
tary or primitive art, from first awkward beginnings. Their
simplicity and spontaneity of effect are those of a complex and
sure art.

To what extent and in what ways that art may have been
brought across by bilingual or trilingual makers in English from
the medieval songs and lyrics they were familiar with in French,
Latin or Provençal is a question which it might be wiser not to
attempt to answer; it is improbable that it could ever be answered.
Both the resemblances and the differences between the songs in the
different languages will immediately strike any reader. It is fairly
clear that the resemblances arise from something deeper than conscious imitation; that there *was* a European community in which
the diverse local communities belonged. R. L. Greene suggests[1]
that the forms of the Latin medieval lyrics were originally derived
from the vernacular carols and not vice versa, although the influence
of Latin and vernacular songs and lyrics was certainly mutual
over several centuries. H. J. Chaytor, in *England and the Troubadours*,
isolates one or two of the connexions between the England of the
early thirteenth century and Languedoc, and seeks thus to account
for the resemblances which he perceives between certain of the
early English lyrics (in the Harley 2253) and those of the troubadours. But there must have been a complexity of other connexions
at a time when Europe had a common life and common forms of
art. There was certainly a perpetual cultural and artistic inter-
change between one country and another as well as, within one
country, between one small local community and another. Songs,

[1] *Early English Carols*, Introduction, III, The Latin Background of the Carol.

because of their very nature—being words that go with tunes—must have travelled particularly light; they would shift across easily from dialect to dialect and even, in an age of widespread bilingualism and trilingualism, from language to language. Translation was probably seldom the highly conscious deliberate activity it now has to be.

But the differences between the lyrics in the different languages are just as striking as the resemblances; and are at least as funda‚ mental since they arise from the differences between the languages themselves, each language having its individual genius and characteristics and having been shaped in expressing a particular people's sensibility and experience. If medieval Europe as a whole was indeed *one* community, it was a community of lesser (many of them quite small) local communities each in itself individual. Every single English song and lyric that has come down to us from before the fifteenth century has done so in a dialect and has therefore, as an essential characteristic, the speech flavour of the folk of some particular locality in England. Yet these so English lyrics have, at the same time, such resemblances to the lyrics of the rest of medieval Europe as to suggest that all medieval lyrics are, in greater or less degree, akin. Thus it may be appropriate to describe the English medieval songs and lyrics as both English and European, local and (in this sense) universal.

But there is another line of consideration which suggests the way in which the songs and lyrics of medieval Europe may have com‚ mon roots. The structures of the carols indicate (as R. L. Greene and others have remarked)[1] that they have evolved from the dance‚ song that accompanied the *carole* which was danced in medieval Europe by both village and courtly folk. The English medieval carols may indeed be described as in their essential nature dance‚ songs, whether or not those that have survived were still being danced to or were simply being sung at the time when they were written down. The age‚old association between poetry, music and dance—ritual dance and game—is still ponderably present, especially in the more traditional songs and lyrics. The impulse of

[1] *Early English Carols*, Introduction, II, cf. E. K. Chambers, 'Some Aspects of Mediaeval Lyric' in *Early English Lyrics*.

the dance animating them may be felt in their movement. A substantial number of the more traditional songs and lyrics evidently
belonged with the seasonal festivals, the rites, dances and dramatic
games of spring and midsummer and Yule or Christmas.

Most of the more traditional of the English medieval shorter
lyrics (not only the comparatively few cases in which the music
has luckily been preserved in the MSS along with the words) are
unmistakably intended to be sung. Word-structures and music-
structures must have evolved in conjunction with each other,
originally perhaps out of the movement and pattern of the dance.
By the fifteenth century, in England, this old association between
song and dance, between words and music, appears to have been
beginning to be less inevitable. The new class of professional
musicians was developing music as a separate art; and the new
men of letters from Chaucer onwards were composing lyric poems
separate from music. Nevertheless the land was still full of songs
and of singing. R. L. Greene, speaking of the carols in his collection—a large number of them from the fifteenth-century MSS—
can say with justice: 'The probability is that most of the pieces
here collected were meant to be sung, at the time they were written
down, much as they would be today, not in a dancing ring, but
in a company gathered for conviviality or for religious praise.
They preserve, however, and it is the secret of much of their
charm, the atmosphere of general participation which the round
dance engenders. The companionship of the dance remained
associated with the form of verse which had the dance-song for its
pattern, even when the singers no longer stepped "hand by hand".'[1]

Music, chiefly vocal but also instrumental, was, we know, a
widespread accomplishment in the island of Britain as on the Con-
tinent before the thirteenth century. The now famous thirteenth-
century English Cuckoo Song, 'Sumer is icumen in', the music
for which has been preserved together with the words, is a *Rota* or
Round for six voices. Both as a musical, as well as verbal, composition it is sophisticated art and, as Wilfrid Mellers has remarked, is 'certainly not an isolated miracle but merely one
recorded example of a style in secular music which must have

[1] *Early English Carols*, Introduction, II, p. 59.

been common'.[1] It is not itself a carol or dance-song but is a spring-welcoming part-song, and as such arises from the same impulse as the *caroles* danced in the spring.

§ 3

The longer and more complex lyrics must, in their turn, have been developed from the shorter songs. Thus 'Lenten is come with love to toune' and 'Bytuene Mersh ant Averil' have clearly taken their origin from the songs and dances celebrating the annual spring-return or triumph of summer over winter. They are in the earliest rich windfall of English songs and lyrics, those in the Harley 2253 MS, a miscellany of Latin, French and English poems collected or copied by monks, it would seem, of Leomin-ster in Herefordshire early in the fourteenth century; they are there-fore probably lyrics of the thirteenth century. R. H. Robbins notes[2] that, even if copied by monks, the collection may be associated with the friar miscellanies because of its Continental or international character as a whole. The English lyrics in the col-lection are none the less as English as can be and are mostly in the dialect of the region—Herefordshire and neighbouring shires—where they were collected or copied; it is probable, however, that at least some of them originated in other parts of England and had shifted across from one dialect to another.

The movement of 'Lenten is come with love to toune'—especially the opening movement announcing spring's return—is one of joyous dance, expressive of the sudden wonder of the spring-return.

> *Lenten is come with love to toune,*
> *With blosmen and with briddes roune,*
>   *That al this blisse bryngeth,*
> *Dayes-eyes in this dales,*
> *Notes suete of nyhtegales;*
>   *Uch foul song singeth.*

---

[1] *Music and Society*, II, 'From Monody to Polyphony', p. 38.
[2] *Secular Lyrics*, Introduction, 1, The Friar Miscellanies.

The threstelcoc him threteth oo;[1]
Away is huere[2] *wynter woo,*
   When woderove[3] *springeth.*
This foules singeth ferly fele[4]
Ant wlyteth[5] *on huere wynter wele,*[6]
   That al the wode ryngeth.

The rose rayleth hire rode;[7]
The leves on the lyhte wode
   Waxen al with wille.
The mone mandeth hire bleo;[8]
The lilie is lossom to seo,
   The fenyl ant the fille.[9]
Wowes thise wilde drakes;
Miles[10] *murgeth*[11] *huere makes.*
   Ase strem that striketh[12] *stille.*
Mody[13] *meneth, so doht mo.*
Ichot ycham on of tho
   For love that likes ille.

The mone mandeth hire lyht;
So doth the semly sonne bryht,
   When briddes singeth breme.[14]
Deawes donketh the dounes,
Deores[15] *with huere derne*[16] *rounes,*
   Domes forte deme.[17]

---

[1] chides over and over.   [2] their.   [3] woodruff.   [4] wondrously many.
[5] whistle, pipe.
[6] The emendation 'wynne wele' has been suggested. If we accept the MS reading 'wynter wele' we must suppose it to be irony, and to mean the opposite of what it says. The birds are joyful at having escaped their winter condition of poverty.
[7] rosy face *or* hue.   [8] sends out her radiance (*or* shows her shining face).
[9] wild thyme *or* chervil.
[10] ? 'wild creatures' (from Welsh 'mil') has been suggested.
[11] make merry.   [12] flows.   [13] the passionate man.
[14] exuberantly, gloriously.   [15] wild animals.   [16] secret.
[17] i.e. to decide their fates. Cf. for the alliteration, 'Ha beoth se wise that ha witen alle godes reades. his runes ant his domes the derne beoth. ant deopre then eni sea dingle' (*Sawles Warde*, c. 1200).

> *Wormes woweth under cloude;*
> *Wymmen waxeth wounder proude,*
> *So wel hit wol hem seme.*
> *Yef me shal wonte wille of on,*
> *This wunne*[1] *weole I wole forgon,*
> *Ant wyht in wode be fleme.*[2]

Spring and love are almost at the point of becoming visible as dancers, partners in a triumphal dance. With blossom and bird-song, they have come back to the world; specifically, to our own immediate and familiar corner of the world—our 'toune' (or homestead). For, as spring works a magical change in plants and birds in the meadows and woods, so it brings love also into the dwellings of the human folk and changes men and women.

But this poem is not simply a communal dance-song welcoming the spring. The movement of joy at the spring-return, though it is the initial and dominant movement, is crossed by a contrary move-ment of personal lover's pain. Thus the poem as a whole expresses a common joy, a personal pain. The individual lover feels that, unless he has his will with 'one', he must forsake all this wealth of universal joy shared with the birds and blossoms, and must for-sake his own community of the human folk (his 'toune') to be-come a fugitive creature, a wild man of the woods.

This is not a medieval poem of courtly love-service, however much we may see a relationship in other respects between it and the lyrics of the troubadours. Here, love is not associated with a castle or court culture but directly with Nature—creative, genera-tive nature, the mating birds, the life-giving and fertilizing dews of spring. In spring all living creatures from the highest to the humblest are subject to love—for they are subject to Nature.

> *Wormes woweth under cloude;*
> *Wymmen waxeth wounder proude.*

The two lines are not, as they may seem, casually juxtaposed. The common earth-worm,[3] the humblest of earth-creatures, is both

---

[1] wealth of delight.   [2] fugitive.

[3] I cannot accept the interpretation 'snakes' for 'wormes' here, nor (instead of 'clods') 'cloud' or 'rock' for 'cloude'—interpretations which seem to me to make virtually nonsense in this context.

associated and contrasted with the young women who in the common mating-season 'waxeth wounder proude'.[1]

'Lenten is come with love to toune' dates almost a century
earlier than 'Whan that Aprille with his shoures sote . . .', the
opening movement of the Prologue to the *Canterbury Tales*. Yet
the resemblances between the two are sufficient to imply essentially
the same kind of English sensibility and the same kind of community, which must therefore have already been there a century
before Chaucer. The same may be felt of another lyric in the
Harley 2253, 'Bytuene Mersh ant Averil'. Even if we allow that
the Julian Calendar had fallen about a fortnight behind and that
therefore 'between March and April' corresponds to mid-April,
the note in these English poems is of the first breaking of spring.

> *Bytuene Mersh ant Averil,*
> > *When spray biginneth to springe,*
> *The lutel foul hath hire wyl*
> > *On hyre lud[2] to synge.*
> > *Ich libbe in love-longinge*
> > *For semlokest of alle thinge;*
> > *He[3] may me blisse bringe;*
> *Icham in hire baundoun.[4]*
> > *An hendy hap ichabbe yhent;[5]*
> > *Ichot from hevene it is me sent;*
> > *From alle wymmen mi love is lent[6]*
> *Ant lyht on Alysoun.*
>
> *On heu hire her[7] is fayr ynoh,*
> > *Hire browe broune, hire eye blake;*
> *With lossum chere he[3] on me loh,[8]*
> > *With middel smal ant wel ymake.*
> > *Bote he[3] me wolle to hire take,*

---

[1] I do not feel that the association of the worm with mortality is relevant here
or present as a warning corrective to the pride of the young women—like Proud
Maisie—in the spring of the year and of their lives. For one thing, the reference to
the worms comes *before* the reference to the women. The poem is singularly un-
touched by the ecclesiastical or moralistic side of the Middle Ages.

[2] in their own language.   [3] she.   [4] dominion, power.   [5] I have had luck.
[6] turned aside.   [7] hair.   [8] laughed.

Forte buen hire owen make,
Longe to lyven ichulle forsake,
Ant feye[1] fallen adoun.

Nihtes when I wende ant wake,
Forthi myn wonges[2] waxeth won.
Levedi, al for thine sake
Longinge is ylent me on.[3]
In world nis non so wytermon,[4]
That al hire bounte telle con.
Hire swyre[5] is whittore then the swon
Ant feyrest may in toune.

Icham for wowing al forwake,
Wery so water in wore.[6]
Lest eny reve me my make,
Ichabbe y-yerned yore.
Betere is tholien whyle sore,
Then mournen evermore.
Geynest under gore,[7]
Herkne to my roun.
An hendy hap ichabbe yhent;
Ichot from hevene it is me sent;
From alle wymmen mi love is lent
Ant lyht on Alysoun.

In this poem the communal spring-welcoming song—while not losing its connexion with its origin as such—has been developed still more completely into a personal love poem. The young woman, the object of the young man's passion, is a bodily presence, not an abstract ideal. One feels about all the Alysouns of the medieval English poems—this Alysoun, the Wife of Bath (when young) and the carpenter's wife in the *Miller's Tale*—that they are much more closely akin to one another than they are to the Bele Aeliz of the French lyrics. The English of this poem—almost a century earlier than Chaucer—is already essentially the

[1] doomed to die.   [2] cheeks.   [3] come upon me.   [4] wise man.
[5] neck.   [6] weir, troubled pool.   [7] gown, i.e. most graceful of women.

same kind of spoken English as that out of which Chaucer made his poetry. (I do not mean that it is in the same dialect.) 'Wery so water in wore' is a simile of essentially the same order as 'She was as digne as water in a ditch' (descriptive of Simkin the miller's wife in the *Reve's Tale*). The images have unmistakably been taken into the poetry direct from the speech of country folk. The lyric—again like Chaucer's poetry—has a dramatic character; it is not a disembodied musical complaint or utterance of devotion to an ideal of remote womanhood. Rather, it is a direct wooing-encounter between a young man and woman—such as, at some earlier stage, might have been enacted in a wooing-dance. At specific moments in the poem *he* addresses *her* directly as in a dialogue, pleadingly.

> *Geynest under gore,*
> *Herkne to my roun.*

There are other seasons than spring, however; and in the same Harley 2253 there is a contrast, a lyric which expresses grief evoked by the onset of winter.

> *Wynter wakeneth al my care;*
> *Nou this leves waxeth bare;*
> *Ofte I sike*[1] *and mourne sare,*
> *When it cometh in my thoght*
> *Of this worldes ioie, hou hit geth al to noht.*

> *Nou hit is, and nou hit nys,*
> *Also hit ner nere ywys.*
> *That moni man seith, soth hit is,*
> *Al goth bote Godes wille.*
> *Alle we shule deye, thah us like ylle.*

> *Al that gren me graveth grene,*[2]
> *Now hit faleueth al by dene.*[3]

[1] sigh.
[2] all that grain (seed) men buried (i.e. that was sowed) green (i.e. vital). Cf. John xii, 24, 25: Nisi granum frumenti cadens in terram mortuum fuerit, ipsum solum manet; si autem mortuum fuerit, multum fructum effert. Cf. also Pearl I, 30: For uch gresse mot grow of graynes dede.
[3] fades in due course.

Jesu, help that hit be sene,
Ant shild us from helle,
For I not whider I shal, ne hou longe her duelle!

As a tree bared of leaves by the winter wind is exposed, so in this poem the individual is exposed to the tragic recognition of the common lot of man that he too shares; there is no stability in earthly joy.

Nou hit is, and nou hit nys,
Also hit ner nere ywys.

(The phrasing is interestingly close to that of Criseyde's reflection on the nature of earthly love in Chaucer's poem almost a century later: 'That erst was no-thing, in-to nought it torneth.')

There is no stability in the whole earthly condition; there is stability only in God's will—so, at least, many people say, and it is true what they say. The vital grain that was buried in the earth and sprang up loses its green now and fades. (Such seems to me to be the best interpretation of the difficult opening of the last stanza.) The recognition of mortality—at the moment of the victory of winter over summer, and the death of the year—evokes finally the desperate cry of appeal: 'Jesu . . . shild us from helle.' This poem, too, becomes a personal cry; involved in the common lot is the individual fate. The desperate situation of being man, the uncertainty of it, is felt personally.

For I not whider I shal, ne hou longe her duelle.

§ 4

Written on a narrow strip of vellum bound up, as if by accident, with the alien miscellaneous matter of the fourteenth-century Rawlinson D 913 MS are a few songs or fragments of songs not all of which are completely decipherable. One or two of these (notably *Ich am of Irlaunde, Maiden in the mor* and the *Hawthorn Tree* song) are songs of a different order from those quoted from the Harley 2253—they have an impersonal or extra-rational quality. It is a fair guess that they are fragments broken off from actual ritual performances, ritual dance-songs or words for dramatic ritual-games. There can be no doubt that they *are* songs to be sung and to be danced to, though the music has not been preserved. The in-cantatory note of these poems—the effect largely of their woven repetitions—makes it seem likely that they actually belonged with the sacred dances of the ancient Nature religion which were still being kept up (whether or not the reasons for doing so were con-sciously realized) as the May and Midsummer rites of the medieval folk.

> *Ich am of Irlaunde,*
> *ant of the holy londe*
> *of irlande.*
>
> *Gode sire, pray ich the,*
> *for of saynte charite,*
> *come ant daunce wyt me*
> *in irlaunde.*

The dancer (and the dance) is instantly a vivid presence to the imagination even of a twentieth-century reader, such is the rhythmical and incantatory power of the song. The dancer (the singer) presents and announces herself[1] as if a *dramatis persona*—as she might in fact have been in some dramatic ritual dance—and invites someone to dance with her. This dancer has come from across the sea, from 'the holy londe of irlande'. Ireland, the Isle of the Saints because earlier it had been the Isle of the Gods, is here sacred still perhaps in a pagan as well as a Christian sense. The dancer from across the sea—from a sacred or magical *other* country —is still perhaps essentially a faery or otherworld visitant (or a human impersonator of such a character in the performed dance). Essentially, or symbolically, the dancer will steal away or abduct her partner.

> *Come ant daunce wyt me*
> *in irlaunde.*

[1] I am assuming that it is a *she* and that the last four lines are uttered by the same person as the first three. Such an interpretation seems to fit rather better. But the possibility cannot be excluded that the song is a fragment of dialogue. Greene regards it as a *carol*. The words may well have been those of a song for a ring-dance, inviting an outsider to join in.

Caught up into the dance such a dancer (the human impersonator) becomes an *other* person, assumes a different, more powerful personality—or, in other words, her own personality is
absorbed into the 'impersonality' of the dance itself (as Yeats
apprehends the identity of the dancer and the dance:

> *O body swayed to music, O brightening glance,*
> *How can we know the dancer from the dance?*[1])

The dancer thus becomes, almost in a literal sense, *enchanted* and
enchanting.[2] This particular song, chiefly by means of its rhythm
and repetitions of sound, suggests to the reader a trance-like or
rapt condition in the dancer whose song it is; consequently, a
supernaturally compelling or appealing power seems to emanate
from the dancer.

The Hawthorn Tree song is another fragment which looks as
though it may have been a song for carollers or sacred dancers on
some festival occasion, and may therefore be quite literally
associated with magic or the faery.

> *Of everykune tre—*
> *of everykune tre—*
> *the hawethorn blowet suotes*
> *of everykune tre.*

> *My lemmon sse ssal boe—*
> *my lemmon sse ssal boe—*
> *the fairest of erthkinne,*
> *my lemmon sse ssal boe.*

This song, to judge from the repeated lines, was a song for
several voices and the singers were dancers round a hawthorn tree

---

[1] *Among School Children.*

[2] We may recall how in Robert Mannyng of Brunne's version of the traditional
tale of the Dancers of Colbek the carollers—who go on dancing the year round
because they are under the priest's curse, and cannot stop—feel neither snow nor hail
nor rain.

> *Frost ne snogh, hayle ne reyne*
> *Of colde ne hote, felte they no peyne.*

Essentially, they are in a state of enchantment.

(or its human impersonator, wreathed in hawthorn, perhaps in a May dance). The song may have belonged with the worship or wooing of the hawthorn tree or its spirit or its human impersonator —the fairest of earth creatures. Even if we regard the 'lemmon' of the last four lines as not identical with the hawthorn tree of the first four, it would still be hard to escape the impression that this more human type of wooing-song had evolved from the earlier type and that it still shares the quality of the earlier type.

Another song belonging to this little group in the Rawlinson D 913 MS—for they do form a group, the one shedding light on the other—is 'Maiden in the mor'.

> *Maiden in the mor lay—*
> *in the mor lay—*
> *sevenyst[1] fulle, sevenist fulle,*
> *Maiden in the mor lay—*
> *in the mor lay—*
> *sevenistes fulle ant a day.*
>
> *Welle was hire mete.*
> *Wat was hire mete?*
> *The primerole ant the—*
> *the primerole ant the—*
> *Welle was hire mete.*
> *Wat was hire mete?*
> *The primerole ant the violet.*
>
> *Welle was hire dryng.*
> *Wat was hire dryng?*
> *The chelde water of the—*
> *the chelde water of the—*
> *Welle was hire dryng.*
> *Wat was hire dryng?*
> *The chelde water of the welle-spring.*
>
> *Welle was hire bour.*
> *Wat was hire bour?*

[1] seven nights.

Carols and other Songs and Lyrics

The rede rose an te—
the rede rose an te—
Welle was hire bour.
Wat was hire bour?
The rede rose an te lilie flour.

Again we may guess this to be a dance-song and—considering the repeated phrases and the question-and-answer formula—that it is a song for several voices, several dancers. The poem almost sings itself and the impulse of the dance is immediate in its movement; the dance-pattern and the song-pattern are one.

Who is this 'maiden' who has spent a seven-nights' vigil on the moor beside a well? It is unlikely that we can ever know exactly, and there is perhaps no need that, as readers of what to us is a *poem*, we should. She is sufficiently defined in the poem for the purposes of our response to the poetry—a child of nature, whether human or faery, her meat the primrose and the violet, her drink the chilled water of the well-spring.

The reference to a well-spring suggests the possibility that the song may originally have had some connexion with the 'well-wakes'—the worship of wells—which, there is abundant evidence, went on all through the Middle Ages. These well-wakes were particularly associated with St. John's Eve and so with the rites, ceremonies and practices of the great Midsummer festival as a whole.

We may guess from what is said in the song that the maiden, if she is human, has been undergoing some rite of initiation or purification. If she is a faery being—or the human impersonator of such in a dramatic dance—she may be the spirit of the well-spring. We know that the word 'maiden' was often used in a special sense as the title of a witch, the leader of a coven, one of the nuns of Diana, as it were.

This song also is evocative of a tranced mood. It has a kind of solemn gaiety, solemn like the gaiety of a child absorbed in what to it is a serious game. This quality would further suggest that this poem may in fact have been connected with rites and dances designed to promote fertility or in some other respect to influence the course of nature magically—in the spring or summer, as the flowers suggest. When we speak, as we well may, of this song's enchanting innocence or magical lightness we may be nearer than we perhaps think to the literal truth.

There are six English lines in a Latin Christian context in another MS (Magdalen College, Oxford, MS 60, of the end of the fourteenth century) which are about another maid beside a well.

> *At a sprynge wel under a thorn*
> *Ther was bote of bale,*[1] *a lytel here a-forn;*
> *Ther by-syde stant a mayde,*
> *fulle of love y-bounde.*
> *Ho-so wol seche trwe love*
> *yn hyr hyt schal be founde.*

In this case the maid—judging by 'bote of bale' and 'trwe love'—is Mary. She has, however, an unmistakable affinity with the maiden by the well-spring, 'the spirit of the fountain'. The lines, though they have lost the movement of the dance and are rhyth-mically uncertain and even flat, illustrate how the imagery of the songs of the earlier religion was being adapted to Christian meanings.

§ 5

Some of the outstanding poems among the specifically Chris-tian songs are in the Sloane MS of the early fifteenth century—another of the rich windfalls of English medieval songs—a century later than the Harley 2253. As the songs in this collection must have been composed at some time before they were collected and written down, they may have been contemporary with Chaucer. They include several of the finest English medieval carols for the great Christmas festival. Whether or not the Sloane 2593 was the song-book of a minstrel (as has been conjectured[2]), this collection is not so international as the Harley 2253; all the songs are in English except three which are in Latin.

[1] cure for grief, remedy for sorrow.
[2] R. H. Robbins, *Secular Lyrics*, Introduction, 7: The Minstrel Collections.

Carols and other Songs and Lyrics

How individual in character the best of the songs in the Sloane
2593 collection can be may be judged from 'Adam lay ibounden'.

> *Adam lay ibounden,*
> *Bounden in a bond;*
> *Four thousand winter*
> *Thoght he not too long;*
> *And all was for an appil,*
> *An appil that he tok,*
> *As clerkes finden*
> *Wreten in here book.*
> *Ne hadde the appil take ben,*
> *The appil taken ben,*
> *Ne hadde never our lady*
> *A ben hevene quene.*
> *Blessed be the time*
> *That appil take was.*
> *Therefore we moun singen*
> *'Deo gracias'.*

Adam, in bonds for four thousand winters, captures one's
imagination as a huge mythological character—a Promethean
figure, a bound giant, enchanted or frozen throughout four
thousand winters.

> *And all was for an appil.*

There is astonishment, incredulity in the voice. An apple, such as
a boy might steal from an orchard, seems such a little thing to have
produced such overwhelming consequences. Yet so it must be
because clerks say so; it is in 'their book' (probably meaning the
Vulgate itself).

But the final and dominant note of the song is one of gladness.
Had it not been for the apple we should not have Our Lady. The
apple produced the Fall which necessitated the Redemption
which gave us Our Lady; thus the divine destiny or love is fulfilled. The singer, therefore, blesses the apple.

> *Blessed be the time*
> *That appil take was.*

God is good after all.

The doctrine of the song is perfectly orthodox—the doctrine of *O felix culpa*[1]—but here it is expressed very individually and humanly. The movement of the song reproduces very surely the movements of an individual human mind.

'Adam lay ibounden' thus turns out to be, in its individual way, a song of gratitude for Mary and so takes its place with the other songs to Mary among the Christmas Nativity songs in the Sloane 2593. These have, of course, their place in the whole body of the medieval lyrics to Mary. Many of these in Latin and the different vernaculars are in essence courtly love lyrics, the difference being that the courtly lady of the troubadours and the trouvères is Mary, Queen of the Court of Heaven. The knight expresses his devotion to his lady—but in this case the lady whom he serves is Mary. There can be no doubt that the influence was mutual, that the hymns to Mary influenced the poetry of courtly love and vice versa. The rose of *Le Roman de la Rose* and the Rose Mary could not but have influenced one another in the medieval mind (though we need not conclude that their significances were confused).

But in the more traditional of the English songs (including those in the Sloane 2593 MS) Mary has something of an older significance, something still of the tree- or flower-goddess or again the spring goddess. In several of the loveliest English carols, evidently for the Christmas festival, she is not simply herself the Rose but the tree out of which the rose-blossom, who is Christ, springs. In those carols also—as in the medieval lyrics as a whole— we are frequently reminded that Mary has the two aspects of mother and maid; she is both the mother goddess and (like Diana) the virgin goddess. In the carols particularly the human and the divine are mutually associated; the natural human tenderness about a mother and child is sanctified when this human child is, miraculously, none other than God. These carols to Mary and her child—who is both God and Man—are so good as poetry partly because out of the traditional imagery inherited from old Pagan myth and ritual is being made the new Christian sym-

[1] A subject recently explored by Herbert Weisinger in *Tragedy and the Paradox of the Fortunate Fall.*

bolism; it must largely account for their strength as well as appealing loveliness. The Christian medieval lyrics generally—but particularly the Christian carols—are just as much as the 'secular' ones rooted in Pagan myth and ritual, in the dances and rites of the seasonal Nature festivals, many of which were still contemporary, still being performed, often alongside and even as part of the Christian feasts and ceremonies.

Before considering one or two of the Christian carols and songs found, together with 'Adam lay ibounden', in the Sloane 2593 MS and in a few other collections, it may be well first to recall— for comparison—a stanza from a fairly conventional type of early vernacular hymn modelled rather closely on the Latin, with Latin lines skilfully interpolated. 'Of on that is so fayr and bright' (found in the Egerton 613 MS together with one or two other lyrics of the early fourteenth or late thirteenth century) is one such hymn.

> *Levedi, flour of alle thing,*
>   Rosa sine spina,
> *Thu bere Jhesu, hevene king,*
>   Gratia divina;
> *Of alle thu berst the pris,*
> *Levedi, quene of Parays*
>   Electa,
> *Mayde milde, moder* es
>   Effecta.

The lovely conventional phrases touch gracefully on several of the principal aspects of Mary. These and other aspects are much more fully developed in the traditional English carols and songs of the Sloane 2593, the Audelay collection, and the one or two other collections which we may associate with these two famous ones.

In the Sloane 2593 MS there is found what is surely the loveliest of all the English medieval songs to Mary; I doubt if there is anything else in English more tenderly lovely.

> *I sing of a maiden*
>   *That is makeles,*
> *King of all kinges*
>   *To her sone sche ches.*

He cam also stille
There his moder was,
As dew in Aprille
That falleth on the grass.
He cam also stille
To his moderes bour,
As dew in Aprille
That falleth on the flour.
He cam also stille
There his moder lay,
As dew in Aprille
That falleth on the spray.
Moder and maiden
Was never non but sche;
Well may swich a lady
Godes moder be.

It is in essence a spring song, but sacred in the new way. The dew in April is the magical life-giving dew associated with that month —the time of the first breaking of the buds, before the exuberance of high summer. The Christian mystery of the Incarnation is here associated with the fall of the dew and thus imaged still in the old way as a marriage of Sky and Earth. Mary, who is both mother and maiden, is still in essence the spring goddess and also the earth-mother. The song expresses with tenderness and reverence the wonder of conception and of natural growth, the gentle silent beginnings of life and growings that are both natural and magical —or miraculous.

The song seems to be for one voice, and it has a kind of single-ness of quality. It is composed of simple statements and repetitions —as though the truth it states is such that it needs only to be stated to be acknowledged and yet is so wonderful that it needs to be repeated many times for the wonder of it to be contemplated. The subject of the song has become completely an object which the singer presents with entire directness.

The simplicity of the song is, however, of the kind that is in itself complex. 'Makeles,' as of a bird without a mate, expresses

Mary's companionless, maiden or virginal state. The meaning of the other word—'without a flaw or blemish, immaculate'—is surely also present. (We may compare the play on 'maskelles' ('spotless') and 'makeles' in *Pearl*, XIII, culminating in the final line (780) 'A makeles may and maskelles'.) It means also, as the poem unfolds, that Mary is without an equal; it indicates her queenly, indeed divine status and uniqueness. 'Sche ches' implies her full, conscious, willing acceptance of the divine will, her entire identification with it; she chooses, as one might choose a lover. As, being 'makeles', she might choose a knight to be her 'make', she chooses the 'king of all kinges' to be her son. God is both her lover and her son; we may compare Dante's paradox *figlia del tuo figlio*. Yet, although he is 'king of all kinges', he comes with no pomp and circumstance, no noise.

> *He cam also stille*

as silently

> *As dew in Aprille,*

the magical, heavenly dew that gives life to plant and tree. We may consciously note, as we must inevitably feel, the upward movement or progression responsive to the dew that falls from Heaven—the grass, the flower, the branch. The song is a beautiful ordered structure; and its order and clarity are not simply those of conscious, anxious ordering. From Mary's singleness and flaw-lessness we pass gradually to a full recognition of her uniqueness. She rises, too, in status. The maiden becomes 'moder and maiden' and a 'lady' who is the mother of no less than God.[1]

---

[1] One of the most original treatments in medieval English poetry of the Incarnation is the passage in Passus I of *Piers Plowman* (B-text) which seems to have grown out of the image of Love as 'the plante of pees' (all there is as yet in the A-text).

> *. . . the plante of pees moste precious of vertues.*
> *For hevene myghte noughte holden it it was so hevy of hym-self,*
> *Tyl it hadde of the erthe yeten his fylle.*
> *And whan it haved of this folde flesshe & blode taken,*
> *Was nevere leef upon lynde lighter ther-after,*
> *And portatyf and persant as the poynt of a nedle,*
> *That myghte non armure it lette ne none heigh walles.*

In the suggestion of the branch heavy laden—the melancholy heaviness of the

Another very lovely English song to Mary, in the same Sloane 2593 MS, is a carol the refrain of which begins 'Of a rose, a lovely rose'.

> *Of a rose, a lovely rose,*
> *Of a rose is all mine song.*
> *Lesteneth, lordinges, bothe elde and yinge,*
> *How this rose began to springe;*
> *Swich a rose to mine likinge*
> *In all this world ne knowe I none.*
>
> *The aungil cam fro hevene tour,*
> *To grete Mary with gret honour,*
> *And seide sche schuld bere the flour,*
> *That schulde breke the fendes bond.*
>
> *The flour sprong in heye Bedlem,*
> *That is bothe bright and schene.*
> *The rose is Mary, hevene quene;*
> *Out of her bosum the blosme sprong.*
>
> *The ferste braunche is full of might,*
> *That sprong on Cirstemesse night;*
> *The sterre schon over Bedlem bright,*
> *That is bothe brod and long.*
>
> *The secunde braunche sprong to helle,*
> *The fendes power down to felle;*

divine Love in pity for the lot of fallen man—bending to the earth we see the concept of the Incarnation, the Word made Flesh, emerging or discovering itself in the imagery. In the C-text, indeed, we find that the phrase 'goten hym-selve' has made its appearance in place of 'yeten his fylle'. Lightened of its burden—in the birth of God as man—Love is now so light and yet so penetrating that, being supernatural, no material force can withstand it. In this poetry thought and image are one, as body and soul; it is in the particular images that the thought takes particular shape or definition—in images that grow significant or symbolic. The poet is, of course, working within the frame of medieval Christian belief, which he has grown up *with* and been instructed in. But in his poetry he is growing *into* this knowledge in which he has hitherto been merely instructed—growing up into it from his own root; he is rediscovering, by means of his poetry, the Way or Christ—as the Plowman.

> *Therein might none sowle dwelle.*
> *Blessed be the time the rose sprong!*

> *The thredde braunche is good and swote,*
> *It sprang to hevene crop and rote,*
> *Therein to dwellen and ben our bote;*
> *Every day it scheweth in prestes hond.*

> *Prey we to her with gret honour,*
> *Sche that bare the blessed flour,*
> *Sche be our helpe and our socour*
> *And schild us fro the fendes bond!*

The opening of the song, 'Lesteneth, lordinges', implies a single vocalist (possibly a minstrel) singing of the glad tidings to a company who may have joined in the refrain—perhaps in the great hall, or perhaps in some humbler place, at Christmas. He sings of the Annunciation, the Nativity, the Harrowing of Hell and the Ascension; he sings, indeed, of events which he has probably witnessed with his own eyes—as Miracle Plays in the great annual cycle, as well as represented in sculpture and wood-carvings in churches, paintings, MS illuminations and stained glass. Thus, as in the Play of the Annunciation,

> *The aungil cam fro hevene tour.*

In this carol Mary is the rose-bush or tree which bears the rose-blossom (Christ).

> *Out of her bosum the blosme sprong.*

The alliteration and assonance intimately bring together 'bosum' and 'blosme'. There is no rose comparable to it in the world—and also none so much 'to mine likinge' is ever found in the world again. It sprang in Bedlem which is so bright and shining (like the Elfin Castle of the romances and ballads) because of the unusual star that signified the newborn *sol verus*. This rose is able to overcome the fiend's power. Though a flower, it is stronger than any material weapon that 'fells'—such as a giant's club; it has magical power over the hostile otherworld (like the Golden Bough), power over the fiend, power to harrow Hell.

Two other (inferior) versions of this carol suggest that the three branches spoken of in our version may originally or at least occasionally have been five and that they may have signified the Five Joys of Mary. In our version the first branch, that sprang on Christmas night, evidently signifies the Nativity; the second, that sprang to Hell and 'felled' the fiend's power, signifies the Harrowing of Hell; the third branch, that sprang to Heaven 'crop and rote therein to dwellen', signifies the Ascension. This third branch is 'our bote', the most potent of healing herbs; it is identified with the bread of the Mass.

Every day it scheweth in prestes hond.

Some of the finest of the English carols for Christmas other than those in the Sloane 2593 collection (made, it has been supposed, in Warwickshire or somewhere in that region) are to be found in the collection made by John Audelay (or Awdlay) in Shropshire, also in the early fifteenth century. 'Sing these caroles in Cristemas' is written on the manuscript (now the Bodleian MS Douce 302), and the carols follow.

Among them is a carol to Mary which offers some parallels to the one just quoted from the Sloane 2593 MS; its refrain begins 'There is a floure sprung of a tree'.

> *There is a floure sprung of a tree,*
> *The rote thereof is called Jesse;*
>   *A floure of price,*
> *There is none seche in Paradise.*

> *This flour is faire and fresche of heue;*
> *Hit fades never, bot ever is new;*
> *The blissful branche this flour on grew*
> *Was Mary mild that bare Jesu.*
>   *A flour of grace.*
> *Ayains all sorow hit is solas.*

The sede hereof was Godes sond,[1]
That God him selve sew with his hond
In Bedlem in that holy londe;
Amedis here herbere there he hir fond.
 This blissful floure
Sprang never bot in Mary's boure.

Two more stanzas describe the Annunciation and the Nativity; the concluding stanzas follow:

Angeles there cam out of here toure
To loke apon this freschele floure,
Houe faire he was in his coloure,
And hou sote in his savoure,
 And to behold
How seche a flour might spring in golde.

Of lilly, of rose of rise,
Of primrol, and of flour-de-lyse,
Of all the flours at my devise,
That floure of Jesse yet bers the pris,
 As most of hele
To slake oure sorows every dele.

I pray youe flours of this cuntre,
Where evere ye go, where ever ye be,
Hold hup the flour of good Jesse
Fore your frescheness and youre beute,
 As fairest of all,
And ever was, and ever schall.

This carol, like the one quoted from the Sloane 2593, again celebrates events which the singer may have witnessed as Miracle Plays—the Annunciation (often associated in medieval art with a vase of lilies or other flowers) and the Nativity; again, as in the Plays,

Angeles there cam out of here toure.

The imagery and symbolism are again largely horticultural. The

[1] sending.

73

branch is Mary and the flower is Christ. God is the husbandman who sowed the seed. The infant Christ of the Nativity is 'this freschele floure'. The image 'spring in golde' (if we accept the reading 'golde' instead of 'mold', the reading in a later MS) might possibly have been directly inspired by medieval paintings or MS illuminations in which there is so much gold. Such is the healing-virtue of the Christ-flower, it is the most potent of medicinal or magical herbs. The 'flours of this cuntre' in the con-cluding stanza correspond (we may surely feel) to Chaucer's 'O yonge fresshe folkes . . .'; a young human life, too, is a flower.

These traditional Christian carols occasionally reach through their symbolism to moments of what might be called metaphysical vision that remind one that they belong to the age of Dante.

> *For in this rose conteined was*
> *Hevene and erthe in litel space,*
> Res miranda.

The rose is again the rose that bore Jesus. The stanza comes from another lovely carol of the Nativity, 'There is no rose of swich vertu', found among a group of thirteen carols in a fifteenth-century MS in Trinity College.

§ 6

Among the carols of the Nativity, the Shepherds' carols form a distinct group and have a close relation to the Shepherds' Plays. The shepherds are recognizably the same characters as the realistic shepherds of the Plays. One or two of these carols appear to be songs that *might* have been sung as an intrinsic feature of the Plays; one or two *did* come in the Plays, as the Salutation of the Shep-herds came at the end of the Towneley Shepherds' Plays. Stanzas from a version of the carol which has the refrain

> *Terly terlow, terly terlow,*
> *So merily the shepardes began to blow*

appear in the text of one of the Coventry Corpus Christi Plays that has survived.

74

Versions of this carol, one of the most attractive of the Shepherds' carols, are found in two famous collections of the late
fifteenth century and the early sixteenth; these are, respectively, a
song-book in a Bodleian MS (Eng. Poet. e.l.) and the miscellany
(Balliol MS 354) of a certain Richard Hill who belonged to the
household of a London alderman. In this latter collection there is
one of the best of the Shepherds' carols, 'The shepard upon a hill
he satt'.

> *The shepard upon a hill he satt;*
> *He had on him his tabard[1] and his hat,*
> *His tarbox, his pipe, and his flagat;[2]*
> *His name was called Joly Joly Wat,*
>> *For he was a gud herdes boy.*
>> *Vt hoy!*
> *For in his pipe he made so much joy.*

This is the first of ten stanzas which tell the story of a shepherd on
the night of the Nativity. In this carol there is less of the wonder
and reverence which, in the Shepherds' carols and Shepherds'
Plays, to some extent restrain the boisterous farcical element; but
it expresses, as the Plays do, the jollity of the folk on a festive
occasion and it has also their homely realistic character. There are
such realistic touches as

> *He swet, he had gone faster than a pace*

and occasional exaggerated gestures, as of an actor on a stage,

> *He put his hond under his hode,*
> *He saw a star as rede as blode.*

Such effects are emphasized by the rhymes throughout. He says
good-bye to each of his sheep individually—to him they are his
fellow-creatures—before descending to Bedlem to salute the newborn one.

> *'Now farewell, Mall, and also Will!*
> *For my love go ye all still*
> *Unto I cum again you till,*
> *And evermore, Will—ring well thy bell.'*

[1] short coat, cape.   [2] flagon.

75

Vt hoy!
For in his pipe he made so much joy.

As in the Plays, the shepherd presents the infant Jesus with homely gifts, bits and pieces of his personal belongings.

'Jesu, I offer to thee here my pipe,
My skirt, my tar-box, and my scripe[1] *. . .'*

The familiarity of this shepherd towards the Holy Family is even less uninhibited than usual.

'Now farewell, mine owne herdes man Wat!'
'Yea, for God, lady, even so I hat;[2]
Lull well Jesu in thy lape,
And farewell, Joseph, with thy round cape!'
Vt hoy!
For in his pipe he made so much joy.

§ 7

A contrast to the carols of the Nativity are the lyrics on the tragic theme of Christ's death. In Richard Hill's miscellany (the Balliol 354 MS on which are the two Shepherds' carols just quoted from) is found the Corpus Christi Carol, surely the most original and poignant English rendering of the theme of the crucified Christ. The sense of irreparable loss is struck as the opening note, the catastrophe of the 'faucon'—the fiend or death perhaps—snatching up and carrying off one's mate.

Lully, lulley, lully, lulley,
The faucon hath borne my make away.

He bare him up, he bare him down,
He bare him into an orchard brown.

In that orchard there was an halle,
That was hanged with purpill and pall.

[1] wallet (for holding food).   [2] am called.

And in that hall there was a bede,
It was hanged with gold so rede.

And in that bed there lithe a knight,
His woundes bleding day and night.

By that bede side kneleth a may,
And she wepeth both night and day.

And by that bede side there stondeth a stone,
Corpus Christi *wreten there on*.

The inspiration is unmistakably the Grail Myth. This Corpus Christi Carol strangely recovers the original significance of the mortally wounded knight (of the Grail romances) as the slain god. The sense of being introduced to a mystery depends partly on the reticence that delays until the very end the recognition that the bleeding knight is Christ and, consequently, that the maiden who weeps both day and night for the slain knight is Mary, his mother. The wounds, we then realize, are those of the crucified body of Christ.[1]

The place is an orchard—a familiar and homely place, and yet it was an apple that brought about the Fall. In the romances and ballads, faery or magical events are apt to happen in an orchard, but in the spring; this is, however, an autumnal or withered orchard—'an orchard brown'. The hall in the orchard hung with purple and pall and, within the hall, the bed hung with gold, suggests some mystery or ceremonial ritual about to take place. The formula of poems of rites—such as the Corpus Christi Carol must surely be—retains in its structure a sense of being initiated by stages, which accounts for their strangely exciting quality. One is led by steps as through a maze until one reaches the centre of the maze, the heart of the mystery. At the end of the Corpus Christi Carol the bed becomes a tomb, as in a dream, for there is a stone beside it—'*Corpus Christi* wreten there on'—and we recognize with a shock that the wounded knight is Christ. (We may then

[1] The association of this carol with the Mass that has been made by some commentators may be a relevant one.

note that the lullaby phrases of the first line already suggest a mother and child.)

Yet the whole mysterious poem is apparently so simple, based on the simplest human situation—a maiden weeping for her new-slain knight, as in a ballad tragedy.

This Corpus Christi Carol was written down at the end of the fifteenth century or the beginning of the sixteenth. Yet it must have continued in oral tradition, continued to be sung, as late as the nineteenth century because what is unmistakably a folk-song version of it, 'All bells in Paradise', was written down in North Staffordshire in 1862.

> *Over yonder's a park, which is newly begun,*
> All bells in Paradise I heard them a-ring;
> *Which is silver on the outside, and gold within,*
> And I love sweet Jesus above all things.
>
> *And in that park there stands a hall,*
> *Which is covered all over with purple and pall.*
>
> *And in that hall there stands a bed,*
> *Which is hung all round with silk curtains so red.*
>
> *And in that bed there lies a knight,*
> *Whose wounds they do bleed by day and by night.*
>
> *At that bed side there lies a stone,*
> *Which is our blessed Virgin Mary then kneeling on.*
>
> *At that bed's foot there lies a hound,*
> *Which is licking the blood as it daily runs down.*
>
> *At that bed's head there grows a thorn,*
> *Which was never so blossomed since Christ was born.*

This version is remarkably close to the medieval poem, except that it introduces the Glastonbury Thorn. (But medieval tradition identified Glastonbury with Avalon, 'the isle of apples'.) Another version, very similar to 'All bells in Paradise', was written down in Derbyshire also in the nineteenth century. Early in the nineteenth century a version more like a Scottish folk-ballad, and with no reference to the wounded knight being Christ, was written down in Scotland by James Hogg.

> *The heron flew east, the heron flew west,*
> *The heron flew to the fair forest . . .*

My attention has been drawn to the rhyme of a children's game[1] which is a striking parallel to the medieval Corpus Christi Carol.

> *This is the Key of the Kingdom:*
> *In that Kingdom is a city;*
> *In that city is a town;*
> *In that town there is a street;*
> *In that street there winds a lane;*
> *In that lane there is a yard;*
> *In that yard there is a house;*
> *In that house there waits a room;*
> *In that room an empty bed;*
> *And on that bed a basket—*
> *A Basket of Sweet Flowers:*
> >Of Flowers, of Flowers;
> >A Basket of Sweet Flowers.
>
> *Flowers in a basket;*
> *Basket on the bed;*
> *Bed in the chamber;*
> *Chamber in the house;*
> *House in the weedy yard;*
> *Yard in the winding lane;*
> *Lane in the broad street;*
> *Street in the high town;*
> *Town in the city;*
> *City in the Kingdom—*
> *This is the Key of the Kingdom.*
> >Of the Kingdom this is the Key.

[1] It will be found in Walter de la Mare's *Come Hither*.

The antiquity of this rhyme is shown by its retention of 'town' with something of the original sense of a walled homestead; the 'weedy yard' may similarly have been the brown orchard of the Corpus Christi Carol, possibly the Garden of Eden overgrown with weeds after the Fall. The Basket of Flowers is either a symbol for Christ—the Easter Christ of the Resurrection—in which case it is a symbol which has replaced Christ just as He did the wounded King of the Grail-cult original; or else the Basket of Flowers is simply a substitute for the centre of the cult that better suited a children's game. The significant point is that this rhyme was actually played and danced; it associates the medieval poem with ritual action—the Corpus Christi Carol may well have been originally a ritual dance—or its descendant a game-song that was made into a Christian carol. Once again, in the children's rhyme one is led on by steps as though through a maze[1] until one reaches the centre—'In that house there *waits* a room'—where one is presented with the Key of the Kingdom, and then the dance unwinds itself again, leading back into the world.

The theme of the crucified Christ enters again into the arresting opening stanzas of 'In a valey of this restles minde', this version of which is found in a Lambeth MS 853 of the early fifteenth century.

> *In a valey of this restles minde*
>   *I soughte in mounteine and in mede,*
> *Trustinge a trewe love for to finde.*
>   *Upon an hill than I took hede;*
>   *A voice I herde, and neer I yede,[2]*
> *In huge dolour complaininge tho,*
>   *'See, dere soule, how my sides blede,*
> Quia amore langueo.'

> *Upon this hill I fond a tree,*
>   *Under the tree a man sittinge;*

---

[1] The actual stone-mazes used in dances no doubt of this kind ever since prehistoric times survive in the British Isles and all over Northern Europe. In the Middle Ages they were called Troys. See Mr. Jackson Knight's *Cumaean Gates*, notably Chap. VII, p. 106 et seq. Also pp. 142, 171.

[2] went.

From heed to foot wounded was he;
  His herte blood I segh bledinge;
A semely man to ben a king,
A graciouse face to loken unto.
  I askede why he had peininge.
He seide 'Quia amore langueo.

'*I am true love that fals was nevere;*
  My sister, mannes soule, I loved her thus;
Because we wolde in no wise discevere,
  I lefte my kingdom glorious.
  I purveide for her a paleis precious;
Sche fleith, I folowe, I soughte her so;
  I suffrede this peine piteous,
Quia amore langueo . . .'

There, again, is the figure of the wounded knight or king whom we recognize to be Christ. This poem also has associations with the romances; the wounded knight who is True Love (or Christ) is the knightly wooer of man's soul.

The opening line indicates that the landscape is an allegorical or symbolical one—an interior landscape of the mind. 'This restles minde' is imaged as a mountainous land; 'in a valey' suggests a mood of despondency (as in the allegory of the *Pilgrim's Progress*) of one who has sought hitherto in vain. The hill and the tree where he does at last find what he seeks are, most likely, Calvary and the Cross.

The man's soul is evidently engaged on a quest—trusting to find a true love. As in a romance or ballad, he comes eventually upon a man sitting under a tree, a wounded knight or king, who utters 'a complaint'. He is True Love (he is that which the man's soul was seeking) and he is the wooer of Man's soul. The reticence of allegory leaves it to us to recognize who this wounded knight really is. He is also the Heavenly Huntsman who has been pursuing, through this mountainous wilderness, the shy Soul. After this very striking opening, the rest of the poem (spoken by True Love) is rather inferior.

§ 8

Side by side with the sacred carols and songs, grave and gay, there are profane songs expressive of the jollity of the folk— Breugel's dancing villagers—at Christmas and other festival occasions. Among the carols in the Sloane 2593, and therefore a song that might be contemporary with Chaucer, there is one that differs from the others in being a profane carol of Yule, in the tradition of the songs of the *clerici vagantes*; there is an element of goliardic parody of the Mass in it.

Kyrie, *so kyrie,*
Jankin singeth merie,
    With eleyson.[1]

As I went on Yole day
    In oure prosession,
Knew I joly Jankin,
    Be his merie tone.
Jankin began the offis
    On the Yole day;
And yit me thinketh it dos me good,
    So merie gan he say
        Kyrieleyson.

Jankin red the pistil
    Full faire and full well,
And yit me thinketh it dos me good,
    As ever have I sel.[2]
Jankin at the Sanctus
    Craketh[3] *a merie note,*
And yit me thinketh it dos me good,
    I payed for his cote.

---

[1] Cf. the following lines from a trope of the Kyrie:

Kyrie,—Rex pie,—Da nobis hodie,—
Veniae—Munus et gratiae! Eleison.

[2] bliss.   [3] sings.

Jankin craketh notes
  An hunderid on a knot,
And yit he hakketh hem smallere
  Than wortes[1] to the pot.
    Kyrieleyson.

Jankin at the Agnus
  Bereth the Pax-brede;[2]
He twinkeled, but said nought,
And on mine fote he trede.
Benedicamus Domino,
  Crist from schame me schilde!
Deo gracias *thereto.*
  Alas, I go with childe.
    Kyrieleyson.

The Christmas service in church is turned privately into a profane occasion by the young clerk and young woman of this carol. The name of the clerk, who thus improves the sacred occasion in a profane sense, is appropriately Jankin, the name of the Wife of Bath's fifth husband (the young clerk whose legs she admired walking in the funeral procession of her fourth). The young woman, too, seems to be a namesake of the Wife of Bath, Alison; the solemn phrase of the Mass as sung by clerk Jankin—*Kyrieleyson*—which becomes a refrain in the carol, almost certainly sounds like her own name to Alison and is probably intended by Jankin to do so—to sound like a wooing-song or lover's call. It is a very human episode, and it has a very natural consequence. The climax of the carol, which Alison herself sings as a *dramatis persona*, is the discovery:

Alas, I go with childe.

We should be careful, however, not to confuse such a profane or goliardic song with the songs welcoming Yule or King Christmas and the songs and carols for the boar-feast or ale-feast as

[1] vegetables.
[2] dish of silver or gilt with a handle and a sacred symbol, used in giving the kiss of peace to the congregation. Its introduction is attributed to the Franciscans.

Christmas still largely was. These latter songs are rooted in the old Pagan religion and are, therefore, not really profane songs. The old Yule feast, all-important for restoring the life and fertility of the year, had simply been given a new and richer significance as the birth-feast of Christ. But it still had a great deal of the character of the old Pagan boar-feast and ale-feast, in which the strength of the boar and the life of the ale entered into the company that partook of them and bound it together.

One of the earliest extant versions of the Boar's Head Carol (still sung as part of the Boar's Head custom at Queen's College, Oxford) appears to be the version in Richard Hill's miscellany (Balliol 354 MS). It was probably sung as the boar's head was borne ceremoniously into the hall, gaily decked like a god—having been indeed originally a divinity for the sacred feast.

> *The bores hede in hondes I bringe,*
> *With garlondes gay and birdes singinge.*
> *I pray you all, helpe me to singe,*
> Qui estis in convivio. . . .

Attempts were evidently made to Christianize even this feature of the Yule feast. Thus one version reads:

> *The borys hede that we bryng here*
> *Betokeneth a Prince withowte pere*
> *Ys born this day to bye us dere* . . .

Another distinct group of traditional songs associated with the ceremonies and dramatic games that clustered round the Christmas feast are the Holly and Ivy Carols. A number of these are found in the fifteenth-century song-book in the Bodleian MS Eng. Poet. e.l. already referred to. In his introduction, R. L. Greene has much of interest to say about the folk-customs connected with the holly and the ivy; he concludes: 'From such a rich background of folk-custom the holly-ivy carol emerges.'[1] It was the custom, for example, until recent times in England and France for two effigies known as the Holly-Boy (carried by the girls) and the Ivy-Girl (carried by the boys) to be burnt at Shrove-

[1] *Early English Carols*, Introduction, IV, The Carol as Popular Song, p. 102.

tide. There can be no doubt that the various holly[1] and ivy customs had an ancestry in ancient fertility rites.

The Holly and the Ivy Carols are clearly songs for the Holly and Ivy debate or flyting-match—a contention between the men (identified with the holly) and the women (identified with the ivy). They contend for the 'maistrie', the one side praising its own tree and mocking the other. This ceremonial contention—it may have taken the form of a dance or game—most probably had its origin in the rites of the old Nature religions. The pattern is seen in its elementary form in the song 'Holver and Heivy made a grete party' (Eng. Poet. e.l.); here the contention ends in reconciliation between the men and the women, essential if life is to go on. A carol in praise of ivy, 'Ivy chefe of treis it is', and one in praise of holly, 'Here commes holly', are found together in this same MS. It seems that in this contention the women were sometimes excluded from the hall. Thus another fifteenth-century carol begins:

> *Holy stond in the hall, fayre to behold;*
> *Ivy stond without the dore; she is ful sore a-cold.*

> *Holy and hys mery men, they dawnsyn and they syng;*
> *Ivy and hur maydenys, they wepyn and they wryng.*

One of the jolliest of these holly-ivy carols is found in Richard Hill's miscellany (Balliol MS 354). Holly is praised, Ivy mocked. Holly's merry men can dance, for example, whereas Ivy's gentle women have not that accomplishment; the song ends with a striking image of the latter's clumsiness.

> *Nay, nay, Ivy!*
> *It may not be, iwis,*
> *For Holly must have the mastry*
> *As the manner is.*

> *Holly bereth beries,*
> *Beris rede ynow;*

[1] The fact that there are both male and female kinds of holly may have been recognized at an early time, in addition to the obvious symbolic value of the fact that it is evergreen.

The thristilcok, the popingay
    Daunce in every bough.
Welaway, sory Ivy!
    What fowles hast thou,
But the sory howlet
    That singeth 'How how'?

Ivy bereth beris
    As blak as any sloe.
There commeth the woode colver,[1]
    And fedeth her of tho;
She lifteth up her taill
    And she cakkes or she go;
She wold not for an hundred pound
    Serve Holly so.

Holly with his mery men
    They can daunce in hall;
Ivy and her jentell women
    Can not daunce at all,
But like a meine[2] *of bullokes*
    In a water fall,
Or on a hot somers day
    Whan they be mad all.

Other carols which express the jollity of the English people on festive occasions are the carols for the ale-feast—and no doubt any convivial gathering might become such. In Richard Hill's miscellany there is a carol in which the butler is called with mock impatience and increasingly desperate urgency, a carol to be acted as well as sung.

Jentill butler, bellamy,[3]
Fill the boll by the eye,
That we may drink by and by,
    With 'How, butler, how!
    Bevis a tout!*[4]
Fill the boll, butler,
And let the cup rout!'[5]

[1] pigeon.   [2] company.   [3] bel ami.   [4] beuvez à tous.   [5] go round.

Here is mete for us all,
Both for grete and for small.
I trow we must the butler call,
  With 'How, butler, how!'

I am so dry I cannot speke;
I am nigh choked with my mete;
I trow the butler be aslepe.
  With 'How, butler, how!'

Butler, butler, fill the boll,
Or elles I beshrewe thy noll.[1]
I trow we must the bell toll,
  With 'How, butler, how!'

In the fifteenth-century song-book, Eng. poet. e.l., there are versions of 'Bring us in good ale' and 'Doll thy ale, doll'.

Bring us in good ale, and bring us in good ale;
For our blessed Lady sake bring us in good ale!
  Bring us in no browne bred, for that is made of brane,
  Nor bring us in no white bred, for therein is no gane,
    But bring us in good ale!
Bring us in no befe, for there is many bones,
But bring us in good ale, for that goth downe at ones,
    And bring us in good ale!
  Bring us in no bacon, for that is passing fat,
  But bring us in good ale, and gife us enought of that;
    And bring us in good ale!
Bring us in no mutton, for that is often lene,
Nor bring us in no tripes, for they be seldom clene,
    But bring us in good ale!
Bring us in no egges, for there are many schelles,
But bring us in good ale, and gife us nothing elles;
    And bring us in good ale!
  Bring us in no butter, for therein are many heres,
  Nor bring us in no pigges flesch, for that will make us bores,
    But bring us in good ale!

[1] noddle.

> *Bring us in no podinges, for therein is all Godes good,*
> *Nor bring us in no venesen, for that is not for our blod;*
> > *But bring us in good ale!*
> *Bring us in no capons flesch, for that is often dere,*
> *Nor bring us in no dokes flesch, for they slober in the mere,*
> > *But bring us in good ale!*

Flesh and fowl—though rejected in favour of ale with an emphasis as of heavy dancing feet thumping the ground—are nevertheless abundantly present as images, together with their farmyard, village common and countryside associations, giving the song its character.

'Doll thy ale, doll' makes a solemn pretence of warning folk against the awful risks of drinking ale, rising to the climax of 'ale make many a man to hang upon the galows'. R. L. Greene actually takes the song seriously; he has the following unbelievable note,[1] apparently having missed the kind of humour the song expresses: 'The vigorous disapproval expressed in this carol of the nearly universal English beverage is surprising, especially in view of the convivial associations of carol-singing. It marks the piece as certainly the work of a moralizing religious, probably, to judge from its realistic observation of drunkenness in humble life, a friar.' The rollicking rhythm alone should have saved Greene.

> *Doll thy ale, doll, doll they ale, doll!*
> *Ale make many a man to have a doty poll.*
> *Ale make many a man to stik at a brere;*
> *Ale make many a man to ly in the miere;*
> *And ale make many a man to slepe by the fiere.*
> > *With doll!*
> *Ale make many a man to stombel at a stone;*
> *Ale make many a man to go dronken home,*
> *And ale make many a man to breke his tone.*
> > *With doll!*
> *Ale make many a man to draw his knife;*
> *Ale make many a man to make grete strife;*

[1] *Early English Carols*, Notes, 423, p. 438.

And ale make many a man to bete his wife.
  With doll!
Ale make many a man to wet his chekes;
Ale make many a man to ly in the stretes;
And ale make many a man to wet his shetes.
  With doll!
Ale make many a man to stombell at the blokkes;
Ale make many a man to make his hed have knokkes;
And ale make many a man to sit in the stokkes.
  With doll!
Ale make many a man to rin over the falows;
Ale make many a man to swere by God and Allhalows;
And ale make many a man to hang upon the galows.
  With doll!

§ 9

The melancholy reflections and moralizings of the Middle Ages
are sufficient in number, even in song. One of the most impressive
longer lyrics of this nature is found in the MS Digby 86 (one of
the Friar miscellanies) which contain poems in French, Latin and
English, and was made probably by Dominicans in the Priory of
Worcester in the late thirteenth century (a little before the Harley
2253). It begins as a rendering of the *Ubi sunt*, the mutability
theme.

> *Were beth they biforen us weren,*
> *Houndes ladden and hauekes beren,*
>   *And hadden feld and wode,*
>   *The riche levedies in hoere bour,*
>   *That wereden gold in hoere tressour,*[1]
>   *With hoere brightte rode?*[2]
>
> *Eten and drounken and maden hem glad;*
> *Hoere lif was al with gamen ilad;*
>   *Men keneleden hem biforen;*
>   *They beren hem wel swithe heye;*[3]

[1] head-dress, caul *or* tresses?.   [2] face.   [3] i.e. very haughtily.

And in a twincling of an eye
Hoere soules weren forloren.

Were is that laghing and that song,
That trayling[1] *and that proude yong,*[2]
Tho hauekes and tho houndes?
Al that joye is went away,
That wele is comen to welaway
To manie harde stoundes.[3]

Hoere paradis they nomen[4] *here,*
And nou they lien in helle ifere;[5]
The fuir hit brennes hevere.
Long is ay and long is ho,
Long is wy and long is wo;
Thennes ne cometh they nevere.

The pride and transience of life are vividly and poignantly presented in these opening stanzas, though touched by a breath of the moralist's scorn for frail humankind: 'They bore themselves high and in the twinkling of an eye they lost their souls; they had their Paradise here on earth.' There is, as the poem goes on to represent, the alternative of Christian salvation. The exhortation, in the succeeding stanzas, to take up the Cross as a staff and the shield of True Belief, like Christian in the *Pilgrim's Progress,* reminds us that here as early as the thirteenth century is Bunyan's tradition. The poem ends with an appeal to Mary to shield us from the Fiend. But as a whole this poem is less personal than 'Wynter wakeneth al my care'. There is something of the preacher in it; one feels that the poet has an illusion of his own relative security as belonging perhaps to a religious order, and can afford to exhort others; he has confidence that he *knows*.

There is, however, an Anglo-Irish cradle-song—'Lollai, lollai, litil child! Whi wepistou so sore?'—which we may more properly associate with 'Wynter wakeneth al my care' because of its individual rhythm and essential bleakness. The song must be

[1] trailing (dresses).　　[2] going, walk.　　[3] pains.　　[4] took.　　[5] together.

nearly contemporary with 'Wynter wakeneth' since it is also found in an MS of the early fourteenth century (Harley MS 913), a miscellany of Latin, French and English poems written down apparently in a Franciscan house in Kildare. It differs from the numerous Lullaby Carols that have been preserved in that the infant is not Jesus but a purely human infant. There could be no greater contrast to the joyous Nativity Carols. It is a sad lullaby to sing to a little child, even though not old enough to understand. The child is born into this world to suffer the lot of man since Adam's fall; it is told, even in its cradle, not to trust the world full of grief and vicissitude.

> *Ne tristou to this world;*
>   *Hit is thi ful fo.*
> *The rich he makith pouer,*
>   *The pore rich also.*
> *Hit turneth wo to wel,*
>   *And eke wel to wo.*
> *Ne trist no man to this world,*
>   *Whil hit turnith so.*
>   *Lollai, lollai, litil child!*
>   *The fote is in the whele.*
>   *Thou nost whoder turne*
>   *To wo other wele.*

Man is born to die; it is a gloomy way of associating birth and death.

> *Deth ssal com with a blast*
> *Ute of a wel dim horre.*

§ 10

Comedy makes its appearance among the extant English lyrics as early as those in the Harley 2253 MS of the beginning of the fourteenth century. Together with 'Lenten is come with love to toune', 'Bytuene Mersh ant Averil', 'Wynter wakeneth' and the other lyrics in this, the Leominster, collection there is a poem in which the Man in the Moon figures as a character, an English countryman gossiped about as if he were a neighbour and, at intervals, addressed and shouted to directly by another country-man. The poem is the dramatic monologue of this latter country-man, who is himself a 'character'; for it is his speaking voice, the very accents and movement of a slow countryman's speech that we hear reproduced in the masterly verse. Almost a century before Chaucer, the poem is a small-scale masterpiece of dramatic comedy. It should be sufficient in itself to make us revise our con-ventional notions about the development of English poetry before Chaucer.

> *Mon in the mone stond ant strit,*[1]
>   *On is*[2] *bot-forke*[3] *is*[2] *burthen he bereth;*
> *Hit is muche wonder that he nadoun slyt,*[4]
>   *For doute*[5] *leste he valle, he shoddreth ant shereth.*[6]
> *When the forst freseth, muche chele he byd;*
>   *The thornes beth kene, is hattren*[7] *to-tereth.*
> *Nis no wyht in the world that wot wen he syt,*
>   *Ne, bote hit bue the hegge, whet wedes he wereth.*
>
> *Whider trowe this mon ha the wey take?*
>   *He hath set is o fot is other to-foren;*
> *For non hihte that he hath*[8] *ne syht me*[9] *hym ner shake,*[10]
>   *He is the sloweste mon that euer wes yboren.*
> *Wher he were o the feld pycchynde stake,*[11]
>   *For hope of ys thornes to dutten is doren,*[12]
> *He mot myd is twybyl*[13] *other trous make,*
>   *Other*[14] *al is dayes werk ther were yloren.*
>
> *This ilke mon upon heh when er he were,*
>   *Wher he were y the mone boren ant yfed,*
> *He leneth on is forke ase a grey frere.*
>   *This crokede caynard*[15] *sore he is adred.*

[1] strides.   [2] his.   [3] forked stick.   [4] does not slide down.   [5] fear.
[6] turns.   [7] his clothes.   [8] effort that he makes.   [9] no one saw.   [10] move.
[11] driving in stakes.   [12] ? to stop up his gaps.   [13] two-edged axe.
[14] either hedge-cuttings make, Or else . . .   [15] idle fellow.

Hit is mony day go that he was here.
   Ichot of is ernde he nath nout ysped,
He hath hewe sumwher a burthen of brere;
   Tharefore sum hayward hath taken ys wed.[1]

'*Yef thy wed ytake, bring hom the trous,*
   Sete forth thyn other fot, stryd ouer sty.[2]
We shule preye the haywart hom to vr hous
   Ant maken hym at heyse for the maystry,
Drynke to hym deorly of fol god bous,
   Ant oure Dame Douse shal sitten hym by.
When that he is dronke ase a dreynt mous,
   Thenne we schule borewe the wed ate bayly.'[3]

This mon hereth me nout thah ich to hym crye;
   Ichot the cherl is def, the Del hym to-drawe![4]
Thah ich yeye[5] *vpon heh nulle nout hye,*[6]
   The lostlase ladde con nout o lawe,[7]
'*Hupe*[8] *forth Hubert, hosede pye!*[9]
   Ichot thart amarscled in-to the mawe.'[10]
Thah me teone[11] *with hym that myn teth nye,*[12]
   The cherl nul nout adoun er the day dawe.

There is a blend of fantasy and realism—the realism having direct reference to the condition and distresses of the peasantry—in the humour and comedy of the poem: for example, the Man in the Moon 'stands and strides', because he is a kind of *picture* of a man striding; he is apparently hard put to it to keep his balance, to prevent himself from falling down; because of the bundle of thorns he carries, he seems 'to wear the hedge'; he has set one foot before the other, yet he has not been seen to move. He is in trouble with the

---

[1] his pledge i.e. security for the payment of a fine.   [2] path.
[3] redeem the pledge from the bailiff.   [4] rend.   [5] call, shout.
[6] he will not hurry.   [7] ? the lazy fellow knows nothing about the law.
[8] hop.   [9] i.e. magpie that looks as if it had hose on.
[10] This line has never been satisfactorily explained. Could it mean, 'I believe you have settled into your own belly' (i.e. within the circle of the moon)?
[11] may be angry.   [12] teeth gnash.

hayward for having cut for his own use a bundle of briars where he should not have done. That is perhaps why, afraid to come home, he has to endure in the moon the winter cold. The countryman who speaks the poem is ready—at this point he addresses the Man in the Moon directly—to make common cause with his unfortunate neighbour now in exile: 'We shall invite the hayward to our house, fill him up with good booze and so get back the "pledge".' But Hubert in the moon appears to be deaf and will not come down.

Several of the most vigorous pieces among the English lyrics have a close relation to the alliterative poetry. A satiric poem (Harley 2253 MS)—alliterative and rhymed in stanzas—on the follies of fashion has much the same texture as a passage on the same subject in the Towneley Play of the Last Judgement (fifteenth-century Towneley MS). Perhaps the most notable alliterative piece among the lyrics is an onomatopoeic flyting against blacksmiths and the din they make.

> *Swarte smekyd[1] smethes, smateryd[2] wyth smoke,*
> *dryue me to deth wyth den of here dyntes!*
> *Swech noys on nyghtes ne herd men neuer:*
> *What knavene[3] cry, and clateryng of knockes!*
> *The cammede[4] kongons[5] cryen after 'col, col!'*
> *and blowen here bellewys that al here brayn brestes.*
> *'huf, puf!' seyth that on. 'haf, paf!' that other.*
> *Thei spyttyn and spraulyn and spellyn many spelles,*
> *thei gnauen and gnacchen,[6] thei gronys togydere,*
> *and holdyn hem hote wyth here hard hamers.*
> *Of a bole hyde ben here barm-fellys,[7]*
> *here schankes ben schakeled for the fere-flunderys;[8]*
> *hevy hamerys thei han that hard ben handled,*
> *stark strokes thei stryken on a stelyd[9] stokke.*
> *'Lus, bus! las, das!' rowtyn be rowe[10]*
> *sweche dolful a dreme[11] the devyl it todryve;*

[1] smoked.   [2] smutted.   [3] of knaves.   [4] snub-nosed? crooked?
[5] changelings, misshapen creatures.   [6] grind and gnash (their teeth).
[7] leather-aprons.   [8] fiery sparks.   [9] steel.   [10] beat, crash in turn.   [11] noise.

the mayster longith a lityl and lascheth a lesse,
twyneth hem tweyn, and towchith a treble.[1]
'Tik, tak! hic, hac! tiket, taket! tyk, tak!
lus, bus! lus, das!'—swych lyf thei ledyn!
Alle clothemerys[2] *cryst hem gyve sorwe,*
may no man for brenwaterys[3] *on nyght han hys rest!*

There is humorous exasperation, but also a strong current of enjoyment and zest in reproducing the sounds and the physical
sense of the huge exertions of the smiths. The noisy, rowdy activity
and the power exerted by the smiths rouse antagonism and yet
release a corresponding life-energy in their disturbed and provoked
neighbour.

Sufficient of the lyric poetry has survived and is there to testify
by itself, even if nothing else had survived, to the variety and
humanity of English medieval literature. To the more traditional
songs and lyrics we should have to add the best of the Chaucerian
and post-Chaucerian lyrics, the lyrics of William Dunbar and
the songs and lyrics that lead up to those of Wyatt—not only
Wyatt's smoother musician's songs but also his more dramatic
and introspective lyrics which point forward to Donne and the
seventeenth-century poets.

NOTE. Those to whom this suggested connexion between
Chaucer, Wyatt and Donne, as masters of colloquial English in
verse, may seem entirely fanciful, might find it worth while to
compare the following passage from *Troilus and Criseyde* (Book
III, stanzas 208-10) with the opening stanza of Donne's *The
Sunne Rising*.

> *'O cruel day, accusour of the joye*
> *That night and love han stole and faste y-wryen,*
> *A-cursed be thy coming in-to Troye,*

---

[1] Sisam suggests as a possible interpretation: 'The master smith lengthens a little
piece (i.e. of hot iron), and hammers a smaller piece, twines the two together, and
strikes (with his hammer) a treble note.'
[2] mare-clothers (i.e. smiths because they clothe horses in armour).
[3] water-burners (i.e. smiths because they plunge hot iron in water).

For every bore hath oon of thy bright yën!
Envyous day, what list thee so to spyen?
What hastow lost, why sekestow this place,
Ther god thy lyght so quenche, for his grace?

Allas! what han thise loveres thee agilt,
Dispitous day? thyn be the pyne of helle!
For many a lovere hastow shent, and wilt;
Thy pouring in wol no-wher lete hem dwelle.
What proferestow thy light here for to selle?
Go selle it hem that smale seles graven,
We wol thee nought, us nedeth no day haven.'

And eek the sonne Tytan gan he chyde,
And seyde, 'O fool, wel may men thee dispyse,
That hast the Dawing al night by thy syde,
And suffrest hir so sone up fro thee ryse,
For to disesen loveres in this wyse.
What! hold your bed ther, thou, and eek thy Morwe!
I bidde god, so yeve yow bothe sorwe!'

III
ROMANCES

III. ROMANCES

§ 1

A NOTE ON THE ENGLISH ROMANCES

The fifty or sixty medieval English romances (like the folk-ballads that were written down in the eighteenth and nineteenth centuries) are not merely an accidental collection of isolated pieces—accidental because survival was not, in the conditions of MS copying and preservation, a necessary consequence of outstanding merit. Each separate piece loses by being read apart from the others. However nearly it approaches completeness in itself, it seems to find its place in a larger whole, a single body of poetry. To regard the medieval romances as composing one larger poem is, then, perhaps the most satisfying way of regarding them; each romance makes more distinct the others by which it is in its turn made more distinct. What seem to be fragments of a single pattern begin to emerge—'the figure in the carpet'—a pattern that begins to be more distinct when seen as common to more than one romance.

It is not simply that the romances share a common art, a common attitude to their subject-matter or method of treating it such as by itself would justify their being regarded as a single *genre*. The diversities among the English romances alone are such as to indicate different schools of makers (and reciters) in different parts of England throughout two or three centuries of change. There are the one or two surviving versions which are alliterative poetry or which, even if rhymed or stanzaic, are under the shaping influence of the alliterative poetry; and these mostly North-West Midland or Northern poems have characteristics which are distinct from the versions that appear to be fairly closely modelled on the French.

What makes it difficult to see clearly the things which the English romances by themselves have in common (they have, of course, the English language in common) is that the versions imply different cultural and social levels as well as different degrees of poetic skill in their makers or adapters. Particularly we have to allow for the injury which many of the versions have evidently suffered in oral transmission or at the hands of copyists. We have to remember that such of the English romances as have survived have done so mostly as 'versions'—like the folk⁄ballads—in varying states of completeness. A number (and these, including the Gawain romances preserved in the Percy Folio MS of about 1650, are not always the least interesting) have survived in a very broken⁄down and fragmentary condition. Generally, therefore, we have to think of each romance that has survived rather as a 'version' than as the one and only, the unique original. The English romances preserve on the whole an anonymity—the names of their makers have sel⁄dom been recorded—almost as complete as that of the folk⁄ballads. They require to be regarded rather as we regard the versions of the ballads than as we regard the literary compositions of personal men⁄of⁄letters.

One might therefore be tempted to conclude that what the romances do have in common is not an art but a subject⁄matter, and that the pattern which begins to emerge from the extant romances is in *that*, a pattern pre⁄existent in the subject⁄matter. But it is not possible to separate subject⁄matter from artistic form. The traditional material out of which the medieval romances were made must already have had some form—no doubt forms that were constantly changing—otherwise it could not have existed, could not have been recited to audiences and transmitted from one generation and place to another. This traditional material must have existed—in the forms in which it did exist—previously to the romances which were made out of it, and independently of them.

The medieval romancers are artists, of varying degrees of skill; and as artists they shape and re⁄shape, select and rearrange their traditional material. They did not themselves invent this material on which they worked; to them it was something given—in some form. It must have had its own themes, and these come out again in the medieval romances, modified and rearranged but still identifiable.

This traditional material consisted, of course, of traditional tales, tales that were told and had been told over long periods of time and in different places. Though continually re-shaped in the process of transmission, such a tale has often persisted as in essentials the same tale. Even when written down, and thus given a literary and less unstable existence, it was liable to be used again for recital to audiences and thence caught back into the stream of oral transmission. Since the medieval makers did not invent the tales they made into romances, we should have to seek for the origin of these tales elsewhere and in an earlier, perhaps ancient, age. But, from an examination of the tales which have been transformed into romances, we can say something about their nature. For the most part, they certainly appear to be the kind of tales that have originated as myths—stories of what happened or what was done in ritual ceremonies.

The tale is greater than the teller; the typical medieval maker feels this and has a respect for the tale that may seem to modern readers at times excessive. We may in this way (allowing also for mere inertia) account for the preservation in later versions of details from earlier versions, even when these details appear no longer to have been understood or to have any intelligible function in the changed tale. Missing details are likely to have been *accidentally* lost. Thus we find in the romances fragments of mythological material untransmuted, apparently no longer understood but still reproduced. The tale appears generally to have been accorded the kind of status we accord to that reconstruction of bits and pieces out of past events which we call history, indeed to have been regarded as a kind of history—not as fiction but as objective truth, having its own rights and its claim to be respected. Only a few makers were daring or original enough to re-shape a tale entirely.

The romances thus come at the end of a long evolution. Tale-telling had long been a developed professional skill and was a principal entertainment of the medieval communities as of the earlier communities from which the medieval had evolved.[1] But 'entertainment' may not be quite the right word as applied even to the medieval romances, their makers and audiences. Even as a medieval romance, the traditional tale appears often to have an aura of 'sacredness' about it, perhaps flowing without a break from a sacred or ritual origin. In such matters we can only judge by 'appearances'; there is nothing else *there* for us to judge by.

What, then, could have been the role of the more original maker working in the tradition of medieval romance-making? At his best—above all as the truly great poet of *Sir Gawayne and the Grene Knight* who handles his traditional material with Shakespearian freedom—he divines the potentialities, the germ of possibilities, in the tale itself; and he shapes the tale in such a way as to bring these out and develop them into new and complex significance. The tale does not, of course, return to what it may have been when it originally came into being, a myth; in the new medieval time, in the hands of a master poet, it becomes again something new, the poem.

§ 2

As we compare the extant romances, we recognize that—in one variation or other—a number of motifs or themes recur in them. The impression grows on the reader that these themes are, many of them, interrelated—

> . . . *workings of the one mind, the features*
> *Of the same face, blossoms upon one tree—*

and that they are fragments of what were originally myths. Anthropologists, and other workers in the field of the origins of literature, have assembled a great deal of evidence that would seem to confirm this impression—even though there remains uncertainty as to what exactly was the mythology (or mythologies) that may have been the principal source even of these traditional tales

---

[1] *Faire ben tales in Compaignye*
Mery in chirche is melodye . . .

(King Alisaunder, *c.* 1300.)

that were made into the Arthurian romances. J. L. Weston in *From Ritual to Romance* and her other books, R. S. Loomis in *Celtic Myth and Arthurian Romance* and C. B. Lewis in *Classical Mythology and Arthurian Romance* (the titles indicate the arguments of the books) at least agree that the medieval romances come at the end of a process of evolution from myth (or ritual). The evidence and arguments of these and other investigators are, cumulatively, impressive; the different pieces fit into place. To avoid taking advantage of their investigations and guesses or intuitions is to risk condemning oneself to an impoverished reading of the romances. Their books are not literary criticism; nevertheless, after reading them, one certainly *notices* things in the romances that one might, or would, have missed and that are (one can now see) really there. The precise significance of some details of the traditional material in the romances may be forgotten—may already have been for-gotten even by the romancers themselves, though it was always liable to be divined or intuitively re-discovered—and may be dis-puted; but the main sense of its significance often remains and is still an effective force in the poetry.

Once the Arthurian romances, and the other romances that may be associated with them, are recognized as being rooted in myths they begin to show themselves more full of *meaning* and thus more interesting as *poetry*. The narrow 'aesthetic' attitude to the romances tends to exclude so much that is actually (on a more alert and sensitive reading) there. The transmutation of traditional tales—and hence of mythical and ritual elements in these tales—into medieval romances is indeed often far from complete, and it cannot be said that the *poetry* always suffers as a consequence. The best episodes poetically are often those in which the original mythical elements are most alive. In the same way those nursery-tales which are in origin folk-tales are frequently found more deeply satisfying both by children and by adults than are the nursery-tales specially fabricated for children in the nineteenth and twentieth centuries. The genuine folk-ballad also—however fragmentary and broken-down the version in which it has survived—is generally felt to be more satisfying than, with one or two notable exceptions, the 'literary' ballad.

The theory that the traditional tales out of which the medieval romances were made originated as myths—the stories of things done, acts performed in rituals—seems borne out if one simply observes those romances themselves and compares a number of them. As romances, of course, they are no longer myths; we must not confuse the myth with the poem. But even as romances the tales are still noticeably rooted in myths; they have not, in many cases, been so severed from these roots that they do not continue to draw, as poetry, some sustenance therefrom. The romance which has developed (or even maintained) some of that mythical signifi-cance is often, to that extent, more fully a poem. It continues to be recognizably more significant than, as we say when we see no significance in a tale, 'just a tale'. New life has in such a case budded out from the old.

The general tendency even of the English romancers, especially those who follow most closely the courtly and literary French models, is of course to rationalize, humanize and Christianize the traditional tales. Yet the less rationalized, humanized and Chris-tianized a romance is (for example, the English *Sir Percevelle*), the more interesting a poem it often is. The gods of ancient mythology have become the medieval knights of the romances; but they have also become the monstrous or otherworld antagonists of the knights, as such retaining their unhuman or otherworld charac-ter. The goddesses—spring, flower, earth or moon goddesses, or fountain, tree, lake or sea spirits—have become courtly ladies, queens or kings' daughters in the romances; but they also have often retained their otherworld character as faery beings. The 'faery mistress', for instance, of many of the romances remains essentially different from the courtly lady of the trouvères; she is frequently the wooer, very forward in contrast to the lady of courtly love poetry, who is so difficult to woo, and sometimes she has magical power over her human lover.

Why the romances—even such as have chanced to survive—seem to compose a single body of poetry may be, therefore, not only because to some extent they share the same principles and conventions of poetic art and reflect the same phase of European civilization and idealism; it may be also because they have evolved

A Note on the English Romances

from traditional tales and tale-telling and are at much the same stage in such an evolution and have common roots in myth and ritual. Most deeply ingrained in the romances certainly appear to be those traditional *motifs* or themes that run right through them. However deep we dig in the romances—through the rationaliza tion, humanization and Christianization—we cannot dig deeper than these themes. Nor can they be ignored in any attempt to appreciate and understand the poems. Not only may separate romances be frequently recognized as different versions of what is essentially one and the same traditional tale; but also different traditional tales are frequently found inextricably interrelated and interwoven in the same romance. Partly, our critical task is to piece together the romances (as we might the versions of a ballad) to see more clearly the whole poem they compose and at the same time to see more clearly each individual piece in relation to the whole. The romances may be regarded as new variations on the old themes of the traditional tales or new developments from them. These themes include those that Shakespeare in his time inherited and made profound use of, especially in his later plays.

§ 3

Mery hit is in halle to here the harpe
Theo mynstral syngith, theo jogolour carpith.

(King Alisaunder)

The extant English romances belong to the period of transition —the thirteenth, fourteenth and fifteenth centuries—from oral poetry to written composition, from poetry for recital (or for being read aloud to a company) to poetry for private reading. They belong to the period of the decline of minstrelsy in England and the emergence (once again in history) of the personal man-of-letters, the *literary* artist. The causes of the decay of minstrelsy are no doubt to be sought in the whole complex of changes in civiliza tion, and are therefore not primarily the business of the literary critic as such. There appears to have been increasing copying of secular poems by clerks; the secular scrivener also (Chaucer's Adam Scrivener, perhaps) makes his appearance. MSS grew in number till finally, in the fifteenth century, printing began to multiply mechanically the copies of books and aided the extension of private reading simply by increasing the opportunities for it. At about the same time the withdrawal of the lord and lady to private apartments[1] in the manor-houses of the fifteenth century must have meant that the audience in the great hall was often no longer there for minstrel recitals; it must have meant that there could no longer so easily be assembled an audience of various degrees of cultivation corresponding to that of the Elizabethan theatres a little later or to that of the Icelandic homesteads in the heyday of the sagas. These circumstances among many others would tend to alter the nature of the romances. But even after the minstrels had ceased to be patronized by the nobles, after the homogeneous audience of diverse social ranks and levels of cultivation in the great hall had dissolved or could no longer be assembled there, and even after what had once been a proud and honoured profession had been reduced virtually to beggary, minstrels must still have been able to collect a fluctuating 'popular' audience to listen to their lays in alehouse or market-place or on the village-green—an audience corresponding more or less, perhaps, to that of the balladists. The versions of Gawain romances preserved in the Percy Folio MS of about 1650 appear to imply just such an audience.

The extant English romances accordingly not only reflect in themselves various social and cultural levels; in reflecting the transition from oral to written poetry they also reflect various degrees of *literacy*. We must not, however, assume that literacy necessarily implies a higher cultural level or a higher level of art than illiteracy. The acquirements of reading and writing do not by themselves bring greater skill in the art of poetry, either in the

---

[1] Cf. in *Piers Plowman* already (B-text, Passus X).

> *Elyng is the halle   uche daye in the wyke,*
> *There the lorde ne the lady   liketh noughte to sytte.*
> *Now hath uche riche a reule   to eten bi hym-selve*
> *In a pryve parloure   for pore mennes sake,*
> *Or in a chambre with a chymneye   and leve the chief halle,*
> *That was made for meles   men to eten inne.*

A Note on the English Romances

art of its composition or in the art of its appreciation. Those English romances which reflect a greater degree of literacy in poet and audience are not always those which show greater art. Certainly, the direct and intimate collaboration of poet and audience in the art of oral poetry is no longer possible when the poet composes in his study and his readers are more or less unknown to him. The advance of literacy did not promote, in the case of the English romances at least, a finer poetic art. The earlier versions (such as *King Horn* and *Sir Orfeo*) and the fourteenth-century versions from the North and West Midlands seem to be those that are closest to still flourishing traditions of oral composition and recital; on the whole they are also as poetic art the surest and finest English romances—if we except Chaucer's *Knight's Tale* and such others of Chaucer's tales as may be regarded as romances.

The broken-down state of the interesting Gawain romances in the Percy Folio MS may more probably be accounted for by a deterioration in the oral tradition than by faulty copying. They appear to be late versions that yet belong as much to oral tradition as do the folk-ballads (perhaps because they belong to a part of the country remote from London). But, as they are found on the Percy Folio MS, they may be regarded as fragments of a poetry that has become in its last stages purely 'popular'. Since the minstrels were themselves in the early Middle Ages the means of transmission of the lays that formed their repertoire, the decline of that professional class in the later Middle Ages must have meant a decline in the means of transmission. There was no longer a professional class of poetic entertainers, of a generally high level of skill and of a high standing in the community, to work creatively on the romances. The minstrels at their best had been so good at transmission (we may reasonably conjecture) because they had done more than simply transmit; they had continually renovated and re-fashioned the lays for successive recitals; they had been—some of them at least *must* have been—not only reciters but makers whose work had been continual re-creation. But, as the profession gradually decayed, we must suppose that the traditional skill of the minstrels declined also; they failed to keep up the artistic level of the lays; the whole art died. The preservation of versions must finally have depended on whoever was interested enough to write them down, on copyists of MSS and on the first printers.

§ 4

Ideally, of course, all the romances of medieval Europe in French, German, English and other languages—and all the tales, Celtic, Norse, Oriental, Greek and Roman, which were made into medieval romances—should be examined together comparatively, as well as each analytically. The English romances form a group (itself breaking up under examination into a diversity of lesser groups) within the larger group of all the medieval romances of Europe. Several of the English romances have been recognized to be renderings from earlier French romances; others have been guessed to be so; and the tendency has been to assume that almost all are. Yet several of the English romances—notably those of the Gawain cycle—are in some respects very different in character from the French romances. Even those English romances which may be regarded as partially continuous, as renderings, from earlier French romances are yet made distinct from the French by their English language with its marked differences of tradition and character. Again, the fact that most of the English romances are anonymous—that no romancers in English comparable to Chrétien de Troyes, Benoit de Ste Maure or Marie de France are known by name (one cannot think of Chaucer as primarily a romancer)—points to some differences in the conditions and, therefore, the nature of English romance-making. Are the majority of the English romances simply derivative from those of the twelfth-century French masters? The French romances themselves circulated, we know, also in England and many of them were actually composed here; Marie de France, for example, lived in England. Were the English versions intended for less sophisticated audiences? Such appears to be the common account. Yet several of the English romances themselves suggest that this account needs to be qualified.

All the medieval romancers, French as well as German and

English, were working on traditional material that was, in itself, mostly not French. But this material did very largely pass through a French phase before it reached the English romancers. The French romancers (notably Chrétien, Benoit and Marie) appear to have been the pioneers in turning traditional tales into medieval romances. What was irrational, unhuman and Pagan in these often primitive tales tended to be rationalized, humanized and Christianized as they were turned by the French romancers into a new kind of courtly and sophisticated art. But qualities were perhaps lost in this softening, refining process that are not lost, or not to the same extent, in some at least of the best English romances—a deeper sense, for instance, of the extra-rational and non-human element in life and occasionally a deeper moral seriousness. The best English romances also are not less works of art though their art is of a rather different kind from the standard French kind.

In surveying the English romances, as in surveying the ballads, it is useful to keep in mind the distinction between poems which are written compositions and those which, though they have been preserved by having been written down, are none the less oral poetry. In the case of the romances this distinction cannot always be simply made. But many of the versions, if not themselves the products of oral composition and recital, are at least the products of a tradition that had fairly recently been still an oral one. Even those versions which we may judge to be written compositions—if not for private reading, then for reading aloud to an intimate circle—come at the end of the phase of minstrelsy and cannot be drastically dissociated from the earlier lays intended for minstrel recital. Here seems to be one of the broad differences between the English and the French romances. Whereas the finer French romances are already literary poems, the finer English romances (apart from Chaucer's) are mostly poems that are, at least to a much greater degree, of the nature of the older oral poetry. Romances that in French are literary poems already in the twelfth and thirteenth centuries generally assume in English (if we may judge from the extant versions of the thirteenth and early fourteenth centuries) the nature of oral poetry. In being translated from one language to another they have been changed back from a tradition that had become more literary into one that was still largely oral. One or two of the outstanding English romances that are extant from the end of the fourteenth century are alliterative poems in a tradition that must have extended back without a break to the older Northern heroic poetry. But many of the English rhyming romances are also—like the alliterative ones—explicitly minstrels' lays for recital.

§ 5

The tales which have been made into the medieval romances appear to have had many and diverse sources—in the East and in the lands bordering the Mediterranean as well as in the north and west of Europe. There are few of them—perhaps none—which it is possible to track down, much less trace to any single or ultimate source, with any confidence. There must have been a great mingling of the tales that flowed together to form the repertoire of the tale-tellers, who were often themselves wanderers. This diversity of origin of the tales circulating in medieval Europe is itself one aspect of the deep-rooted international character of the literature— a literature that is both local in character and at the same time international. We should not underestimate the distance that could, apparently, be traversed by particular tales in medieval Europe and the obstacles that could be overcome in their rapid dissemination from one sea-board of Christendom to another. French romances turn up in Norway and are changed into Norse. They turn up in Wales—itself often regarded as one of the lands of origin of the tales that were made into Arthurian romances— and are changed, it seems, into one or two of the Welsh tales found in the *Mabinogion* alongside the more primitive mythical tales that have not apparently passed through a 'French' stage. The minstrels and poets appear to have been themselves the principal media of this kind of communication, agents of transmission and dissemination, translators, often remarkably far-travelled men and often equally at home in two or more languages.

The channels through which so many and diverse tales flowed into the literature of medieval Europe must also have been many and diverse. By focusing attention on some particular one of these channels, to the exclusion of possible others, scholars may have suggested too simple a picture.

R. S. Loomis in his chapter on 'Celtic Story Channels and Story Ways'[1] indicates one channel by which Celtic tales could have passed into French romances and so into German and English—namely, the Breton *raconteurs*. As Bretons they would have inherited the tales of their own Celtic race that had their origin (Loomis supposes) in Ancient Celtic myth and ritual. But outside Britanny they would have told their Breton tales in French, the language that would be understood by their audiences. These bilingual Breton *raconteurs* would thus have been uniquely placed and equipped (if Loomis is right) to unlock the stores of Celtic tales for the audiences and poets of Europe. Loomis seems to think that the principal or original *locus* of the ritual and myth from which the Celtic tales evolved may have been in Ireland, although the whole of the Celtic West probably had at one time a religion and culture more or less in common and kept up intercommunications. It may well have been in some such ways as Loomis conjectures that the Celtic tales (if they *are* Celtic) became accessible to Chrétien de Troyes to be made into his French romances, and to Marie de France to be made into her Breton *lais*. In being made into French romances the Celtic tales were inevitably much 'civilized', modified particularly by the concepts and conventions of chivalry and courtly love.

C. B. Lewis, for his part, shows in his very logical and well documented *Classical Mythology and Arthurian Romance*[2] how Greek myths from the regions that had been the Eastern provinces of the Roman empire, and were later the Byzantine empire, could have become accessible in some form to the French romancers of the twelfth and thirteenth centuries. He considers in some detail, for example, what would have been the effect of the wonders of Constantinople, Asia Minor and Crete on the Crusaders and the pilgrims to the Holy Land and on the minstrels and other professional entertainers who accompanied the Crusaders and later returned to all parts of the Western world. In this

[1] *Celtic Myth and Arthurian Romance*, III.   [2] *Ibid.*, VIII.

way the romancers of the West could have been provided with fresh wonders—ancient and yet freshly discovered.

It is evident that in Chrétien's own century Classical and later literary sources were drawn upon by Benoit de Ste Maure in his *Roman de Troie* and by the authors of the *Roman d'Eneas* and the *Roman de Thebes*. Ovid was, of course, one of the great sources, perhaps the great souice, of the knowledge of Greek myth. But C. B. Lewis makes out a good case for supposing that there was also a continuous oral tiadition in tale telling from GraecoRoman times and that it is by no means impossible that the Ancient Greek myths went on being tales that were told—in one form or another circulating throughout the whole of Europe; and that they turned up in later times as Norse or Celtic tales, changed almost beyond recognition, the names of their characters and their place names localized as Norse or Celtic names. C. B. Lewis goes so far as to suggest that the tales which were made into the Arthurian romances may have been only superficially Celtic and that their great original source is the ritual (and myth) of the Ancient Greek world.[1] He examines Chrétien's *Ivain* in some detail in relation to the possible ultimate sources of its central episodes. Thus the episode of the storm raising fountain, which in *Ivain* is placed in the forest of Broceliande in Brittany, is related back by Lewis to rain making rites at the shrines of Zeus in the sacred grove at Dodona and in Crete. The gong used in the ancient thunder making rites (if we follow Lewis's theory) persists in *Ivain*, though with an altered function. Beside the fountain there is a basin which, when filled with water and emptied on an emerald stone, does—in the medieval romance as in the ancient rain making rites—produce a thunder and rain storm. There is also a tree full of singing birds beside the fountain, and Lewis traces these back very plausibly to the sacred tree and the sacred birds in the groves of Zeus at Dodona and in Crete and to the gilded tree behind the

[1] 'There is good reason to believe that, throughout the sixth, seventh, and eighth centuries, a knowledge of Greek, as well as a considerable familiarity with Latin classics, survived among the Irish.'—Bertrand Russell, *History of Western Philosophy*, Chapter VIII, p. 421. See R. R. Bolgar, *The Classical Heritage*, Chapter III.

Emperor's throne at Byzantium with its mechanical golden birds (the tree that figures in Yeats's *Sailing to Byzantium* and *Byzantium*). As for the Monster Herdsman who appears in *Ivain* and in other medieval romances, Lewis identifies him as originally an animal god or king wearing an animal mask—in particular, according to Lewis's argument, the Minotaur. We may feel when we read Lewis's book that he has on the whole established his case in relation to *Ivain*, and yet we may also feel that to have done so in relation to one romance is not enough. As it happens, one of the best of the English romances, *Ywain and Gawain*, is a version of Chrétien's *Yvain*, made in the north of England in the fourteenth century, and is as much illuminated by Lewis's discussion as is Chrétien's poem itself.

'YWAIN AND GAWAIN'
FIRST EPISODE

Ywain and Gawain is a mid-fourteenth-century Northern English version—expressly intended for recital—of Chrétien de Troyes' *Yvain, ou Le Chevalier au Lion*. The poem begins by providing a setting for the adventures which are to be its subject. Arthur has celebrated the feast of Whitsun 'at Kerdyf, that es in Wales'. After the feast, as the knights Gawayn, Kay, Ywaine, Colgrevance and others keep the door of the King and Queen's chamber, the Queen herself comes and sits down among them. Provoked by Sir Kay, who in this as in other romances is 'of his tong a skalde' and prone to brag, Sir Colgrevance passes the time by telling a tale of an adventure that befell him.

He tells how he was riding alone in a wood when he picked up a path

> *ful thik and hard*
> *With thornés, breres, and moni a quyn.*[1]

Journeying on, he comes finally to a plain and in the plain a tower.

> *And on the drawbrig saw i stand*
> *A knight with fawkon on his hand.*

He is the keeper of the hold and conducts Sir Colgrevance into the hall. In the hall hangs a board and beside it a hammer with which to strike it. This is the board which C. B. Lewis conjectures may be a reminiscence in medieval romance of the thunder-producing gongs of Dodona or Crete.

> *I saw no man of moder born.*
> *Bot a burde*[2] *hang us biforn,*
> *Was nowther of yren ne of tre,*
> *Ne i ne wist whareof it might be;*
> *And by that bord hang a mall.*[3]
> *The knyght smate on thar with all*
> *Thrise . . .*

---

[1] whin. [2] board. [3] hammer.

114

In this version, however, it is simply the signal for a company of courteous people to enter, some of whom lead Sir Colgrevance's steed to stable. Among them there is a lovely lady who attends to the guest, unlaces his armour, leads him into a chamber, clothes him in purple and ermine, leads him back into the hall and attends him at supper. It is all very ceremonious and rather mysterious as it customarily is in these castles where the knight is received as a guest, and which are somehow connected with the 'adventure' that is about to befall him; it suggests some pre-arranged ceremony or ritual rather than an accidental series of events.

In the morning Sir Colgrevance, having taken leave of his host, enters a forest which is full of beasts. There he encounters the keeper of the beasts, the Monster Herdsman (a figure who appears in several romances). This uncouth fellow carries a great mace, which may possibly correspond to the Green Knight's Danish axe or to Thor's hammer. The description in the poetry is certainly such as might well suggest that his original in tradition was an animal god or an impersonator of such, a king wearing an animal mask.

> *His hevyd, me thoght, was als grete*
> *Als of a rowncy[1] or a nete:[2]*
> *Unto his belt hang his hare . . .*
> *His face was ful brade and flat;*
> *His nese was cutted als a cat;[3]*
> *His browes war like litel buskes[4]*
> *And his tethe like bare[5]-tuskes;*
> *A ful grete bulge opon his bak;*
> *Thare was noght made withowten lac;[6]*
> *His chin was fast until his brest;*
> *On his mace he gan him rest.*
> *Also it was a wonder wede*
> *That the cherle yn yede;*
> *Nowther of wol ne of line[7]*
> *Was the wede that he went yn.*

[1] horse. [2] ox. [3] slit like a cat's. [4] bushes.
[5] boar. [6] defect. [7] linen.

Since he is clad neither in wool nor in linen, are we perhaps to understand that he is clad in an animal's skin? His behaviour, as well as his appearance, suggests rather some kind of beast than a man.

> *. . . als a beste than stode he still.*

The knight asks him: 'What ertow?' He answers that he is a man —an answer that would be necessary enough if he really is a man in an animal disguise.

> *He said again, 'I am a man.'*
> *I said, 'Swilk saw i never nane.'*
> *'What ertow?' alsone said he.*
> *I said, 'Swilk als thou here may se.'*

The knight's answer signifies that he is what he appears to be; *he* is not disguised.

The function in this poem of the Monster Herdsman—who has such power over the wild beasts of the forest that none dares disobey him—appears to be simply to direct the knight to what he seeks, to an adventure or marvel. Frequently in traditional tales of this pattern—and therefore possibly in an earlier version of this tale—such a character is none other than the antagonist himself in one of his diverse shapes or disguises who directs his challenger to the place where the contest is to be. Although in the poem as we have it nothing of the kind is made explicit, it is possible that audiences accustomed to such a pattern would have guessed that the Herdsman had at least some connexion with the antagonist himself.

At the place to which the knight is directed there is a well. This well proves to be no ordinary one; it turns out, later, to be indeed a storm-raising fountain. Overhanging it there is a tree, and nearby there is 'a chapel'—the place is evidently a sacred place—and beside the well there is a basin. This basin, when used to pour water on the stone, certainly produces rain; it produces indeed a dreadful thunderstorm. The mysterious Herdsman first describes to the knight what will happen.

Ywain and Gawain—First Episode

The well es under the fairest tre
That ever was in this cuntré;
By that well hinges a bacyne
That es of gold gude and fyne . . .
Thare es a chapel nere tharby,
That nobil es and full lufely.
By the well standes a stane;
Tak the bacyn sone onane,
And cast on water with thi hand;
And sone thou sal se new tithand.
A storme sal rise, and a tempest,
Al obout, by est and west;
Thou sal here mani thonor-blast
Al oboute the blawand fast;
And thare sal cum slik slete and rayne,
That unnesse[1] sal thou stand ogayne.

Is this episode a pure creation of the fancy? The conjecture that what we have here is an episode that, in origin, was an account of a rain-making rite—whether or not it can be traced back to the particular rites at the shrines of Zeus at Dodona and in Crete—has only to be stated in relation to the particular passage of the poetry to appear much more convincing. But what difference, it may be asked, does that make to the poetry? It means that the episode is really more serious than simply a sport of fancy and not less mysterious if it has its origin in an actual 'mystery'—a sacred rite—even though *we* may no longer suppose ourselves to take sympathetic magic seriously. It means that we might have to correct our way of taking these episodes as if they belonged to something of the order of a boy's adventure story—taking them, that is, too easily. It may be argued, however, that neither Chrétien nor the poet responsible for our English version knew the origins of the episode they had inherited in a tale which they conceived themselves as re-telling. Even if they did not know of these origins, they surely inherited with such episodes something of the traditional attitude of reverence towards them, a sense of their mystery, a sense too of the mystery of all life. Even if not under-

[1] scarcely.

stood, these episodes are recounted in detail, and they preserve a suggestion of a hidden power. Only the very few greater poets are able to give a new significance to the old episodes. These adventures, if no longer recognized as accounts of initiation and other rites and ceremonies, may be—probably were—felt as some kind of parable of life. It may be ventured that this is the way also for the modern reader to respond to them. The truest reading, surely, is the one which releases the maximum of the significance that is actually there, as it is organized in the poem. Works of imagination require to be responded to by the imagination—and the imagination is the *seeing* what is there in the order in which it is there.

The Monster Herdsman concludes his account of what is to happen, and what the knight must do, by saying that if having raised the storm the knight comes away unharmed he will be luckier than any of his predecessors. He will in fact have (unknowingly) challenged the keeper of the well—originally, the old rain-maker priest or king (human impersonator of a god); he will, reverting to the ritual conception that underlies the episode, have challenged the old rain-maker by proving that he himself can produce rain.

It all happens to Sir Colgrevance exactly as the Monster Herdsman has foretold—as if in fact it were some prescribed and pre-arranged rite. The tree is discovered to be an evergreen thorn; the stone on which the water is poured from the basin is an emerald based on four rubies that light up the land.

> *I toke the bacyn sone onane*
> *And helt water opon the stane.*
> *The weder wex than wonder blak,*
> *And the thonor fast gan crak;*
> *Thare come slike stormes of hayl and rayn,*
> *Unnethes i might stand thareogayn;*
> *The store[1] windes blew ful lowd:*
> *So kene come never are of clowd;*
> *I was drevyn with snaw and slete:*
> *Unnethes i might stand on my fete;*
> *In my face the levening[2] smate.*

[1] fierce.   [2] lightning.

When fair weather returns the most wonderful things are the singing birds on the tree. (Birds do, of course, sing when the sun shines
again after rain; but, if Lewis's whole theory is right, the ancestors
of these birds that alight so thickly upon that tree and sing so
wonderfully were—it may account for the feeling of wonder—the
sacred birds in the sacred grove at Dodona or, later, the golden
birds on the gilded tree behind the Emperor's throne at Byzantium.)

> *Than saw i sone a mery syght:*
> *Of al the fowles that er in flyght*
> *Lighted so thik opon that tre*
> *That bogh ne lefe none might i se;*
> *So merily than gon thai sing*
> *That al the wode bigan to ring . . .*
> *Thare herd never man none swilk.*

The rain in fact does seem to have done good, to have been a
blessing. But then, preceded by a noise as of many horsemen,
comes the keeper of the well, whose function as rain-maker has
been usurped, to answer the challenge. But in this medieval
romance he is of course a *knight*, and he gives other *reasons* for his
annoyance.

> *He bad that i sold tel him tite*
> *Whi i did him swilk despite,*
> *With weders wakend him of rest,*
> *And done him wrang in his forest.*

In the combat Sir Colgrevance is overthrown, but is received
again as a guest at the castle. Thereafter (as in other romances, for
example, *Eger and Grime*[1]) another knight, in this case Ywain,
undertakes the adventure.

[1] Even in the late and broken-down version preserved in the Percy Folio MS and
in a chap-book printed in Aberdeen in 1711 *Eger and Grime* is another interesting
romance in which a knight penetrates into a forbidden country, an 'uncouth' land,
and by so doing challenges the keeper of the land. The latter is a Red Knight
called Graysteele, one of those figures who, as they are described in the poetry, have
something about them of the sun. In Graysteele's country there is also a 'perilous
princess', one of those whom one must risk one's life to win, the Lady Loosepaine,
whom he keeps in the typical otherworld castle. As her name suggests, she is a
healer, one of those faery women who have the magical power not only to heal
wounds but even to bring the dead to life. The adventure, undertaken first by Eger,
then by Grime, has again something of the character of an initiation.

All happens as before—as Colgrevance has described. But this time the keeper of the well is defeated and pursued into the 'city'. This city has certain features which suggest a labyrinth or maze. For example, the pursuing Ywain is trapped within the mechanism of the entrance gate; a door opens behind him and a damsel appears. Although this damsel, Lunet, is *not* the lady of the castle or city, her role is that of the damsel who aids the hero, like Ariadne and the other helpful maidens of the myths—and now of the medieval romances. Lunet informs Ywain that his antagonist is dead and is mourned for by his widow, and that the people of the city or castle seek Ywain to slay him and avenge their lord. Lunet lends Ywain one of those magical rings which render the wearer invisible and invulnerable; she gives him food and drink and in other ways assists him. The people go in procession to bury the dead man with a 'doleful din' and a lady, white as milk, follows the bier, wringing her hands and weeping. Ywain longs to have sight of this mourning lady. When Lunet reveals the sight to him, he immediately falls in love with this lady whom he himself has widowed. This may be all against reason but is exactly in accordance (if not with human nature) with the ancient myth and ritual pattern in which the victor marries the queen (or goddess) of the slain king (or god). On the other hand, the sophistications and delicacies of the French romance—arising from the recognition that the widow of a knight would shrink from marrying the slayer of her husband—are reproduced in the English version. The primitive tale has been given a contemporary setting, and the people have contemporary manners and ways of feeling. With the contemporary setting have been introduced the complications of a new civilization and morality. The repugnance of the lady, who may be supposed rather to nourish thoughts of revenge, has to be overcome. This is Chrétien's theme. The handling of this theme makes the romance at this point something like a sketch or embryo of parts of the wooing of Criseyde in *Troilus and Criseyde*, although there is nothing here of the subtle Chaucerian creative life and genius. The damsel who assists the hero through his perils is in this case other than the damsel whom he is to wed. Her role here is not unlike that of Pandarus. She seeks to promote Ywain's marriage with her mistress. With this object she counsels her mistress. Who will now defend the widowed lady and her land? It will be remembered that similar considerations of prudence are suggested to Criseyde. The lady understands what her maid is hinting at and, angry, sends her away; but afterwards she sits (not unlike Criseyde) in a reverie, pondering her maid's counsel. The maid reappears and (again not unlike a faint pre-shadow of Pandarus) calls her a child for mourning.

> . . . *Trowes thou the flowre of chevalry*
> *Sold al with thi lord dy,*
> *And with him be put in molde?*
> *God forbede that it is so solde!*
> *Als gude als he and better bene.'*

When the widowed lady asks where is such another man as was her husband, Lunet puts the riddle:

> '. . . *Yf twa knyghtes be in the felde*
> *On twa stedes, with spere and shelde,*
> *And the tane the tother may sla,*
> *Whether es the better of tha?'*

Her mistress has to answer that the living victor is better than the dead man, but again orders Lunet out of her sight. Nevertheless she ponders all through the hours of darkness on the fact that she has now no knight to protect her. When her maid comes again in the morning there is a reconciliation. Ywain, bathed and clad in scarlet and gold and precious stones, is led by Lunet into the presence of the widowed lady of the eastle. He kneels and asks forgiveness for having slain her lord. She forgives him, he confesses his love. Her barons counsel her to take a husband and lord, and Ywain is thereupon presented to them as her new husband. Thus Ywain is wedded to the lady Alundyne. The whole episode culminates in a feast in the castle at which Arthur is the honoured guest—the wedding-feast of the victor.

> *And damysels danceand ful wele*
> *With trompes, pipes, and with fristele.*[1]
> *The castel and the ceté rang*
> *With mynstralsi and nobil sang.*

[1] flute.

'SIR PERCEVELLE OF GALLES'

Sir Percevelle of Galles, a version of the Perceval story in Northern English of the latter half of the fourteenth century, is one of the more fascinating of the English romances, partly *because* its mythological substance is less overlaid by the conventions of the French medieval courtly romances. In its character it has more in common with the English Gawain romances and—though it is no complete work of art—with *Sir Gawayne and the Grene Knight* itself than with the French romances. Expressly intended for recital to a company it is evidently a minstrel's lay. Unlike the French version of Chrétien de Troyes and his successors, and unlike the German *Parzival* of Wolfram von Eschenbach, this English *Percevelle* is not specifically a Grail romance, though there is a cup in it which Brown describes as 'an undeveloped Grail' and Loomis as a 'faded Grail'.

One of the first things that the English maker or minstrel says will interest his hearers in the tale of Perceval is that

> *He was fosterde in the felle,*
> *He dranke water of the welle.*

It has been suggested that in earlier or more primitive versions of the tale Perceval's mother may have been a waterspirit. Certainly the life of mother and child beside a well is enlarged upon in this version, and indeed the mother persists in living beside the well throughout the period of the tale, as if it were her natural habitat.

But one of the main tasks which in this version Perceval has to perform when he grows to manhood is to avenge the death of his father (old Perceval). The tale is therefore partly one of those tales of a son under an obligation or destiny to avenge his father. [1] At young Perceval's birthfeast old Perceval was challenged and slain by an intruder called (because of his colour) the Red Knight, evidently an otherthanhuman antagonist like the Green Knight of *Sir Gawayne and the Grene Knight.*

After his father's death the child Perceval is brought up in the woods by his mother.

[1] Gilbert Murray's *Hamlet and Orestes* essay illuminates also Perceval.

Sir Percevelle of Galles

Sall he no thyng see
Bot the leves of the tree
*   And the greves[1] graye,*
Schall he nowther take tent[2]
To justes ne to tournament,
Bot in the wilde wodde went,
With bestes to playe.

In these circumstances it is not surprising that Perceval grows up as a 'wild man', a 'fole in the filde', a naïve child of nature, a holy innocent. It is a fascinating theme, and full of suggestiveness for a reading of some of Wordsworth's poetry or of Blake's *Songs of Innocence*. We again come across the old theme with a new significance in Dostoyevsky's *The Idiot*, as Ernest Rhys recognized in an introductory note to the novel. 'The tale-writer was reapplying an ancient formula and a motive known in Oriental and Celtic folk-tale, that of the Fool of Nature, the Peredur or Percival, or the Gaelic Great Fool, who acts as the agent of Heaven and the master-spirit in certain trying episodes that prove his rarer faculty and unfoolish mind.'

His mother takes with her into the woods a 'tryppe of gayte', and Perceval acts as a goatherd and himself wears a goat-skin in this pastoral world that recalls that of the primitive wood-gods and goat-gods. He hunts in the woods with 'a lyttill Scottes spere', 'a darte' (according to French and Hale,[3] a talismanic weapon which is to be the means of accomplishing the death of the Red Knight.)

Thus he welke in the lande,
With hys darte in his hande;
Under the wilde wodde-wande
*   He wexe and wele thrafe.*
He wolde schote with his spere
Bestes and other gere,
As many als he myghte bere;
*   He was a gude knave!*

[1] groves.　　[2] i.e. know.　　[3] *Middle English Metrical Romances.*

> *Smalle birdes wolde he slo,*
> *Hertys, hyndes also;*
> *Broghte his moder of thoo.*

The child is clearly a kind of untutored prodigy of nature and something of an infant god as yet unrecognized.

> *Fyftene wynter and mare*
> *He duellede in those holtes hare;*
> *Nowther nurture ne lare*
> *Scho wolde hym none lere.*

His naïve questions lend the poetry its peculiar quality of combined wonder and humour. Thus, one day his mother bids him acknowledge God by praying to God's son. He questions her with the innocence of a young pagan who has never heard of Christ.

> *'Swete moder,' sayde he,*
> *'Whatkyns a godd may that be*
> *That ye nowe bydd mee*
> *That i schall to pray?'*
> *Then byspakke the lady even:*
> *'It es the grete Godd of heven . . .'*
> *'And i may mete with that man . . .'*

So he leaves his mother and his goats to seek the great God.

> *There he levede in a tayte*[1]
> *Bothe his modir and his gayte,*[2]
> *The grete Godd for to layte,*[3]
> *Fynde hym when he may.*

Instead of the great God he meets, as he walks in the 'holtis hare', three knights of Arthur—Ywain, Gawain and Kay, 'clothede all in grene'. They, for their part, are confronted on the forest path with a 'childe', wearing nothing but a goat-skin, who asks which of them is the great God of whom his mother has told him. Gawain answers that such they are not. Again there is the peculiar blend of wonder and humour which is characteristic of this poem.

[1] left eagerly.   [2] goats.   [3] seek.

There is the unexpectedness, the incongruity of the meeting, the mutual surprise of the civilized or experienced knights and the child of nature or holy innocent (who is potentially dangerous), their enormous ignorance of each other, the apparently preposterous self-assurance of the *enfant terrible*, and in general the clash between nature and nurture, innocence and experience.

> Than saide the fole one the filde,[1]
> Was comen oute of the woddes wilde,
> To Gawayne that was meke and mylde
>   And softe of ansuare,
> 'I sall sla yow all three
> Bot ye smertly now telle mee
> Whatkyns thynges that ye bee,
>   Sen ye no goddes are.'

Sir Kay (whose habitually brusque, sarcastic or bragging tone is a foil in the romances to the unfailing courtesy of Gawain) asks the boy his name in such a manner as to rouse his anger.

> 'Who solde we than say
> That hade slayne us to-day
>   In this holtis hare?'
> At Kayes wordes wexe he tene
> Bot a grete bukke had bene—
> Ne hadd he stonde tham bytwene,—
>   He hade hym slayne thare.

The great stag that thus opportunely, as if from nowhere, interposes itself between Perceval and Kay seems to be essentially magical. Gawain, ever in contrast with Kay, speaks gently to the boy and tells him that they are knights of Arthur's court. The boy asks if Arthur will make *him* a knight, and Gawain counsels him to go himself to Arthur and ask.

Alone in the woods again, the boy sees a stud of wild colts and mares and recognizes the 'things' the knights rode upon though he does not know their name.

---

[1] fool in the field.

Swilke thynges as are yone
Rade the knyghtes apone;
Knewe i thaire name . . .

He out-runs the biggest wild mare and rides homeward bareback upon it, having thus won his horse.

And saide, 'Thou sall bere me
To-morne to the Kynge.'

When his amazed mother catches sight of her child riding on the mare, she acknowledges that knightly 'nature' will out.

Scho saw hym horse hame brynge;
Scho wiste wele, by that thynge,
That the kynde wolde oute sprynge.

When she utters the word 'mare' he learns for the first time the name of the 'thing' he rides on. But henceforth he supposes that all horses are 'mares'. He tells his mother that he will go to the King 'to-morne'.

Bot-if the Kyng make me knyghte,
To-morne i sall hym sloo!

Such is the astonishing confidence of this *enfant terrible*, whether arising from consciousness of superhuman powers or from simple ignorance. His mother pleads with him against his perilous undertaking, and in her pleadings there is further interplay be-tween 'nature' and nurture. 'Lyttill thou can of nurtoure.' She tells him to try to be well-mannered, having hitherto entirely neglected his education in that as in other respects.

'There thou meteste with a knyghte,
Do thi hode off, i highte,
And haylse hym in hy.'

She shows him knightly clothing so that he should know a knight when he sees him, for, as he says, he has never yet seen a man. (This, which flatly contradicts his meeting with the three knights, French and Hale conjecture to be a survival from an earlier ver-sion of the tale in which Perceval's otherworld mother inhabited a land of women to which men did not have access and where she brought up her son.)

In the morning, which (it seems) is 'forthirmaste Yole-day', Perceval sets out on his adventure, mounted on his mare, with a bridle improvised out of a withy or willow-shoot,[1] carrying his talismanic spear and wearing a ring[2] given him by his mother. This ring, he exchanges, for some reason unexplained in our version, with a ring on the finger of a sleeping lady in the first episode of his adventures. This episode is one which, in different variations, frequently recurs in the romances, particularly in those of the Grail cycle. The adventurer comes to a hall or castle. He rides straight in without hindrance and, though there is apparently no one there, he finds a banquet spread and provision for a horse.

> *He went in withowtten lett;*
> *He fande a brade borde sett,*
> *A bryghte fire, wele bett,[3]*
> *Brynnande therby.*

He helps himself to half of the bread and wine and gives his mare half of the corn provided, because he remembers that his mother had bade him be of 'mesure'. It may be that Perceval is being tested, though the idea of testing is not made explicit in this version. Perceval certainly appears to be doing something that he *must* do, and do correctly. (In the Grail romances the mysterious banquet is regularly associated with the Grail itself as life-giving vessel.) Perceval then penetrates farther into the house and finds a lady, richly clad, asleep on a bed. Without awakening her he makes the mysterious exchange of the rings.

> *Ther he kyste that swete thynge;*
> *Of hir fynger he tuke a rynge;*
> *His awenn modir takynnynge[4]*
> *He lefte with that fre.*

[1] Cf. the Knight without a Bridle of other romances.

[2] French and Hale note that 'Brown conjectures that in the original form of the story the mother advises Perceval to exchange rings with a damsel, because the mother, a fairy, knows that she can so direct him that he will secure a ring making him invulnerable'.

[3] well kindled.   [4] mother's token.

Wearing this ring and carrying his spear, Perceval proceeds on his destined journey and rides into Arthur's hall where the first course has just been served. Arthur asks the 'faire childe' whence he comes and what is his will.

> *Than saide the fole of the filde,*
> *'I ame myn awnn modirs childe,*
> *Comen fro the woddes wylde . . .'*

He then declares that unless the King will make him a knight he will slay him. All wonder that the King should allow such rude‑ness. But the King sees in the boy the resemblance to old Perceval, who married his sister, and he knows that only old Perceval's son can slay old Perceval's slayer, the Red Knight, who is also Arthur's enemy. Gradually Arthur arrives at the virtual recogni‑tion that the boy is indeed old Perceval's son, brought up in the woods in a kind of Garden‑of‑Eden state of innocence outside the knowledge of good and evil.

> *The childe hadde wonnede in the wodde:*
> *He knewe nother evyll ne gude;*
> *The Kynge hymselfe understode*
> *He was a wilde man.*

The boy sits down to the banquet but, before he has begun to eat, the Red Knight himself, mounted on a red steed, rides into the hall.

> *So commes the Rede Knyghte in*
> *Emanges tham righte than,*
> *Prekande one a rede stede;*
> *Blode‑rede was his wede.*
> *He made tham gammen full gnede,[1]*
> *With craftes that he can.*

The Red Knight is clearly an otherworld visitant whose 'craftes' are magical. Everyone seems to be powerless against him—except young Perceval whose role it is to slay him who is (though the boy himself does not know it) his father's slayer. But young Perceval

---

[1] sorry sport.

has another, perhaps more significant, task besides that of revenge, and this is now provided for him.

The Red Knight, having first in the manner of all his kind taunted the company as cowards, seizes the cup of red gold, full of wine, that is set before Arthur. He drinks the wine and, to the sorrow of Arthur, rides off with the cup. We may agree with Brown and Loomis that the cup is no ordinary cup and that, until it is recovered, Arthur's realm will decline. In this respect, as a life-giving vessel or source of vigour, it has undoubtedly a connexion with some of the significance of the Grail. When next in our poem we hear how Arthur has fared in the absence of the cup, we learn that he has taken to 'care-bed' and is in much the same plight as the sick king of the Grail myth. The cup must be recovered if the King and the kingdom are to be restored.[1] It becomes apparent that young Perceval has been undergoing an education from a state of nature to become the hero fit to recover the cup, restore the King and the kingdom and perform other tasks beyond the power of ordinary mortals.

Young Perceval's task, then, is not only to slay the Red Knight but, perhaps more essentially, to recover the cup. For this twofold purpose he has been equipped with, as it seems, the protective ring and the talismanic spear. (If such tales had their ultimate source in myth and ritual, the three objects—the cup, the ring and the spear—may have been associated symbols with some such ceremonial uses and significances as Miss Weston conjectured. Even if the original precise significance of these objects had been lost for the maker of this version and his audiences, the sense that they were *significant* must have continued to be an essential part of the poetic effect for people for whom ceremony and ritual were still immensely important.) Perceval, mounted on his mare and clad

---

[1] It seems that the Red Knight has been a regular visitant, every five years in fact, and has regularly absconded with such a cup—three in the fifteen years since old Perceval's death.

> *Fyve yeres has he thus gane,*
> *And my coupes fro me tane.*

But all the cups appear to be each the one essential cup.

only in a goat-skin—'a fole als he were'—goes in pursuit of the Red Knight and, overtaking him, demands back the cup. The Red Knight puts up his visor and addresses the strange boy in the well-known *flyting* manner of Herod, the Turkish Knight, and all the others of his kind.

> He sayde, 'Come i to the, appert fole,
> I sall caste the in the pole,
> For all the heghe days of Yole,
>   Als ane olde sakke.'

The unorthodox combat and slaying are half-humorously described. Thus, when the Red Knight falls dead from the saddle, the child does not know that he *is* dead. On his mare he first pursues the riderless steed of his late antagonist.

> The stede was swifter than the mere,
> For he hade no thynge to bere
> Bot his sadill and his gere . . .
> The mere was bagged with fole;
> And hirselfe a grete bole.

The child thereupon takes to his own feet, and he is once again so superhumanly swift that he outruns the steed and restores him to the corpse. There is here that strange buffoonery in the presence of death which is characteristic of traditional or popular life, literature and customs. The child addresses the dead man and bids him mount his steed.

> The knyghte lay still in the stede:
> What sulde he say, when he was dede?

The child knows no better way of obtaining the Red Knight's armour than by burning him out of it. He is kindling a fire of birch and oak when Gawain rides up, anxious about the child, and unlaces the Red Knight. Young Perceval, arrayed in the red armour, admires himself; he may now indeed pass for a knight. The body of the Red Knight is cast upon the fire—an act that is a relic, it has been suggested, of the funeral custom of a previous age; but the point here *may* be that burning was regarded as the appropriate or only effective means of disposing of an enchanter as of a witch.

Young Perceval's next adventure is, in fact, a meeting with an old witch, the Red Knight's mother. She mistakes the knight in red armour for her son and tells him that if he had been dead she would have brought him to life again. Evidently it is a long-standing practice of hers, a way she has had of collaborating with her son. Perceval casts her on the same fire. Before riding on and meeting the witch, Perceval had given Gawain the recovered cup. So it is Gawain who bears back the cup to Arthur.

But the Red Knight proves not to be one but many—in the sense that there are many who are much of his kind. A brood of uncouth or other-than-human characters provide a succession of antagonists whom the young hero has each in turn to overcome. There is (1) a Sowdan, Golrotherame, and his army of Saracens from whom the Lady Lufamour has to be rescued. When he is slain there is (2) his brother, a giant eager to avenge his death. Finally there is (3) a Black Knight who has become involved in the affair of the exchange of rings.

First, however, after the encounter with the old witch, the comedy of mistaken identity continues. Perceval, in the red armour, comes upon an old knight and his nine sons who fly for their lives before him, mistaking him for the Red Knight. He overtakes them, puts up his visor and is revealed as the slayer of him who he had himself *seemed* to be. Fifteen years ago the old knight's brother was slain by the Red Knight. (Is it a coincidence that the old knight's brother was slain by the Red Knight in the same year as Perceval's father, or were they one and the same?) Throughout these fifteen years the Red Knight has sought to slay the nine sons, fearing that one of them would grow up to slay him. The old knight and his sons entertain their deliverer to a banquet in their hall. In the midst of the banquet a messenger arrives from the Maydenlande[1] and reveals that the Lady Lufamour of that land is besieged in her city by a Sowdan (Golrotherame) who, having slain her father, uncle and brothers, wants to take her as

---

[1] The name has been taken to indicate a land of women. Here it might well be a fairy country and the Lady Lufamour a fairy queen.

his wife. Thus is introduced Perceval's second principal task, the deliverance of the besieged lady and his winning of her—essentially perhaps one of those besieged (or abducted) women (or goddesses) of tradition, like Helen of Troy—as his bride.

The messenger continues on his journey to Arthur's court to ask for *his* help. Arthur's sickness, which in earlier versions would almost certainly have been ascribed to the loss of the cup, seems here rather to be ascribed to his grief at the absence of Perceval. At any rate the messenger's mention of Perceval seems to dispel Arthur's sickness, and Arthur, too, sets out for the Maydenlande —to save Perceval.

Meanwhile Perceval rides on alone in the traditional role of the 'unknown knight' (a role played again by Edgar in *King Lear* when he appears against his brother after the trumpet, so suggestive of the Judgement, has sounded).

> *Als he were sprongen of a stane,*
> *Thare na man hym kende,*
> *For he walde none sold hym ken.*
> *Forthe rydes he then,*
> *Amanges uncouthe men*
> *His maystres to make.*

Perceval crosses what appears essentially to be the mountain barrier to the Otherworld, a waste of moor and mountain.

> *Over more and mountayne,*
> *To the Maydenlande.*

When he approaches the city he fights his way through the Saracens, the lopping of the Saracens' heads being rendered in that spirit of caricature humour characteristic of this tradition.

> *Made the Sarazenes hede-bones*
> *Hoppe als does hayle-stones*
> *Abowtte one the gres.*

Tired after such exertions, his steed standing beside him, he sits down under the walls of the besieged city which, like Troy, has its Helen. At dawn she comes upon the walls, the Lady Lufamour, and looks down. She sees the heads and helmets strewn on the grass. She wonders who could have done such a deed, and the 'unknown knight' is discovered.

> *Thay luked undir thair hande,*
> *Sawe a mekill horse stande,*
> *A blody knyghte liggande*
> *By a rede stede.*

It is thus, as a Red Knight and apparently a wounded knight in need of succour, that her deliverer first appears to the Lady Lufamour. She speculates as to whether he is dead, asleep or a prisoner.

> *'Owthir es yone man slane,*
> *Or he slepis hym allane,*
> *Or he in batelle es tane,*
> *For blody are his wede.'*

She promises him herself and the kingdom if he slays her oppres' sor, and entertains the young champion splendidly as her guest.

> *In a chayere of golde,*
> *Bifore the fayrest, to byholde.*

As if to put him to the test, the alarm bell rings. She arms him, and in full view he scatters the Saracens a second time from before the walls.

Then Perceval rides against four unknown knights whom he sees approaching the city. They are Arthur, Ywain, Gawain and Kay, who cast lots as to which of them shall fight the unknown knight. The lot falls to Gawain. The tragic issue, sister's son slain by sister's son, which might in this case have resulted from non-recognition, is averted by Gawain recognizing in time his unknown opponent.

> *By the wordis so wylde*
> *At the fole one the felde,*
> *He wiste wele it was the childe.*

At the feast that follows—yet another in the succession of Homeric feasts in this, as in other romances—the Lady Lufamour wonders at Perceval who does not know how to dine politely, he 'couthe so littill of nurtour'. Arthur explains—

> *Fully feftene yere*
> *To play hym with the wilde dere:*
> *Littill wonder it were*
> *Wilde if he ware.*

Next morning the combat between Perceval and Golrotherame to decide who shall have the 'maystry' takes place under the walls. The combat is again of the unorthodox kind but ends by Perceval cutting off the Saracen's head and winning the lady and the land. The episode concludes with the wedding of Perceval and Lufamour.

After spending a twelvemonth with Lufamour, however, Perceval remembers his mother by the well and is filled with longing to see her. The song-like quality of the stanzas of this romance (including the effect of the echoing of the last line of a stanza in the first of the succeeding one) may be well illustrated by the poetry here which expresses how Perceval forgets and then remembers his mother.

> *Thus he wonnes in that wone*
> *Till that the twelmonthe was gone,*
> *With Lufamour his lemman:*
>   *He thoghte on no thyng,*
> *Nor on his moder that was,*
> *How scho levyde with the gres,*
> *With more drynke and lesse,*
>   *In welles, there thay spryng;*
>
> *Drynkes of welles, ther thay spryng,*
> *And gresse etys, withowt lesyng!*
> *Scho liffede with none othir thyng*
>   *In the holtes hare;*
> *Till it byfelle appon a day,*
> *Als he in his bedd lay,*
> *Till hymselfe gun he say,*
>   *Syghande full sare,*

Sir Percevelle of Galles

> The laste Yole-day that was,
> Wilde wayes i chese:
> My modir all manles[1]
>   Leved i thare.'
> Than righte sone saide he,
> 'Blythe sall i never be
> Or i may my modir see,
>   And wete how scho fare.'

The life of the mother beside the well as here described resembles, perhaps not accidentally, that of the maiden who spends seven nights on the moor, whose drink is water of the well and whose food is the primrose and the violet in the song 'Mayden in the mor lay'.

Against the wishes of Lufamour—indeed as if breaking the spell of her who tries to hold him—Perceval departs to seek his mother.

> Faire scho prayed hym even than,
> Lufamour, his lemman,
> Till the heghe dayes of Yole were gane,
>   With hir for to bee;
> Bot it served hir of no thyng.

It is as though Lufamour were the faery mistress of many traditional tales and medieval romances, and as though she has detained Perceval with her under a spell, causing him temporarily to forget everything, including his mother. After Perceval's departure from her there is no further mention of Lufamour in the poem. A twelve months' sojourn with the Lady Lufamour in Maydenlande seems to be all that his 'marriage' with her amounts to.

Before Perceval can recover his mother it seems necessary that he should recover the ring she gave him. This involves him in an adventure. There is considerable involvement in the tale—outside the understanding of the characters concerned, if not of the reader—but it might be dangerous for the modern reader to conclude that there is no overall design (as in some involved tapestry pat-

---

[1] i.e. without a man to protect her.

tern), artistic as well as fateful. As Perceval rides alone through a wood, he knows not where, he hears a woman cry.

> *As he come thurgh the wode,*
> *A ferly he fande,*
> *A birde, brighteste of ble,*
> *Stode faste bonden till a tre.*

He asks who has bound her to the tree. She answers, 'Sir, the Blake Knyghte'. We may have suspected her from the first of being a fay. It turns out that she is none other than the sleeping lady in the mysterious castle with whom Perceval exchanged the rings 'appon the laste Yole-Day'. The Black Knight, her lord, has bound her to the tree because of her 'fault' in losing the ring. The ring is (as she now reveals) a magical ring with protective powers. Perceval recognizes that he himself has brought the lady into this 'bale'. He unbinds her, an act which almost seems to have the effect of causing the Black Knight to materialize—as the plucking of a branch, fruit or nut in various traditional tales and ballads sets the faery powers in action, has the effect of a challenge. Scarcely has Perceval, suddenly weary, laid his head upon the lady's knee after her release from her bondage than she bids him flee.

> *'For yonder comes the Blake Knyghte;*
> *Dede mon ye be!'*

But Perceval (he still wears the protective ring, perhaps) over-throws the Black Knight, and the latter is only saved by the lady coming between them—like the stag of a previous episode. Perceval explains about the rings, reconciling the lady and the knight, and offers to change back the rings. But his mother's ring—necessary perhaps to the recovery of his mother—has been given by the Black Knight to a giant, the lord of that land, who is the brother of Golrotherame.

Perceval now has the task of recovering the ring from the giant.

> *The geant stode in his holde . . .*
> *'I se a bolde man yare*
> *On my lande ryfe.'*[1]

[1] come trespassing.

He has a brother to avenge—'I had no brothir bot hym ane'. He goes forth against Perceval (who is still wearing the protective ring) with an enormous iron club, a weapon of the same uncouth character as the Green Knight's axe or Thor's hammer, perhaps originally a thunder-making instrument. The antagonists meet on a brown moor. The sound of the tremendous blows they rain on each other does indeed, as rendered in the poetry, suggest thunder.

> *The dales dynned thaym bytwene*
> *For dynttis that thay gaffe bydene.*

Perceval leaves the giant headless on the ground and rides into the giant's hold. The Porter, who in this as in other episodes in the romances, is no ordinary personage—as befits one who no doubt is in origin the Porter of the Otherworld[1]—guides Perceval through the castle to the giant's treasure chest. Perceval empties it, and the ring rolls out. The Porter tells him that his lord had offered it to a lady dwelling near-by whom he loved. This lady recognized the ring as one she had given to her son and, supposing her son to have been slain, has run mad in the woods; she is none other than Perceval's mother. The Porter concludes his melancholy tale—

> *Now es the lady wode*[2] ...
> *Bot alsone als scho sees me,*
> *Faste awaye dose scho flee.*

She has become a shy creature of the woods who flees from anyone who comes near her.

On foot, clad once again in a goat-skin, Perceval goes to seek his mother in the same wood where a twelvemonth earlier he left her. He seeks for a 'seven-night' and on the ninth day comes to the well and drinks of it. As if a consequence of this act, he becomes aware of his mother.

> *Than was he warre, hym besyde,*
> *Of the lady so fre.*

She tries to hide, not recognizing her son, though she perceives the

---

[1] *Vide* Loomis's chapter on 'The Porter of the Other World', *Celtic Myth and Arthurian Romance*, Chap. II.

[2] mad.

resemblance—'Siche a sone hade i'. Calling her 'mother' (in a way that may remind the modern reader of the line in *Ash Wednes-day*, 'Blessed sister, holy mother, spirit of the fountain . . .') he gets so near her that she can no longer flee. She leaps upon him, but his strength is the greater; he holds her firm, overpowers her and carries her into the castle. The elusiveness of Perceval's mother is not unlike that of Proteus, the Old Man of the Sea; she here re-tains something of the quality of her origin, perhaps, as a water spirit—as, in fact, *water*, the elusive element.

In the castle Perceval and the Porter clothe her and give her, from a spring, a drink which the giant is said to have made. It evidently has medicinal or magical potencies—it puts her to sleep for three nights and three days. When she awakes she is restored to her right mind and has recovered her lost son. Thus, in the great Shakespearian scene, Lear, awaking from sleep, is restored to his right mind—indeed knows himself for the first time, is virtually new-made, re-born—and simultaneously recognizes his lost and recovered daughter. 'Sleep', as induced by a magical potion or as the condition of suspended being while such a potion is doing its magical work, seems in such episodes in the romances to have dimly the kind of value it more profoundly has in Shakespeare. In Shakespeare, 'sleep' is 'natural' (in the full Shakespearian sense); it works in with 'great creative Nature'; it restores, renews, re-creates, so that the sleeper is re-born in sleep almost magically (as in the traditional tales and romances). In the episode in our romance 'a riche bathe' is made for Perceval's mother, to com-plete the restorative process of her magically induced sleep.

> *A riche bathe for to ma*
> *And made the lady in to ga*
> *In graye and in grene.*

(We learn that green, the colour of vegetation and the faery, was recognized in medieval medicine, as we also recognize it, as a colour possessing a soothing and restoring power; grey is associated with green in the romances as conventionally the colour of wild vegetation—'holtes hore'.) Thus mother and son—as in *King Lear*, *A Winter's Tale* and *Pericles*, father and daughter—are at the end of our poem restored to one another.

FOUR BRETON LAYS
IN ENGLISH

§ 1

Within the whole body of the English romances we can distinguish certain lesser groups. Apart from the Gawain romances
(which hardly form a very homogeneous group as they now exist)
the most interesting single group is perhaps the one which is made
up of the so-called 'Breton lays' in English. Three of these—*Sir
Orfeo, Sir Degare, Le Freine*—are extant in the Auchinleck MS of
the early fourteenth century and are apparently the earliest survivors
of this group. Of these, only the lay *Le Freine* is a translation from
the French of an extant lay by Marie de France. But they appear to
be the poems in English nearest to the Breton lays of Marie and are
(like hers) in rhymed octo-syllabic couplets. We may associate
with these lays in the Auchinleck MS two later lays—*Sir Launfal*
and *Emare*—extant on a fifteenth-century MS. *Sir Launfal* may be
regarded as an English successor of Marie's *Lanval*; but it is not a
direct translation of her poem and may be an elaboration (by a
poet whose name is given, Thomas of Chester) of an earlier, more
direct English version. These later, more elaborated, lays are in
stanzas, though they appear to be still intended for minstrel recital.

§ 2

'SIR ORFEO'

In the lay of *Sir Orfeo* the legend of Orpheus and Eurydice,
known throughout the Middle Ages from Ovid and other
sources, having been caught into the stream of medieval tale-telling,
has emerged as a tale of a changed nature. How far afield and
across what stretches of time the streams of tale-telling could carry

a tale is proved by the fact that fragments of a ballad version of *King Orfeo* were collected in the Shetlands late in the nineteenth century. (The written and oral traditions were not isolated from one another; they continually filched tales from one another—as the ballads also prove.) More particularly, *Sir Orfeo* is proof that the tradition in which the 'Breton lays' belong might adopt a tale from another tradition and might shape it by association with them into a tale so similar in character that it has become a typical 'Breton lay'. Its association with these apparently Celtic tales could have been neither accidental nor incongruous. Whatever connexions—in their ritual origins or at later stages—there may have been between the different mythologies, Mediterranean, Norse, Celtic, from which numberless tales circulating in medieval Europe appear to have evolved, the similarities of pattern between them have frequently been remarked on. The tale-tellers and poets who wove afresh the legend of Orpheus and Eurydice according to the patterns of those Celtic tales, by which their own minds and imaginations were fashioned, could do so the more readily because in that legend itself, in its imagery and symbolism, were felt affinities, intimate resemblances as well as differences between it and their own tales.

In being changed into a Celtic fairy-tale, the legend of Orpheus and Eurydice could retain not only part of the detail but a large part of the main outline of its original pattern and yet be changed in its nature. As the lay of *Sir Orfeo*, it is one of those tales of a mortal queen who is abducted from a spring meadow or, in this instance, orchard by the King of the Otherworld and ultimately, after many privations and distresses suffered by her husband in quest of her, won back from the Otherworld. A radical change is that the Greek kingdom of the dead, the shadowy abode of the shades, has become the Celtic Otherworld or fairyland, a shining realm that suggests rather the abode of the sun-god than that of the king of the shades. (Schofield notes[1] that it is in accord with this medieval conception that in Chaucer's *Merchant's Tale* Pluto is spoken of as 'king of the fayerye' and in Dunbar's *Golden Targe* as 'the elrich incubus in cloak of green'.) Another radical alteration

---

[1] *English Literature from the Norman Conquest to Chaucer*, V, p. 185.

is that the tragic and beautiful close of the Greek legend—Eurydice but half-regained, lost again irrevocably at the moment of restoration, of emergence into the light—has been replaced by the more common complete restoration of the lost one.

A device of the medieval minstrel, as of any tale-teller endeavouring to bring home his *aventure* to his audience, is to say that it happened in their town or country. Accordingly, in the English *Sir Orfeo* the tale is localized in England. Orfeo is King of England—and, like Horn and Tristram (and presumably the minstrel reciter of the tale) a harper. Some lines added to the poem on an MS copy of a date later than that in the Auchinleck MS (early fourteenth century) emphasize—perhaps out of concern for the prestige of the profession of minstrelsy fallen on evil days—that Orfeo was a king and also himself a harper, and that he delighted to honour harpers.

When May—the month of the triumph of spring—is come and the fields are filled with flowers, Orfeo's queen, Herodis, goes a-maying with two of her maidens.

> *Bifel so in the comessing of May,*
> *When miri and hot is the day,*
> *And oway beth winter-schours,*
> *And everi feld is ful of flours,*
> *And blosme breme[1] on everi bough*
> *Overal wexeth miri anough,*
> *This ich[2] Quen, Dame Herodis,*
> *Tok to[3] maidens of priis*
> *And went in an undrentide[4]*
> *To play bi an orchardside,*
> *To se the floures sprede and spring*
> *And to here the foules sing.*

Like Proserpina and all the other young women who gather flowers in spring meadows and are abducted by otherworld wooers, Herodis is clearly in the line of descent from the flower or spring or earth goddesses. She falls asleep in the orchard under a

[1] glorious.   [2] same.   [3] two.
[4] originally 'mid-morning' but came to mean 'about noon'.

tree—always a dangerous thing to do if one would avoid falling under the power of the fairy. *Something* does in fact happen in her sleep. She wakes crying out, as if possessed. What makes her outcry the more mysterious and terrifying to others is that she either cannot or will not explain its cause.

In this stricken condition she is brought back to the palace. There she looks upon her husband as if he were a stranger or worse, she 'loketh so man doth on his fo'. At last she breaks the news to him that a power which cannot be resisted is drawing her away from him. Orfeo answers in words which will remind the modern reader of those of Ruth in the Authorized Version (and that the makers of the English medieval romances and of the Authorized Version have a language in common).

> *Whider thou gost, ichil with the,*
> *And whider y go, thou schalt with me.*

Herodis then tells him what happened to her under the tree.

> *As ich lay this undertide*
> *And slepe under our orchardside,*
> *Ther come to me to fair knightes*
> *Wele yarmed al to rightes*
> *And bad me comen an heiying[1]*
> *And speke with ther lord the King.*

When these otherworld messengers had failed to move her, the King of the Otherworld himself had come with more than a hundred knights and a hundred damsels riding on snow-white steeds—typically, the fairy cavalcade.

> *The King hadde a croun on hed;*
> *It nas of silver no of gold red,*
> *Ac it was of a precious ston:*
> *As bright as the sonne it schon.*

The precious stone that (as it is described in this quartet which read by itself might be from a ballad) shines as bright as the sun is a regular feature of the Otherworld King of the romances and

[1] in haste.

ballads. If (as Loomis and others have conjectured) the original of the Otherworld King was the sun-god, his stone would originally have been the sun itself or its symbol; he is still in *Sir Orfeo* resplendent and of superhuman power. Herodis tells how he rode away with her.

> *And schewed me castels and tours,*
> *Rivers, forestes, frith[1] with flours,*
> *And his riche stedes ichon.*

Having shown her his otherworld country, as if intending that its superior charms should woo her away from the world of men, he had brought her back to the tree, but on the understanding that he would come to fetch her away finally on the following day at the same hour from under the same tree. The experience is partially rationalized in that it has happened in sleep and might be a dream, yet it is reality. The following day in the orchard—the appointment, it seems, must be kept—Orfeo surrounds his queen with a solid phalanx of armed men. But right from the midst of the armed men Herodis is snatched away.

> *Ac yete amiddes hem ful right*
> *The Quen was oway ytwiht,[2]*
> *With fairi[3] forth ynome,[4]*
> *Men wist never wher sche was bicome.*

A power which no human strength, no material weapons can withstand and which compels her away is a power like that of death (as it is in the original Greek legend) but is explicitly, in the medieval poem, 'magic'.

Did this shift from the conception of death to that of magic arise simply from the natural tendency of the human fancy to soften the edge of the fact of death? Thus in De la Mare's poem *The Ghost* the fact is softened, half-hidden away by the gentle associations of fairyland; the grave becomes 'the root of the dark thorn'. But in the medieval romances Fairyland—the Otherworld—is itself much more actual than in nineteenth-century romantic dream poetry, and 'magic' is still conceived as something

---

[1] woodland.   [2] snatched.   [3] magic.   [4] taken.

of a practical science or as one of those powers which such science manipulates, powers destructive or creative.

Bereft of his queen, Orfeo forsakes his kingdom and goes into the wilderness taking only his harp which, it would appear, has magic powers, even over the Otherworld. Orfeo's ten years' sojourn in the wilderness is, as it turns out, not purposeless; it is a kind of quest. To find again what is lost, to bring back the dead to life seems still, in our poem, to be felt obscurely as having some con-nexion with nature. This relation between the waste land and the lost one is not made explicit. But there seems to be an emotional logic at work in the poem. It is perhaps not simply the pathetic fallacy that, immediately supervening on the loss of Herodis, there should be in the poem·a recrudescence of the waste land or, at least, a wilderness.

> *Now on hard hethe he lith,*
> *With leves and gresse he him writh*[1] . . .
> *Now, thei it comenci to snewe and frese,*
> *This King mote make his bed in mese*[2] . . .
> *Now may he al day digge and wrote,*[3]
> *Er he finde his fille of rote.*
> *In somer he liveth bi wild frut*
> *And berien bot gode lite;*[4]
> *In winter may he nothing finde*
> *Bot rote, grases, and the rinde.*

Under these deprivations 'al his bodi was oway duine'; he grows withered, shaggy and uncouth.

> *His here of his berd, blac and rowe,*[5]
> *To his girdel-stede*[6] *was growe.*

Then the note of the poetry begins to change towards a renewal of joy—responding to that same inner emotional logic—in a succession of episodes that lead up to the first fleeting reappearance of Herodis. When the weather turns clear and bright, Orfeo takes out his harp from the hollow of a tree and makes music—a harping

---

[1] covers. [2] moss. [3] root in the earth. [4] of little worth. [5] rough. [6] waist.

that magically charms the wild beasts and birds (this feature of the
original Greek myth has persisted).

> *That alle the wilde bestes that ther beth,*
> *For ioie abouten him thay teth.*[1]
> *And alle the foules that ther were*
> *Come and sete on ich a brere,*
> *To here his harping afine,*[2]
> *So miche melody was therin.*

From now on Orfeo catches occasional glimpses of the faery
riding by (as they do in the romances and in ballads). At one
time he sees the faery hunt all about him; at another time, a
warrior host; at another time, knights and ladies dancing to music
—the rhythm changes to suggest, together with the repetition of
'queynt', their dance movement.

> *Oft in hot undertides,*
> *The King o fairy with his rout*
> *Com to hunt him al about*
> *With dim*[3] *cri, and bloweing,*
> *And houndes also with him berking.*
> *Ac no best thai no nome,*
> *No never he nist whider thai bicome.*
> *And otherwhile he might him se*
> *As a gret ost bi him te,*[4]
> *Wele atourned*[5] *ten hundred knightes,*
> *Ich yarmed to his rightes,*[6]
> *Of cuntenaunce stout and fers,*
> *With mani desplaid baners,*
> *And ich his swerd ydrawe hold,*
> *Ac never he nist whider thai wold.*
> *And otherwhile he seiye other thing:*
> *Knightes and levedis com daunceing*
> *In queynt atire, gisely,*[7]
> *Queynt pas and softly;*
> *Tabours and trunpes yede hem bi*
> *And al maner menstraci.*

[1] draw near.   [2] to the end.   [3] faint.   [4] went.
[5] equipped.   [6] as he should be.   [7] skilfully.

Finally—the glorious climax of these visions—he sees a company of sixty ladies ride hawking by a river where there is great plenty of wildfowl. There is no man among them (a recurrent feature in the romances that might be a memory of the huntress Diana and her company, the land of the Amazons, or the Celtic land of women).

> *And on a day he seiye him biside*
> *Sexti levedis on hors ride,*
> *Gentil and iolif as brid on ris,*[1]
> *Nou̇ght o man amonges hem ther nis.*
> *And ich a faucoun on hond bere*
> *And riden on haukin bi o rivere;*
> *Of game thai founde wel gode haunt:*
> *Maulardes, hayroun, and cormeraunt.*
> *The foules of the water ariseth,*
> *The faucouns hem wele deviseth:*[2]
> *Ich faucoun his pray slough.*

Orfeo had often taken part in this sport of kings, and he laughs for joy—a sign indeed of a reviving interest in life—and makes as if to join in. Then, among this company of women, he sees his lost queen. There seems, however, to be some sort of invisible barrier between them that prevents or forbids speech; they move each in a separate world. But there is a moment of mutual recognition, and she weeps—which would indicate that she loves him still and longs to return. But the other women compel her away with them.

Orfeo follows after the women riders—possibly we are to under-stand that his magic, the magic of his harp, gave him the power to do so with such speed and to enter the Otherworld. When they ride in at a rock—through the rock barrier between this and the Otherworld, or into a cave which is, in the romances as in tradi-tional belief generally, the entrance to the Otherworld—Orfeo still follows. In the rock he discovers a green and shining country, as bright as the sun on a summer's day, in the midst of which is a shining castle all of precious stones and with a hundred towers.

The conjecture that such a castle—so frequently met with in the

[1] bough.   [2] descry.

romances—was in the original myths the abode of the sun-god, or the sun itself, seems a plausible one; this association is still active in the poetry, for this otherworld castle is what gives light to that country.

> *Al that lond was ever light,*
> *For when it schuld be therk[1] and night,*
> *The riche stones light gonne,*
> *As bright as doth at none the sonne.*

Orfeo (like Thomas of Ercildoune on a similar occasion) mistakes this castle for Paradise.

> *Bi al thing, him think that it is*
> *The proude court of paradis.*

The implication is that it is not, that it is an elfin castle.

Orfeo must gain entrance to this castle, which the ladies have entered. He knocks at the gate which is opened by a porter—the Porter of the Otherworld—and introduces himself with his harp as a wandering minstrel (as Horn and others do in similar circumstances). In the courtyard Orfeo is confronted by a kind of Madame Tussaud's or Bluebeard's Chamber of Horrors. In initiation rites, at a certain stage in the tests, the aspirant is suddenly confronted with just such horrors of physical death. Certainly, if the medieval tale were following the original Greek legend of Orpheus and Eurydice here, this should be the house of the dead into which Orpheus has descended through the cave from the upper world. But in the medieval tale the idea of enchantment has replaced, though not quite entirely, the idea of death. Some of the distorted and mutilated figures in the courtyard could not indeed appear to be more dead—headless, strangled, drowned, or burnt. Yet they are 'thought dede and nare nought'. Each figure is fixed, as if frozen, in the attitude and appearance of the moment of apparent death, abduction or even madness.

> *And seiye liggeand within the wal*
> *Of folk that were thider ybrought*
> *And thought dede and nare nought:*

[1] dark.

Sum stode withouten hade,[1]
And sum non armes nade,
And sum thurch the bodi hadde wounde,
And sum lay wode, ybounde,
And sum armed on hors sete,
And sum astrangled as thai ete,
And sum were in water adreynt,[2]
And sum with fire al forschreynt;[3]
Wives ther lay on child-bedde,
Sum ded, and sum awedde;[4]
And wonder fele ther lay bisides,
Right as thai slepe her undertides;
Eche was thus in this warld ynome,
With fairi thider ycome.

The idea of death—since each was brought thither by magic—has clearly been absorbed, partially at least, into the idea of enchant-ment. If the dead are not dead but enchanted, they are capable of being disenchanted or brought to life again. Among these figures Orfeo sees his own wife, Dame Herodis, asleep under the orchard tree in her aspect when abducted.

The tale differs from many others of the kind in that Herodis, though abducted by the King of the Otherworld, has not apparently become his mistress or bride. When Orfeo with, or by means of, his harp enters the King's hall he sees before him the King and Queen of the Otherworld (who is not Herodis) all shining.

Her crounes, her clothes schine so bright,
That unnethe bihold he hem might.

The shining quality of the Otherworld Queen, characteristic of the faery, would certainly be more appropriate to a bride of the sun than to a queen of the dead.

The Otherworld King asks Orfeo what manner of man he is who dares make his way into that hall.

'Y no fond never so folehardi man,
That hider to ous durst wende . . .'

[1] head.   [2] drowned.   [3] shrivelled.   [4] crazed.

Orfeo answers:

> 'Y nam bot a pouer menstrel,
> And, sir, it is the maner of ous
> To seche mani a lordes hous;
> Thei we nought welcom no be,
> Yete we mot proferi forth our gle.'

Orfeo's harping, as it had charmed the wild beasts and birds, now charms the King of the Otherworld himself so that he promises Orfeo whatever he may ask—the rash promise of the traditional tales. When Orfeo asks for

> That ich levedi, bright on ble,
> That slepeth under the ympe-tre

the Otherworld King appears to be shocked at the idea of such an ill-matched couple.

> 'For thou art lene, rowe,[1] and blac,
> And sche is lovesum withouten lac.'[2]

The irony is that they are husband and wife (though it may be we are to understand that Herodis throughout her sojourn in the Otherworld has retained her youth while Orfeo has grown old). The promise must, however, be kept. Thus, in the lay of *Sir Orfeo*, Herodis is recovered and brought back completely.

Orfeo returns to his kingdom with Herodis and, disguised as a beggarman, to his palace—again (as in *King Horn*) in accord with the ancient pattern of which Odysseus's return is the classic type. His shaggy appearance, like a withered tree, is again remarked on.

> 'Lo,' thai seyd, 'swiche a man!
> How long the here hongeth him opan!
> Lo, how his berd hongeth to his kne!
> He is yclongen[3] also a tre!'

As in those tales of kings and gods who wander in disguise among men, finding out who is truly generous and loyal, Orfeo too must test his people before revealing himself. The steward

---

[1] rough.   [2] flaw.   [3] withered.

(who has had charge of the kingdom during the ten years of the king's absence) proves true.

> *'Everich gode harpour is welcom me to*
> *For mi lordes love, Sir Orfeo.'*

Orfeo takes his place, as a beggar minstrel, among the harpers in the hall. His harp excels all others in its music. The steward recognizes the harp, and complete recognition follows. The tale ends with the restoration of the King and Queen to their kingdom.

> *Thai brought the Quen into the toun,*
> *With al maner mentraci.*

It would seem that in this tale two magics act counter to one another. For Orfeo, too, has his magic—the magic of his harp with which he virtually compels the Other world to yield up his Queen.

§ 3

'SIR DEGARE'

Degare, whose name signifies 'the almost-lost one', is one of the heroes who, having been exposed in infancy, is brought up by foster-parents in ignorance of his true parentage. The tasks of the hero, in the English version, are to find his mother and, having found her, his father. In the course of his quest for the latter, an additional task is imposed on him: to win—by releasing her from an oppressor—one who appears to be essentially a faery mistress or otherworld bride.

Our poem is a version of the tale of one who was born of a union between a mortal and an otherworld being. This strange union begins the tale's sequence of events. A king's daughter and two of her maidens lose themselves in a forest 'in the west'.

> *The wode was rough and thikke, iwis,*
> *And thai token the wai amys.*

The princess's two maidens fall asleep at noon under a chestnut tree. The princess strays from her sleeping companions, gathering flowers, and so loses herself still more.

> *She wente aboute and gaderede floures,*
> *And herknede song of wilde foules,*
> *So fer in the launde she goht, iwis,*
> *That she ne wot nevere whare she is . . .*
> *'Allas!' hi[1] seide, 'that i was boren!*
> *Nou ich wot ich am forloren!*
> *Wilde bestes me willes togrinde,*
> *Or ani man me sschulle finde!'*

At this moment of distraction there suddenly appears to her a marvellous stranger, a faery knight.

> *A robe of scarlet he hadde upon;*
> *His visage was feir, his bodi ech weies;[2]*
> *Of countenaunce right curteis;*
> *Wel farende[3] legges, fot, and honde:*
> *Ther nas non in al the Kynges londe*
> *More apert[4] man than was he.*
> *'Damaisele, welcome mote thou be;*
> *Be thou afered of none wighte:*
> *Ich am comen here a fairi knyghte . . .'*

Though, in this case, there is no abduction, the union is a forced one. There is, in our version, what may seem a curious dis-crepancy between the faery knight's reassuring address to the for-lorn maiden and his violent act, between his initial 'courtesy' and his rude conduct. This may be explained if we have here a primitive tale to which the touches of 'courtesy' have been added by the medieval romancers. The otherworld wooer, having be-come a medieval knight, has to speak somewhat like a courtly lover, though he must still act as in the traditional tale, if the tale is not to be altered in its essentials. His abrupt appearance and equally abrupt departure—'Have god dai: i mot gon henne'—are characteristic of the faery. He has, moreover, the foreknowledge of his kind. Before he departs, he foretells that the child she is des-

---

[1] she.   [2] in every way.   [3] well-shaped.   [4] seemly.

tined to bear him will be a son, and he gives her a gift for her son, a broken-pointed sword. When the child has grown to manhood and seeks his father, the broken-pointed sword—an object that plays a part in many traditional tales and medieval romances—will prove essential to his recognition by his father, just in time, in our version, to avert the tragedy of the son slaying the father or vice versa (the Oedipus situation).

The second episode concerns the child who is born, the hero of the poem who is—typical of the traditional hero—supernatural or semi-divine in origin. The birth is (also typical) a concealed birth, in this case because the King must not know what has befallen his daughter (whom he is guarding with very peculiar care from possible husbands). The newborn infant is taken right away by one of the princess's maidens. But first the mother provides the infant with gifts such as are always found beside the exposed infant of tradition. These include gold and silver and a letter tied with a silken thread. This letter, explaining that the child is of noble birth and that the treasure is to pay for his upbringing, is clearly a late addition in a tale of this kind. But the most interesting and essential gift, in our version of the tale, is a pair of gloves.

> *And seththen she tok a paire glove*
> *That here lemman here sente of fairi londe,*
> *That nolde on no manne honde,*
> *Ne on child ne on womman she nolde,*
> *But on hire selve wel she wolde . . .*
> *And biddes him, wharevere he go,*
> *That he ne lovis no womman in londe*
> *But this gloves willen on hire honde;*
> *For siker on honde nelle thai nere[1]*
> *But on his moder that him bere.*

The gifts found beside the exposed infant in traditional tales are necessary not merely to pay for his upbringing (that may be a later rationalization) but to provide for his ultimate recognition as in origin divine or royal. In this case, the fairy gloves that fit only the mother are essential for the recognition of the son by the mother—

[1] they would never (fit any hand except his mother's).

just in time to avert the wedding of mother and son (again the Oedipus situation).

The infant is left—after a winter-night's journey by the princess's maiden—outside a 'hermitage', the habitation of a 'holi man', a cave in a rock. In our version this holy man is a Christian hermit who will have the infant he finds at his door brought up as a Christian.

When the child, whom he has christened Degare, has grown to manhood the holy man reveals to him that his origin is a mystery. Armed with an oak sapling (like young Perceval) the youth sets out to seek his mother with the gloves as his clue. After an initial testing adventure, in which he slays a dragon with his oak sapling, and after many women have tried on the gloves in vain, Degare chances to hear of a king who has the peculiar custom—though not uncommon in traditional tales—of challenging every one of his daughter's suitors to fight with him. Whoever overthrows the king is to win his only daughter and the kingdom, but the king has so far slain all comers. He evidently wants to prevent his daughter from marrying anyone and to keep himself king. If time in traditional tales and medieval romances bore any relation to time by the clock or sun, this king's daughter would have been young no longer. We were told at the beginning of our poem that the king whose daughter encountered the faery knight in the forest had such a custom. It is therefore not difficult to guess that the king's daughter of whom Degare hears will turn out to be his mother. Degare fights and overthrows the king; he is about to wed the latter's daughter when she recognizes her son by means of the gloves that fit her alone. She reveals to him the mystery of his father and provides him with his father's gift, the broken sword.

Thus armed, Degare sets out to find his father; his quest takes him through the same forest in the West where he was begotten. Towards nightfall he comes to a castle.

> Thenne he sey a water cler,
> And amidde a river,
> A fair castel of lim and ston:
> Other wonying was ther non.

What happens there is typical of the Otherworld Castle. It is wide open, as if Degare were an expected guest; he rides straight in but finds apparently no one there, though there is plenty of oats and hay in the courtyard for his horse. He passes into the great hall and still finds no one, though in the middle a fire burns. He argues, with admirable sense, that whoever has kindled the fire will come home to it, and meanwhile he makes himself at home.

> '*Par fai,*' *he saide, 'ich am al sure*
> *He that bette that fure*
> *Wil comen hom yit to-night;*
> *Abiden ich will a litel wight.*'
> *He sat adoun upon the dais,*
> *And warmed him wel eche wais.*

Then four women enter, in appearance huntresses. They remain mysteriously silent.

> *Four dammaiseles, gent and fre;*
> *Ech was nakked to the kne.*
> *The two bowen an arewen bere,*
> *The other two icharged were*
> *With venesoun, riche and god.*
> *And Degare upstod*
> *And gret hem wel fair aplight,*[1]
> *Ac thai answerede no wight,*
> *But yede into chaumbre anon*
> *And barred the dore after son.*

They depart as mysteriously as they came. A dwarf enters and, also mysteriously silent, lights torches and prepares a banquet.

> *Ther com a dwerw into the halle.*
> *Four fet of lengthe was in him;*
> *His visage was stout and grim;*
> *Bothe his berd and his fax*[2]
> *Was crisp an yalew as wax;*
> *Grete sscholdres and quarre;*[3]

---

[1] indeed. [2] hair. [3] square.

> *Right stoutliche loked he;*
> *Mochele were hise fet and honde*
> *Ase the meste man of the londe.*

Apart from this dwarf—the uncouth, though richly clad, attendant of the women—this castle appears to be tenanted only by women. When the banquet has been set out there enters the lovely lady of the castle, attended by ten women. She, too, at first maintains a mysterious silence.

> *A dammeisle of gret honour;*
> *In the lond non fairer nas;*
> *In a diapre clothed she was.*
> *With hire come maidenes tene,*
> *Some in scarlet, some in grene,*
> *Gent of bodi, of semblaunt swete,*
> *And Degarre hem gan grete;*
> *Ac hi ne answerede no wight,*
> *But yede to the soper anon right.*

We may guess already (if we have read other romances) that she and her women are under some enchantment or oppression from which Degare is destined to release them. At the silent banquet he falls under the lovely lady's spell in the common meaning of the word, if in no other.

> *At the soper litel at[1] he,*
> *But biheld the levedi fre,*
> *And sey ase feir a wimman*
> *Als he hevere loked an,*
> *That al his herte and his thout*
> *Hire to love was ibrowt.*

Clearly this lady of the castle is essentially the faery mistress or elfin queen of the romances and ballads.

After the banquet Degare listens to her playing on a harp in her chamber. Harps in fairyland have magical powers and on occasions lull their mortal hearers magically asleep. Although,

[1] ate.

like Gawain, 'couthe of corteisie' Degare falls asleep in spite of himself.

> *The levedi on here bed set,*
> *And a maide at here fet,*
> *And harpede notes gode and fine;*
> *Another broughte spices and wine.*
> *Upon the bedde he set adoun*
> *To here of the harpe soun.*
> *For murthe of notes so sschille.*
> *He fel adoun on slepe stille;*
> *So he slep al that night.*

In the morning the lady makes game of him for having slept, and he is ashamed of his discourtesy.

> '*For godes love, forgif hit me!*
> *Certes the murie harpe hit made . . .*'

At length he asks her the questions essential to unravelling the mystery of the castle.

> '. . . *Who is louerd of this lond?*
> *And who this castel hath in hond?*
> *Wether thou be widue or wif,*
> *Or maiden yit of clene lif?*
> *And whi her be so fele[1] wimman*
> *Allone, withouten ani man?*'

If the lady has something of the quality of the faery mistress under whose spell Degare has temporarily fallen, her role is here more specifically that of the abducted or oppressed lady of myth and traditional poetry whom it is the task of the hero to release from bondage. She reveals that she is oppressed by a grim knight who has slain all her own knights and would compel her to marry him. Scarcely has she obtained Degare's promise to champion her than her enemy approaches. Under the walls of the castle Degare slays the oppressor in combat. The lady begs the victor to dwell with her and offers him herself and her land. It is all (as in *Sir Percevelle of Galles*) according to the ancient pattern. But Degare cannot

---

[1] many.

immediately reply. He must continue his quest for his father, though he promises to return to her in a twelvemonth.

During the twelvemonth he does indeed find his father. As he rides through a forest in the West—doubtless again the same forest in which he was begotten—he meets an unknown knight who challenges him as an intruder.

> '*Velaun, wat dost thou here,*
> *In mi forest to chase mi dere?*'

But the father—for the unknown knight is none other—recognizes, just in time, the sword with the broken point. The mutual recognition of father and son averts the tragedy. (Here the romance breaks off; there are some leaves missing from the MS at this point.)

§ 4

'EMARE'

Emare is a partially rationalized, Christianized and much overlaid version of the primitive traditional tale which seems to be the original also of the tale of Constance (which Chaucer and Gower found already transformed into the likeness of a saint's legend and moral fable in an Anglo-French chronicle). Emare, in our version, similarly suffers persecution and calumny, first as a daughter and thereafter as a wife. She too is set floating across the sea in a boat on two occasions, on the second of these with her newborn child. She too undergoes a long cycle of separation ending in restoration both to her father and to her husband.

We can still apprehend in our version the feeling or suggestion that Emare is a supernatural or otherworld being, a faery. Probably in the original tale one parent at least was a faery, and the more likely conjecture is that it was the mother. Emare's mother is in our version said to be dead. That may well be a rationalization, since the children of the faery if they are brought up among mortals are necessarily brought up by foster-parents (as Emare is). Then, in our version, very much is made of a richly embroidered and bejewelled cloth sent by the King of Sicily to the Emperor who is Emare's father. The cloth and the love-motifs embroidered on it are described throughout seven stanzas. In the original tale this may have been a magic gift bestowed on the child by the faery. The suggestion persists in our version for the Emperor says of it

> *'Sertes, thys ys a fayry,*
> *Or ellys a vanyte!'*

There is no such cloth in Christendom; it was made in Heathendom. This could mean simply that it came from the East (associated with magic and sorcery), but in the romances Heathendom undoubtedly often stands for the Otherworld. The cloth has been seven winters in the making, as was the embroidery for Gawain when he sets out on his quest in *Sir Gawayne and the Grene Knight*. 'There's magic in a web of it', as in Desdemona's handkerchief. If indeed it acts as a love-charm, like the magic potion in the Tristram romances, this cloth could explain (though, in our version, this explanation is not invoked explicitly) the Emperor's incestuous passion for his daughter, Emare. He has a robe made for her out of the cloth.

> *And when hyt was don her upon,*
> *She semed non erthely wommon*
> *That marked[1] was of molde.*

She *seemed* no earthly woman perhaps because in the original tale she *was* no earthly woman.

When she resists her father's persecution he is so angered that he sets her afloat, wrapped in her gold mantle, on a boat which is clearly the magical boat that recurs in the romances because, though without anchor or oar, without food or drink, it conveys her across the sea to a far-distant country.

The landfall is in itself a recurrent marvel in traditional tales and romances, the mystery of a boat that floats a precious burden— perhaps an otherworld being—to the shore of a sea or river. These landfalls in romance and in myth and ritual may all be connected (the Maid of Astolat floating into Westminster and the effigy of

[1] created.

Adonis floating ashore near Alexandria in the ancient rite described by Miss Weston[1]), and they have gathered associations
from one another. In our lay of *Emare* the boat's burden is a lovely
lady in a glistening mantle. A knight is 'playing' by the shore
when the boat comes to land—Sir Kadore, a knight of 'that
country' (Galys), who lives in a castle by the shore. (In the original
tale Emare may have returned to her faery mother's country, the
castle by the shore being again the Otherworld. More likely, perhaps, it was Emare herself who was the faery visitant.)

> *A boot he fond by the brym,*
> *And a glysteryng thyng theryn.*

The 'glysteryng thyng' is the mantle of gold wrapped round the
lady and, in the context of the romances, it suggests faery treasure
and a faery being. She says her name is Egare, apparently the
same as the name of the hero in *Sir Degare*, meaning the lost one or
the outcast. Sir Kadore carries the 'lady of the see' into his castle
where, when she has been revived,

> *She tawghte hem to sewe and marke*
> *All maner of sylkyn werke;*
> *Of her they wer full fayne.*

Her unusual skill in sewing (perhaps magic designs) may be
another hint or vestige of faery origin. In the Irish *Tochmare Emere*
(The Wooing of Emer) the women at court learn needlework
from Emer.

Sir Kadore holds a feast for the King of Galys, and at this feast
the King sees Emare in her mantle.

> *The cloth upone her shone so bryght,*
> *When she was theryn ydyght,*
> *She semed non erdly thyng.*

Almost certainly, she *was* no earthly thing in the original tale. The
irresistible love which the King of Galys instantly feels for her
could again be explained—may have been so explained in the
original tale—as the effect of the magic mantle. The King determines to wed her and make her his queen.

[1] *From Ritual to Romance*, IV, 44.

But the Old Queen, his mother, has to be reckoned with. When she sees her son's bride—

> *She was bryght as someres day,*
> *The clothe on her shon so bryght—*

the Old Queen has no doubt that she is not human (and she may be right).

> *'I sawe never wommon*
> *Halvendell so gay!'*

She tells her son that his bride is a fiend, and forbids the wedding. But the King weds Egare, and the Old Queen goes home angry.

The tale now modulates into that of the malign mother-in-law and the calumniated wife. In the absence of the King at the wars Emare gives birth to a son (born with a double king-mark, which would appear to signify that *both* his parents are royal). But the Old Queen makes mischief. By the device of the exchange of letters she causes the King to receive the false news that his queen has given birth to a fiend and—by the device of yet another exchange of letters—causes the mother and child (like Constance and her child) to be cast adrift in a boat.

> *The lady and the lytyll chylde*
> *Fleted forth on the water wylde.*

There are great waves; the child weeps. But magically (though in our version it is not *said* that it is magic) the boat is carried after seven nights to Rome. Thus the episode of the magical boat is doubled in this romance, and also the finding of a boat at the water's edge with a precious cargo—on this occasion by a merchant of the city.

> *The cloth on her shon so bryght*
> *He was aferde of that syght,*
>   *For glysteryng of that wede;*
> *And yn hys herte he thowght ryght*
> *That she was none erdyly wyght.*

She says again that her name is Egare. He takes her and her child to his house and acts as the child's foster-parent till the boy is seven years old, at which age he is distinguished by unusual beauty.

> *He wax the fayrest chyld on lyfe.*

The romance ends with the recognition of his son and wife by the King of Galys, and of his daughter by the Emperor. Thus the lost daughter is restored to her father, the lost wife to her husband, and the lost son to his father.

§ 5

'SIR LAUNFAL'

Thomas Chestre's *Sir Launfal* breaks the anonymity of most of the English lays by announcing in its final stanza the name of its maker. Composed in stanzas, some time after 1350, it looks like an amplified and elaborated version of some earlier English transla-tion—contemporary perhaps with the lays in the Auchinleck MS —of Marie de France's *Lanval*.

The principal themes of the lay are the persecution of Launfal by Gwennere, Arthur's Queen, and, on the other hand, the love for him of an otherworld being who is also a kind of Lady Bountiful or Fairy Godmother, the source of the miraculous pros-perity which for a time he enjoys. The favour of his faery mistress (Dame Tryamoure) is dependent, however, as is usual in such cases, on his not breaking a certain taboo.

In the early part of the poem Launfal is virtually an exile from the Court of Arthur because of Gwennere's antagonism. In this, as in other romances, she is not a very reputable character. (There is indeed some suggestion that she too is a faery, and perhaps for that reason not very reliable; she may have attachments in the faery country from which she comes. She has been fetched from across the sea, it is said in *Sir Launfal*, from Ireland.) Attended by only two knights, Launfal comes to Karlyoun (Caerleon), the Mayor of which is, in this romance, a somewhat comic character. When he understands that Launfal is out of favour at court he makes excuses for not putting him up, but finally lets him have a chamber beside his orchard. There Launfal falls into such poverty that even his two knights are compelled to leave him. At the lowest ebb of his fortune—possibly, in the original tale, because of some magical malign influence or hostility emanating from Gwennere—his faery wooer intervenes.

It happens exactly as such an event always does in the lays. Launfal rides towards the West (having borrowed saddle and bridle from the Mayor's good daughter) and rests in the hot 'undern-tyde' under a tree. Two maidens appear out of the wood, faery messengers, richly attired, one bearing a gold basin, the other a towel (apparently ritual objects, at least in their original significance).

> *He sawe come out of holtes hore*
> *Gentyll maydenes two;*
> *Har kerteles were of Inde-sandal[1]*
> *Ilased smalle,[2] iolyf, and well:*
> *Ther myght noon gayere go.*
>
> *Hare manteles were of grene felwet,*
> *Ybordured with gold, ryght well ysette,*
> *Ipelured with grys and gro.[3]*
> *Hare heddys were dyght well withalle:*
> *Everych hadde oon a iolyf coronall*
> *With syxty gemmys and mo.*
>
> *Hare faces were whyt as snow on downe;*
> *Har rode was red, here eyn were browne:*
> *I sawe nevir non swyche!*
> *That oon bare of gold a basyn,*
> *That other a towayle, whyt and fyn,*
> *Of selk that was good and ryche.*

They bid him come and speak with their lady, Dame Tryamoure. He goes with them courteously, and they lead him into the wood to a splendid pavilion surmounted by an eagle of burnished gold whose eyes are carbuncles shining like the moon. (Lady Try-

---

[1] Indian silk.   [2] laced tight.   [3] trimmed with grey-and-white squirrel's fur.

amoure may in her mythological origins have been, like Diana, a goddess of the woods and of the moon.) Within the pavilion he finds a lady so preternaturally lovely that she is clearly a faery personage.

> *He fond yn the pavyloun*
> *The Kynges doughter of Olyroun,*
>   *Dame Tryamoure that hyghte;*
> *Here fadyr was kyng of fayrye . . .*
> *Sche was as whyt as lylye yn May*
> *Or snow that sneweth yn wynterys day . . .*
> *The rede rose, whan sche ys newe,*
> *Agens here rode nes naught of hewe.*[1]

With the forwardness characteristic of the faery lady she is the wooer and promises Launfal rich and magical gifts if he becomes her sweetheart. These gifts include a purse of silk and gold perpetually replenished (the purse that recurs in traditional tales), magical preservation of her knight in battle and tournament, and, for his own use, her steed Blaunchard (clearly a descendant of the magical steed which the hero of tradition rides). She spreads a banquet before him. The whole scene might indeed be an eyewitness report of one of those 'faery' feasts and rites which Dr. Margaret Murray[2] and others have suggested were still celebrated by the devotees of some pre-Christian fertility cult in woods and wildernesses in medieval Europe. Finally, Tryamoure becomes Launfal's mistress, but, as usual, there is a taboo imposed on the mortal lover. In this case it is that he must never boast of her.

From that hour Launfal is enriched by the faery and enjoys a marvellous prosperity. The Mayor changes his tune now that Launfal is rich, and invites him to dinner. Launfal becomes a source of bounty to others and feeds the poor. In feats of arms he also prospers under the protective magic of his faery mistress. Finally he is invited again to Arthur's Court at St. John's Mass (the midsummer festival).

---

[1] i.e. would seem colourless by comparison.
[2] *God of the Witches*, II, The Worshippers, p. 42 *et seq.*

> *And Syr Launfal also*
> *Wente to daunce upon the grene,*
> *Unther the toure ther lay the Quene,*
> *With syxty ladyes and mo.*

The Queen sees him go in the dance, and she and her ladies join in the mazes of the midsummer dancing.

> *To daunce they wente alle yn same:*
> *To se hem play, hyt was fayr game,*
>   *A lady and a knyght.*

> *They hadde menstrales of moch honours—*
> *Fydelers, sytolyrs,*[1] *and trompours . . .*
> *There they playde, for sothe to say,*
> *After mete the somerys day.*

The Queen is overpowered by love for Launfal. In the evening she declares to Launfal that she has loved him for seven years (the seven years in which he has loved Tryamoure). He refuses her love. Angry, she taunts him:

> *'That thou lyvest, hyt ys pyte;*
> *Thou lovyst no woman, ne no woman the!'*

Stung to retort, Launfal rashly boasts and so breaks the taboo.

> *'I have loved a fayryr woman*
> *Than thou evir leydest thyn ey upon,*
> *Thys seven yere and more!'*

The angry Queen withdraws into her tower and plots revenge. When the King returns from hunting she plays the part of Poti-phar's wife and turns the King against Launfal.

From the moment that he rashly boasted of his faery mistress a disastrous change has come over Launfal. With the loss of his mistress's favour his prosperity withers away, deprived of its source, her magic; his splendour fades as the year itself does.

---

[1] players on the citole.

Sir Launfal

Hys armur, that was whyt as floure,
Hyt becom of blak coloure.

His purse is empty, and he is 'forlorn'.

Launfal must now substantiate his boast (this is a theme of several traditional tales, notably of one or two of the Gawain cycle). He is given a twelvemonth and a fortnight in which to produce his 'lemman . . . that he made of swych yelpynge'. This, it would seem, is Tryamoure's opportunity to cast down Gwennere. The latter has further played into the hands of her rival by invoking a hypothetical curse upon herself—in the traditional tales, always a dangerous thing to do.

'Yf he bryngeth a fayrere thynge,
Put out my eeyn gray!'

The appointed day becomes the occasion of the shining triumph of Tryamoure. Ten maidens come riding each of whom might be a queen; then another ten. The preternatural brightness of these harbingers of Tryamoure shows that they are faery beings, and

They ryd upon ioly moyles¹ of Spayne,
With sadell and brydell of Champayne;
Hare lorayns² lyght gonne leme.³

Finally Tryamoure herself comes riding through the town on a white palfrey.

Gentyll, iolyf as bryd on bowe,
In all manere fayre inowe
To wonye yn worldly wone.
The lady was bryght as blosme on brere,
With eyen gray, with lovelych chere;
Her leyre lyght schoone.

As rose on rys here rode was red;
The here schon upon here hed
As gold wyre that schynyth bryght.

¹ mules.   ² bridlereins.   ³ brightly gleamed.

Sche hadde a crounne upon here molde[1]
Of ryche stones and of golde,
  That lofsom lemede lyght.

The lady was clad yn purpure palle,
With gentyll body and myddyl small,
  That semely was of syght.
Her mantyll was furryth with whyt ermyn,
Ireversyd[2] iolyf and fyn;
  No rychere be ne myght.

Her sadell was semyly set:
The sambus[3] were grene felvet,
  Ipaynted with ymagerye;
The bordure was of belles
Of ryche gold, and nothyng elles,
  That any man myghte aspye.

In the arsouns,[4] before and behynde,
Were twey stones of Ynde,
  Gay for the maystrye;
The paytrelle[5] of her palfraye
Was worth an erldome stoute and gay,
  The best yn Lumbardye.

A gerfawcon sche bar on here hond;
A softe pas here palfray fond,
  That men here schuld beholde.
Thorugh Karlyon rood that lady;
Twey whyte grehoundys ronne hyre by;
  Hare colers were of golde.

The description is that of a principal figure in a ritual or pageant. Compared with Tryamoure, the Queen is said to be as the moon to the sun in daytime. The faery is, however, not content with triumphing over her rival. She takes a terrible revenge on her; she

---

[1] top of her head. [2] trimmed. [3] saddle-cloths.
[4] saddle-bow. [5] breast-trappings.

blows on Gwennere such a breath that the latter is blinded for ever. It is indeed dangerous to fall foul of the faery. After her terrible act of vengeance Tryamoure rides disdainfully away.

> *The lady lep an hyre palfray*
> *And bad hem alle have good day.*

Launfal on his steed follows her

> *Fere yn to a iolyf ile,*
> *Olyroun that hyghte.*

It seems that, in our version, he is reconciled to her and dwells with her in the Otherworld.

> *Every yere, upon a certayn day,*
> *Me may here Launfales stede nay,*[1]
> *And hym se with syght.*

[1] neigh.

A BALLAD-ROMANCE:
'THOMAS OF ERCILDOUNE AND
THE QUENE OF ELF-LAND'

The ballad-romance of *Thomas of Ercildoune and the Quene of Elf-Land*, in spite of its fragmentary and disordered condition as it has survived on three fifteenth-century MSS, is an extraordinarily fine rendering, as poetry, of those traditional subjects: the union of a mortal man with an otherworld being and his journey to the Otherworld.

What gives the poetry its more than usual imaginative depth and its poignancy is the interplay of Pagan and Christian feeling and symbolism. Two mythologies are co-present and to some extent in conflict in the demands they make, the obligations they impose on the individual curious of experience. The old themes are rendered particularly complex by the new knowledge of the *soul* and the consequent concern for the soul. The mortal man now adventures into the faery realm at the risk not only of the destruction of his body but of his soul. There is more than a suggestion of the Faust theme of breaking into the circle of forbidden knowledge and risking damnation. Man has his own proper place in the scheme of things, and to presume to step outside it may be disastrous for his soul as well as his body. There is also something here of the Promethean myth of risking divine retribution in order to wrest from inaccessible or forbidden places, for the benefit of mankind, some hidden or secret knowledge; thus prophetic knowledge is brought back from the otherworld, won from the faery by Thomas. But deeply present in the poem is the sense that everything, every experience, must be paid for. One who dares make any choice, who dares take any step into the unknown, must be prepared to pay the penalty by setting in motion a train of unforeseeable and uncontrollable consequences.

In all three fifteenth-century MSS the poem opens in the first person, then shifts into the third person to speak of Thomas. This narrator in the first person and the Thomas thereafter spoken of appear to be one and the same. There may be a conjunction of more than one earlier version in the poem we have; yet it is appropriate that a vision vouchsafed to a solitary person should be reported by himself in the first person, and the introductory section of the poem is virtually such a vision. The circumstances are the customary, perhaps necessary or prescribed ones, and are reminiscent not only of the 'visions' of the romances but of the more massive alliterative vision-poems (*Wynnere and Wastoure, The Parlement of the Thre Ages*). The man to whom the vision or faery pageant appears wanders alone on a May morning through woods full of birds, and rests under a tree.

> *In a mery mornynge of Maye,*
> *By Huntle bankkes my selfe allone.*

> *I herde the jaye, and the throstelle,*
> *The mawys meuyde of hir songe,*
> *The wodewale[1] beryde[2] als a belle,*
> *That alle the wode abowte me ronge.*

> *Allone in longynge, thus als I laye,*
> *Undre nethe a semely tre,*
> *Saw I whare a lady gaye,*
> *Came ridand over a longe lee.*

The gay lady, it will be noted, is all shining—she is richly bejewelled—and she is a huntress (like Diana).

> *Hir palfraye was a dappill graye;*
> *Swilke one I saghe ne never none:*
> *Als dose the sonne, on someres daye,*
> *That fair lady hir selfe scho schone.*

> *Her sette it was of reuylle bone;[3]*
> *Full semely was that syghte to see!*

[1] wood pecker?   [2] rang out.   [3] ivory.

169

Stefly sett with precyous stone,
And compaste all with crapote.[1]

Stones of Oryente grete plente;
Hir hare abowte hir hede it hange;
Scho rode over that lange lee,
A whylle scho blewe, a nother scho sange.

Hir garthis[2] *of nobyll sylke thay were;*
The bukylls were of berelle stone;
Hir steraps were of crystalle clere,
And all with perelle over by gone.[3]

Hir payetrelle[4] *was of iralle*[5] *fyne;*
Hir cropoure was of orfare;[6]
And als clere golde hir brydill it schone;
One aythir syde hange bellys three.

Scho led three grehoundis in a leeshe;
And seven raches[7] *by hir fete rone;—*
Scho bare a horne abowt hir halse;
And undir hir belte full many a flone.[8]

After this presentment of her, the shift from the first person of the narrator to the third person takes place; it is now said that it was Thomas who saw this sight under a tree. Thomas mistakes the lady for Mary, Queen of Heaven. This mistake in identifying the lady (it occurs frequently in medieval literature and occurs again in the folk-ballad versions of our poem three hundred years later) first indicates the 'point of intersection', as it were, of the Pagan and Christian symbolism between which there continues to be an interplay at poignant moments throughout the poem. Thomas feels he must speak to her, but to do so (as if this first sight of her were simply a fleeting vision) it seems he has certain obstacles to cross 'hir for to mete at Eldone tree'. He has to cross a mountain—the mountain barrier between the human world and the Other-

[1] toad stone.   [2] girths.   [3] covered.   [4] horse's breast-trappings.
[5] ?   [6] gold embroidery.   [7] hounds.   [8] arrow.

world.[1] There, under a branch of that sacred tree—sacred, however, according to another religion than Christianity—he kneels to the lady and, addressing her as Queen of Heaven, asks for her 'pity'.

And sayd, lufly ladye! rewe one mee.

The phrase is in itself ambiguous, for it is as much used in the profane love-poetry as in the religious poetry of the Middle Ages. The lady corrects his error, denying that she is Queen of Heaven or anyone of such high degree; she is of 'ane other con-tree'. Thus, it would seem, the Elfin Queen here acknowledges Mary as a higher power.

Having learned that the lady is not Mary, Thomas asks for her love. In this case it is the mortal man who woos—or thinks he does (for it was she who first presented herself to him, perhaps not accidentally). But not only is the faery lady in this case not *apparently* the wooer—an unusual feature—but she actually first of all warns the mortal man that union with her, which she calls 'that synne', will 'for-doo' all her beauty. But he recklessly persists in asking 'now, lufly ladye, rewe on mee' and rashly promises to dwell with her for ever 'wethir thu will in heven or helle'. In effect he is prepared to give away his soul, to risk damnation, as Faustus does. She warns him a second time that he, a 'man of molde', will mar her.

Man of molde, thu will me merre.[2]

It is this which lends a moral and indeed tragic depth to the event. She herself has disabused him of his error that she is Queen of Heaven, and she has warned him of the consequences of the act he then contemplates. Yet he persists—under her spell—in choosing what she herself calls the worse ('and trowe it wele thu chewys the werre'). She grants him his will 'undir nethe that grene wode spraye'.

The effect upon the faery of union with a mortal is a disastrous

[1] It would appear that the name 'Eldone' may originally have been Halydown or Halidon, which would mean the holy hill.

[2] The line might have been spoken by the grave child—with looks as grave as those of a duke or earl—in the vision of *Pearl*.

change in her appearance. Her beauty and brightness have faded; the colour and the light in her have drained away.

> *Hir hare it hange all over hir hede,*
> *Hir eghne semede owte, that are were graye.*

> *And all the riche clothynge was a waye,*
> *That he by-fore sawe in that stede;*
> *Hir a schanke blake, hir other graye,*
> *And all hir body lyke the lede.*

> *Than sayd Thomas, allas! allas!*
> *In faythe this es a dollfull syghte;*
> *How arte thu fadyde thus in the face,*
> *That schane by-fore als the sonne so bryght!*

A similar transformation happens to Lucifer in the Miracle Play of the Fall of Lucifer. The episode is the reverse of that of the withered hag who is disenchanted or metamorphosed back into the lovely lady she originally was by the embrace of a courteous knight, as in *The Wedding of Sir Gawain and Dame Ragnell,* Chaucer's *Wife of Bath's Tale* and Gower's tale of the *Knight Florent.* The faery withered or blighted by the embrace of a mortal is more tragic, if not more imaginative.

There are consequences for Thomas, too, a penalty to be paid. He is compelled to go with her to the Otherworld. His soul and body are (like Faustus's) no longer his own; thay have passed into the keeping of another. She bids him take leave of the sun and moon and of the leaf that grows on the tree. He shall not see middle-earth for a twelvemonth (it turns out to be seven years, perhaps again because of an imperfect conjunction of differing versions of the poem). Thomas kneels and prays to 'Mary mylde' to have mercy on him, using again the phrase that he had used in a profane sense, 'Lady, but thou rewe on mee'; and he entrusts his soul to Christ ('My saulle, Jhu, by-teche I the') wherever it may happen that his body shall go. He thus prepares himself for his dread journey, clearly recognizing that his soul as well as body is in peril.

> *I trewe my dedis will wirke me care.*

Thomas may indeed be 'lost' in a more significant sense than is usual in the traditional tales. Two supernatural powers or systems of necessities, Pagan and Christian, to some extent acting counter to one another, are bearing upon the human mortal in his now critical predicament.

Such mythical journeys to the Otherworld may have corresponded originally to the progression of rites and tests in some grave initiation ceremony. Such a hypothesis seems to work, in that it seems to make the poetry here more understandable and yet certainly not less significant and profound. The entrance to the Otherworld is, as is customary, a cave or shadowy hollow.

> *Scho ledde hym in at Eldone birke,*
> *Undir nethe a derne lee;*
> *Whare it was derk als mydnyght myrke,*
> *And ever the water till his knee.*

There is, as is also customary, the necessity of crossing a water barrier (like the Styx). For three days—

> *He herd bot swoghyne of the flode.*

Among these perils and tests there is one that is reminiscent of the grapes of Tantalus. She who has become his otherworld guide leads him into a garden full of fruits which he is forbidden to eat though he is famished with hunger.

> *Scho lede hym in till a faire herbere,*
> *Whare frute was growyng gret plentee:*
> *Pere and appill, bothe rype thay were,*
> *The date, and als the damasee.*
>
> *The fygge, and als so the wyneberye;*
> *The nyghtyngales lyggande on thair neste;*
> *The papeioyes faste abowte gan flye;*
> *And throstylls sange, wolde have no reste.*
>
> *He presed to pulle the frute with his hande;*
> *Als man for fude that was nere faynt.*

Scho sayd, Thomas, thu late tham stande,
  Or ells the fende the will atteynt.

If thu it plokk, sothely to say,
  Thi saule gose to the fyre of helle;
It comes never owte or Domesdaye,
  Bot ther in payne ay for to duelle.

The garden and the forbidden fruit suggest inevitably the Garden of Eden; but the interplay of Pagan and Christian symbolism and significances reaches a momentary climax in the poetry when she warns him that the Fiend will have him, his soul go to Hell, if he plucks the fruit. The Christian concern for the soul has given a new significance and depth to the Pagan notion (so frequent in traditional tales) of a taboo the breaking of which must entail the most dreadful consequences.

The Elf-Queen has become, for love of Thomas, not only his guide but (like Medea or Ariadne when they assist the hero) his guardian spirit through the perils of his journey, a protective and not destructive power. Thus she prevents him from plucking the fruit by making him lay his head on her knee and showing him a Christian vision—a vision of Heaven and Hell and Purgatory.

Seese thu nowe yone faire waye,
  That lyggis over yone heghe montayne?—
Yone es the waye to heven for aye,
  When synfull sawles have duryd ther payne.

Seese thu nowe yone other waye,
  That lygges lawe by nethe yone rysse?[1]
Yone es the waye, the sothe to saye,
  Unto the joye of paradyse.

Seese thu yitt yone thrid waye,
  That lygges under yone grene playne?
Yone es the waye, with tene and traye,[2]
  Whare synfull saulis suffirris thare payne.

[1] bough.   [2] sorrow, vexation.

Thomas of Ercildoune and the Quene of Elf-Land

Bot seese thu nowe yone fourt waye,
That lygges over yone depe delle?
Yone es the waye, the sothe to saye,
Unto the brennande fyre of hell.

There is, however, yet another possible destination—the Elfin or Otherworld castle. It is Thomas's destination, as it is Gawain's and that of other knights who journey on quests. In the Grail romances it is the Grail Castle.

Seese thu yitt yone faire castelle,
That standes upone yone heghe hill?
Of towne and towre it beris the belle;
In mydul erthe es non lyk ther-till.

It is the castle of the King of that other country. The lady now says that the King must not know that she (who is evidently the Queen) is Thomas's mistress. This is the *reason*, at least, that she gives for imposing on her mortal lover another taboo—the taboo of silence. He must speak to no one even when addressed. She will say she took away his speech 'by yonde the see'.

As she approaches the magical castle a second change comes over the lady—she recovers or reassumes her original beauty and brightness; like many of the faery and of the divinities of mythology she is subject to transformations, a shape-shifter.

Scho come agayne als faire and gude,
And al so ryche one hir palfraye.

Hir grehundis fillide with dere blode;
Hir rachis couplede by my faye;
Scho blewe hir horne with mayne and mode,[1]
Un to the castelle scho tuk the waye.

In our version it had not been remarked that the blood of her grey-hounds had been drained away, that they had become shadows, bloodless and without substance, when she herself and all her finery faded; but we may now assume that to have happened.

[1] spirit.

Now they are filled again mysteriously with precious ('dere') blood.

There are many marvels in the castle, but the greatest is said to be that there are fifty harts—the spoils, it seems, of some hunt—being prepared for a banquet, and that dogs are lapping their blood. It seems more than probable that the blood of the harts may be associated with the 'dere' blood which marvellously restored the greyhounds of the Elf-Queen. If so, the life-blood of the harts is no ordinary blood; it has a life-giving or life-restoring effect like the blood of the sacrificed one of ancient cults and, in relation to the life of the soul, the wine of the Christian sacrament. The hart, we know, became a symbol of Christ in medieval tradition and the hart's blood the blood of Christ. There is certainly an underlying, though not overt, connexion between the harts' blood in this castle and the Grail. It is hardly necessary to remark that the Grail itself is a symbol in which Christian and Pagan significances are involved: it has healing or life-giving powers; it has the effect of a horn or cauldron of plenty, promoting abundance of food and drink; and it has taken on a Christian mystical significance as the vessel that holds the blood of Christ. In the castle of our poem, as in the Grail Castle, the banquet for which the fifty harts are prepared—

> *Cokes come with dryssynge knyfe*

—appears to have the character of a sacramental or sacred feast. There is music and dancing as in some festival.

> *Harpe and fethill bothe thay fande,*
> *Getterne and als so the sawtrye;*
> *Lutte and rybybe[1] bothe gangande,*
> *And all manere of mynstralsye ...*

> *Knyghtes dawnsede by three and three,*
> *Thare was revelle, gamen, and playe,*
> *Lufly ladyes faire and free,*
> *That satte and sange one riche araye.*

[1] ? rebeck.

Thomas of Ercildoune and the Quene of Elf-Land

When Thomas has dwelt 'in that solace' for seven years (although he imagines he has been there for only three days) his time is up—in two possible senses, either that the seven years of his destined sojourn in the Otherworld are ended or that after the seven years' cycle of his specially favoured condition he is liable to become a human sacrifice. His faery mistress warns him that he must go because the time has again come round—evidently a seven-year cycle—when 'the fende of helle' (like the Minotaur in the Cretan myth or ritual) will seek his 'fee'.

> To morne of helle the foulle fende
> Amange this folke will seche his fee;
> And thu arte mekill man and hende;[1]
> I trowe full wele he wolde chese the.

(The reminiscence or reference to some rite of human sacrifice is preserved also in the folk-ballad version and in the ballad of *Tam Lin*—

> But ay at end of seven year
> They pay a teind to hell.)

The Elf-Queen fears that, because he is so handsome, Thomas will be chosen. Once again the otherworld being proves the guardian of her mortal lover. She brings him back to the Eldone tree.

The essential poem is now ended. The succession of prophecies —answers of the faery lady to Thomas's questions as she turns to go and he seeks to detain her—are by way of something added, though they amount to two more *fits*. Their relation to the significance of the poem is that they are wisdom which Thomas has brought back from the Otherworld (originally perhaps from his initiation), in the sense that he has obtained them from his faery mistress.

---

[1] courteous, gentle.

'MATTER OF ENGLAND'

§ 1

'KING HORN'

King Horn, as found on an MS of the end of the thirteenth century and on two MSS of the beginning of the fourteenth, appears to be a Southern English version of about 1250 or earlier, and it is generally regarded as the earliest version of an English medieval romance that has chanced to survive. There is a twelfth- or early thirteenth-century Anglo-Norman version, *Horn et Rimenhild*. But there appears to be no direct connexion between it and the English *King Horn*, and the tale itself out of which these French and English medieval romances have been made must be older still. The nature of the tale has suggested a possible origin in a Norse saga. But it may have passed through a French medieval stage before becoming the English lay we now have. On the other hand, it remains sufficiently independent of the Breton lays and the Arthurian romances and has been classified with *Havelok the Dane*, another English romance which has Scandinavian associations, as the two earliest English survivors among the romances that deal with the so-called 'Matter of England'.

The English *King Horn* is expressly a song to listen to—

A sang ihc schal you singe

—a minstrel's lay to be recited or sung to an audience, probably to the accompaniment of the harp, as Horn himself, in one of the episodes, is described as doing. The metrical lines are shorter than the usual octosyllabic lines of the French romances and of the English romances in rhyming couplets and, as in the half-line of the alliterative verse, there are normally in reading two stressed words in each line. These stresses, rather than the number of syllables, are what regulate the movement and the meaning in recital.

King Horn

The lay of *King Horn* is distinguished among medieval romances, particularly the more literary specimens, by its spareness and directness, its comparative freedom from elaborations, accretions and digressions. The telling of the tale itself is clearly the absorbing preoccupation that has burnt away irrelevances. On the other hand, there is occasionally that economy of using again the same phrase or image—as, for example,

> *The se bigan to flowe*[1]
> *And Horn child to rowe*

—which is characteristic of traditional poetry from the Homeric poems to the ballads. Further, there is a doubling or paralleling of whole episodes. This latter may, of course, be explained as the result, in this collaborative art, of audiences having been so pleased by an episode that they demanded or were willing to hear it, or something not quite the same but like it, twice over. But such an explanation does not do justice to the way in which the paralleling or doubling, always with skilful variation, seems to play a part in the formation of a satisfying and interesting total pattern. The critical modern reader may well conclude that this doubling of certain episodes in *King Horn* is done by artistic design, not merely as repetition but as significant patterning.[2]

The tale of Horn is one of the tales of the exile and wanderings of a king's son, unrecognized as such, and how he wins his bride and then, having also avenged his slain father and proved his manhood, returns and wins back his kingdom. The images in which the young hero is initially visualized in the poem—as a child fairer than rain on flower, fairer than the sun shining, as bright as glass, white as a flower, rose-red—are those conventionally used in the descriptions of heroes and heroines in the medieval romances. They belong to a descriptive convention that certainly appears to be more appropriate to a divinity (a young sun-god or a spring-goddess) than to a human child, even though a king's son. Horn's father (Old Horn) is king of a kingdom in the West called in the

---

[1] i.e. it was flood-tide.

[2] A supreme instance is the parallel tales of Lear and his daughters and of Gloucester and his sons in *King Lear*. See Yeats's essay, 'The Emotion of Multitude' in *Ideas of Good and Evil*.

poem Suddene (identified by Schofield[1] and others as, in this particular poem, the Isle of Man); he is slain by giant Saracen invaders from the sea while Horn is still a child. They usurp the kingdom. Thus the tasks which young Horn will be under an obligation to perform when he arrives at manhood will be (like Hamlet and Orestes) to avenge his slain father and win back his kingdom.

The 'Saracens' will be recognized by the historically schooled modern reader not only as the Moslem enemies of Christendom of the period of the Crusades but also as here possibly a reminiscence of the pagan Viking marauders of the period of the Norse invasions of the British Isles. But more essentially (or universally) they are simply the *others*, the antagonists of the hero, like the Turkish Knight of the Mummers' Play.

The Saracens in *King Horn* foresee that 'in seven years' time' young Horn, having assumed manhood, will avenge his father's death. It is of the essence of custom or ceremony (as of tragedy) that everything is in this way prearranged or foredoomed. Thus a poetic quality—the sense of fate in this poem—may be rooted in something extra-poetic. Like the King Herod of the Miracle Plays, therefore, the Saracens set about putting out of the way the child born to be king. With his twelve companions Horn is cast adrift in a boat without rudder or sail.

Thus *King Horn* becomes at this point one of the group of traditional tales in which a child is cast adrift in an open boat which none the less conveys him to the country where, in fulfilment of his destiny, he is to be brought up by foster-parents until he returns to his own people. In other tales it is a woman—or a mother with her child—who undergoes this cycle of events. The boat in *King Horn* is no ordinary boat; it has something of the quality still of a magical boat which, of its own volition, conveys the child hero where his destiny lies; as if it were alive, it is sent back by itself with a message for the Queen, Horn's mother, who has taken refuge in a cave. The whole episode is, however, to some extent rationalized in the poem. Horn is committed to the waves apparently as a convenient way of getting rid of him while

[1] *English Literature from the Norman Conquest to Chaucer*, V, 262.

avoiding the guilt of shedding his blood; and it appears that the rowers make use of some current or tide which carries the rudder-less boat with mathematical precision to the destined shore.[1]

> *The se bigan to flowe*
> *And Horn child to rowe.*

The boat makes a landfall at daybreak on the shores of an un-known country which in its essence, as it is described, might— like the green earth that reappears at the end of the Noah Play—be any country in which the day or the spring has returned after night or winter.

> *Til hit sprang dai-light*
> *Til Horn saw on the stronde*
> *Men gon in the londe.*
> *'Feren,'[2] quoth he, 'yonge,*
> *Ihc telle you tithinge.*
> *Ihc here fogeles singe*
> *And that gras him springe.'*

This new country is Westernesse (thought by Schofield and others to be probably Wirral or somewhere in the north-west of Eng-land). In a passage of almost ceremonial question and answer, the King of Westernesse asks Horn where he has come from and who he is, and he finally adopts the unknown one as his 'fundling'. Apart from acquiring the usual noble accomplishments, Horn becomes, like Sir Orfeo (who is also a king) and Sir Tristram, a harper.

The King of Westernesse has a daughter, Rymenhild. She is the king's daughter who, in accordance with destiny, falls in love with the unrecognized king's son and is eventually to be his queen.

---

[1] The boat and the crossing of water are symbols that recur in the medieval romances. The boat may, in the original myths, have been a magical conveyance, a conveyance to the Otherworld across the barrier of water, as the very special horse the hero rides may have been originally a magical conveyance across (or through) the mountain barrier between the human world and the Otherworld. In many apparently different traditions there is some such boat—Charon's ferry-boat, Noah's Ark, Wade's boat, the boat that conveys the wounded Arthur across the lake to Avalon—a boat plying between two worlds.

[2] comrades.

Unlike the lady of troubadour poetry, but like the forward faery mistress of many of the romances or like some of the bold women of the Old Norse and Germanic literatures, Rymenhild is the wooer and asks him to take her as his wife. But the young man answers that he is a thrall and a foundling whereas she is a king's daughter. Accordingly, Rymenhild sends a cup and a ring to the Steward who thereupon persuades the King to knight Horn. She gives Horn a gold ring—the magic ring (or sometimes girdle) of traditional tales and medieval romances which has the power to protect the wearer. Horn rides out singing, does battle with a Saracen (conveniently landed from a ship), cuts off the Saracen's head and bears it, like the boar's head or the Turk's head, to the King's hall as a trophy. He has proved his manhood.

Then, one morning, while the King has ridden forth hunting, Horn finds Rymenhild in her bower distracted. She has had a dream that she cast her net into the sea and caught a great fish which broke the net. The dream is used in a later episode by Horn to bring about his recognition by Rymenhild. Meanwhile, it portends trouble. Among Horn's twelve companions there is a Judas-like traitor, Fykenhild. Envious and false, he tells the King that Horn plans to kill him, wed his daughter and so, presumably, make himself king. Thus calumniated, Horn is banished and for a second time must cross the sea to 'uncuthe londe'—this time to Ireland.

For the second time a king's daughter—this time the King of Ireland's—falls in love with the unknown stranger from the sea. The resemblance between the names of the rival women, Reynild and Rymenhild, is not accidental, if we may judge from the usage in other romances; in *Tristram*, indeed, both have the same name. Such a 'doubling' of an episode may be a feature of a deliberate design, as is a Shakespearian sub-plot. On this occasion the hero must remain loyal to his previous love, and does. The situation thus becomes a new kind of testing for him. Horn goes under the name of 'Cutbeard' during his probationary seven years' exile in Ireland. The King on this occasion would gladly have approved the wedding and made the young hero his successor in the king-ship; for, as 'Cutbeard', Horn has a second time proved his manhood. At Christmas there enters the King's hall (as in many traditional tales and medieval romances and as in a Yuletide ritual play or Christmas 'game') a giant. He brings news that many other pagans like himself have landed from the sea, and he presents a challenge which Cutbeard accepts. At daybreak, looking upon the ring, Horn vanquishes the three champions of the giants single-handed. In so doing he avenges his father; it is discovered that he has in fact slain his father's slayers. (This idea may have been introduced at this point in order to assist in making the whole Irish episode seem more relevant to the main theme. Horn's revenge is only complete at the end of the poem when he returns to his own kingdom and scatters his enemies. Meanwhile, in Ireland, Horn has proved himself—like Gawain or Thor—a match for the giants.) The long-established traditional pattern is not, however, on this occasion followed in this particular poem. The victor does not accept the bride and the kingdom he has won. It may be said that there has to be this variation simply because Horn is already pledged to Rymenhild and has to be loyal to her who is indeed ultimately to be his bride and queen. But this episode may also be regarded as a test of his loyalty. He need not have been loyal, and the tale *might* have been a different tale. Surprisingly also the good King of Ireland and his good daughter are not offended and continue to entertain the young hero generously.

It is in a forest of Ireland while hunting the stag that—when the seven years have passed—Horn is confronted by a messenger who has come from Rymenhild across the sea. She is about to be married against her will to a king from the North. On his voyage back from Ireland to herald Horn's return, the messenger is drowned. Rymenhild finds his body washed up on the seashore. She concludes that her messenger has never reached Horn. Meanwhile Horn, having obtained the King of Ireland's permission to depart, is on his way.

The return of Horn across the sea just in time to prevent the wedding, his presence in disguise at the wedding feast and his recognition form the climax of the poem—a climax that is repeated with variations to form a double climax. It is not for nothing that this episode lingered longest in the memory of the folk, if we may judge from the ballad versions, *Hynd Horn*, written down in Scotland in the beginning of the nineteenth century. In these the episode has been virtually dramatized and at the same time evidently been intended to be sung or chanted. The resemblances between this repeated episode in *King Horn* and the return of Odysseus will not fail to be noticed by the modern reader and to arouse speculation as to whether there could possibly have been any connexion. All the chances seem to be against there having been even a remote connexion. Yet it is clear that the essentials of the episode—related perhaps to the myth of a returning god in disguise or before his recognition—wandered about for centuries in the tale-telling of the West. Among the English medieval romances we have already come across it—or elements of it—in the return of Orfeo to his kingdom in *Sir Orfeo*.

The episode, as we find it doubled in *King Horn*, is well worth considering in detail. There is first the voyage back from Ireland and the landfall (for the second time in the poem) in Westernesse.

> *The wind him gan to blowe*
> *In a litel throwe.*
> *The se bigan to posse*
> *Right into Westernesse.*
> *Hi strike seil and maste*
> *And ankere gunne caste.*

Horn, newly landed and having left his companions 'under wude side', goes on alone and meets a palmer from whom he learns news of the wedding—

> *'I come fram o brudale'*

—and of how the bride 'wepeth sore'. Against all good custom, the palmer has been shut out from the wedding feast. Horn exchanges clothes with him and further disguises himself by blackening his face.

> *Horn tok burdon[1] and scrippe[2]*
> *And wrong[3] his lippe.*
> *He makede him a ful[4] chere,*
> *And al bicolmede[5] his swere.[6]*

[1] staff.   [2] pilgrim's wallet.   [3] twisted.   [4] foul.   [5] blackened.   [6] face.

Horn's blackened face is, of course, part of the elementary—or conventional—disguise. But if in the original pattern of the tale (in the myth before it became the tale) Horn was the returning god before his recognition, the blackened face may here have some further significance or associations. The modern reader may be assisted towards these associations if he in his turn associates Horn's blackened face (as surely he may) with the blackened faces of figures that belong to the rites and popular beliefs of centuries later than the thirteenth—the God of the Witches, the Morris Dancers, and the Chimney-sweep (about whom there were superstitions).

Horn reveals something of his concealed strength in his hand-ling of the rude porter at the gate.

> *Horn threu him over the brigge.*

Having thus gained entry, he takes his place unobtrusively among the beggars in the hall.

> *He sette him wel lowe,*
> *In beggeres rowe;*
> *He lokede him abute*
> *With his colmie snute;*[1]
> *He sey Rymenhild sitte*
> *Ase heo were of witte,*[2]
> *Sore wepinge and yerne.*

Meanwhile Horn's loyal companion, Athulf, whom he had left behind with Rymenhild when he had to cross the sea to Ireland, is in the watchtower looking out for Horn's ship, apparently in vain.

> *Athulf was in the ture,*
> *Abute for to pure*[3]
> *After his comynge,*
> *Yef schup him wolde bringe.*
> *He sey the se flowe*
> *And Horn nowar rowe.*

The bride, as was the custom, moves through the hall pouring wine and ale for the guests, who include the beggars.

[1] blackened nose.   [2] as if she were out of her wits.   [3] look intently.

Rymenhild ros of benche,
Wyn for to schenche:[1]
After mete in sale,[2]
Bothe wyn and ale.
On horn he[3] *bar anhonde,*
So lawe was in londe.

Horn, sitting among the beggars, becomes impatient and calls out
that the beggars are thirsty.

Horn sat upon the grunde;
Him thughte he was ibunde.[4]
He sede, 'Quen so hende,[5]
To meward thu wende;
Thu yef us with the furste:[6]
The beggeres beoth of thurste.'

She sets down the white horn from which the gentlefolk are given
to drink, and fills the brown bowl for the greedy beggarman who
has so rudely called out to her.

Hure horn heo leide adun,
And fulde him of a brun,
His bolle of a galun,
For heo wende[7] *he were a glotoun.*

But Horn will not drink from the brown bowl like the other beggars. He demands the horn from which the gentlefolk drink. This
is not simply assertion of personal pride on Horn's part. It is the
beginning of a series of riddles which he puts to Rymenhild, leading up to her recognition of him. Such riddling passages are a
feature of traditional poems and tales that may have had their
origin in rites. Thus Horn goes on to allude to her dream of the
fishing-net until she begins to take up his thread of meaning.

Thu wenest i beo a beggere,
And ihc am a fissere,
Wel feor icome bi weste
For fissen at thi feste:

[1] pour. [2] hall. [3] she. [4] i.e. overpowered.
[5] courteous, gentle. [6] serve us among the first. [7] she supposed.

King Horn

Mi net lith her bi honde,
Bi a wel fair stronde.
Hit hath ileie there
Fulle seve yere.
Ihc am icome to loke
Ef eni fiss hit toke.
Ihc am icome to fisse:
Drynke null y of dyssh:
Drink to Horn of horne.

Though she does not yet recognize him she willingly drinks to
Horn, understanding the allusion. Wondering what the seeming
beggarman knows of Horn, she asks him

If thu evre isiye
Horn under wude liye.

He drops the ring, which she had once given him, into the horn;
when she returns to her bower she finds it—'a ring igraven of
golde'—at the bottom of the horn. She recognizes it and summons
the beggar to her bower. Horn first tests her, telling her of his death.
The effect is as he would wish; she attempts to kill herself. He rubs
the black off his face. The recognition takes place.

The three significant symbols in the episode, and indeed in the
whole poem, are clearly the horn, the fish in the net, and the ring.
The riddling play with the horn, the ring dropped into it and the
allusion recalling the dream of the fish caught in the net are devices
used to lead Rymenhild towards the eventual recognition. The
connexion between the name of the hero and the drinking-horn is
explicitly made in what is perhaps the most significant line in the
poem—'drink to Horn of horne'. As a drinking-horn, it is certainly related to the horn of plenty of the mythologies, as is the
Christianized symbol, the Grail itself. The horn-of-plenty meaning does not, of course, exclude other meanings. It will be recalled
that in the early part of the poem, when the King of Westernesse
questions the youthful stranger newly landed on his shore, the
name Horn is at once associated by the King with a horn that is
blown; even so, it is no ordinary horn.

'*Horn, thu go wel schulle*[1]
Bi dales and bi hulle;
Horn, thu lude sune,[2]
Bi dales and bi dune;
So schal thi name springe
Fram kynge to kynge,
And thi fairnesse
Abute Westernesse,
The strengthe of thine honde
Into evrech londe . . .'

Further, it cannot be accidental that in Rymenhild's dream, which Horn recalls in leading her towards his recognition, he is a fish caught in a net (the net being Rymenhild herself); the fish is, of course, an ancient fertility symbol (*piscis*) that came to be a symbol of Christ himself, the Heavenly King. When, in his riddling, Horn speaks of himself not only as a fish but a fisher—'and ihc am a fissere'—his connexion with the Fisher King of the Grail myth becomes almost explicit. The implication in the poem is that the apparent beggarman is really of royal (therefore divine) origin and status. Finally, the ring of course figures in many traditional tales and medieval romances as a talisman or as a means of recognition. In this poem, it is both. Besides being a pledge of love, it magically protects Horn in battle and ultimately it is a means of his recognition.

After the recognition and Horn's rescue of Rymenhild there is, however, a postponement of the final *dénouement*. Before Horn weds Rymenhild and makes her his queen he must win back his kingdom of Suddene.

Horn gan to schupe drawe
With his Yrisse felawes . . .
That schup bigan to crude,[3]
The wind him bleu lude.

They land at midnight and find a knight, a Christian, on the shore watching. Horn blows his horn, and his people after so many years recognize it as Horn's horn and rally to him.

[1] musically. [2] sound loudly (imper.). [3] make way.

King Horn

Horn gan his horn to blowe;
His folk hit gan iknowe.

In a great battle before dawn Horn vanquishes the Saracens,
finally avenges his father and wins back his kingdom. He seeks
his mother in the cave where she had withdrawn after his father's
death, and provides corn—'corn he let serie'—for a feast.

Meanwhile Rymenhild has been abducted (or virtually so). As,
in so many traditional tales and medieval romances, Proserpine,
Guinevere, Dame Herodis and many another maiden, queen or
goddess are abducted by the King of the Otherworld or of the
Shades, so Rymenhild is shut up by Fikenhild in his gloomy
castle by the sea.

Strong castel he let sette,
Mid see him biflette,[1]
Ther ne mighte lighte
Bute foghel with flighte.
Bute whanne the se withdrowe,
Mighte come men ynowe.

Fikenhild's castle by the sea has something of the quality of the
castle of the King (or Demon) of Darkness. Correspondingly,
Fikenhild himself has something of the quality of the King (or
Demon) of Darkness, antagonist of the rising or youthful Sun.
Surely this is what the poetry directly suggests.

Fikenhild, or the dai gan springe,
Al right he ferde to the Kinge,
After Rymenhild the brighte,
To wedden hire bi nighte.
He ladde hure bi the derke[2]
Into his nywe werke.
The feste hi bigunne
Er that ros the sunne.
Er thane Horn hit wiste,
Tofore the sunne upriste,
His schup stod under ture
At Rymenhilde bure.

---

[1] surrounded by the sea.   [2] in the darkness.

Whether or not poetry (as some think) originated in myths and rites, the imagery here is certainly such as could have been kindled by the reflection still of some ancient myth of the sunrise, of the young sun crossing the sea and dispelling the power of darkness.

Horn has learned of what was happening by a dream and, for a second time, the pattern of Horn's return in the nick of time to rescue his bride from a forced wedding to another is repeated. On this occasion, after sailing to land under Fikenhild's tower, it is as a harper (like Orfeo) that Horn makes his entrance into his antagonist's castle.

> *Harpe he gan schewe,*
> *And tok felawes fewe,*
> *Of knightes suithe snelle*[1]
> *That schrudde*[2] *hem at wille.*
> *Hi yeden bi the gravel*[3]
> *Toward the castel;*
> *Hi gunne murie singe*
> *And makede here gleowinge.*[4]
> *Rymenhild hit gan ihere,*
> *And axede what hi were.*
> *Hi sede, hi weren harpurs,*
> *And sume were gigours.*[5]
> *He dude Horn in late*[6]
> *Right at halle gate.*
> *He sette him on the benche,*
> *His harpe for to clenche.*[7]
> *He makede Rymenhilde lay,*
> *And heo makede walaway.*
> *Rymenhild feol yswoghe,*[8]
> *He was ther non that loughe.*
> *Hit smot to Hornes herte*
> *So bitere that hit smerte.*
> *He lokede on the ringe*
> *And thoghte on Rymenhilde:*
> *He yede up to borde*

[1] active, brave.　　[2] clothed, i.e. disguised.　　[3] i.e. the beach.　　[4] i.e. music.
[5] fiddlers.　　[6] she caused Horn to be let in.　　[7] pluck.　　[8] in a swoon.

Havelok the Dane

With gode suerdes orde:[1]
Fikenhildes crune
Ther he fulde adune,
And al his men arowe[2]
Hi dude adun throwe.

Then Horn sails away to his regained kingdom with the bride he has finally won. The tale, in its present form a kind of chant, has clearly something of the character of myth—as have many folk-tales—only partially rationalized and humanized. This is the source of half its appeal.

§ 2

'HAVELOK THE DANE'

It seems natural for modern readers to associate *Havelok the Dane* with *King Horn*, though the version of *Havelok* (extant on a unique MS of the beginning of the fourteenth century) appears to be the later of these two thirteenth-century English romances. The scholarly discussion on the name Havelok at least indicates, once again, how international such tales had become, even if it establishes nothing as to the origin of the tale. In the French versions Havelok is called Cuaran; and Cuaran (we are told) is a Celtic word meaning 'a sock or a brogue of untanned leather or skin' and is the surname of a famous Viking, Olaf Sictricson—no doubt associated in tradition or in the popular mind with other Olafs. Havelok (we are also told) is a form of the Celtic name Abloc which is often substituted for the Norse name Olaf. Nevertheless, there is no obvious connexion between the tales of Havelok and of Olaf Sictricson. Certainly the English version is full of Norse words, as might be expected of a poem which is substantially in the English of the North-East Midlands where there were many Danish settlements. It has indeed a strong *local* character as a tale that has become associated specifically with the towns of Grimsby and Lincoln. It embodies what appear to be memories

---

[1] sword's edge.   [2] in a row.

of the historical relationship between England and Denmark in pre-Norman times; but as a whole—and basically—this tale is again mythical rather than historical.

The English version has no direct connexion with the extant French version, and is almost entirely lacking in courtliness; it has, rather, the character of a tale intended for a 'popular' audience. The opening lines seem to imply not only minstrel recital but also the necessity of first attracting and holding an audience out of a fluctuating crowd, perhaps, in some public place—a village green, market, or ale-house.

> *Herknet to me, godemen,*
> *Wives, maydnes, and alle men,*
> *Of a tale that ich you wile telle,*
> *Wo-so wile here and ther-to duelle[1] . . .*
> *At the biginning of ure tale,*
> *Fil me a cuppe of ful god ale.*

It is to be a tale of Havelok, unfortunate as a child and strong and true as a man—just such a character as would make a popular appeal, the typical popular hero.

The tale begins with the portrayal of a good king (Athelwold), his kingdom of England well governed and at peace, followed by an impressive and moving description of the death and obsequies of this good king. Funerals have always been popular occasions. He leaves behind him an only child, an infant daughter, Golde-boru, in the power of a foster-father, Godrich, the first of the two Judas-like villains in the tale. Godrich's soliloquy—one of several effective soliloquies in this poem—establishes understandable motives and creates a character the movement of whose thought and feeling is made audible and embodied.

> *Tho bigan Godrich to sike,[2]*
> *And seyde, 'Wether she sholde be*
> *Quen and levedi over me?*
> *Hwether sho sholde al Engelond,*
> *And me, and mine, haven in hire hond?*

---

[1] linger. [2] sigh.

Havelok the Dane

Datheit hwo it hire thave![1]
Shal sho it nevere more have.
Sholde ic yeve a fol, a therne,[2]
Engelond, thou sho it yerne? . . .
Shal it nouth ben als sho thenkes:
Hope maketh fol man ofte blenkes.[3]
Ich have a sone, a ful fayr knave:
He shal Engelond al have!
He shal be king, he shal ben sire,
So brouke i evere mi blake swire![4]

He imprisons the maiden princess in a castle by the sea (Dover Castle).

This situation in the Kingdom of England is paralleled, with sufficient variation to continue the interest, by that which is described as existing in Denmark—a repetition in the pattern rather like those in *King Horn*. In Denmark the King (Birkabeyn) dies and leaves two young daughters and a son, Havelok, in the keeping of the second Judas-like villain in the poem, Godard, a deeper-dyed villain still than Godrich. Such tales are clearly among the stuff out of which some of the Elizabethan plays were made. Godard imprisons the three children in a tower where they suffer hunger. The episode has much the same character as that of the children in the Tower in *Richard III* which so captured the popular imagination of later times, and may have been influenced by Herod's Massacre of the Innocents. The two girls are brutally murdered by Godard; but the boy, almost miraculously, is spared. The crime, in its naked horror and pathos, is presented with the grim directness that one meets occasionally in the ballads.

Hwan that was thouht, onon he ferde
To the tour ther he woren sperde,[5]
Ther he greten for hunger and cold.
The knave, that was sumdel bold,

---

[1] Cursed be he who puts up with it from her.   [2] a servant girl.
[3] i.e. Hope often plays tricks with a foolish man.
[4] So may I continue to enjoy the use of my white neck.
[5] where they were locked in.

Kam him ageyn, on knes him sette,
And Godard ful feyre he ther grette.
And Godard seyde, 'Wat is you?[1]
Hwi grete ye and goulen[2] *nou?'*
'For us hungreth swithe sore,'
Seyden he, 'We wolden more . . .
Wo is us that we weren born!
Weilawei! nis it no korn
That men mihte maken of bred?
Us hungreth: we aren ney ded!'
Godard herde here wa,
Theroffe yaf he nouht a stra,
But tok the maydnes bothe samen,[3]
Also it were up>on his gamen[4]—
Also he wolde with hem leyke,[5]
That weren for hunger grene and bleike.[6]
Of bothen he karf on two here throtes,
And sithen hem al to grotes.
Ther was sorwe, wo>so it sawe,
Hwan the children bi the wawe[7]
Leyen and sprauleden in the blod:
Havelok it saw, and ther bi stod.
Ful sori was that seli[8] *knave;*
Mikel dred he mouhte have,
For at hise herte he saw a knif
For to reven him hise lyf.

Two of the principal characters in the poem are then introduced. They are Grim, the fisherman, and his wife (Leve) who are to be the good foster-parents of the boy. Grim is the legendary founder of Grimsby. This Grim may well be not simply a namesake but a humanized version of the giant god Grim of Norse mythology. Godard (like Herod) fears that the boy Havelok may grow up to be King in his place, and he therefore commands the poor fisher-man to drown the boy in the sea at night.

[1] What is the matter with you?   [2] cry.   [3] together.   [4] as if . . . in sport.
[5] play.   [6] wan.   [7] wall.   [8] innocent.

As they are described, Grim and his wife—originally perhaps the giant god and his wife—may surely be regarded as predecessors of such types in the Cycle Plays as Mak and his wife or Noah and his wife. Grim arrives at his hut with the child in a bag on his back, much as Mak arrives at his hut with the stolen sheep.

> *In a poke, ful and blac,*
> *Sone he caste him on his bac,*
> *Ant bar him hom to hise cleve,*[1]
> *And bitaucte him*[2] *dame Leve,*
> *And seyde, 'Wite*[3] *thou this knave,*
> *Also thou with me lif have:*
> *I shal dreinchen him in the se . . .'*

Grim's wife, as she appears at first, is a savage creature. She

> *. . . caste the knave so harde adoune,*
> *That he crakede ther his croune*
> *Ageyn a gret ston, ther it lay.*

In the middle of the night Grim rises to do the deed. He bids his wife to blow the fire and light a candle. At this moment a light like a sunbeam issues from the child's mouth.

> *Als she shulde hise clothes handel,*
> *On forto don, and blawe the fir,*
> *She saw therinne a liht ful shir,*[4]
> *Also briht so it were day,*
> *Aboute the knave ther he lay.*
> *Of hise mouth it stod a stem*[5]
> *Als it were a sunnebem.*

The mysterious light brings about the recognition by Grim and his wife of Havelok's royal—no doubt originally divine—origin. The recognition is confirmed by the king-mark which they discover on the child's shoulder. They have indeed found a rich treasure in the forlorn child brought home in a bag. They hasten to provide the famished boy with 'bred an chese, butere and milk, pastees and flaunes'. Godard, when told by Grim that his

[1] hut. [2] gave him in charge. [3] guard, keep. [4] bright. [5] there issued a ray.

instructions have been (as of course they have not been) carried out, breaks his promises like a true villain and treats the instrument of his crime with contempt and menaces.

Grim prepares to flee across the sea with his wife, children and Havelok. In making ready his fishing-smack for this voyage across the North Sea he is doing something more; he is (like Noah) making ready a vessel for the preservation of precious life in a new world.

> Hise ship he greythede wel inow:
> He dede it tere,[1] an ful wel pike,[2]
> That it ne doutede sond ne krike;[3]
> Ther-inne dide a ful god mast,
> Stronge kables, and ful fast,
> Ores gode, an ful god seyl;
> Therinne wantede nouht a nayl.

Once again the pattern of this tale is to be that of the boy born to be king who crosses the sea to another country, is brought up there in a poor man's hut, wins his bride, returns to his own country, is recognized as king and finally (in this poem) wins his bride's kingdom also.

A wind carries the ship 'fraught with precious souls' to the Humber. There Grim lands and builds a hut of earth; thus Grimsby is founded. At first Grim the fisherman prospers; 'the mackerel-crowded seas' yield their abundance. The fisherman's life is described with the particularity of one familiarly acquainted with it.

> Mani god fish therinne he tok,
> Bothe with net, and with hok.
> He tok the sturgiun and the qual[4]
> And the turbut and lax[5] withal;
> He tok the sele and the hwel[6] . . .
> Keling[7] he tok, and tumberel,[8]
> Hering and the makerel,
> The butte,[9] the schulle,[10] the thornebake,[11]
> Gode paniers dede he make,

[1] tar.   [2] pitch.   [3] creek.   [4] whale.   [5] salmon.   [6] eel.   [7] cod.   [8] porpoise.
[9] flounder? cf. halibut.   [10] plaice.   [11] skate.

On til him, and other thrinne[1]
Til hise sones, to beren fish inne
Up o-londe, to selle and fonge;[2]
Forbar he neyther tun ne gronge[3]
That he ne to yede with his ware;
Kam he nevere hom hand-bare[4]
That he ne broucte bred and sowel[5]
In his shirte, or in his couel;
In his poke benes and korn;
Hise swink ne havede he nowt forlorn.
And hwan he tok the grete laumprei,
Ful wel he couthe the rithe wei
To Lincolne, the gode boru;
Ofte he yede it thoru and thoru.
Til he havede al wel sold,
And therfore the penies told.
Thanne he com thenne, he were blithe,
For hom he brouhte fele sithe[6]
Wastels,[7] simenels with the horn,[8]
Hise pokes fulle of mele an korn,
Netes flesh, shepes, and swines;
And hemp to maken of gode lines,
And stronge ropes to hise netes,
That in the se he ofte setes.

This romance is an interesting combination of the realistic and the legendary. Havelok is a true hero of the people, who grows up in a poor man's hut and willingly shares the toil of his foster-father and foster-brothers.

Goddot! y wile with hem gange,
For to leren sum god to gete;
Swinken ich wolde for mi mete.
It is no shame forto swinken . . .
On the morwen, hwan it was day,
He stirt up sone, and nouht ne lay;

[1] i.e. one basket for himself and three others for his sons.   [2] take (money).
[3] grange, farm-house.   [4] empty-handed.   [5] relish.   [6] many times.
[7] fine bread.   [8] cakes twisted to look like a horn?

> *And cast a panier on his bac,*
> *With fish giveled[1] als a stac.*

The cycle of the years of plenty—twelve years of abundant harvests of the land and sea—is succeeded by a dearth both of corn and fish. Young Havelok has to go to Lincoln to find work—an interesting variation of the young hero setting forth into the tough world to prove his manhood, to bring back plenty, or to win his kingdom. Grim clothes him in a sail.

> *He tok the sheres of the nayl,*
> *And made him a couel of the sayl,*
> *And Havelok dide it sone on.*
> *Havede he neyther hosen ne shon,*
> *Ne none kines other wede;*
> *To Lincolne barfot he yede . . .*
> *Two dayes ther fastinde he yede,*
> *That non for his werk wolde him fede;*
> *The thridde day herde he calle:*
> *'Bermen, bermen,[2] hider forth alle!'*
> *Poure that on fote yede*
> *Sprongen forth so sparke of glede.[3]*
> *Havelok shof dune nyne or ten*
> *Rith amidewarde the fen,*
> *And stirte forth to the kok,*
> *Ther the erles mete he tok*
> *That he bouhte at the brigge:*
> *The bermen let he alle ligge,*
> *And bar the mete to the castel.*

The scene has again the stamp of authenticity, is done from the daily life of the people. The episode is repeated; another day the earl's cook, having bought fish at the market beside the bridge, calls for a porter, and Havelok again pushes over all who stand in his way.

> *And bigan the fish to kippe.[4]*
> *He bar up wel a carte-lode*

---

[1] heaped up.   [2] porters.   [3] live coal.   [4] seize.

Havelok the Dane

Of segges,[1] *laxes, of playces brode,*
Of grete laumprees, and of eles;
Sparede he neyther tos ne heles.[2]

He bears this burden on his head to the castle. The cook recognizes the young man's merits and employs him as a kitchen boy. Thus Havelok, a king's son, has to pass through a testing phase, like other heroes, and perform menial tasks such as fetching water and wood, washing dishes, kindling fire, skinning eels; he does it willingly. Havelok is a great favourite with children. Gradually it begins to appear that he is no ordinary man; he turns out to be outstandingly strong and handsome.

One of the most vivid episodes in the poem is that of the games. They are the typical games of the village green, though the strong men of all England, of all ranks and conditions, both barons and ploughmen, have assembled. At putting the weight Havelok performs prodigies of strength, and the king's son unrecognized is the unrivalled champion of the village green. The ability to cast huge stones has often been attributed to gods and heroes, as well as to devils and giants, and perhaps something of Havelok's divine original shows again in this; but strong muscular men have always been the darlings of the people.

The fame of Havelok's feats of strength reaches the ears of Godrich who determines to wed him to Goldboru. His motives are cunningly wicked—in an elementary way. He will fulfil his promise to the late king by wedding Goldboru to the strongest man in England, and at the same time he will effectively exclude her from the crown by her marriage to a 'cherles sone'. The villain thus unintentionally fulfils Havelok's and Goldboru's destiny. On the wedding night, in Grim's hut, the mysterious light again issues from Havelok's mouth, and thus his royal origin and destiny are revealed to Goldboru.

Shortly after this episode there is a leaf missing from the MS; but we may understand, when the text is resumed, that Havelok has sailed back to Denmark with Goldboru and with Grim's three sons as companions. Havelok has evidently assumed the disguise

[1] cuttle-fish?   [2] i.e. he went so fast.

199

of a pedlar (as Horn, Orfeo and Odysseus returning assumed disguises). After a variety of complications, Havelok is recognized by
means of the mysterious light which again issues from his mouth,
and by the king-mark. The lords of Denmark acknowledge him
as king, and the villain Godard is slain. Finally Havelok returns
to England, which in its turn acknowledges him and Goldboru
as King and Queen. Godrich, the other villain, is also slain to
make the tale complete.

TWO GAWAIN ROMANCES
FROM THE PERCY FOLIO MS

§ 1

'THE TURK AND GAWAIN'

In the Percy Folio MS (about 1650) are versions of one or two Gawain romances, *The Turk and Gawain, The Carle of Carlile, The Wedding of Sir Gawain and Dame Ragnell, The Green Knight* (in addition to several ballads and romances, *King Arthur and King Cornwall, Libius Disconius* and *Eger and Grime,* all of which may be associated in one respect or another with the Gawain romances). *The Turk and Gawain* and *The Carle of Carlile* are, like others in the Percy Folio MS, in a very battered and broken-down condition, whatever thay may have been like at an earlier stage of the oral tradition in which they evidently belong. But they may be interesting to a reader of literature because there may be seen in them, as in the versions of the Folk Plays, the shattered remains of something that may have been greater, and because they embody even in their degenerate state traditional legendary material that has an affinity with that out of which *Sir Gawayne and the Grene Knight* and others of the finer romances were earlier shaped. (*The Green Knight* is clearly a very degraded version of the same tale as that of *Sir Gawayne and the Grene Knight. The Wedding of Gawain* is a version of the traditional tale which, as *The Wife of Bath's Tale*, was made into one of the triumphs of Chaucerian art.)

One is tempted to guess that these tales are at least as much Norse as Celtic in origin and character. The adventures of Gawain among the giants of the Isle of Man as described in *The Turk and Gawain* bear a family resemblance to Thor's adventures among the giants in Jötenheim as described in the *Eddas.* The Carle in *The Carle of Carlile* is a humorous character whose not so remote original may well have been a Norse giant god; the tone and spirit of the episode are again reminiscent of the episodes in the *Eddas* between Thor and the giants. There must have been constant coming and going across the Irish Sea between the Norse settlements there were in Ireland and those in the north-west of England; to a seafaring race the sea would not divide but would facilitate communication. It is not difficult to conceive the importance which the Isle of Man would have had in such circumstances—an island (holy in itself) situated midway between the Irish, English and Scottish shores. The comings and goings across the Irish Sea, and the mixture of peoples and cultures around its shores, might help to account for the apparent mixture of Norse and Celtic elements in some of those traditional tales that were made into the English romances of the north-west.

§ 2

The Turk and Gawain, though a very late and very garbled version of a tale that may well have been told for centuries, is still expressly intended for recital. It tells of Gawain's adventures with the giants in the Isle of Man.[1]

While King Arthur sits in his hall feasting there enters a 'turke' —meaning, evidently, a dwarf. The Turk proposes an exchange of buffets. Gawain, we may surmise (half a page is missing here), must have obliged the Turk by dealing him the blow he asked for, and so started a train of events; the dwarf seems to be, as a consequence, bound to Gawain as the latter's supernatural servant and guide to the Otherworld, and Gawain seems equally to be bound to go with the dwarf. At any rate, Gawain rides away with the Turk who promises Gawain that he will thoroughly scare him before he gets back.

The two ride northward through what is evidently a version of the Waste Land or Utgard where Gawain suffers hunger and thirst, taunted by the Turk—'Where is all thy plenty?' Because he

---

[1] Until recently there were traditions in the island about a race of giants who had overcome the primitive inhabitants, had themselves been enchanted by Merlin, and now lie spell-bound in huge subterranean caves.

had given the Turk a buffet instead of food (so the Turk now says)
he shall have 'mickle care'. They enter a hill in which there are
thunder and winter.

> *The earth opened and closed againe,*
> *Then Gawaine was adread;*
> *The merke was comen and the light is gone;*
> *Thundering, lightning, snow and raine . . .*

Within this hill, it seems (again half a page is missing) there is a
castle where—as is usual in the otherworld castle and was also
Thor's experience—they find a board spread with food and drink
although no one appears to be there. The famished Gawain would
have helped himself had not the dwarf warned him not to.
Gawain marvels that out of such great plenty nothing can be
spared; but then the Turk himself serves Gawain. When Gawain
has satisfied his hunger and thirst he asks for his return-buffet and
then to be allowed to go his way.

Again half a page is missing. But when the text is resumed
Gawain and the Turk have come to a boat by the seashore and,
leaving his steed on the shore, Gawain enters the boat. As the
steed has been a conveyance through the mountain-barrier, so the
boat is now a conveyance through the water-barrier to the Otherworld (the Isle of Man appears in this tale to have something of
that character). Gawain and the Turk cross the sea to a castle
where dwells the King of Man.

> *With him he hath a hideous rout*
> *Of giants . . .*

These giants spend their time, very much as the champions of a
village green might do, putting the weight. It may well have been
that in earlier versions—or the original—of this tale the giants had
more of a purpose and were engaged in the manufacture of thunder. In particular they roll a huge ball around (as in the Elizabethan
theatres thunder was produced by similar methods).

> *Thou shalt see a tenisse ball*
> *That never knight in Arthurs hall*
> *Is able to give it a lout.*

The Turk enters into a bargain to help Gawain—to be in fact Gawain's familiar spirit—in the tasks he must perform.

After another gap in the MS, it appears to be the King of Man who is speaking. As is in the character of one whose original may have been a pagan god, he has a hatred of 'Bishop Bodwin' and indeed all the clergy whom he threatens to burn because they 'will not let his goods alone'. However, he invites Gawain to sit down at his board. But Gawain first wants to witness some 'adventure'. The King calls for his tennis ball. He will play; in other words (or so it might have been in the original of the tale) the thunder-god will make thunder, and the ball is a thunderstone. It is brought in by a 'hideous rout of giants', each of whom is half as tall again as Gawain.

> *All thought Gawaine but little good.*

The 'tennis ball' is a ball of brass made for a giant's hand—

> *There was noe man in all England*
> *Were able to carry it . . .*

We gather, after another gap in the MS, that Gawain has to per-form a series of tasks in the giants' hold—in the original myth perhaps in order to find out whether the young hero was capable of being a thunder-god—tasks which the Turk, evidently in-visible, is performing for him. There is in the King's hall a big fire of coal and wood burning in a huge brazier. Gawain is com-manded to lift it—'Gawaine, begin the play!' Gawain's 'boy', the invisible Turk, seizes it and swings it thrice round his head so that 'the coals and red brands . . .' But we cannot tell how exactly the whirling coals and brands behave, because half a page is again missing. When the poem is resumed, the King of Man appears to be threatening to slay Gawain but is overheard by the latter's in-visible guardian, the Turk ('he was cladd in such a weede'). Gawain is led to a boiling cauldron in front of which stands a giant with an iron fork in his hand. This is of course the cauldron which has descended from that which appears in various myths, Irish, Norse, Greek, and which has had many diverse significances and uses, as, for example, the cauldron of plenty, of destruction, of creation, of thunder-brewing, of prophesying. The giant with the fork has his counterpart also in the Devil in Hell. The King says to the giant, 'Here is none but wee tow'. But, in addition to their victim, there is an unexpected *third* in the room (though the effect of dramatic surprise is largely missed in this version); the Turk has also entered, invisible (again, 'he was cladd in such a weede'); he throws the giant into the cauldron and holds him down with his own fork. Gawain then requires the King of Man to agree 'unto our law', otherwise he will have eaten his last meal. The King spits on Gawain, at which the Turk pitches him headlong into the fire and declares to Gawain

> *Noe force, master, all the perill is past.*

When the tale is resumed after another gap of half a page, the Turk has evidently produced a basin of gold and a sword—objects which figure as two of the symbols in the Grail romances. He begs Gawain, as a favour and a reward for his services, to strike off his (the Turk's) head with the sword. Gawain refuses; he would not have the Turk slain for all the gold so red. But the Turk insists and says he has no fear provided Gawain lets him bleed into the basin. The basin is there, as we may have expected, to catch the blood—another resemblance to the Grail. Gawain does as he is asked. The beheading act has the effect on the Turk of disenchantment and of renewal.

> *And when the blood in the bason light,*
> *He stood up a stalwortht knight.*

The stalwart knight sings *Te Deum* and blesses Gawain. Together, they release many captives, both men and women—the enchanted ones of the otherworld castle of so many romances and (in another context) the imprisoned souls of the Harrowing of Hell. They all sit down to dine; then they all go to King Arthur, who makes the former Turk King of Man; and the tale ends, as a minstrel's lay should, with a blessing on the company who have listened.

§ 3

'THE CARLE OF CARLILE'

The Carle of Carlile is another of those traditional tales which appear to have originated as accounts of initiation rites. As such an account, it is very garbled; as a medieval romance, the version preserved in the Percy Folio MS is in much the same broken-down state as is *The Turk and Gawain*. Nevertheless it is not without interest; at least, it assists the understanding of the other romances to which it may be related. It is again a tale expressly intended for recital.

The tale begins—as this type of tale commonly does—with a deer hunt. Arthur and his knights ride with greyhounds in pursuit of the deer.

> *For now its grass time of the yeere.*

By noon a hundred harts lie on the earth. But Sir Gawain, Sir Kay and Bishop Baldwin—the same knights who principally figure in the fourteenth-century *Avowing of Arthur*—pursue a red deer which leads them into a forest where a thick mist descends. They lose both the red deer and their way. The red deer has fulfilled its function; it has guided them—it may originally have been the form assumed by an otherworld guide—towards the place where an 'awntyr' will happen.

The Bishop says he knows of a Carle who keeps a castle in that waste.

> *Here dwelleth a Carle in a Castele,*
> *The Carle of Carlile is his name . . .*
> *Was there never man yett soe bold*
> *That durst lodge within his hold.*

He is one of those keepers of castles who prove no easy hosts for their guests—'If his guest escape with his life' he will have done well. Kay declares that he will go to the Carle's hold and, true to his traditional character, boasts of what he will do to the Carle.

The Carle of Carlile

For and the Carle be never soe bolde,
I thinke to lodge within his hold.
For if he jangle and make it stout,
I shall beate the Carle all about.

But Gawain says they will first try fair speech. The traditional contrast between the courteous Gawain and the rude Kay is still here in this late version.

As Thor has a hammer and the Green Knight an axe, the Carle of Carlile too has a hammer—hanging at his gate.

When they came to the carles gate,
A hammer they found hanging theratt.

The knocking on the gate with this hammer is, perhaps, as much a challenge to the inmates (though not intended by Gawain, who 'courteously' knocks, to be so) as it is a request for admission. The porter at the gate of this version of the otherworld castle demands who is so bold as to knock. Gawain answers courteously that they are two of Arthur's knights and a bishop, tired out with hunting and seeking a night's lodging. Won over by Gawain's courtesy and in spite of the rudeness of the crabbed Kay, the porter communicates Gawain's request to the Carle. The Carle expresses regret that his guests have been kept waiting; their steeds are taken to stable, and they enter a hall where the Carle is sitting.

The Carle is an uncouth character, unhuman in appearance, with the recognizable features both of a primitive giant god and the Monster Herdsman.

Heere the Carle sate in his chaire on hye,
With his legg cast over the other knee;
His mouth was wyde, and his beard was gray,
His lockes on his shoulders lay;
Betweene his browes, certaine
It was large there a spann,
With two great eyen brening as fyer.
Lord! hee was a lodlye syer!
Over his sholders he bare a beard
Three taylors yards, as clarkes doe reade;

> *His fingars were like to teddar stakes,*
> *And his hands like breads that wives may bake;*
> *Fifty cubitts he was in height;*
> *Lord, he was a lothesome wight!*

He is the keeper of a kind of menagerie. By the fire there crouch four angry beasts, a bear, a boar whetting its tusks, a roaring bull, a lion that 'gapes' and 'grens'. If the original of the otherworld castle was (as Loomis has argued) the abode of the sun god (and thunder-maker), these beasts would perhaps correspond to the Signs of the Zodiac, the 'eyrish bestes'. The Carle—surely he has an affinity with the Monster Herdsman—orders the beasts to be quiet, and they creep under the table.

Despite the Carle's forbidding appearance, Gawain salutes him courteously; the Carle welcomes them—for Arthur's sake, as he says, though he and Arthur have ever been foes. The board is spread with the abundance characteristic of the hospitality of the otherworld castle. There enters the lovely lady of the castle whom we have also come to expect (if we have read other romances). The abducted or enchanted one or the Queen of the Otherworld of other tales is here simply the Carle's wife.

> *Downe came a Lady faire and free,*
> *And sett her on the carles knee;*
> *One whiles shee harped, another whiles song,*
> *Both of paramours and lovings amonge.*

There is an air of free jesting and rough-and-tumble farcical mirth about this tale, as there is also about some of the encounters between Thor and the giants in the *Eddas*. Thus Gawain says of the fair lady, seated on the Carle's knee, that her bedfellow will be a lucky man; the Carle reproves him.

> *'Sir,' said Gawaine, 'I sayd nought.'*
> *'No, man,' said the carle, 'more thou thought.'*

The first of the series of events in the castle is the visit to the stable which each of the three guests in turn pays in order to see how his horse has fared. The first to go there is Kay who finds that his horse has both corn and hay, but also finds the Carle's palfrey next to his, and thrusts it out 'with a clout'. He has not observed that the Carle himself is standing near-by.

> *The carle raught Kay such a rapp*
> *That backwards he fell flatt.*

The second guest to go to the stable is the Bishop, and much the same performance is repeated. He too thrusts the Carle's palfrey out 'with a clout' and

> *Sais, 'wend forth, fole, in the devills way!*
> *Who made thee soe bold with my palfrey?'*

The Carle, who has again been standing by unseen, knocks the Bishop over.

> *He hitt the Bishopp upon the crowne,*
> *That his miter and he fell downe.*

The Bishop reminds the Carle that he is a holy clerk.

> *'Mercy!' said the Bishopp, 'I am a clarke!*
> *Somewhatt I can of Christs werke.'*
> *He saith, 'By the Clergye I sett nothing,*
> *Nor yett by thy miter nor by thy ringe . . .'*

The Carle is clearly a pagan.

Gawain is the third who goes to the stable. With his own mantle of green he covers the Carle's horse which has been in the rain, and bids it eat away—'thy Master payeth for all that wee heere gett'. The Carle reveals himself and thanks Gawain for his courtesy. Gawain alone has passed this test.

The Carle conducts his guest back into the hall and calls for a bowl of wine.

> *Seventy bowles in that bowle were,—*
> *He was not weake that did itt beare.*

The Carle drinks fifteen gallons from the bowl at one draught—as Thor among the giants drinks out of an inexhaustible horn, inexhaustible because the other end is in the sea.

Gawain has, it seems, qualified to go on with the tests or ritual games or contest. The Carle bids him take a long spear and mark his (the Carle's) face with it.

> *'A long speare see thou take in thy hand,*
> *Att the buttrye dore take thou thy race,*
> *And marke me well in middest the face.'*

Gawain charges the Carle with this spear which the latter dodges.

> *Gawaine raught the wall such a rapp,*
> *The fyer flew out, and the speare brake.*

The spear, however, strikes fire from the wall. Possibly the meaning is (or was) that Gawain has at least proved that he can produce fire (originally lightning?).

The Carle next conducts Gawain to his wife's bed and bids him get in and kiss her (she had from the beginning seemed to Gawain desirable) but 'doe no other villanye'. In this chastity test —with which we may compare the testing of Gawain by his host's wife in *Sir Gawayne and the Grene Knight* and the jealousy test on Baldwin in *The Avowing of Arthur*—Gawain is successful. The Carle has also a daughter, who is there to provide a bride for Gawain in the end.

Next day, the Carle conducts Gawain into a chamber in which he is confronted with the horrors of physical death. There are many a 'bloody serke' and a heap of dead men's bones—the bones of those who have been slain by the Carle. If the basis of this tale was an account of initiation rites, a confrontation with the horrors of physical death is here associated (as, J. L. Weston remarks, was commonly the case in such ceremonies) with initiation—by means of the Carle's wife and daughter—into the facts of generation.

Gawain prepares to take his leave and thanks the Carle and the two ladies. But the Carle insists 'we will first dine' and, after dinner, leads Gawain into a gay chamber where swords are hanging. The Carle presents Gawain with a sword—evidently a very special sword for a very special task—and requests him to strike off his (the Carle's) head. Gawain refuses, the Carle insists; he will strike off Gawain's head if Gawain does not do him the favour he asks. Finally, Gawain beheads him. It proves to be (as in *The Turk and Gawain* and many other tales) an act of disenchantment, and therefore indeed a favour. The Carle stands up a proper man, no longer a monstrous giant. For forty winters he has been enchanted, indeed metamorphosed, and he could be disenchanted and restored only by being beheaded by one of Arthur's knights. Kay and Baldwin, having apparently proved unworthy from the first, because of their rudeness to the Carle's horse, Gawain alone proved to be fit for the task.

During those forty winters the Carle's whole nature had apparently been changed. He and his beasts had slain everyone who lodged in his castle unless he did his bidding. Now he will 'leave that lawe' and is indeed converted into a good Christian.

The three knights of Arthur ride away with the Carle's daughter, gorgeously arrayed on a white palfrey, as Gawain's bride.

> Then they rode singing by the way
> With the Ladye that was gay;
> They were as glad of that Lady bright
> As ever was fowle of the day-lyght.

At the dawn of the following day they return with Arthur to the castle. The tale concludes, again in the manner of such tales, with a wedding feast.

> And minstrells sate in windowes faire,
> And playd on their instruments cleere.

IV
ALLITERATIVE ROMANCES
AND POEMS

IV. ALLITERATIVE ROMANCES AND POEMS

'SIR GAWAYNE AND THE GRENE KNIGHT'

Sir Gawayne and the Grene Knight is a great English poem. It has not been simply neglected so much as it has suffered a wrong kind of attention that has perpetuated its essential neglect as a poem. For it would be hard to say what in the nature of the poem itself has ever been attended to. The attention has not been that of literary criticism, the kind that is appropriate to a poem. It has been of the kind that has tended to obscure rather than to expose the poem itself, a directing of attention away from the poem towards extrinsic matters, an interposition of pedantic irrelevances between the poem and the reader, an elaborate evasion of its significance. The poem has never been attended to as what in itself it is uniquely.

The mere mechanics of deciphering the text are, it may be admitted, troublesome. That is not simply because its language is a dialect of English (that of the North-West Midlands) which is not the dialect that became our English; it is because (to speak out bluntly) of the way in which the poem has been edited. The edition at present used by students and on which they are examined (it is the *edition* rather than the *poem* they are examined on) merely slavishly reproduces the deficiencies, confusions and inconsistencies of the copyist's spelling in the Cotton Nero AX MS. The introduction and lengthy, mostly irrelevant notes, which further overlay the poem in this edition (as in most other editions of so-called Middle English texts), illustrate again the depressing technique of interposing extrinsic 'points of interest' between the reader and the poem and so distracting attention from the poem itself to these; as if the significance of a great poem were not in itself the most difficult thing in the world to grasp without the deliberate obtrusion and exaggeration of external 'difficulties'.

What little show of criticism of the poem there has been seems to have been governed by the determination to relate it to the medieval French romances. But the place of *Sir Gawayne and the Grene Knight*—and *because* it is a great poem it is a central place—is in the English tradition. It belongs to the first great creative moment of (I shall dare to say) *modern* English literature—the moment of the *Canterbury Tales* and of *Piers Plowman*. These three English poems, though quite independent from each other, are not accidentally contemporary. Their very unlikeness to each other is a guarantee of the integrity, the individuality, the uniqueness of each. They are each different, as Ben Jonson is different from Shakespeare. But they have the same kind of relation to each other —and indeed to Shakespeare and to Ben Jonson—as Ben Jonson has to Shakespeare. When the important regional differences have been allowed for, they remain English poems; they have in common what is, as a whole, the same English community; they are nourished (allowing fully for their regional differences) by a common English soil. For *Sir Gawayne and the Grene Knight* is the crown, the masterpiece of a whole school of poetry—the alliterative poetry of the north-west of England—contemporary with Chaucer and Langland, distinct from either, but equally an important, though less recognized, element in the English tradition. I refer not only to the poems which appear in the same MS with *Sir Gawayne and the Grene Knight*—*Cleanness, Patience* and *Pearl*[1]—but also to such poems as the alliterative *Morte Arthure, The Awntyrs of Arthure, The Destruction of Troy, Wynnere and Wastoure, The Parlement of the Thre Ages*.

The concern to derive this superb English poem from French romances (even if the very existence of these has to be hypothetical), while allowing that somehow it goes one better than they do, has been such as, in effect, to belittle it. By establishing the 'derivative-

[1] To suppose as a matter of course or probability that because these poems appear in the same MS and dialect they are—on these grounds alone—by the same author is quite uncritical. What can be said is that in this particular locality there was a whole school of poetry; and that the quality of that poetry is such that it implies a cultivated society.

ness' of any given poem, or the limiting 'conditions' within which it had to be composed, it becomes more easy safely to do it down, to ignore its uniqueness, what it does that no other poem does. To attend to an assortment of French romances and Celtic tales[1] is not at all the same thing as to attend to *Sir Gawayne and the Grene Knight*; just as to attend to Holinshed's Chronicle is not at all the same thing as to attend to *Macbeth*. To summarize the 'plots' of these French romances and of *Sir Gawayne and the Grene Knight* and to attend to and compare these summaries is still less the same thing as to attend to and compare the poems themselves.

There is no need to deny that the author of *Sir Gawayne and the Grene Knight* may have had a French romance before him, just as Shakespeare had *his* 'sources'. It is unlikely that he did *not* read (or listen to) French romances. But even if we establish that a French romance (or group of romances) was the poem's *literary* source, we have got no nearer the poem itself. The poem is clearly not *simply* a courtly romance, and it is totally a very different kind of thing from a French romance. Yet the sheer unlikeness of the English alliterative poem to all the French romances we have has not discouraged the attachment of apparently supreme importance to the relating of it to 'French Romance'. It is as if the placing of some of Shakespeare's plays in the context of the 'Italian Novel' were to be regarded as the function of Shakespearian criticism. The particular French romances which are not there for *Sir Gawayne and the Grene Knight* to be derived from are lightheartedly assumed to have been there and to have been lost.[2] These hypo-thetical romances are discussed in relation to the poem almost as if they, rather than it, had a real existence.

Our task is to see the object, the English poem as what it is, and that is not, of course, the abstracted 'story'. If the value were in the 'story' in itself, then our editors' summary of it in the forefront of their edition would be all that we should require to read. It is what is made of the 'story', how it is realized, the kind of signifi-

[1] The Old Irish tale of *Bricriu's Feast* (MS *c.* 1100) certainly offers a striking parallel.

[2] One of the curiosities of Tolkien and Gordon's introduction is a diagram in which letters of the alphabet represent French originals that do not exist but are assumed to have existed.

cance it is made to bear, what the poem totally communicates or does that is our object. Thus to judge from the abstracted 'story' Morgan le Fay is the *cause* of all the events. Yet in the poem itself she is not at all felt to account for these events. To do so she would have had to be realized as Lady Macbeth is realized. Her envy of Guinevere would have had to be as real a force, present in the texture of the poem, as the Macbeths' ambition. But it is not. The old woman of the Second Fit of the poem *is* realized, and at the end of the whole poem Gawain is told that she was Morgan. But where the old woman occurs the point is not that she is Morgan, but simply that she is an old woman. What the significance of the old woman is, in contrast to the young woman, will, of course, have to be considered in any critical analysis of the poem. The 'explanation'—Morgan's envy of Guinevere—introduced rather perfunctorily at the end of the poem (from the 'source' or 'authority', perhaps) is, in effect, no more than a bone for the rationalizing mind to play with, and to be kept quiet with.

Yet though we may dismiss the abstracted 'story' as of no value in itself, we may well ask how it is that this particular rendering of the 'story' (or combination of 'stories') has turned out to be a great unified work of art. For the English poem has the unity of a very completed, very deliberately constructed and finished work of art. But the unity is more than a construction; it has the character of an organic unity, a unity of growth. A conscious and deliberate artist (bearing, perhaps, the same kind of relation to his subject-matter as we imagine Homer does) the poet has constructed. But in so doing he has, as it were, co-operated with some inner organizing, unifying and realizing principle of life and growth. The result is both a satisfying surface completeness and a full-bodied, matured completion or fulfilment. We may perhaps legitimately begin by inquiring generally what this principle of life might be that has activated the genius of the poet and made the poem the remarkable Shakespearian unity it is, though only an analysis of the poem itself can more exactly define its nature.

It is a case in which the literary critic may appropriately find his initial hint in some of the observations of the anthropologists, provided he recognizes that this does not relieve him from his own responsibility and function of criticism of the particular poem in itself. Miss J. L. Weston's *From Ritual to Romance* and *The Quest of the Holy Grail*—to a lesser extent the chapters on the Folk Drama in E. K. Chambers's *Mediaeval Stage*—provide exactly the hint we may have been looking for. Our poem is clearly a midwinter festival poem. The seasonal theme (as any detailed analysis of the poem will bear out) is the poem's underlying, indeed pervasive theme.

The Green Knight whose head is chopped off at his own request and who is yet as miraculously or magically alive as ever, bears an unmistakable relation to the Green Man—the Jack in the Green[1] or the Wild Man of the village festivals of England and Europe. He can be no other than a recrudescence in poetry of the Green Man. Who is the Green Man? He is surely a descendant of the Vegetation or Nature god of almost universal and immemorial tradition (whatever his local name) whose death and resurrection are the myth-and-ritual counterpart of the annual death and re-birth of nature—in the East the dry and rainy seasons, in Europe winter and spring. The episode (the First Fit of our poem) in which the Green Knight rides into the hall of Arthur's castle among the courtly company at the Christmas feast and demands to have his head chopped off is exactly a Christmas pageant play or interlude—a castle version of the village Folk Play—become real. The central episode of the traditional Folk Play, SwordDance and Morris Dance was (as Chambers shows[2]) a mock beheading or slaying followed by a revival or restoration to life (often by the Doctor who administered to the corpse the contents of a bottle—the elixir of life).

A recent book by C. J. P. Cave, *Roof Bosses in Mediaeval Churches,* demonstrates the vitality of the Green Man in medieval England. Mr. Cave's photography has revealed carvings on the roofs of cathedrals and parish churches which could previously

---

[1] Represented by the lad wreathed in hawthorn, a walking bush, in the May Day village festivals. The leafy screens carried by the restoration army in *Macbeth*, Birnam Wood advancing on Macbeth's castle, have possibly a related symbolic significance.

[2] E. K. Chambers, *The English Folk Play* and *The Mediaeval Stage*, Bk. II, Folk Drama; R. J. E. Tiddy, *The Mummers Play*.

only be clearly distinguished through field-glasses, or in some cases, because in shadow, have never been very noticeable till this day. The photographs reveal a face with leaves sprouting from the corners of its mouth, its eye-lids, eyebrows and ears, the face of the Green Man.[1]

The Sir Gawain of our poem is correspondingly related to a traditional Gawain who (Miss Weston says[2]) was the hero, the agent who brought back the spring, restored the frozen life processes, revived the god—or (in later versions) cured the king.[3] (Though there is no mention of that in our poem, there are other poems in which Sir Gawain is mysteriously spoken of as having the skill of a healer or doctor—not one of the usual skills of courtly knighthood.) The subject of our poem is a kind of contest—not the orthodox kind of knightly contest but a kind of ritual contest in which the two antagonists are Gawain and the Green Knight. Further, Gawain must engage in a quest and must pass certain tests; thus the whole has very much the character of a story of an initiation.

The winter landscape through which, in our poem, Sir Gawain rides on his quest for the Green Chapel, where on New Year's Day he is to renew his acquaintance with the Green Knight, is again the northern European Waste Land, the land that has been (not, as in the East, dried up) frozen up. If it is (implicitly) 'enchantment' which the land suffers from in our poem, it is the kind it suffers from every winter in the north of Europe.

Sir Gawayne and the Grene Knight is of course a Christian poem.

---

[1] It can scarcely be accidental that so many village pubs in England are called The Green Man.

[2] *The Quest of the Holy Grail* and *From Ritual to Romance*, notably Chap. II, 'The Task of the Hero', also Chap. VIII, 'The Medicine Man'.

[3] There are some unexpected underground resemblances (which may be glanced at here in transition) between Sir Gawain and Piers. Piers the Plowman—in one part of Langland's poem described as 'the leche of life' and associated with the seasonal cycle—is identified with Christ, and Christ is the hero who (in Passus XVIII) harrows Hell, releases imprisoned life, restores the dead,

> Lord of life and of light.

It is the Easter theme; the dreamer, appropriately, awakes to the sound of the Easter bells. The episode has *its* dramatic counterpart, too, the Harrowing of Hell of the Miracle Plays.

But it is Christian rather as some of the medieval Christmas carols are, as Christmas itself is; Christian in harmony with pre-Christian nature belief and ritual, a Christian re-interpretation of these. It is Christian to about the same depth as it is a courtly romance. The value of 'courtesy'—Sir Gawain is among other things the pattern of courtesy, the most courteous of Arthur's courtly company—is certainly one of the values defined in the poem and brought out in relation to the other values in their order, Christian and pre-Christian; and these other values are pre-courtly.

The fundamental *knowledge* in the poem, the hidden source which the poet has tapped, the ultimate source of the poem's actuality, strength and coherence, is the knowledge, which the age-old experience of the race has turned into an assured knowledge, that there is life inexhaustible at the roots of the world even in the dead season, that there is perpetually to be expected the unexpected spring re-birth. The whole poem is, in its very texture—its imagery and rhythm—an assertion of belief in *life* as opposed to winter deprivation and death; and it seems finally to discover, within the antagonism between man and nature, between the human and the other-than-human, a hidden harmony, expressed in the kind of humorous understanding that develops between the Green Knight and Gawain.

There might be no great impropriety in describing as Eliza-bethan the poem's delighted acceptance and vivid consciousness of what takes the senses in rich colour and decorative pattern, in costly magnificence of costume and tapestry, jewellery and em-broidery, in elaborate and subtle craftsmanship in metal, wood and stone; and of life also as it expresses itself in ceremonial ban-queting, pageantry, music and 'carolling' (dancing and singing in unison) and in the strenuous physical exertions and hazards of tourneying and hunting; gay, Homeric laughter recurs throughout the scenes, the Homeric feasts, in the castles. Yet the rich and exuberant imagery of the poem is strictly controlled by the inner intention; it has its symbolic value in relation to the main, the 'life' significance. The jewellery and embroidery, for example, are related to the underlying fertility theme, contrasted with the chastity theme, as the feasting and generous hospitality in the castles contrast with the winter dearth.

The poem depends for its local effects largely upon its wealth of vocabulary, sheer weight and heaped-up pressure of language—a piling-up of language that contrasts with Chaucer's civilized simplicity—masses of bright colours and concatenations of differentiated sounds. But it is not simply lavishness and excess; it is all built into an art as firm as Ben Jonson's; it is even Shakespearian in the way it is all unfalteringly, unerringly controlled towards an inclusive significance.

The poem is in four fits. It opens at once on the note of the indestructibility and perpetual renewal of life. Arthur's castle is placed in history as one of the phoenixes of Troy, the utterly destroyed city—

> *The borg brittened[1] and brent to brondes and askes*

—from which the so many new cities and kingdoms of the Western World have sprung.

> *On mony bonkkes ful brode Bretayn he settes wyth wynne.[2]*

Among these there is this kingdom of Britain where joy and trouble—like winter and spring—have many times alternated.

Then the poem begins to move with a superb impression of the Christmas and New Year festivals at Arthur's castle.

> *This kyng lay at Camylot upon Krystmasse*
> *With mony luflych lorde, ledes[3] of the best,*
> *Rekenly of the Rounde Table alle tho rich brether,*
> *With rich revel oryght and rechles merthes.*
> *Ther tournayed tulkes[3] by tymes ful mony,*
> *Justed ful jolile thise gentyle knightes,*
> *Sythen kayred[4] to the court caroles to make.*
> *For ther the fest was ilyche[5] ful fiften dayes,*
> *With alle the mete and the mirthe that men couthe avyse;[6]*
> *Such glaum[7] ande gle glorious to here,*
> *Dere dyn upon day, daunsyng on nyghtes,*

---

[1] broken.   [2] joy, delight.   [3] men.   [4] rode.
[5] i.e. went on without ceasing.   [6] devise.   [7] noise.

Sir Gawayne and the Grene Knight

Al was hap[1] upon heghe in halles and chambres
With lordes and ladies, as levest him thoght.
With alle the wele of the worlde thay woned ther samen,[2]
The most kyd[3] knyghtes under Krystes selven,
And the lovelokkest ladies that ever lif haden,
And he the comlokest kyng that the court haldes;
For al was this fayre folk in her first age, on sille,[4]
    The hapnest[5] under heven,
    Kyng hyghest mon of wylle;
    Hit were now gret nye to neven[6]
    So hardy a here on hille.[7]

Wyle New Yer was so yep[8] that hit was new cummen,
That day doubble on the dece was the douth[9] served,
Fro the kyng was cummen with knyghtes into the halle,
The chauntré of the chapel cheved[10] to an ende.
Loude crye was ther kest of clerkes and other,
Nowel nayted[11] onewe, nevened ful ofte;
And sythen riche forth runnen to reche hondeselle,[12]
Yeyed[13] yeres-yiftes on high, yelde hem bi hond,
Debated busyly aboute tho giftes;
Ladies laghed ful loude, thogh thay lost haden,
And he that wan was not wrothe, that may ye wel trawe.
Alle this mirthe thay maden to the mete tyme;
When thay had waschen worthyly thay wenten to sete,
The best burne ay abof,[14] as hit best semed,
Quene Guenore, ful gay, graythed[15] in the myddes,
Dressed on the dere des, dubbed al aboute,
Smal sendal besides, a selure[16] hir ouer
Of tryed tolouse,[17] of tars tapites[18] innoghe,
That were enbrawded and beten wyth the best gemmes

---

[1] happiness.   [2] together.   [3] famous.   [4] in hall.   [5] most fortunate.
[6] difficulty to name.   [7] company, host on a hill (i.e. castle-hill).
[8] eager.   [9] company.   [10] came, drew.   [11] celebrated.   [12] New Year's gifts.
[13] called, proclaimed.   [14] i.e. they were seated in order of worth.
[15] set.   [16] canopy.   [17] fine cloth of Toulouse.
[18] silken tapestries (of Tharsia or Turkestan).

That myght be preued of prys wyth penyes to bye, in daye.[1]
   The comlokest to discrye
   Ther glent with eyen gray,
   A semloker that ever he sye
   Soth moght no mon say.

Bot Arthure wolde not ete til al were served,
He was so joly of his joyfnes,[2] *and sumquat childgered:*[3]
His lif liked hym lyght, he lovied the lasse
Auther to longe lye or to longe sitte,
So bisied him his yonge blod and his brayn wylde.

The fullness and vividness of life are there both in the imagery and in the rhythm. The alliterative lines build up into massive stanzaic paragraphs each concluding with a quartet of short rhymed lines which releases the reader momentarily before he is again caught up into the rhythmic energy of the succeeding paragraph. This superb poetry does not merely describe; its strong ringing rhythm *communicates* the enjoyment of maximum life in its flowering prime. The youthfulness of Arthur and of Arthur's folk[4]—

For al was this fayre folk in her first age

—introduces the theme of youth in contrast to age which is an aspect of the spring⁄winter (or New Year⁄Old Year) theme. The poem thus launched is sustained right through as a Christmas⁄New Year festival poem. The note of feasting—contrasted with the winter deprivation experienced by Gawain on his journey in the Second and Fourth Fits—keeps recurring. The poem expresses the jollity, the confident belief in life of the medieval English folk (one need not in this respect differentiate the castle folk from the village folk).

Arthur looks for a marvel, Christmas being the season of mar⁄vels (what could be more marvellous than a birth in the dead season?) and indeed the ceremonial banquet has hardly com⁄

---

[1] i.e. that could ever be bought with money.   [2] youth.
[3] childlike in behaviour, boyish.   [4] Cf. The Celtic Land of Youth.

menced, the first course brought in with 'crakkyng of trumpes', when

> *Ther hales in*[1] *at the halle dor an aghlich*[2] *mayster.*

He is no mummer disguised as a Green Knight who rides into the hall; he *is* the Green Knight.

The huge impression, larger than life—the Green Knight on the green horse—is massively built up. He is not only faery but robustly substantial and a fiercely humorous character. The emphasis on his glittering array—the jewel-like greenness of his green colour and that of his horse, the glittering green jewellery, the rich embroidery of multiplied 'bryddes and flyghes'—is unmistakably significant of life resurgent. It is as though the summer has entered. But more considered recognition of this significance had better be postponed till we come to the counterpart, in the structural balance, of the description of the Green Knight, the arming of Sir Gawain in the Second Fit. This predilection for jewels, for example, is certainly not simply the influence of the lapidaries or an interest in what the contemporary jewellers and goldsmiths had to offer.

The 'vegetation' aspect of the Green Knight will be immediately recognized. His green beard is like a bush, and together with his long green hair covers his chest and back all round down to his elbows. He carries a holly branch in one hand—

> *a holyn bobbe*
> *That is grattest in grene when greves are bare*

—and in the other a huge axe (a thunder weapon, like Thor's hammer).[3] He is as green as green verdure. It would indeed be singular not to feel that (in one of his aspects at least) he is a reappearance in poetry of an old vegetation god. After his head has been chopped off he is as vigorously alive as before, like a pollard tree, like John Barleycorn in the old ballads against whom came 'three kings from the West, their victory to try', and who, though killed and buried, 'sprang up again. And that surprised them all.'

My own experience is that the reader instinctively feels him to be

---

[1] i.e. bursts in.   [2] terrifying.   [3] Cf. 'He loked like the layt' (the lightning).

an intruder from a pre-Christian, pre-courtly world. Something of the old untamed, unreclaimed north of Europe has come back here (though the Green Knight will be discovered not merely to typify the destructive, menacing aspects of wild nature hostile to pioneering humans in their struggle to maintain their clearings in forests and swamps). He carries no knightly arms but wields a Danish axe—the stress is on the primitive and heathen nature of the weapon. A 'salvage' intruder, he 'breaks the good feast', disturbs the ceremonious courtly order with his presence and his challenge; the contrast is, at one level, between 'nature' and 'sophistication'. He evokes a half-amused, half-horrified fascination. If he is life, he is wild, uncouth, raw life. His demeanour and his behaviour in this castle of courtesy are outrageously discourteous; he behaves, as if radically a 'villeyn', with contemptuous humorous rudeness. In essence he is the *other*—the other than human.

> *The renk*[1] *on his rouncé*[2] *hym ruched*[3] *in his sadel,*
> *And runischly*[4] *his rede yen he reled aboute,*
> *Bende his bresed*[5] *browes blycande*[6] *grene,*
> *Wayved his berde for to wayte quo-so wolde ryse.*
> *When non wolde kepe hym with carp he coghed ful hye,*
> *Ande rimed hym*[7] *ful richley, and ryght hym to speke:*
> *'What, is this Arthures hous,' quoth the hathel thenne,*
> *'That al the rous renes of*[8] *thurgh ryalmes so mony?*
> *Where is now your sourquydrye*[9] *and your conquestes,*
> *Your gryndellayk*[10] *and your greme,*[11] *and your grete wordes?'*

The challenge, to who will, to chop off his head—'For it is Yol and New Yer'—on condition that he who dares to do so will submit to have his own head chopped off on New Year's Day a year hence by the survivor (if the Green Knight *should* survive with his head off) is accepted by Gawain, Arthur's sister's son, the pattern of courtesy, the Prince ('the glass of fashion and the mould of form!').

The dismembering act is gruesome enough. There is blood in

---

[1] man.   [2] horse.   [3] turned.   [4] fiercely.   [5] bristling?   [6] flashing.
[7] puffed himself out.   [8] that all the fame is about that spreads.
[9] pride.   [10] fierceness.   [11] anger.

the Green Man ('For the red blood reigns in the winter's pale').[1]
The courtly company kick away the head as it rolls towards them.
That is not cruelty or even, perhaps, simply horror; the head of the
sacrificed beast in fertility rituals was believed pregnant with
magical powers.[2]

> *That the bit of the broun[3] stel bot on the grounde.*
> *The fayre hede fro the halce hit to the erthe,*
> *That fele[4] hit foyned wyth her fete, there hit forth roled;*
> *The blod brayd[5] fro the body, that blykked[6] on the grene;*
> *And nauther faltered ne fel the freke[7] never the helder,[8]*
> *Bot stythly he start forth upon styf schonkes,*
> *And runyschly he racht out, there as renkkes stoden,*
> *Lacht to[9] his lufly hed, and lyft hit up sone;*
> *And sythen boges to his blonk,[10] the brydel he cachches,*
> *Steppes into stelbawe[11] and strydes alofte,*
> *And his hede by the here in his honde haldes.*

The impacts of the axe and of the head on the ground are felt in
the 'bit ... bot ... hit' of the first and second lines. This is poetry
that must be read with the body; it conveys directly a sense of
physical actions and movements.

The chopping off of his own head is to this amazing fellow but
a 'Crystemas gomen'. With a savage yell ('a runisch rout') he
flings out of the hall, fire struck from the flints by his horse's
hooves. The roar and flash of his departure suggest that *one* of his
aspects is that of a thunder-and-lightning god; and the thunder
gods (we are told) were often identical with the sun or sky gods.
Fire, later, is also struck from the hooves of Gawain's horse; and
the flicker of fire in the *other* castle (of the Second and Third Fits)
is too frequent to have an accidental significance.

The opening paragraphs of the Second Fit, superbly conveying
an impression of the changing seasons, the revolving year, are not

---

[1] Autolycus's song in *A Winter's Tale*.
[2] The anthropologists tell us that our game of football is derived from the struggle
for possession of the head which, buried in the earth, would make the land fertile,
the crops rich. In this case, however, the head is (very naturally) spurned.

[3] bright.   [4] many.   [5] spurted.   [6] gleamed.   [7] the fellow.
[8] never the more for that.   [9] seized.   [10] horse.   [11] stirrup-iron.

mere decoration. They are integral to the poem; they rise from the core of the unifying seasonal experience. We are not just told that a year has passed; we experience the year changing, the alternating pattern of the seasons; everything is in movement, and we live through the year.

> *Bot thagh the ende be hevy, haf ye no wonder;*
> *For thagh men ben mery in mynde when thay han mayn drynk,*
> *A yere yernes ful yerne,[1] and yeldes never lyke,[2]*
> *The forme to the fynisment foldes ful selden.[3]*
> *Forthi this Yol overyede, and the yere after,*
> *And uche sesoun serlepes[4] sued after[5] other:*
> *After Crystenmasse com the crabbed lentoun,*
> *That fraystes flesch wyth the fysche[6] and fode more symple;*
> *Bot thenne the weder of the worlde wyth wynter hit threpes,[7]*
> *Colde clenges adoun, cloudes uplyften,*
> *Schyre[8] schedes the rayn in schowres ful warme,*
> *Falles upon fayre flat, flowers there schewen,*
> *Bothe groundes and the greves[9] grene ar her wedes,*
> *Bryddes busken to bylde, and bremlych syngen*
> *For solace of the softe somer that sues therafter bi bonk;*
> > *And blossumes bolne[10] to blowe*
> > *Bi rawes[11] rych and ronk,*
> > *Then notes noble innowe*
> > *Ar herde in wod so wlonk.[12]*
>
> *After, the sesoun of somer wyth the soft wyndes,*
> *When Zeferus syfles[13] hymself on sedes and erbes;*
> *Wela wynne[14] is the wort that waxes theroute,*
> *When the donkande dewe dropes of the leves,*
> *To bide a blysful blusche of the bryght sunne.*

[1] runs quickly away. [2] never the same.
[3] the beginning seldom matches the end.
[4] in turn. [5] pursued.
[6] tries the flesh with (having to eat) fish. (A play in the meanings of 'flesh'.)
[7] contends. [8] bright (i.e. in falling through sunshine?).
[9] meadows and woods. [10] swell. [11] in rows (or hedgerows?). [12] lovely.
[13] breathes (cf. 'Zephirus . . . inspired hath', *Canterbury Prologue*).
[14] very joyous, delightful.

Sir Gawayne and the Grene Knight

Bot then hyes hervest, and hardenes hym sone,
Warnes hym for the wynter to wax ful rype;
He dryves wyth droght the dust for to ryse,
Fro the face of the folde to flye ful hyghe:
Wrothe wynde of the welkyn wrasteles with the sunne,
The leves lancen from the lynde and lyghten on the grounde,
And al grayes the gres that grene was ere;
Thenne al rypes and rotes that ros upon fyrst,
And thus yirnes the yere in yisterdayes mony,
And wynter wyndes agayn, as the worlde askes . . .

There is continual struggle. Summer contends ('threpes') with
Winter and wins, but then again Winter contends ('wrastles')
with Summer and wins and the earth again loses its greenness.
The Shakespearian phrases (al'rypes and rotes' . . . 'in yisterdayes
mony') remind the modern reader that the language of the poem
is radically the same language as Shakespeare's. The analogy
with human life—human life has its seasons—an analogy familiar
to us in Shakespeare underlies the melancholy note of transience.
The harmony between man and nature is here a harmony in their
common fate of transience. Spring and summer, though vividly
rejoiced in, are episodes in the perpetual process of change. The
day approaches when Gawain must set off on his quest for the
Green Chapel to keep his tryst with the Green Knight on New
Year's Day and take the return blow. The concluding emphasis
is on the waning of the year. The year's revolution has, however,
again brought round the Christmas-New Year season. The poem
is thus maintained right through as a Christmas and New Year
festival poem.

The arming of Sir Gawain, which (as already observed) corresponds, in the structural balance, to the description of the Green
Knight, is also not mere decoration; it is not simply the medieval
romancer's, and his castle audience's, interest in knightly accoutre-
ment, armour and weapons. The representatives of life, including
the youthful hero whose task it is to bring back life, have always
(the anthropologists tell us) been glittering figures arrayed as for
some ceremony rather than in what we should regard as practical

'battle-dress'. The throng of dancing youths who in the ancient rituals accompanied the god, the Maruts of India, the Corybantes and Couretes of the Greeks, the Salii of the Romans—the predecessors of the Sword Dancers and Morris Dancers of more recent folk festivals—were glitteringly arrayed; in their dances, designed to stimulate the reproductive energies of nature, they carried flashing weapons. In Sir Gawayn's array, and that of his horse,[1] red colour, as distinguished from the gleaming green of his opposite, and gold—

> *That al glytered and glent as glem of the sun*

—predominate. This aspect suggests that Gawain's original *may* (as Loomis thinks) have been the young sun-god. To borrow, from another context, one of Gilbert Murray's phrases, Gawain, too, has 'a touch of the sun in him'. There is again a profusion of jewels and a silk embroidery of birds—'papiayes' and 'tortors'—

> *As mony burde theraboute had ben seven wynter.*

Perhaps 'There's magic in a web of it.' His array thus associates Gawain with life resurgent.

Nor is it accidental that Sir Gawain's emblem is the pentangle, an ancient life-symbol. It appears as one of the figures on the Tarot Pack. It was believed (Miss Weston tells us) to 'give power over the other world'.[2] The Sword Dancers, as they enclose the head in their mock beheading, make the figure of the pentangle; as the dancers 'hold up the sign, they cry triumphantly "A nut! a nut!"'[3] In *Sir Gawayne and the Grene Knight*, the pentangle has acquired a Christian significance; but the pre-Christian significance unmistakably underlies and is active in the poem.

---

[1] It is interesting to note that the name of Gawain's horse, Gringolet, is a name also given to Wade's boat. The hero's horse is a conveyance to the Otherworld, across the mountain-barrier, as the boat is across the water-barrier.

[2] The significance of the pentangle (Faust's 'Druid's foot' that kept Mephisto from crossing the threshold) is preserved in the 'Five for the symbol at your door' of the old English counting-song *Green Grow the Rushes O*, where also Two is 'for the lilly-white boys clothèd all in green, O'.

[3] *From Ritual to Romance*, Chap. VII, 'The Sword Dance', p. 93. 'Nut' means 'knot'—as in the game 'nuts in May' which means 'breast-knots or nosegays in May'; in our poem it is said that the English call the pentangle 'the endeles knot'.

Sir Gawayne and the Grene Knight

The winter landscape through which Gawain now rides on his quest for the Green Chapel is not mere decorative background to a romance; it is the northern European Waste Land, the Utgard of Norse mythology. That is to say, it is actual winter as it may be experienced among the mountains of North Wales after a blizzard. The geography of Gawain's search for the Green Chapel is, and is intended to be, significant. Why else should we be told in such detail how he left the court in Somerset (Arthur's court representing the centre of Christian culture and civilization) to search Wales? And right through Wales to Anglesey—the Druid country, the home of the pre-Christian culture, the ancient religion of Britain, and where Gawain was the favourite hero and whence, perhaps, the original Gawain legend came—and so to the Wirral? After that the whereabouts of his wanderings become necessarily a mystery. The point is that Gawain *expected* the Green Chapel and the Green Man to be where the cult belonged, perhaps survived. And this specification of the real countryside of the quest makes Gawain's subsequent wanderings in the waste full of monsters more blood-chilling: it prevents the reader from feeling he is merely in the stock fairy-tale world of romance and can discount the horrors—Gawain's waste is felt to be real and perilous indeed.

The actuality of the experience of desolation—Gawain's experience of being a stranger in a mountainous frozen region—depends upon the actuality of this winter landscape. The experience is distinct because the landscape is distinct (in contrast to the indefinite dream landscapes of the *Faerie Queene*). It is a landscape from which God (originally perhaps the god) appears to have withdrawn, a landscape desolate of humans, inhabited by unhuman creatures, beasts and monsters against which Gawain must hazard his life. The succession of tests which Gawain will undergo has commenced. 'The test preceding and qualifying for initiation into the secrets of physical life, consisted in being brought into contact with the horrors of physical death'. (J. L. Weston, *The Quest of the Grail*.)

The actuality of this ice-bound universe is itself dependent upon distinctness and accuracy of sensation, on the sharpness or piercingness of the sensory impressions and the subtlety with which these are distinguished and differentiated.

> *When the colde cler water fro the cloudes schadde,*
> *And fres er hit falle myght to the falé erthe;*
> *Ner slayn wyth the slete he sleped in his yrnes*
> *Mo nyghtes then innoghe in naked rokkes,*
> *Ther as claterande fro the crest the colde borne rennes,*
> *And henged hegh over his hede in hard iisse-ikkles.*

'In his iron . . . on the naked rocks'—no acuter impression of the cold endured by Gawain could be conceived or communicated in words.

But from among these rocks, on the morning of Christmas Eve, Sir Gawain enters a forest. The trees of the Sacred Wood (they are the traditionally sacred trees) are full of suffering, half-frozen birds.

> *Of hore okes ful hoge a hundreth togeder;*
> *The hasel and the hawthorne were harled¹ al samen,*
> *With roghe raged mosse rayled² aywhere,*
> *With mony bryddes unblythe upon bare twyges,*
> *That pitosly ther piped for pyne of the colde.*

The intimate medieval fellow-feeling for the birds seems to restore a whole range of human feeling; sympathetic feelings that had been frozen up un-freeze.³ The Christian knight, remembering that it is Christmas Eve, prays to Christ and Mary for some lodging where he might hear mass and matins on Christmas morning.

> *To se the servyse of that syre, that on that self nyght*
> *Of a burde was borne oure baret⁴ to quelle;*
> *And therfor sykyng he sayde, 'I beseche the, lorde,*
> *And Mary, that is myldest moder so dere,*

¹ tangled.   ² clothed.

³ The moment is nearly analogous to the moment in the *Ancient Mariner* when 'A spring of love gushed from my heart . . .' The albatross which suddenly appeared in the icy desolation ('Thorough the fog it came, As if it had been a Christian soul . . .') is life, and in destroying it the Mariner committed a crime against life. The moment, in the purgatorial process, has come when the Mariner suddenly recovers his love for living creatures. 'The self-same moment I could pray . . .'

⁴ sorrow.

Sir Gawayne and the Grene Knight

Of sum herber ther heghly I myght here masse,
Ande thy matynes to-morne, mekely I ask.'

As if in answer to his prayer he is confronted with the miracle of a castle. It is an ancient experience of the race. You are crossing a desert; you look again and (as by magic) the desert is a garden, a paradise—as desert land may (often does) become quite suddenly after rainfall. So here, unexpectedly, in the Waste Land is a castle where the knight, after deprivation, will be entertained with abun⁄ dance of food and drink. The castle is unmistakably a version of the Grail Castle. (There is no mention of the Grail in our poem; but always associated with the fleeting appearances of the Grail, the life⁄giving vessel, are just such windfalls of food and drink.) The castle is seen first as like the sun shining through the trees—

> *It shemered and schone through the brode okes*

—a touch that *could* have come from its possible original, the abode of the sun⁄god.

In contrast to the 'naked rokkes' the castle is as if faery, as if it might vanish again as suddenly as it appeared.

> *Chalkwhyt chymnes . . .*
> *That pared out of papure purely hit semed.*

But it is multiplex in detail, a multiplicity of towers and turrets, suggesting again, perhaps, fertility —as innumerable stalks thrust upward from the ground in spring—and various as flowers are. It is islanded by water, oasis⁄like in effect. Gawain is here nearer than he knows to the hidden source of life.

In the structural balance of the poem this castle balances, on the one hand, the Green Chapel of the Fourth (and final) Fit— Gawain has come first not to a chapel but a castle—on the other hand, Arthur's castle. The lord of this *other* castle (Sir Bercilak de la Hautdesert—the surname is perhaps significant) will, in the Fourth Fit, turn out to be the Green Knight. Between the robust and boisterous lord of the castle, a huge man of mature age, and the Green Knight, there is a concealed resemblance, allowing that the colour of his beard is now reddish brown and not green.

> *Brode, brycht, was his berde, and al bever-hued.*
> *Felle face as the fyre . . .*

His association with fire has unmistakably the same kind of significance that the fire festivals (really sun-festivals) had; the flicker
of fire—fire-light and torch-light—is (as previously remarked)
characteristic of this castle. Gawain and the Green Knight of the
First Fit have here in the Second Fit in some respects changed
places. After he has been clothed in fresh garments[1] the youthful
Gawain looks like the spring.

> *The Ver by his visage verayly hit semed*
> *Welnegh to uche hathel, alle on hues,*
> *Lowande[2] and lufly alle his lymmes under . . .*

It is as if the spring itself has come to the castle and been welcomed.
As a guest, Gawain is restored to the warmth of hospitality
before the Yule fire.

> *A cheyer byfore the chemne, ther charcole brenned.*

As the plentiful food and drink with which—in this hostelry of
the Green Man—Gawain is generously refreshed contrasts with
the winter deprivation, so also the domestic comfort and sump-
tuousness of the interior of the castle contrasts with the inhospitable
rocks. In return, Sir Gawain is to the folk in the castle the pattern
of courtesy, 'the fyne fader of nurture'.

There are in the castle a young woman and an old woman. The
lady hostess, Sir Bercilak's wife, is youthful and lovely.

> *Thenne lyst the lady to loke on the knyght,*
> *Thenne com ho[3] of hir closet with mony cler burdes.*
> *Ho[3] was the fayrest in felle,[4] of flesche and of lyre,[5]*
> *And of compas[6] and colour and costes[7] of alle other,*
> *And wener[8] then Wenore, as the wyghe thoght.*

[1] We may compare those who have 'suffered a sea-change' in *The Tempest*.
'But the rarity of it is, which is indeed almost beyond credit . . . that our garments,
being, as they were, drenched in the sea, hold notwithstanding their freshness and
glosses, being rather new-dyed than stained with salt-water.'
The rebirth significance of the change of garments will be familiar enough.
[2] glowing.   [3] she.   [4] skin.   [5] cheek.   [6] size, proportions.
[7] qualities, ways.   [8] more lovely.

She is accompanied, however, by another lady who in contrast to
her is old and withered.

> *An other lady hir lad bi the lyft honde,*
> *That was alder than ho,[1] an auncian hit semed,*
> *And heghly honored with hatheles aboute.*
>
> *Bot unlyke on to loke tho ladyes were,*
> *For if the yonge was yep,[2] yolwe was that other;*
> *Riche red on that on rayled[3] ayquere,*
> *Rugh ronkled chekes that other on rolled;*
> *Kerchofes of that on, wyth mony cler perles,*
> *Hir brest and hir bryght throte bare displayed,*
> *Schon schyrer[4] then snawe that schedes on hills;*
> *That other wyth a gorger[5] was gered over the swyre,[6]*
> *Chymbled[7] over hir blake chyn wyth chalkwhyte vayles,*
> *Hir frount folden in sylk, enfoubled[8] ayquere,*
> *Toret and treieted[9] with tryfles aboute,*
> *That noght was bare of that burde bot the blake browes,*
> *The tweyne eyen and the nase, the naked lyppes,*
> *And those were soure to se and sellyly blered.*

The realism of that reminds one of Villon's hags. Whoever this
withered ancient is in the 'story' (she is, as we happen to be told at
the very end of the poem, Morgan the Goddess), the point here is
immediately the contrast between youth and age, which has its
significance in relation to the underlying seasonal theme. Winter is
the season when the year has lost its vigour, spring when the year
recovers its youth; the year grows old in winter, young again in
spring. The one woman is what the other turns into; age is what
youth turns into. But in relation to the seasonal theme the order is
here also reversible; the young woman supplants the old. The old
year (in this respect there is doubtless an underground connexion
with the envy of Morgan) works the mischief, produces the frozen
world simply by being old. Underlying the old woman and the
young woman are the Old and the New Year.[10]

---

[1] she.   [2] fresh.   [3] spread, i.e. mantling, glowing.   [4] brighter.
[5] neckerchief.   [6] neck.   [7] wrapped.   [8] muffled.   [9] tricked out, decked.
[10] Such figures were familiar features of the annual folk festivals. The Romans had
their Mamurius Veturius and his female counterpart, Anna Perenna.

When the feast of Christmas draws to a close Gawain's host tells him he knows where the Green Chapel is—it is close at hand —and bids him rest in the castle for the three days that remain. Again there is a bargain. During each of these three days the lord of the castle proposes to be abroad hunting. Each evening Gawain will exchange whatever he may have won during the day in the castle for whatever his host may have won in the chase.

The events of these three days before New Year's Day—the day of Gawain's tryst at the Green Chapel—are the subject of the Third Fit. They are days of apparent rest for Gawain but really of most perilous testing. The peril is the greater because Gawain does not know he is being tested. On his success or failure in these days of testing by the gay, youthful lady, his distractingly lovely hostess, will depend, though he does not guess it, his success or failure, indeed his life, at the Green Chapel. Though the original, and still the underlying, purpose of the diverse tests—to find out whether or not Gawain is a fit agent to bring back the spring—is resolved into the conception of a testing of fitness for Christian knighthood, chastity has here nothing very particularly to do with monastic asceticism. Chastity has immemorially been a requirement in fertility—or nature—ceremonies and initiations. The chastity theme is here complementary to the fertility theme.

The hunts, besides being realistic hunts, are certainly also sym-bolic parallels to the encounters in the castle between the lady and Gawain. The shy deer, the ferocious (yet courageous) boar, the cunning fox are the qualities of the natural man which Courtesy has to vanquish or, at least, civilize. Gawain's first natural reaction when the lady first steals into his chamber—like a huntress, 'with naked fote, stalking in my chamber'[1]—is to pretend to be asleep and evade the issue if he can (the deer); but he overcomes his shy-ness and is victorious by changing it into the exercise of a beautiful tact, a skilful and adroit courtesy. At her second visit she seeks more directly to provoke his 'corage', the fierceness of his instincts (the boar); he is victorious on this occasion by the *moral* courage with which he directly opposes his almost irresistible beautiful opponent without falling into discourtesy. But on the third occa-

[1] Wyatt. 'They fle from me . . .'

236

sion Gawain in ignorance partially identifies himself with the
cunning (the fox) of the proffer of the Green Girdle—which later
in the poem he recognizes as having been a snare—by accepting
and concealing it. The hunts are thus a symbolic parallel of what
Gawain is doing in the castle, in the way of self-conquest, to maintain the ideal of the Christian knight. The poem implies an
audience trained to be on the alert for a symbolic—as well as a
literal—meaning; it is what made the poem possible as both
sophisticated art and a popular poem. The hunts move successively to a climax which is symbolic; the boar, we should think,
would follow the fox, if the crescendo were literal-dramatic and
not, as it is, spiritual-symbolic.

Further, the spoils of each day's hunt both correspond, in the
exchange, to the kisses of the lady and provide in midwinter
the foison, the plenty that is consumed at each evening's feast; for the
note of feasting continues right through the Third Fit. The Green
Man now appears as a huntsman. The intimate association of
vegetable and animal life, of crops and herds, has always been
recognized. The three hunts of our poem provision the successive
ceremonial feasts. Each hunt has its own character corresponding
to the character of the creature hunted; the first day's is a deer-hunt,
the second a boar-hunt, the third a fox-hunt.

The three episodes of the testing of Gawain by the lady who
each morning steals into his chamber are interwoven with the three
hunts. These slow-motion, gay but slyly perilous bedchamber
scenes contrast with the vital activity and rush of the hunts. If we
consider only the interweaving and the glowing colours we may be
reminded of a tapestry-piece; yet the analogy is inadequate because
these scenes are not *simply* picture, or processional pageantry, as the
scenes in the *Faerie Queene*, so easily dissociable from their intended 'moral' meaning, readily become. The scenes and the
people involved in *Sir Gawayne and the Grene Knight* are substantial,
alive and individual; the people—and even the boar and the fox—
are real characters.

There is a further complication of rhythm or pattern in this Fit
composed by the rotation of each day, slow—dangerously slow—
in the castle in Gawain's chamber, swift in the hunt; each day

opens with its dawn scene and closes with its evening feast after the day's hunt.

The Third Fit opens with a lively enactment, in strong 'pausing' rhythm, of the animation, the vital movement of the departing guests on the first morning of the lord's three hunts.

> *Ful erly bifore the day the folk uprysen,*
> *Gestes that go wolde hor gromes thay calden,*
> *And thay busken up bilyve[1] blonkkes to sadel,*
> *Tyffen[2] her takles, trussen her males,*
> *Richen[3] hem the rychest, to ryde alle arrayde,*
> *Lepen up lyghtly, lachen her brydeles.*

The startling effect produced on the wild creatures and the timid deer by the first sounds intimating a hunt is sympathetically apprehended.

> *At the fyrst quethe[4] of the quest[5] quaked the wylde;[6]*
> *Der drof in the dale, doted for drede.*

Yet it is the exhilaration of the chase that is primarily communicated; and sounds, concatenations of sounds, have their full values.

> *The hindes were halden in with hay! and war!*
> *The does dryven with gret dyn to the depe slades[7] ...*
> *Hunters wyth hyghe horne hasted hem after*
> *Wyth such a crakkande kry as klyffes haden brusten.*

There is a great plenty of deer (many being 'hindes barayne').
Meanwhile the gay lady steals into Gawain's chamber.

> *And as in slomeryng he slode, sleyly he herde*
> *A litel dyn at his dor, and derfly upon;[8]*
> *And he heves up his hed out of the clothes,*
> *A corner of the cortyn he cast up a lyttel,*
> *And waytes warly thiderwarde quat hit be myght.*
> *Hit was the ladi, loflyest to beholde,*
> *That drow the dor after hir ful dernly and stylle,*

[1] quickly.   [2] made ready.   [3] prepared (themselves), dressed.
[4] outcry.   [5] i.e. the questing hounds.   [6] the wild creatures.   [7] glens.
[8] and (heard it) quickly open.

238

And boged towarde the bed; and the burne schamed,
And layde hym doun lystyly,[1] and let as he slepte;
And ho stepped stilly and stel to his bedde,
Kest up the cortyn and creped withinne,
And set hir ful softly on the bed-syde,
And lenged there selly longe to loke when he wakened.
The lede lay lurked a ful longe quyle,
Compast in his concience to quat that cace myght
Meve other amount—to mervayle[2] hym thoght,
Bot yet he sayde in hymself, 'More semly hit were
To aspye wyth my spelle[3] in space quat ho wolde.'
Then he wakenede, and wroth,[4] and to hir warde torned,
And unlouked his eye-lyddes, and let as hym wondered,
And sayned hym, as bi his saye the safer to worthe,[5] with hande.
   Wyth chynne and cheke ful swete,
   Bothe whit and red in blande,[6]
   Ful lufly con ho lete[7]
   Wyth lyppes smal laghande.

'God moroun, Sir Gawayn,' sayde that gay lady,
'Ye ar a sleper unslye,[8] that mon may slyde hider;
Now ar ye tan astyt! Bot true us may schape,[9]
I schal bynde yow in your bedde, that be ye trayst':
Al laghande the lady lanced tho bourdes.[10]
'Goud moroun, gay,' quoth Gawayn the blythe . . .

The humanity of the scene, the humour of Gawain's embarrass-
ment and of his pretending at first to be asleep, distinguishes it
from the 'temptation' scenes in the *Faerie Queene*; the gay laughing
lady has more affinity with some of Chaucer's wives.[11] She is (it
transpires at the end of the poem) in league with her husband to
test the unsuspecting Gawain. The chastity test is complicated not
only by its being a test of loyalty—the loyalty of guest to host—but

---

[1] slyly.   [2] a great marvel.   [3] i.e. to inquire, to ask.   [4] stretched himself.
[5] so as to be the safer by his prayer.   [6] blent.   [7] conduct herself.
[8] unwary.   [9] unless we can arrange a truce.   [10] uttered these jests.
[11] The 'gay wives' of Dunbar's *Twa Marrit Wemen and the Wedo* are also real
enough, but by comparison are savage, merciless creatures of instinct.

also (much more difficult) a test of courtesy. Gawain has to resist the lady while at the same time not being discourteous to her. There is nothing unreal about this situation. The problem of how to resist different kinds of demands made upon one, without being discourteous, is a very real problem of civilized social behaviour in any community in any age. The theme of the inter⁄ play between 'nature' and civilized behaviour—Sir Gawain being the pattern of civilized behaviour or 'courtesy'—attains its maxi⁄ mum insistence in the episode between Sir Gawain and the lady.

Immediately supervening on Gawain's first day's successful resistance we are present at the 'breaking up'—an elaborate ritual —of the finest of the slain deer.[1] Gawain's success each day thus synchronizes in the poem with the death of the hunted beast for which he faithfully exchanges the lady's kisses; there are one kiss to be exchanged on the first day, two on the second, three on the third.

On the second day's dawn the castle is awakened by the crow⁄ ing of a cock (that most medieval of birds) in this Christmas festival poem. In the richly orchestrated poetry that renders the strenuous rushing action of the boar⁄hunt, our consciousness of sounds, given substance as they are by imagery of impetuous physical movement, again plays a large part.

> *Thenne such a glaver ande glam² of gedered rachches³*
> *Ros, that the rokkeres rungen aboute;*
> *Hunteres hem hardened with horne and with muthe.*
> *Then al in a semblé sweyed togeder,*
> *Bitwene a flosche⁴ in that fryth and a foo cragge.*

The boar is a really formidable antagonist.

> *On the sellokest swyn swenged out there . . .*
> *Ful grymme when he gronyed,⁵ thenne greved mony,*
> *For thre at the fyrst thrast⁶ he thryst to the erthe,*
> *And sparred forth good sped boute spyt more.*

---

[1] We may compare this episode, as also the deaths of the boar and fox, with the animal sacrifice at the cave—the entrance to the underworld—in Book VI of the *Aeneid*; the Green Chapel also is a cave.

[2] babel and din.   [3] hounds.   [4] pool.   [5] grunted.   [6] thrust.

Sir Gawayne and the Grene Knight

Thise other halowed hyghe! ful hyghe, and hay! hay! cryed,
Haden hornes to mouthe, heterly rechated;[1]
Mony was the miyry mouthe of men and of houndes . . .

The second of the critical bedchamber scenes—the second visit of the 'mere wyf', who on this occasion, after she has failed to provoke him to constrain her by force, presses Gawain to teach her the art of courtly love-making in which, as a knight of Arthur's court, he is erudite—is interposed in this contrasting context; the peril for Gawain is even deadlier than on the first day.

At the moment of our assurance at last of his second day's success we are present at the death of the boar. The terrible event is not merely told about; its savagery is experienced.

Bot the lorde ouer the londes launced ful ofte,
Sues his uncely[2] *swyn, that swynges bi the bonkkes*
And bote the best of his braches[3] *the bakkes in sunder . . .*
He gets the bonk at his bak, bigynes to scrape,
Whetes his whyte tuskes. . . .

The lord dismounts and, sword in hand, himself tackles the ferocious and maddened beast in a deadly duel; he also, as Gawain does, hazards his life.

The wylde was war of the wyghe with weppen in honde,
Hef hyghly the here,[4] *so hetterly he fnast*[5]
That fele ferde for the freke,[6] *lest felle hym the worre.*
The swyn settes hym out on the segge even,[7]
That the burne and the bor were bothe upon hepes
In the wyghtest of the water; the worre hade that other,
For the mon merkkes hym wel, as thay mette fyrst,
Set sadly the scharp in the slot[8] *even,*
Hit hym up to the hult, that the hert schyndered . . .
There was blawyng of prys in mony breme horne,
Heghe halowing on highe with hatheles that myght . . .

[1] vigorously sounded 'the recall'.
[2] ill-fated.   [3] hounds.   [4] raised up his bristles.
[5] fiercely he snorted.   [6] many feared for the man.   [7] rushes straight at . . .
[8] hollow at the base of the throat (vulnerable spot).

241

The boar's head of the traditional yule feast is brought home to the castle in triumph.

> *And sythen on a stif stange¹ stoutly hem henges.*
> *Now with this ilk swyn thay swengen to home;*
> *The bores hed was borne bifore the burnes selven.*

The 'hoge hed'—exchanged for the two kisses—graces the evening's seasonal feast among flickering torch-light and fire-light.

> *. . . clere lyght thenne*
> *Wakned bi wowes,² waxen torches . . .*
> *Aboute the fyre upon flet, and on fele wyse*
> *At the soper and after, mony athel songes,*
> *As coundutes³ of Krystmasse and caroles newe.*

There is quite evidently a cunning relation between the boar's head and the heads of the Green Knight and of Gawain.

On the frosty dawn of the third day, as the sun rises redly against drifting clouds, the horns of the final hunt sound.

> *Ferly fayre was the folde, for the forst clenged;*
> *In rede rudede⁴ upon rak rises the sunne,*
> *And ful clere costes⁵ the clowdes of the welkyn.*
> *Hunteres unhardeled⁶ bi a holt syde,*
> *Rokkeres roungen bi rys⁷ for rurde of her hornes.*

The strenuous exertions of this day's hunt are evoked by a fox; that fox is a character, Reynard, the well-known rascally character of the Beast Fables, a rascal to his end. Dogs and men

> *Runnen forth in a rabel in his ryght fare.⁸*

The fox

> *. . . fyskes hem before; thay founden hym sone,*
> *And when thay seghe hym with syght thay sued hym fast,*

---

¹ pole.   ² walls.
³ Medieval Latin, *conductus*. Old French *condut*. Here, songs for Christmas.
⁴ reddened, glowing red.   ⁵ coasts, i.e. passes close by.   ⁶ unleashed hounds.
⁷ in the woods.   ⁸ track.

Wreyande[1] *hym ful weterly*[2] *with a wroth noyse;*
And he trantes[3] *and tornayees thurgh mony tene greve,*
Havilounes,[4] *and herkenes bi hegges ful ofte.*
At the last bi a littel dich he lepes ouer a spenne,
Steles out ful stilly bi a strothe rande,[5]
Went haf wylt[6] *of the wode with wyles fro the houndes;*
Thenne was he went, er he wyst, to a wale tryster,[7]
Ther thre thro at a thrich thrat hym[8] *at ones, al graye.*

He blenched agayn bileve
And stifly start on-stray,
With alle the wo on lyve
To the wod he went away.

Thenne was hit lif upon list[9] *to lythen*[10] *the houndes,*
When alle the mute[11] *hade hym met, menged togeder:*
Suche a sorwe at that syght thay sette on his hede
As alle the clamberande[12] *clyffes hade clatered on hepes,*
Here he was halawed, when hatheles hym metten,
Loude he was gayned[13] *with garande*[14] *speche;*
Ther he was threted and ofte thef called,
And ay the titleres[15] *at his tayl, that tary he ne myght;*
Ofte he was runnen at, when he out rayked,[16]
And ofte reled in agayn, so Reniarde was wylé.
And ye he lad hem, bilagged[17] *men, the lorde and his meyny.*

Gawain's third and last test with the lady is meanwhile in progress. On this, the day before he must keep his tryst with the Green Knight at the Green Chapel, she wakens him from dreams that have been very naturally gloomy. But she is as gay and as distracting as ever.

In a mery mantyle, mete to the erthe . . .
Hir thryven[18] *face and hir throte throwen al naked,*
Hir brest bare bifore, and bihinde eke . . .
The lady luflych com laghande swete . . .

[1] accusing, denouncing.　　[2] clearly.　　[3] dodges.　　[4] doubles back.
[5] edge of a wood.　　[6] escaped.　　[7] choice, good hunting-station.
[8] three fierce dogs at a rush attacked him.　　[9] joy ('lif upon list'—brave sport).
[10] hear.　　[11] pack.　　[12] clustering.　　[13] greeted.　　[14] snarling.
[15] 'ticklers' (hounds pressing him).　　[16] made for the open.　　[17] muddied.　　[18] fair.

Now let Mary be mindful of her knight, for his fate at the Green Chapel will depend on how successfully he resists the gay lady here and now. This is the decisive test, before his venture into the unknown and unpredictable. He is human. He fails in a minor respect. He successfully resists the lady for the third time but—though he refuses a rich jewelled ring blazing like the sun—she at the very end slyly induces him to accept from her a simple-seeming lovelace, her Green Girdle, which she tells him magically preserves life. He accepts it not as a love-gift and not from essential cowardice, but because he positively wants life—in the poetry so vividly apprehended through every nerve and sense—if he can honourably have it, honour being dearer to him still than life.

The death of the fox is equivalent to Gawain's partial success, partial failure.

> *As he sprent ouer a spenne to spye the schrewe,*
> *Ther as he herde the houndes that hasted hym swythe,*
> *Renoud com richchande thurgh a roghe greve,*
> *And alle the rabel in a res ryght at his heles.*
> *The wyghe was war of the wylde, and warly abides,*
> *And braydes[1] out the bryght bronde, and at the best castes.*
> *And he schunt[2] for the scharp, and schulde haf arered;*
> *A rach rapes hym to, ryght er he myght,*
> *And ryght bifore the hors fete thay fel on hym alle,*
> *And woried me this wyly wyth a wroth noyse.*
> *The lorde lyghtes bilyve, and laches hym sone,*
> *Rased hym ful radly out of the rach mouthes,*
> *Haldes heghe ouer his hede, halowes faste,*
> *And ther bayen hym mony brath[3] houndes.*

A requiem is sounded for Reynard's soul.

> *Alle that ever ber bugle blowed at ones,*
> *And alle thise other halowed that hade no hornes;*
> *Hit was the myriest mute[4] that ever men herde,*
> *The rich rurd[5] that ther was raysed for Renaude saule.*

(Tomorrow, we may remember, it may be Gawain's turn.)

[1] draws.   [2] flinched.   [3] fierce.   [4] baying of hounds.   [5] clamour.

Gawain, not to implicate his hostess, says nothing about her gift of her Green Girdle; and the lord apologetically exchanges the pelt of the fox—a mere fox—for the three kisses.

> *For I haf hunted al this day, and noght haf I geten*
> *Bot this foule fox felle—the fende haf the godes!*

The Third Fit draws to a close with the New Year's Eve feast and some natural preoccupation about the morrow.

Gawain's journey through winter in quest of the Green Chapel is resumed in the Fourth (and last) Fit; in the structural balance the Fourth Fit corresponds in this aspect to the Second Fit, as in the final encounter between Gawain and the Green Knight it corresponds to the First Fit. The opening paragraph itself corresponds to the two opening paragraphs of the Second Fit conveying the experience of a year's revolution. The sense of time passing is again conveyed—on this occasion the passing of Old Year's Night into the wintry dawn of the New Year—and it is conveyed in particular terms of the wild weather outside the castle as Gawain listens to it on his bed with foreboding, conscious that his meeting with the Green Knight is now imminent.

> *Now neghes the New Yere, and the nyght passes,*
> *The day dryves to the derk, as Dryhten[1] biddes;*
> *Bot wylde wederes of the worlde wakned theroute,*
> *Clowdes kesten kenly the colde to the erthe,*
> *Wyth nye[2] innoghe of the northe, the naked to tene;*
> *The snaw snitered ful snart, that snayped the wylde;[3]*
> *The werbelande wynde wapped fro the hyghe,*
> *And drof uche dale ful of dryftes ful grete.*
> *The leude[4] lystened ful wel that ley in his bedde,*
> *Thagh he lowkes his liddes, ful lyttel he slepes;*
> *Bi uch kok that crue he knewe wel the steven.[5]*

Gawain then rides out again through winter as it may be actually experienced any winter among the mountains.

> *They bogen bi bonkkes ther boghes ar bare,*
> *Thay clomben bi clyffes ther clenges the colde.*

[1] God.　　[2] bitterness.　　[3] pinched the wild creatures.　　[4] man.　　[5] hour.

The heven was up halt, bot ugly ther-under;
Mist muged¹ on the mor, malt² on the mountes,
Uch hille had a hatte, a myst-hakel³ huge.
Brokes byled and breke bi bonkkes aboute,
Schyre schaterande on schores, ther thay doun schowved.

One variation is that on this occasion Gawain is accompanied by a guide—the guide provided by his host—and knows that the Green Chapel is at hand. As they draw near the place this guide warns Gawain of the peril and proposes a way of escape. It may be that the guide is well-meaning, or it may be that he, too, is in league with his master. (In a number of romances the Antagonist himself in disguise acts as guide.) But whether or not deliberately engineered this is certainly yet another test, a test that Gawain at once shows there is no danger of his failing in; he will go on, though courteously he thanks the fellow for his apparently friendly but dishonourable counsel. The guide rides off, leaving Gawain to go on alone.

Just as no event ever turns out to be exactly as one had expected it, but comes always with the shock of a difference, so the Green Chapel turns out to be quite different. It is not a chapel at all; it is 'nobot an olde cave'.

And ouergrowen with gresse in glodes aywhere,
And al was holwe inwith, nobot an olde cave.

Its being a cave—that immemorial symbol and sacred place—is more richly significant than if it had been a chapel. Gawain is here at the hidden, secret source of life. If the cave is the entrance to the underworld, that entrance is in our poem realized not as the devourer of life but as the source of life, the entrance through which life *returns* to the earth. The place—it is essentially an experience of a place—is felt as holy, enchanted, taboo; it is *sacer*. Possibly in the wilder regions of Britain (as J. L. Weston thinks[4]) such ancient shrines of an earlier worship were still places of worship—certainly of veneration or fear—as late as the fourteenth

---

¹ drizzled (cf. muggy).   ² melted (i.e. dissolved into rain).   ³ mist-cloak.
⁴ *From Ritual to Romance*, XIII, The Perilous Chapel, e.g. p. 173.

century. The cave (possibly a tumulus or barrow) is certainly more appropriate than a Christian chapel to that wild mountain universe, to unreclaimed, unredeemed nature.

The equivocal attitude of the medieval Church to nature seems to be reflected in Sir Gawain's attitude. He feels—it is the ancient feeling—that the place is *sacer,* but he feels not simply that; he is not at all sure how to take it, how as a Christian knight he *ought* to take it. The Church's attempt to outlaw the old cults was (we know) what turned them into black magic and devil worship;[1] in Sir Gawain's first reaction to the place we see reflected the kind of attitude that by outlawing the surviving remnants of a nature cult produced witchcraft. Perhaps (Sir Gawain thinks) the cave is the Devil's kirk.

> *Here myght aboute mydnyght*
> *The dele his matynnes telle!*

Perhaps the Green Man is after all the Devil (perhaps nature is the Devil!) who has lured him there in order to destroy him.

> '*This oritore is ugly,*[2] *with erbes ouergrowen;*
> *Wel bisemes the wyghe wruxled*[3] *in grene*
> *Dele here his devocioun on the develes wyse.*
> *Now I fele hit is the fende, in my fyve wyttes,*
> *That has stoken me*[4] *this steven to strye*[5] *me here.*
> *This is a chapel of meschaunce, that chekke*[6] *hit bytyde!*
> *Hit is the corsedest kyrk that ever I com inne!*'

Gawain's fears are totally disproved by the event. The experience that immediately follows is of a sudden, overwhelming release of life-energies, as of some sudden thaw in which the pent-up, gigantic life beneath the frozen earth bursts free or as of thunder among the mountains; suggestions of rushing water and wind powerfully contribute to the exhilaration of the experience.

---

[1] Recently Christianized peoples could not at once imagine their old gods as not existing; the gods persisted, though outlawed by the Christian Church and turned into devils. The identification of the Green Man with the genial outlaw Robin Hood is significant of the viewpoint contrary to the official ecclesiastical one.

[2] forbidding, terrifying.   [3] changed into . . .   [4] imposed on me.
[5] destroy.   [6] ill-luck (cf. checkmate).

> *Thene herde he of that hyghe hil, in a harde roche*
> *Biyonde the broke, in a bonk, a wonder breme[1] noyse.*
> *Quat! hit clatered in the clyff, as hit cleve schulde,*
> *As one upon a gryndelston hade grounden a sythe.*
> *What! hit wharred and whette, as water at a mulne;*
> *What! hit rusched and ronge, rawthe to here.*

It is the Green Man sharpening his axe. Presently he comes

> *Whyrlande out of a wro[2] wyth a felle weppen,*
> *A Denes ax newe dyght, the dynt with to yelde*

and leaps hugely across the intervening stream. The chief actors in the poem—essentially the hero and the god, man and nature—now again, as in the First Fit, confront each other. The final test is executed by the Green Man with grim humour—two feints and a blow that merely grazes the skin, shedding a few symbolic drops of blood on the snow. For the Green Man turns out not to be such a bad fellow after all. He could have destroyed Gawain, but does not. In effect, therefore, he gives Gawain his life; he does not, as he so easily could, take it away, though it remains certain that if Gawain had failed in the tests with the lady he would have forfeited his life. (The three aims with the axe appear to correspond to the three encounters with the lady down to some of the details of Gawain's reactions.) Gawain's life is really in the balance and there is uncertainty, suspense while he is in the Green Knight's power. The graze is for his fault in accepting and concealing the Green Girdle.

> *Bot for ye lufed your lyf; the lasse I yow blame.*

There follows immediately an impression as of a re-birth.

> *And when the burne segh the blode blenk on the snawe,*
> *He sprit forth spenne-fote[3] more than a spere lenthe,*
> *Hent heterly[4] his helme, and on his hed cast,*
> *Schot with his schulderes his fayre schelde under,*

---

[1] fierce.   [2] nook.
[3] i.e. he sprang from his kneeling position, kicking out with his feet.
[4] seized vigorously.

Sir Gawayne and the Grene Knight

Braydes out a bryght sworde, and bremely he spekes—
Never syn that he was burne borne of his moder
Was he never in this worlde wyghe half so blythe.

What is achieved seems to be a kind of adjustment, if not reconciliation[1], between man and nature, between the human and the
other than human. In a more limited sense, the courtly order has
been put to the test of nature. As a consequence Gawain recognizes his own nature, knows himself.

The Christian significance of the poem is that Gawain emerges
from the whole succession of tests—having its basis, possibly, in
an account of an initiation ceremony—as nearly the perfection of
Christian knighthood as that condition is humanly attainable. For
though he has failed in minor respects—he accepted and concealed
the Green Girdle, he shrank a little at the first descent of the axe—
he could not humanly be more nearly the perfect Christian knight
than he is; he is human, and human nature (according to Christian
doctrine) is imperfect, only perfectible through grace. But Gawain
is now sensitively conscious of his human imperfection and, therefore, does not fail in the essential Christian virtue of humility.
In this respect the Gawain of our poem—who belongs to 'the
noblest fellowship of Christian knights'—differs from the pre-
Christian hero. He wears the Green Girdle as a garment of
penitence.

Once we begin to realize how closely worked is the art of the
poem, how complex the poem is in its significances as a work of
art, it should be possible to avoid the error of regarding it simply as
a recorded myth, the record of the story of a ritual. 'Myth is the
new intellectual fashion', as an American reviewer of some recent
books about myth and literature puts it.[2] The recent tendency in

---

[1] 'In the final development of the story [the Grail story] the Pathos is shared alike
by the representative of the Vegetation Spirit and the Healer, whose task involves a
period of stern testing and probation.' (*From Ritual to Romance*, p. 104.)

The Green Man and Gawain of the first fit again appear in some respects to
have changed places in the last fit. Gawain withstanding the blow is compared to
a 'stubbe' ... 'That ratheled is in roché grounde with rotes a hundreth.'

[2] Stanley Hyman, 'Myth, Ritual and Nonsense', *The Kenyon Review*, summer,
1949.

criticism, under the influence of anthropology, to interpret a work
of art too simply by disinterring its buried myth and leaving it at
that, seems to involve an unhappy confusion between myth and
art. Unless we can see very exactly the relation between the myth
and the art in the case of each individual work of literary art (where
there is a myth *there* at all), the 'anthropological approach' to
literature becomes only the latest technique for irrelevance. To discuss a poem as though it were a myth is only another way of
evading the poem.

The same reviewer helpfully sums up what appear to be the
findings at the stage at present reached, of the school of anthropologists who have explored the ritual theory of myth: 'Myth is
neither a record of historical fact nor an explanation of nature. It is
the spoken correlative of a ritual, the story which the rite enacts or
once enacted.' The poet of *Sir Gawayne and the Grene Knight* was
evidently a very conscious artist, conscious of what he wanted to
do and of what he was doing. It seems possible that he had consciously in mind—may have himself witnessed—the ritual the
story of which underlies the poem. This underlying ritual and the
poet's belief in its value as myth is what gives the poem its life. But
it is not what has made the poem a complex work of art and not
simply a record of a ritual. A conscious artist, the poet *begins* from
a myth; he *ends* with the poem we have.

The poem—the work of a highly conscious and sophisticated
artist—implies also a conscious and sophisticated audience. If we
required evidence that there existed in England in the fourteenth
century not only a vivid local life but—in what we regard as a remote locality—a higher degree of *civilization* than exists anywhere,
perhaps, in the twentieth century we need only point to this poem.
Thoroughly *local* as the poem is there is nothing provincial in a
limiting sense about it; it is, in the best sense, sophisticated. It implies, as Shakespeare does, a highly refined and complex literary
art, which engages at all levels, thus testifying to the existence of a
truly integrated public, trained to respond.

The miracle of the poem is indeed that it has so consciously held
and made the best of such diverse worlds, composed these without
loss of diversity or substance in the very inclusive harmony of a

superb work of art—a firmly rooted, multiple-branched, gnarled but symmetrical northern oak. It should be as well known to us as Eliot's *Waste Land*; it equally belongs to the great English tradition. Its imagery and symbolism have also underlying affinities that are certainly not accidental with the characteristically Shakespearian.

'THE AWNTYRS OF ARTHURE
AT THE TERNE WATHELYN'—
FIRST EPISODE

The poem which is in some ways most akin to *Sir Gawayne and the Grene Knight* is *The Awntyrs of Arthure at the Terne Wathelyn*. Not only does it come from the same region of England at about the same time, but the texture of the poetry is closer to that master-piece than to any other extant poem of the same alliterative school. The masterly verse—the alliterative lines building up into elaborate rhyming stanza-structures in what seems a splendidly easy and un-forced art—is comparable to that of *Sir Gawayne and the Grene Knight*; so also is the exuberant and often vivid imagery and the generous creativeness issuing in large-scale massive effects, scenes and situations, movements and activities in which, as 'wonders' or 'marvels', the human and the unhuman aspects of life are spectacularly opposed. *The Awntyrs*, then, is almost as magnificent poetry, and poetry of much the same kind, as *Sir Gawayne and the Grene Knight*; but because of its incompleteness as a poem it cannot be placed so high in the scale as the latter. It remains a remarkable fragment of the same kind of poetic art, but a fragment only. It consists, as it stands, of two episodes which have not been made into an inclusive whole. The first of these episodes is the more striking of the two. It has some noticeable affinities in theme and characteristics with the *Parlement of the Thre Ages*, as well as with *Sir Gawayne and the Grene Knight*, and even with parts of the Towneley Cycle Play of the *Last Judgment*. The Pride of Life is confronted with its opposite, an image of death and after-death.

The poem opens with a dazzling and massive impression of the Pride of Life, a glowing hunting-scene comparable with those in *Sir Gawayne and the Grene Knight* and *The Parlement of the Thre Ages*. Arthur and his 'erles' ride out from the Court at Carlisle into the forest to hunt; Dame Gayenour (Guinevere) the Queen rides with Gawane at her side—like that other pair, Dido and Aeneas, on the great hunting occasion which also is interrupted by a storm. The buoyant rhythmic movement expresses the joyous, free, onward sweep of the riders. The tone is one of spring-like gaiety, carefree and careless. Visually, Gawane is a gay figure in green, and Dame Gayenour is a glittering jewelled figure decked with rubies, sapphires and ribbons.

> *Thus to the wode are thay wente, the wlonkaste*[1] *in wedys,*
> > *Bothe the Kynge, and the Qwene,*
> > *And all the doghety by dene,*[2]
> > *Schir Gawane gayeste one grene,*
> *Dame Gayenour he ledis.*

> *And thus Schir Gawane the gay, dame Gayenour he ledis,*
> *In a gletterande gyse, that glemet full gaye . . .*
> > *One a muyle als the milke,*
> *Gayely scho glydis.*

(The short lines at the end of each stanza speed up the movement, and the frequent repetition of the final phrase of a stanza in the first of the following one links them together, often with some felicitous effect.)

Though Gayenour might have been mistaken for the Elfin or Summer Queen, she is (as we discover) human enough; her flesh is frail human flesh, and she is Pride that is about to be taught a lesson by means of a grisly visible *exemplum*. Gawane and she ride away by themselves alone until, finally, she alights near a laurel tree.

> *He ledde that lady so lange by these landes sydys,*
> *Sythen so neir a lorere scho lyghte lawe by a felle.*

As we have seen, it is always, in these tales, dangerous to rest under a tree; one is peculiarly liable to come under the influence of the supernatural there.

At the same time as Gawane and Gayenour are dallying under the laurel tree, Arthur and his Erles are hunting the deer and the

---

[1] loveliest, most splendid.   [2] together.

boar. Of course, they are hunting because they have to be got out of the way; but, further, it is as if there were some underlying con‚ nexion between the deer and boar slaying and the vision or what‚ ever it is that happens to the solitary pair.

> *They questys and quellys*[1]
> *By frythis and fellis,*
> *The dere in the dellys,*
> *Thei droupen and dare.*[2]

> *Alle darkis the dere in the dim schowys,*
> *And for drede of the dede drowpys the daa,*
> *And by the stremys so strange, that swythly swoghes,*[3]
> *Thay wery the wilde swyne, and wyrkkis tham waa;*
> *Thay hunte and halowes, in hurstis and huwes,*[4]
> *And till thaire riste, raches*[5] *relyes on thaire raye;*[6]
> *Thay gafe to no gamen no grythe,*[7] *that one grownde growes,*
> *Grehundis in the green greves full gladly gan gaa.*

When the horn blows the recall they all seek the king again—all except Gawane.

> *Hy levys with dame Gaynoure in those greves grene:*
> *Undir a lorere scho laye, that lady so smalle.*

Indeed, as far as Gawane and Gaynoure are concerned, the blow‚ ing of the horn, unheeded by them, seems to be the signal for the extraordinary event, the 'awntyr'—as, when the horn sounds again later, it seems to dispel that event.

> *Faste byfore undrone,*[8] *this ferly gan falle.*

There is a change—a change in the key of the poem—intro‚ duced by a sudden storm. There is darkness in daytime, winter in summer; and youth and life in their splendour are confronted by age, death and the terrors of hell.

> *The daye woxe als dirke,*
> *Als it were mydnyghte mirke.*

---

[1] kill. [2] cower, lie still. [3] flow swiftly with rushing sound.
[4] woods and hills. [5] hounds. [6] array? [7] peace, respite.
[8] before noon (originally, 'mid‚morning').

Gawane and Gayenoure (again like Aeneas and Dido in the famous storm) seek shelter from the storm of sleet and snow that is so unexpected and portentous when woods are green.

> *Thay rane fast to the roches, for reddoure[1] of the rayne,*
> *For the slete and the snawe, that snappede[2] tham so snelle.*

The storm is associated with something that rises out of the lake (the Tarn Wadling, among the Cumberland hills). It is as if the storm itself has arisen out of that water[3] as a prelude to the grisly ghost, in the 'lyknes of Lucyfere', that now rises like an exhalation from the storm and the lake. The mere-dweller, reptile-monster or otherworld inhabitant of the lake, as (like Grendel's mother) it would have been in the old Northern poetry, is in our poem a soul in torment. If the lake is not a lake of Hell, it is at least an entrance to Hell or Purgatory, since a soul suffering the pains of Hell or Purgatory now issues from it.

> *Thare come a lawe[4] one the loughe, in lede[5] is noght to layne,[6]*
> *In the lyknes of Lucyfere, lauyst in helle,*
> *And glyddis to dame Gaynoure, the gatis[7] full gayne,*
> *Yolland ful yamyrly,[8] with a many lowde yelle;*
>   *It yellede, it yamede[9] with vengeance full wete;*
>   *And said, aftre syghande full sare,*
>   *'I bann the body that me bare,*
>   *Allas! now kyndyls my kare,*
>   *I gloppyn[10] and I grete!'*

> *Thane gloppynde and grett dame Gaynoure the gay . . .*

Gawane comforts the Queen, with knightly considerateness, by explaining what has happened as an eclipse of the sun.

> *It is the clippus of the sune I herde a clerke saye.*

It is at any rate a portentous and, as it turns out, prophetic event

---

[1] violence.   [2] nipped.
[3] Cf. the storm-raising fountain of *Iwain and Gawain* and other romances.
[4] flame.   [5] language.   [6] conceal, deny.   [7] ways, paths.
[8] yelling dolefully, lamentably.   [9] lamented.   [10] wail.

such as might well have been associated with an eclipse of the sun.[1] Gaynoure laments that all the other knights of Arthur have deserted her on what she now supposes to be her death-day.

> *That thus me hase lefte in this erthe at my dede daye,*
> *With the gryselyeste gaste, that ever herde I grete!*

But Gawane, as the hero whose task it is to contend with the un-known and to be the spokesman of humankind, boldly undertakes to speak with the spirit (we may be reminded of Hamlet's 'I'll speak to it').

> *I salle speke with yone sprete,*
> *In yone wayes so wete.*

The full horror of the appearance is now visible at close quarters as a *body* risen from the grave, the body of what was a woman. The poetry here is similar in imagery and effect to the Lazarus episode in the Towneley Cycle—and also in some respects to such ballads as *The Wife of Usher's Well* and *The Lyke-Wake Dirge*.

> *Bare was hir body, and blake to the bane,*
> *Alle by claggede in claye, un-comlyly clede:*
> *It weryit, it wayemettede, lyke a Woman . . .*
> > *One the chefe of the cholle,[2]*
> > *A tade pykit one hir polle,*
> > *Hir eghne ware holkede full holle,*
> > *Glowand als gledis.*

It is as if a candle in a hollow skull were glowing balefully through the eye-sockets; the suggestion is that it is an infernal or subterra-nean fire from the bottom of the lake—or whatever is the habitat of the ghost—that is burning in those hollow eyes. The hero with drawn sword threatens—but makes no visible impression on—'the body'; contrastingly, the effect of the 'body' on the beasts and birds is the *natural* one.

---

[1] Cf. in *King Lear*, Gloucester's 'These late eclipses in the sun and moon portend no good to us . . . love cools, friendship falls off, brothers divide: in cities, mutinies, in countries, discord; in palaces, treason; and the bond crackt 'twixt son and father . . . there's son against father: the king falls from bias of nature; there's father against child. We have seen the best of our time: machinations, hollowness, treachery, and all ruinous disorders, follow us disquietly to our graves.'

[2] top of the jowl.

> *The hundes hye to the hillys and ther hedus hydus*
> *The grewhundes were agayste, for that grym bere,*[1]
> *The birdes on the bewes,*
> *That one that gaste gewes,*[2]
> *Thay scryken in the clewes,*[3]
> *That herdus myghten hom here.*

Gawane, calling on Christ Crucified to save us from sin, con-
jures the ghost to say why she 'walkes thies woddis with inn'. She
answers:

> *I was of fegure, and of flesche, the fayereste of alle,*
> *Christenede and krysmede,*[4] *with kynges in my kyn:*
> *I hafe kynges in my kyn, knawen for kyde full kene,*
> *God hase sent me this grace,*
> *To dre my paynes in this place,*
> *And now am I commen a passe,*
> *To speke with youre Qwene.*

It is none other than the ghost of Gaynoure's mother, the ghost of the
old Queen come as a grisly warning to its daughter and successor.[5]
It was once as Gaynoure is now, and is what Gaynoure will
become—unless she mends her life. So the young woman is confronted with the old, the living with the dead, the splendour of life
with the horror of death. Each is confronted with herself in the
other—the daughter as she will be, and the mother as she once
was.

> *Qwene was I whilome, wele bryghtere of browes*
> *Than Beryke or Brangwayne, the byrdis so balde;*
> *Of any games or gudis, that one the grownde growes,*
> *Wele grettere than Gaynoure of garsomes*[6] *and of golde,*
> *Of pales, of powndis, of parkis, of plewes,*[7]
> *Of tounes, of towris, of tresoures un-tolde . . .*
> > *Now gyffe me anes a syghte*
> > *Of Gayenour the gaye.*

---

[1] tumult.   [2] look.   [3] cliffs.   [4] chrysomed.

[5] There are suggestions in other romances that Guinevere was of faery origin;
but in this poem the supernatural mother from being a faery, a lady of the lake, if
she ever was, has become a ghost, a soul in torment.

[6] treasures.   [7] plough-lands?

In such ghastly circumstances do mother and daughter meet; so changed out of recognition is the mother that the effect of the familiar greeting 'Welcome, Waynoure' (as, at the end of the interview, 'Hafe gude daye, dame Gaynoure') is one of grim irony. She who was redder than the rose in the rain now dwells with Lucifer in the depth of the lake.

> *Thus am I lyke to Lucefere, takis witnes by mee*
> *For all youre fresche favoure,*
> *Now meyse¹ one this mirroure,*
> *For bothe Kynge and Emperoure,*
> *Thus sall ye bee.*

She warns Gayenour—perhaps seeking to save her daughter from becoming as she is—and in warning Gayenour she warns everyman to beware of pride and to have pity on the poor.

> *When thou es richely arrayed, and rydes in a rowte,*
> *Hafe than peté, and mynd one the pore, for thu arte of powere.*
> *Beryns and byrdis are besye the abowte,*
> *When thi body is bawmede, and broghte appone bere,*
> *Than will thay leve the lyghtely, that nowe will lowte,*
> *And than helpes the no thynge, bot halye prayere:*
> *The prayere of the pore, purchases the from helle,*
> *Of thase that yellis at the gate . . .*

The necessity of caring for the poor, if the soul is to be saved from Hell, is insisted upon in this dialogue (as it is, still more terrifyingly, in *The Lyke-Wake Dirge*). In *King Lear* also, it will be remembered, there is the same traditional Christian idea, more profoundly understood; in the midst of Lear's purgatorial *agon* on the heath, one of the first signs of his re-birth or redemption, of his beginning to know himself, is when he takes thought for others besides himself, when he takes thought for the poor.[2] At her death hour, Gayenour too will be deserted by all who now surround her—as Everyman is, by all except his Good Deed, and as Lear the

---

¹ muse.
² Cf. the passages on the poor in *Piers Plowman*, notably in Passus VI, VII, XIV (B-text).

King also is gradually stripped to naked man. Then the prayers of the poor (like Everyman's Good Deed) may intercede for her soul and alone can save it from Hell. The mother—perhaps with a touch of the envy the dead have sometimes been supposed to feel for the living—compares her own present lot with her daughter's, once her own; the fawning courtiers correspond now, in her present case, to pursuing fiends.

> *There folowes me a ferde[1] of fendis full fell:*
> *Thay harle[2] me unhendely,[3] and hewys me one hyghte.*

Gayenour has pity for the soul—or 'body'—in torment, her mother, though unrecognizable, and is ready to put the machinery of the Church in motion to engineer her release.

> *Gyff matyns or messes myghte oghte menden thi mysse,*
> *Or any mobylls[4] on molde, my myrthis ware the mare;*
> *Or bedis of bechopes myghte brynge the to blysse;*
> *Or conventis in cloysters myghte kere the of care.*

The poem now takes the form of a question-and-answer dialogue in which there emerges more distinctly the idea that Gayenour has the power, by seeing to the performance of the proper religious rites, to release her mother's soul from Purgatory. The dead have their dues and claims, and may suffer if neglected. Thus, if the mother has performed a service to her daughter in being herself a warning to her, the daughter may in her turn perform a kindly service to her mother.

Gayenour *sees* the hell-hounds[5] (in the poetry an echo of the hunt of the poem's opening movement) seeking to devour her mother.

> *Bot of thase balefull bestis, that one thi body bytys,*
> *All blendis my blode, thi blee es soo blake.*

The beasts appear to correspond to the paramours and passions of the ghost's earthly days—her 'days of nature'—judging from the ghost's answer:

---

[1] crowd, throng. [2] hurl, drag. [3] discourteously, ungently. [4] property.
[5] Cf. the shapes like hounds which Aeneas meets near the entrance to the Underworld—visaeque canes ululare per umbram. *Aeneid* VI, 257.

This es it to luffe paramoures, and lustys, and litys,[1]
That gerse me lyghte and lenge so lawe in this lake.

She explains precisely what is needful to be done to release her.

Were thritty trentalls[2] *done,*
By twyxen undrone and none,
My saule were salvede full sone.

There is at this point a beautiful appeal to Christ and His Mother in the traditional English medieval phrasing, and again the reminder:

Gyffe nowe fast of thy gude,
To folke that fayles the fude,
Whylls that thou erte here.

The question-and-answer dialogue has risen to a more spiritual plane—not unlike that between father and daughter in *Pearl*. Gayenour asks what most grieves God; the answer is: Pride, an answer which goes home to the questioner, a proud rider as seen in the poem's opening. Finally Gayenour asks what is needful for salvation; her own personal salvation she now recognizes is at stake as well as her mother's. The ghost answers—

Mekenesse and mercy, scho saide, tho are the moste,
Hafe peté on the pore, thane plesys thou owre Kynge.

Having thus answered the essential question, the ghost refuses to be questioned more on such spiritual matters; Gayenour now knows all that it is needful for her, a mortal woman, to know.

It is then Gawane's turn again to address the apparition. He asks how such as himself, a member of the military class, the class of those who make conquests and win wealth and honour by force and often against right, shall be judged.

How sall we fare, said the freke,[3] *that fowndis so fyghte,*
That ofte foundis the folkes, in fele[4] *kyngis landis;*
That riche rewmes over rynnes agaynes the ryghte,
And wynnes wirchippis and welthis by wyghtenes[5] *of handis.*

---

[1] vices. [2] masses for the dead. [3] man. [4] many. [5] strength.

This is a new attitude to the old ideal—the ideal of the old heroic poetry—of the warrior king and his followers winning lands, wealth and honour by war. Surprisingly, this new attitude of doubt is here expressed by the hero himself, a Gawane morally troubled, it seems; he is at the point of change from the pagan hero to the Christian knight. The ghost's answer is as applicable to Edward III as to Arthur—and is, perhaps, intended by the poet to be so.

> *Yowre Kynge es to covetous, I tell the, Schir knyghte . . .*
> *Fraunce hafe ye frely with your fyghte wonnen . . .*

The ghost here assumes the prophetic role—joins the awful company of prophetic ghosts—and prophesies Arthur's downfall; the image is that of Fortune's Wheel, the theme Mutability and the Fall of Princes, and the tone that of *contemptus mundi*. Finally, she prophesies Arthur's last battle, the destruction of the noble fellowship of the Round Table, and the death of Gawane himself. There is the implication that these oncoming events are nemesis, a just retribution for guilt—'yowre Kynge es to covetous'.

> *And al the rial rowte of the Rounde Tabille*
> *Thei shullen dye on a day, the doughty be dene[1] . . .*
> > *In kyng Arthures haulle*
> > *The childe plays hym at the balle*
> > *That sall owttraye[2] yow alle,*
> *Full derfely[3] a daye.*

Having cast these terrible foreshadowings of doom, the ghost bids Gayenour good day.

> *Hafe gude daye, dame Gaynoure, and Gawane the gude;*
> *I hafe no langare tyme, mo tales to telle,*
> *For I mun wende one my waye, thorowte this wode . . .*
> > *And thus with a grysely grete*
> > *The gaste awaye glydis.*

It might have been a vapour, a mist that had temporarily risen from the lake. As the ghost glides away 'with a grysely grete', the

---

[1] together. [2] destroy. [3] powerfully.

sun shines out, the King blows his horn. Life recovers, after the warning vision of death in the temporary night, and resumes its normal round.

> *The prynces prowdeste in palle,*
> *Dame Gaynoure, and alle,*
> *Wente to Rendolfe sett haulle*
> *To thaire sopere.*

'WYNNERE AND WASTOURE'
AND
'THE PARLEMENT OF
THE THRE AGES'

§ 1

The indications are that *Wynnere and Wastoure* was composed in (or about) 1352; if so it comes at the beginning of what is known as the alliterative 'revival' of the fourteenth century. The accuracy of speaking thus of a 'revival' may be doubted even from a consideration of this poem alone, although it may well be its earliest surviving example. *Wynnere and Wastoure* does not, any more than any other of the surviving alliterative poems of the fourteenth century, read like the production of a self-conscious archaic revival. Far from reading like an effort, however successful, to reconstitute what by that time was felt to be an archaic mode, the poem has as the living core of its interest, the nerve-centre of its 'technique', the concern of the poet with a contemporary problem of state-craft and social and moral behaviour. The problem is presented with such masterly ease and vigour in the traditional alliterative mode that we feel the poet could have had no doubt that this mode was still simply the accepted and natural contemporary one both for himself and his audience.

The Parlement of the Thre Ages, a Midland alliterative poem which possibly preceded *Wynnere and Wastoure,* may be associated with the latter not merely because these two poems happen to have been preserved on the same fifteenth-century MS, but because they have certain striking features in common. In both poems, but particularly in *Wynnere and Wastoure,* we may observe the tradition in which *Piers Plowman* belongs. At the same time we may recognize certain features in these poems which they have in common with *Sir Gawayne and the Grene Knight,* and other Midland or

North/West Midland alliterative poems that have chanced to be preserved.

The fact that these poems of the alliterative 'revival' have sur/vived virtually by accident on unique MSS—apart from the exceptional case of *Piers Plowman*—should make us hesitate to assume that there had been no such poetry immediately before them. Because no such poetry has survived we should not assume that no such poetry was composed.[1]

Wynnere and Wastoure is so maturely accomplished that it cannot have been an isolated and fortuitous phenomenon. It implies the existence not only of a whole social order with an individuality of its own, a unique human community, but also a tradition of poetic art and an audience trained to listen to poetry in that tradi/tion. *Wynnere and Wastoure* is thus itself the evidence—and this is confirmed by each one of these fourteenth/century alliterative poems that has survived—that there had long been, and still was, a living and flourishing tradition, in the English of the Midland regions, of such poetry as it is itself. The survival of even one such poem makes nonsense of much of the literary and social history of medieval England as we have too easily accepted it. The poem— if we respond to it—is sufficient in itself to force us to revise our conventional ideas of the civilization of medieval England.

Even when the poet laments (as he does in his prologue) that in these degenerate times the true poets or makers are being sup/planted in the favour of the lords by inexperienced and unskilled minstrels, it is evident that he is proudly conscious of belonging to a succession of poets who for generations were accustomed to command the attention of noble audiences.

> *Whylome were lordes in londe that loved in thaire hertis*
> *To here makers of myrthes, that matirs couthe fynde,*
> *Wyse wordes with/inn, that writen were never*
> *Ne redde in no romance that ever renke[2] herde.*

[1] If it had not been for a few enthusiasts who began the work of collecting the folk/ballads, we should not now know of even the existence of the majority of our best ballads. The whole vast folk/ballad literature might by now have perished almost without a trace.

[2] man.

Wynnere and Wastoure

Bot now a childe appon chere, with-owtten chyn wedys,
That never wroghte thurgh witt three wordes to-gedire,
Fro[1] he can jangle als a jaye, and japes can telle,
He schall be levede[2] and lovede and lett[3] of a while
Wele more than the man that makes hym-selven.

Further, it is evident from *Wynnere and Wastoure* that a poem in this tradition could be both regional in character and, at the same time, a national poem. The Midland poet could evidently feel that he might count in the conduct of affairs in the kingdom, that he might expect to be listened to by those who were responsible for the government. He handles with complete confidence, as a poet, a delicate social and economic problem that was the concern and responsibility of the King himself. The implication seems strong, therefore, that the poem was intended to be heeded by the King himself and his counsellors. If so, the poet was addressing (in the reign of Edward III) as noble an audience as Chaucer addressed so differently only a generation later (in the reign of Richard II principally). In English it was rather the Chaucerian modes which were, it would seem, the innovations. *Wynnere and Wastoure* and its successors prove at least that in Chaucer's England there flourished a whole conservative school of alliterative poetry in the Midland regions, having an individuality of its own quite distinct from that of Chaucer's poetry. They prove that in a region remote from, yet evidently in touch with, the capital there were tradition-ally rooted poets of great accomplishment—certain of responsive audiences that were different from those of the capital and court. So it was, perhaps, throughout medieval Europe.

Piers Plowman, among the successors of *Wynnere and Wastoure*, has equally the character of a national poem, though it hardly im-plies an audience of the nobles but makes its appeal more broadly to humbler—as well as to instructed—folk. Midland poems though they are, *Piers Plowman* and *Wynnere and Wastoure* both show their poets' familiarity with London; and there seems every reason to suppose that they were current there. The evidence of the MSS certainly indicates that *Piers Plowman* was known in widely

---

[1] as soon as, because.   [2] believed.   [3] esteemed.

different parts of the country (and, the MSS suggest, in widely different forms). It would be unwise, therefore, to assume that *Wynnere and Wastoure* was known only in the Midlands.

But it is with *Sir Gawayne and the Grene Knight* (rather than with *Piers Plowman* which is a special case) that *Wynnere and Wastoure* and *The Parlement of the Thre Ages* take their places as the last English masterpieces of the oral tradition of early northern European poetry. These poems are not the less characteristically oral poetry because they have been written down. Very possibly we have no predecessors of these poems from the thirteenth cen-tury[1] simply because these predecessors were never written down. The assumption that there were no such poems seems more un-reasonable than the assumption that there were, and that either they were not written down or—if some at least were—the MSS have not survived (as should not be surprising). There is ample evidence not only that in the early communities poetry was oral but that there was a class of men, highly honoured by nobles and kings for their skill and insight, whose whole occupation in life was poetry, and who composed and recited long poems which they did not write down and many of which were never written down.[2]

Our poems are in their very nature oral poetry; and oral poetry, as B. S. Phillpotts (in *Edda and Saga*) has stressed, was a social function. Oral poetry could not be enjoyed by the individual alone. He had to join a company if he wished to listen to a poem. The poet himself had to find a company before he could practise his art by reciting a poem; for the role of the poet and the reciter was, at this stage, one. There was thus an immediate relationship —indeed collaboration—between the poet and his audience, as there was between Shakespeare and his theatre audience. There was no need for the literary critical reviews of modern times; the audience could tell the poet directly what they thought of the

[1] The existence of the live tradition in the thirteenth century is witnessed by both *King Horn* (South Midland, *c.* 1225) and *Havelok the Dane* (North-east Midland, *c.* 1285).

[2] The reader may be referred to Professor Chadwick's note 'On the Heroic Poetry of the Slavonic Peoples' in *The Heroic Age*, and to Chap. III, 'Celtic Story-channels and Story-ways' in Loomis's *Celtic Myth and Arthurian Romance*.

poem, and he could see for himself its effect on his audience. Moreover, though our poems were evidently intended to be listened to by nobles and their ladies, everyone in the great hall down through the various 'degrees' there assembled must have had to listen too. Thus one effect of an oral literature was that it 'brought about a general levelling-up of interests and culture' (B. S. Phillpotts[1] makes this point in regard to the Sagas and the audience in an Icelandic homestead). The audience in the great hall could not have been dissimilar in this respect from the audience in an Elizabethan theatre. So, for this reason also, our poems, aristocratic and sophisticated as they are, have a truly national character.

It would be a mistake to think of the poet simply as an entertainer and these poems as after-dinner entertainment of however fine a quality. Whether or not recitals of poetry originated as ritual recitals, the conception of the poet as prophet or seer whose insights require to be attended to even by the king himself is very persistent. The poet of *Wynnere and Wastoure*, and indeed also of *The Parlement of the Thre Ages*, still regards his role as that of the seer. Chaucer would not think of giving himself such airs. This is one of the differences between the conservative alliterative poet and the more modern Chaucerian poet. Visions are what the poet as seer appropriately sees. There was no need for the alliterative poet to borrow the dream-vision convention from *Le Roman de la Rose*. In the Elder Edda, *Völuspa* (Sibyl's Dream) is a prophetic vision of the end of the world.

The old-fashionedness of the poet of *Wynnere and Wastoure*, his belonging to a dying culture, is perhaps what makes him feel the social problem of his contemporary England so acutely. He inherited two contradictory and incompatible ideals. The ideal of the King as a victorious warrior, an open-handed giver of gold, came to him by way of his poetic tradition from the past when the peoples were battling not only for land but for treasure and honour. (It seems a mistake of modern theorists to suppose that peoples have ever been governed by purely economic considerations.) But by the fourteenth century the English people as a whole had settled down to agriculture and trade (merchants were becoming

[1] *Edda and Saga*, VII, pp. 161–2.

influential). War—specifically the French campaigns of Edward III—was beginning to be regarded by many as a ruinous dis‑ turbance. The new settled order required peace, the hard work of all classes and an ideal of thrifty toil. Christianity seemed to sanction this latter ideal, while the Pagan heroic ideal that was still immediate in the poetry sanctioned the former. The scene was further complicated by the Church not practising what it preached. The old‑fashioned poet of *Wynnere and Wastoure* (and Langland follows him in this respect) falls back on satire and dramatizes his perplexities, at the same time offering his vision as guidance in the old high manner.

§ 2

Wynnere and Wastoure and *The Parlement of the Thre Ages* are not, of course, what we call plays; they are not intended for dramatic performance by costumed actors; they are recitative (though the professional minstrel—or the poet himself—in rendering them before an audience, may be assumed to have dramatically animated the dialogues and monologues in which each poem so largely consists). Nevertheless, each poem in its structure and in several of its characteristic features has unmistakable resemblances to a species of drama. It is as if the poet were describing a dramatic performance or pageant play he is in the act of witnessing and were reproducing dialogues and monologues as overheard by him in the act of being spoken by the costumed actors he describes. He represents himself as having luckily, or perhaps magically, been favoured to witness this performance while in a dream or trance. The convention of the dream‑vision (whether or not it was bor‑ rowed by the alliterative poets, as it was by Chaucer, from the French—and it seems unlikely that it was) is here used partly as a device for securing both the detachment of the dramatic pageant and 'the suspension of disbelief' in it. The 'space' within which the imagined events happen is distinctly marked off from the audience's every‑day environment. A landscape and a pageant of costumed actors, as seen by the poet‑spectator in his dream‑vision, are sharply visualized in the poem. There is no dream-like or trance-like quality, no vagueness of enchantment, about the spectacle; it is vision—clarity of intense and ordered visualization —rather than dream. The central episode of both poems is a *flyting* in which the principal figures of the pageant engage, a satiric word-contest and not—as at first seems possible—a physical combat. This dialogue contest, in the contemporary colloquial English of the Midland region, is vigorously realistic within the formal structure of the whole.

We cannot be satisfied to suppose that the fourteenth-century poet personally invented the well-defined basic structure of such a poem any more than he invented the alliterative mode itself. We are bound to inquire how a structural form so reminiscent of that of some species of drama originated or evolved. The explanation that the poet is in fact describing a dramatic pageant he has witnessed—or constructing his poem with the aid of a reminiscence of such a performance—is probably too simple. There were, of course, contemporary pageants, ceremonies and rituals, both among the courtly folk and the village folk; there were such surviving fragments of ancient ritual drama as the predecessors of the Mummers' Play and the Wooing Play (Plough Play), and there were the Mystery Cycles. But it would not be safe to guess, on the existing evidence, that either *Wynnere and Wastoure* or *The Parlement of the Thre Ages* was directly modelled by its poet on any of these contemporary performances, though it might well have been influenced by them. It seems much more likely that the poems and the contemporary dramatic performances belong to traditions that had become independent but had all ultimately (if they could be traced back far enough) a common origin in ancient dramatic ritual. This is not in itself saying very much because it may be that all poetry and all drama has had a common origin in dramatic ritual. There are, however, poems which appear to have retained, in their very structure, more of the features of a ritual origin than others. Our two poems are such that a recollection of what we happen to know about ancient ritual drama seems at once to illuminate their basic structure and to explain why it is so and not otherwise. Our poems no doubt reflect aspects of contemporary pageantry;[1] but that in itself is not sufficient to explain their basic structure. It seems indeed much more likely that our poet (or poets) inherited the basic structure of that kind of poem from the poetic tradition in which he was working, whatever modifications he might himself introduce.

F. M. Cornford in *The Origin of Attic Comedy* and B. S. Phillpotts in *The Elder Edda and the Ancient Scandinavian Drama*, each working in apparently divergent fields, have shown how poetry—both in its dramatic and non-dramatic variations— evolved originally from ancient dramatic rituals. Miss Phillpotts's work is more particularly relevant to the study of poems which belong, as *Wynnere and Wastoure* and *The Parlement of the Thre Ages* do, with the alliterative poetry of northern Europe. By a process of an exact critical analysis of the Elder or Poetic Edda[2] Miss Phill-potts shows that 'the Norwegian Eddic poems bear the unmistak-able stamp of dramatic origin. . . . Yet these poems are not the remains of folk-drama in the modern sense of the word. Modern folk-drama is a degenerate descendant of the ancient religious drama, whereas these poems are the actual shattered remnants of ancient religious drama.' If one turns from reading Miss Phill-potts's book to examine the structure of *Wynnere and Wastoure* or *The Parlement of the Thre Ages* one cannot fail to be struck with the correspondences between that structure and certain features of the ancient ritual drama as she describes it, correspondences too close to be merely fortuitous.

We will at once observe, on the one hand, the pronouncedly cere-monial or ritualistic aspect of both our poems and, on the other, their largely dialogic and monologic character; the realistic collo-quial dialogue develops in both poems within a frame of ballet-like stylized formality. Further, the vividly visualized principal figures undoubtedly resemble, if they are not reminiscent of, the costumed actors—the impersonators of the gods—of ritual drama. Rich cos-

---

[1] 'The Northern muse of the ninth and tenth centuries loved more than any other to dwell on the stately pageant of court life, and had a real gift for reproducing im-pressions of colour and form and movement.' (B. S. Phillpotts, *The Elder Edda and the Ancient Scandinavian Drama.*)

[2] The Codex Regiius MS on which the *Edda* has been preserved has been dated *c.* 1250 but these poems appear to be in a tradition that is much older.

tume was no doubt a feature of contemporary courtly ceremonies, themselves in the tradition of ritual kingship; it is also a characteristic feature of the traditional literature that seems to derive originally from the ancient dramatic rituals, as Lord Raglan (in his convincingly reasoned book *The Hero*) does not fail to note: 'It is a feature of all ritual that great importance is attached to the clothes and ornaments worn by the actors. . . . Whereas in history there is very seldom any mention of what anyone wore, in the traditional narrative detailed descriptions of costume often occur, and this gives us another reason to believe that traditional narratives are accounts of dramatic ritual.'[1] He instances the fact that 'all those who took part in the May Day festivities, even the King, wore Lincoln green, and this ritual costume appears in the ballads'.

Above all, we will take account, in this connexion, of the fact that the central episode of each of our poems is a *flyting*. The *flyting* is, of course, a regular feature of medieval poetry. Much earlier, however, it was a regular feature of the ancient fertility drama in localities as far apart as Scandinavia (as Miss Phillpotts shows) and Greece (as Cornford shows). 'The flyting, the slaying, the love-scene', says Miss Phillpotts,[2] 'are the integral parts of the most widespread drama in the world. . . . It represents the contest of the Old and New Year.' Cornford sees the *agon* of an Aristophanic comedy as a literary development from the flyting match that was the regular preliminary of the combat between the two antagonists in the ritual drama. In this respect, our two poems may be regarded as corresponding to the *agon* of an Aristophanic comedy. To assume that the *flyting*, *estrif* or *debat* was imported into medieval English alliterative poetry from French or Latin is therefore a large assumption, if one remembers how nearly universal the feature has been and that satiric poetry may well have developed from the flyting. There was in fact no need for English alliterative poetry to import the flyting from French or Latin. We may perhaps add that in *Wynnere and Wastoure* and *The Parlement of the Thre Ages* we may observe one of the traditions that converge in the Shakespearian drama.

[1] *The Hero*, XXIII.
[2] *The Elder Edda and the Ancient Scandinavian Drama*, XIV, 144.

§ 3

The melancholy meditation on the degeneracy of the times with which *Wynnere and Wastoure* opens—the sense of the work of creation undone, degree overthrown, the approach of Doomsday —is no doubt itself in accordance with an ancient convention, though in this specific poem evidently too deeply felt and person, ally endorsed to be merely 'conventional'.

> *When .wawes[1] waxen schall wilde, and walles bene doun,*
> *And hares appon herthe,stones schall hurcle in hire fourme,[2]*
> *And eke boyes of no blode, with boste and with pryde,*
> *Schall wedde ladyes in londe, and lede at hir will,*
> *Thene dredfull domesdaye it draweth neghe aftir.*

It is too simple to regard such meditations as exclusively medieval Christian; there is, for example, in *Völuspa* and Snorri Sturluson's *Prose Edda* a sublime impression of the destruction of the world evidently in accordance with ancient Scandinavian mythology. The old Norse vision of society gone to pieces, of social and moral upheaval and shifting of the landmarks which precedes the universal disaster, is indeed unmistakably what recurs here; as it recurs in *Lear* and the other tragic plays of Shakespeare (together with much else that is 'medieval' and pre,medieval). The poet here feels that total ruin will follow on these ominous signs of disturbance of the social order, if he and the king do not do their duty, the poet's duty being to reveal the situation in its true light to the King who is the source of honour and social concord.

In this prologue, too, the poet identifies himself with the view, point of the country gentlemen of the West who distrustfully re, gard the more fashionable South (where the metropolis is) as having a baneful influence on the younger generation; this is cer, tainly in accord with the concluding passage of the whole poem in which we see rich 'passers through' the metropolis become the companions of Waster to their cost. The prologue concludes with the lament that poets are no longer favoured by the lords as they

[1] waves.　　　　　　[2] crouch in their lairs.

once were. The impression is conveyed that the times are such that many grievous problems, social and moral, arise. Among these there is the problem with which the poem will be specifically occupied.

The first fit opens on a summer landscape that contrasts with the broodings and forebodings of the prologue as summer contrasts with winter. From this opening right through the poem the similarities, even in the phrasing, between it and *Piers Plowman* are distinctly noticeable, and we cannot but be convinced that the two poets were working in a common tradition and that, possibly, the later poet was acquainted with the work of the earlier. Both poets are wandering in the West when the 'dream' happens to them; perhaps that is not simply because the West was the country of their origin, but because there were places in the West —shrines of an earlier worship—where sacred associations still lingered. In this much wilder landscape than the enclosed garden of the tradition of *Le Roman de la Rose* the poets wander and fall asleep by a running stream. The trees (to follow *Wynnere and Wastoure*) are the traditionally sacred hawthorn and hazel; and there is God's plenty of all kinds of birds.

> *As I went in the weste, wandrynge myn one,*
> *Bi a bonke of a bourne, bryghte was the sone,*
> *Undir a worthiliche wodde, by a wale¹ medewe;*
> *Fele² floures gan folde ther my fote steppede.*
> *I layde myn hede one ane hill, ane hawthorne be-syde:*
> *The throstills full throly they threped³ to-gedire;*
> *Hipped⁴ up heghwalles⁵ fro heselis tyll othire;*
> *Bernacles with thayre bills one barkes thay roungen;*
> *The jay janglede one heghe, jarmede the foles⁶*
> *The bourne full bremly rane the bankes by-twene;*
> *So ruyde were the roughe stremys, and raughten⁷ so heghe,*
> *That it was neghande nyghte or I nappe myghte,*
> *For dyn of the depe watir, and dadillyng⁸ of fewllys.*

¹ pleasant, delightful.　　　² many.　　　³ sharply contended, debated.
⁴ hopped (hallooed?—see Gollancz's note in his edition).　　⁵ woodpeckers.
⁶ chanted the birds.　　⁷ reached.　　⁸ chattering.

These assemblies of birds and (in other poems) beasts may well have taken their origin, if the ritual theory of myth is correct, in the assemblies of humans impersonating birds and beasts in the fertility rituals.[1] Certainly the birds in *Wynnere and Wastoure*, recurring in different settings throughout the dream, are a diversity of creatures and an aspect of the wealth of high summer and the bounty of nature hoarded by Winner and expended by Waster.

A pageant presents itself to the dreamer; two armies oppose each other in glittering battle array; the scene is a grassy space between hills, a natural stage. The impression certainly is of an impending ritual battle or tournament rather than of an actual historical battle; at a higher elevation, on a cliff suspended over the hostile armies, the dreamer sees a resplendent royal pavilion, a dazzling and dominant feature of the whole spectacle, decked with blue and gold garters. Worked in blue on the pavilion is the motto, in English, of the Order of the Garter (recently founded by Edward III). Conspicuous beside the pavilion there stands a 'wild man'. He *may* be (as Gollancz suggests[2]) the Garter Herald or the Master of the Ceremonies. He has himself no active part to play in the poem. But as a 'wild man'—or a knight impersonating a 'wild man'—he has his place in the symbolism of the poem as the birds have and is, as such, a significant figure of the pageantry.

Within the pavilion a king sits in formal state, crowned and enthroned. It is by now quite clear that the poem is no simple realistic depiction of a battle about to be joined; for a king to sit thus, in formal state, between two hostile armies would show no practical sense. The king is apparently Edward III; but he is here conceived in an essentially ritualistic role. The birds reappear as

[1] 'It seems probable', says Miss Phillpotts (in *The Elder Edda*, Chap. XVI, 'The Chorus'), 'that the Eddic drama, too, had some sort of chorus in animal disguise, and that this chorus sang or made music and probably danced in a ring round the chief performers as in the later dramatic games so widespread in Scandinavia. We can perhaps trace some memory of this chorus in the motley crowd of animals which are present at Baldur's funeral.' Lord Raglan has a chapter in *The Hero* in which he argues, convincingly, that the innumerable traditional tales of talking animals and of shape-shifting arose from the custom of humans wearing animal disguises in dramatic rituals.
[2] in his edition of the poem.

embroidered birds on his costume, expressive of the traditional fertility-god aspect of a king.

> *Bery-brown as his berde, brouderde with fewlys*
> *Fawkons of fyne golde, flakerande¹ with wynges . . .*
> *A brighte belte of ble, broudirde with fewles,*
> *With drakes and with dukkes, daderande² tham semede*
> *For ferdnes³ of fawcons fete, lesse fawked⁴ thay were.*

The actions that follow are essentially ceremonial. The King ceremonially bids a 'beryn'—recognizably the Black Prince—descend to the armies and command them to keep the peace. The Prince arms; his arming is described in detail as having itself a symbolic import; then

> *He brake a braunche in his hande . . .*

The branch corresponds to the holly branch which the Green Knight carries into Arthur's hall as a symbol of peace (cf the golden bough which Aeneas breaks off and bears with him as an offering to Proserpina to safeguard him on his journey through the underworld).

The rest of the first Fit consists of a monologue by the Prince as 'messenger', in which he not only delivers his message, but describes the appearance of the two opposing armies and tells us (the audience) who they are. They are such as could not come together on any actual field of battle; for they are the army of the Winners and the army of the Wasters.

There are folk of France, Lorraine, Lombardy, Spain and various other lands besides England in the army of the Winners, who appear to be chiefly merchants and churchmen. This motley allied army includes the army of the Pope himself and contingents of the monastic orders, each arrayed behind a heraldic banner.⁵ The wasters are said to include many good men-at-arms—knights

---

¹ flapping.   ² trembling (doddering).   ³ fear.   ⁴ pounced upon.
⁵ The banner of the Dominicans, for example, is black with a ball in the middle.

> *Reghte siche as the sone es in the someris tyde,*
> *When moste es the maze one Missomer Even.*

The Augustinian banner is, on the other hand, 'whitte als the whalles bone'.

and squires—members of the feudal nobility, the landed gentry of England.

Each army produces a spokesman. This Winner and this Waster are the two antagonists in the flyting match which is to take the place of an armed combat.

> *I holde hym bot a fole that fightis whils flyttynge may helpe.*

Both acknowledge the King who provides them with food and clothing.

> *Well knowe we the kyng; he clothes us bothe,*
> *And hase us fosterde and fedde this fyve and twenty wyntere.*

The King calls for wine; the poet also (as minstrel) calls upon *his* company to fill up the goblets

> *Full freschely and faste, for here a fitt endes.*

It is the conventional ending of each Fitt—evidently indicating a pause—and corresponds to the curtain at the end of an act in the modern theatre.

But the call to drink in unison at intervals here (as in *Sir Gawayne* and elsewhere) also distinguishes the dramatic poem which had a ritual origin and was intended for recitation to a convivial but attentive company; it distinguishes it from the 'art' poem in the modern sense like *Pearl*, which was not public but private, and from the homiletic poem, like *Cleanness* or *Patience*, which (though meant as improving literature for an audience) had little social function. This drinking at stated intervals is clearly in the tradition of the ritual drinking that had originally been an essential feature of the old religion of the Scandinavian and Teutonic societies and that explains the obstinate practice of heavy drinking in northern Europe against which preachers inveighed throughout the Middle Ages. These drinking rites were retained by the medieval guilds of northern Europe, undoubtedly with some memory of their original solemnity as binding a company together (according to degree) and promoting blessing and luck in a household. The banquet in the great hall had a similar significance, and still has in Shakespeare. Undoubtedly our poet, too, is here play-

ing upon this traditional memory to draw his audience more completely into his poem's action.

Within this formal setting (established in the first Fit) the
flyting match—a duologue occupying the second and third of the
three Fits of the poem—takes place before the King as judge. The
flyting, though satiric, is no mere farcical exchange of rowdy
abuse. The opposing aspects of a problem of the greatest contemporary relevance—the problem of the *right* relation between
economy and expenditure in the kingdom—are presented in the
concreteness of this dramatic duologue, responsibly and intelligently debated and, as a consequence, more clearly apprehended.
The problem is one on which it was indeed for the King himself
to judge; the poem presents the various considerations which
might enable him to come to the right decision.

The advantage of this treatment of such a problem is exactly
that it is a poetic-dramatic treatment. The poem is no mere
political-economic discussion abstracted from the way actual
people live and feel, from any realization of what they live for and
what are the possible ends of living, such abstraction as perhaps
accounts for the unreality of modern political and economic discussions. (It is not true that we attain precision of thought, any
more than we attain precision of feeling, by a process of abstraction, by dissociating discourse from living sensation and images.)
The duologue between Winner and Waster is not one of those
discussions in which it makes no odds what kind of character each
of the opponents is. The opposition is not simply one of ideas but
of persons; two opposing ways of life are balanced against each
other. The flyting has thus the dramatic aspect of a quarrel between two mutually repellent individuals; it springs from a clash
of character and temperament, from a natural antipathy between
two opposite types of personality and not merely from a difference
of opinion. The life of the traditional contest between summer and
winter still underlies and lends some of its force to this new contest which, with its different or more complex significance, has
evolved from the old.[1]

[1] The old summer and winter contest unmistakably underlies the thirteenth-
century English debate poem, *The Owl and the Nightingale*, the Owl being the bird

Nevertheless, though the flyting between Winner and Waster springs from a mutual antagonism, the arguments of these well-matched opponents are as full of sense as they are lively and sharp. Sound reasons, evolved from the concrete experience of daily living, are put forward and tested against each other; the colloquial English of the duologue is saturated with proverbial wisdom, crystallized from a people's experience. We listen to English as it must actually have been spoken; its rhythms are caught up into the rhythms of the poetry. The contemporary life enters with this colloquial English and is vividly present in the imagery. A total wisdom of broad human experience emerges from the poem; the social and economic problem debated is realized as involving real human and moral issues.

Both antagonists appeal not only to economic laws but to the same traditional religious morality; the pattern of the Seven Deadly Sins, familiar from innumerable sermons, underlies their opposing arguments. Winner accuses Waster not only of disregard for worldly prudence and of socially irresponsible neglect of his inherited estate but of sinfully wasteful Pride. Waster recklessly wastes through Pride what Winner prudently labours to win.

> *Alle that I wynn thurgh wit he wastes thurgh pryde;*
> *I gedir, I glene, and he lattys goo sone;*
> *I pryke and I pryne, and he the purse opynes.*
> *Why has this cayteffe no care how men corne sellen?*
> *His londes liggen alle ley,[1] his lomes[2] aren solde,*
> *Downn bene his dowfehowses, drye bene his poles;[3]*
> *The devyll wounder the wele he weldys at home,*
> *Bot hungere and heghe horses and howndes full kene!*

of winter, the Nightingale the bird of summer. In the eighth-century Latin *Conflictus Veris et Hiemis*, Hiems is a Winner in that he enjoys the contemplation of the accumulated wealth of the year, a Waster in that he feasts on it.

> *Sunt mihi divitiae, sunt et convivia laeta . . .*
> *sed placet optatas gazas numerare per arcas*
> *et gaudere cibis simul . . .*

Ver reminds him, however, that spring and summer provide him with the wealth he enjoys.

[1] fallow.   [2] tools.   [3] pools.

Hunger is the inevitable accompaniment of the young lord's pride in keeping horses and hounds.

But Waster, on his side, also accuses Winner of violating the traditional morality. If the sin of the Wasters is Pride, the sin of the Winners is Avarice. When wealth is hoarded the poor suffer, and the soul of the hoarder, unmindful of the poor and over-anxious about worldly possessions, is in danger of Hell.[1]

> *For siche a synn haste thou solde thi soule in-to helle.*

Christ's injunction, 'Lay not up for yourselves treasure upon earth where moth and rust doth corrupt...', is here echoed unexpectedly by one of the Wasters of the world (as it is echoed, with an individual distortion of her own, by the Wife of Bath).

> *When thou haste waltered and went[2] and wakede alle the nyghte,*
> *And iche a wy in this werlde that wonnes the abowte,[3]*
> *And hase werpede[4] thy wyde howses full of wolle sakkes,—*
> *The bemys benden at the rofe, siche bakone there hynges,*
> *Stuffed are sterlynges[5] undere stelen bowndes,[6]—*
> *What scholde worthe[7] of that wele, if no waste come?*
> *Some scholde rote, some ruste, some ratones fede.*
> *Let be thy cramynge of thi kystes, for Cristis lufe of heven!*
> *Late the peple and the pore hafe parte of thi silvere.*

The sense is conveyed of laboriously amassed winter stores and wealth glutting and overloading the house ('the bemys benden at the rofe...').

If Waster can describe Winner as wakeful at night, preoccupied with the accumulation of wealth, Winner in his turn can describe Waster also as 'wakynge in winteres nyghttis' dissipating wealth 'in angarte of pryde'. Waster, the prodigal reveller, devours his substance in riotous living with companions clothed in finery that costs an estate,[8] piles up a tavern bill that can only be paid by

---

[1] This note of concern for the hungry poor has become much more insistent in *Piers Plowman.* (Passus VI, VII, XIV—B-text.)

[2] tossed and turned?   [3] i.e. and all who live near you.   [4] stored.

[5] pounds sterling.   [6] bands.   [7] become.

[8] Cf. 'lordships sold to maintain ladyships' (*The Revenger's Tragedy*). The medieval morality tradition, which is more than simply the tradition of the Morality Plays, persists, as has been remarked, through Elizabethan and Jacobean drama.

selling his land. Winner illustrates his argument with a realistic impression of Waster and his companions in a tavern.[1]

> *Thou ledis renkes in thy rowte wele rychely attyrede;*
> *Some hafe girdills of golde, that more gude coste*
> *Than alle the faire fre londe that ye by-fore haden.*
> *Ye folowe noghte youre fadirs that fosterde yow alle*
> *A kynde herveste to cache, and cornes to wynn,*
> *For the colde wyntter and the kene with clengande frostes,*
> *Sythen dropeles drye in the dede monethe.*[2]
> *And thou wolle to the taverne, by-fore the toune-hede,*
> *Iche beryne redy withe a bolle to blerren thyn eghne,*
> *Hete the*[3] *whatte thou have schalte, and whatt thyn hert lykes,*
> *Wyfe, wedowe, or wenche, that wonnes there aboute.*
> *Then es there bott 'fille in' and 'feche forthe', Florence to schewe,*
> *'Wee-hee', and 'worthe up', wordes ynewe.*
> *Bot when this wele es a-waye, the wyne moste be payede fore:*
> *Than lympis yowe weddis to laye,*[4] *or youre londe selle.*

Waster's prodigality is set against the prudent traditional way of life, gathering in and conserving the harvest as one's fathers did, laying in stores of food and fuel for the winter, careful manage-ment and improvement of one's estate; the lord of the manor has in these respects a responsibility towards his people.

> *Teche thy men for to tille and tynen*[5] *thyn feldes;*
> *Rayse up thi rent-howses, ryme up*[6] *thi yerdes,*
> *Owthere hafe as thou haste done, and hope aftir werse—*
> *That es firste the faylynge of fode, and than the fire aftir,*
> *To brene the alle at a birre,*[7] *for thi bale dedis:*
> *The more colde es to come, als me a clerke tolde.*

Waster's self-justification is the rather unexpected one that with his feasts he feeds the poor, which is pleasing to Christ. His argu-ment in general is that wealth expended benefits everyone, in-

---

[1] We may again compare the scene in *Piers Plowman* when Gluttony on his way to church drops into the ale-house instead. (Passus V.)

[2] Afterwards the dropless drought in the dead months.

[3] proffer you *or* order yourself.   [4] Then you must lay pledges, give bonds.

[5] fence.   [6] enlarge.   [7] at a blast.

cluding the poor, whereas wealth hoarded—hid away from the
sun—benefits no one.

> *With oure festes and oure fare we feden the pore;*
> *It es plesynge to the Prynce that paradyse wroghte;*
> *When Cristes peple hath parte hym payes[1] alle the better*
> *Then here ben hodirde[2] and hidde and happede in cofers,*
> *That it no sonn may see thurgh seven wynttter ones.*

Pope, after describing with distaste the Italianate magnificence of
Timon's villa, his vain extravagance, can add a comment, on a
different note of serious sincerity,

> *Yet hence the poor are clothed, the hungry fed.*

The Popeian ironic wit clearly indicates, however, that Timon
fulfils the divine will in a regulated universe without knowing he
is doing so and, indeed, by his very vices.

> *. . . What his hard heart denies*
> *His charitable vanity supplies.*

What counterpoises Waster's account of himself, supplements and
critically places it—in that respect doing what Pope's irony does—
is simply Winner's satiric account of Waster. But in his reference
to sharing with the poor, who are Christ's people, Waster has
evidently spoken with due sincerity; the medieval Waster is indeed
a simpler, more spontaneous and more human sinner than the
Augustan great lord whose expenditure on his outsize mansion
and gardens is a form of Pride more megalomaniac and less spontaneous than Waster's.

It is appropriate therefore that Waster should accuse Winner of
being no lover of 'mirth', a word which had a richer and fuller
value in medieval English than in modern.

> *. . . thou durste never*
> *Mawngery[3] ne myndale,[4] ne never myrthe lovediste.*
> *A dale[5] aftir thi daye dose the no mare*

---

[1] it pleases him. [2] covered up. [3] feast.
[4] wake, commemoration feast (mind-ale). [5] dole, gift to charity.

Than a lighte lanterne late appone nyghte,
When it es borne at thi bakke . . .[1]

Wanhope (according to Waster) is the brother of Winner. The force of that statement will only be realized if it is remembered that according to medieval Christian tradition Wanhope (Despair) is itself, as implying a failure of faith in the divine grace, a sinful condition. It is Faustus's condition at the end of Marlowe's play; the Doctor cannot be saved because he does not believe he can be saved; it is the final, deadliest condition of the lost.[2] Waster, the goliard, goes recklessly beyond what is ordinate, however, when he wishes not only Winner and Wanhope drowned in the deep sea but all the fast-days of the Church as well. His argument (in this Fit) concludes with a challenge to actual combat and with a couplet on the proverbial timidity of property owners.

> *The richere of ranke wele, the rathere will drede:*
> *The more havande that he hathe, the more of hert feble.*

Waster has not, however, the last word in the second Fit. An impression by Winner of one of Waster's extravagant and immoderate feasts is the grand climax of this Fit. The feast may surely be regarded as another of the poem's traditional features rather than *simply* a reflection of the social life of the time. It is a recurrent feature of epic poetry—both Homeric and Northern—and also of West and North Midland alliterative poetry.[3] The chief difference in *Wynnere and Wastoure* is that the feast is *disapprovingly* described by Winner who, indeed, weeps for sorrow at such sinful extravagance. This impression of Winner weeping at the imagination of a feast which might be expected rather to produce a mirthful effect, as of Yule, is not without a comic aspect. It is doubtful who

---

[1] Cf. in *Piers Plowman* 'chastity without charity' likened to an unlighted lantern. (Passus I—B-text.)

[2] So also the Seven Deadly Sins in *Piers Plowman*, Passus V, sorry for what they are, are themselves despairing.

[3] Possibly it goes back to the feast that celebrated the sacred marriage of the goddess (or queen) with the victor in the ritual contest. Thus Cornford observes that at the feast with which an Aristophanic comedy characteristically concludes a mute bride, who has not previously appeared among the *dramatis personae*, almost invariably turns up to accompany the hero in the *comos* or triumphal procession.

gains or loses more in the argument by the evocation of the feast, Winner or Waster. Winner declares himself miserable at the sinful waste and excess of the gluttonous feast; but, as he contrasts his own frugal meals, there is perhaps an element of envy in his grief. It is as if Winner feels himself to be something of a loser. He takes his revenge, perhaps, by reminding his audience of the uncomfortable effects of gluttony; it burns the bowels. Gluttony is another of the Seven Deadly Sins, and Winner has doubtless both prudence and the preachers on his side in his condemnation. On the other hand, among the flesh and fowl in plenty of the great feast we recognize once again the birds—translated now to the table.

> *The bores hede schall be broghte with bayes appon lofte,*
> *Buk-tayles full brode in brothes there be-syde,*
> *Venyson with the frumentes,[1] and fesanttes full riche,*
> *Baken mete ther-by one the burde sett,*
> *Chewettes of choppede flesche, charbiande fewlis,[2]*
> *And iche a segge that I see has sexe mens doke ...*
> *Roste with the riche sewes,[3] and the ryalle spyces,*
> *Kiddes cleven by the rigge,[4] quartered swannes,*
> *Tartes of ten ynche, that tenys[5] myn hert*
> *To see the borde over-brade with blasande dисches,*
> *Als it were a rayled rode[6] with rynges and stones ...*
> *And ye will hafe birdes bownn one a broche[7] riche,*
> *Barnakes and buturs[8] and many billed snyppes,*
> *Larkes and lyngwhittes,[9] lapped in sogoure,*
> *Wodcokkes and wodwales,[10] full wellande hote ...*

The music at the feast is, to Winner's mind, another form of boastful and blasphemous pride.

> *Me tenyth[11] at your trompers, thay tounen so heghe*
> *That iche a gome in the gate[12] goullyng[13] may here:*
> *Than wil thay say to them-selfe, as thay samen[14] ryden,*
> *Ye hafe no myster[15] of the helpe of the heven kyng.*

[1] wheat boiled in milk.   [2] grilled chicken.   [3] sauces.   [4] back.   [5] pains.
[6] Cross adorned (with rings and stones).   [7] broached on a spit.
[8] bitterns.   [9] linnets.   [10] woodpeckers.   [11] it pains me.
[12] each wayfarer.   [13] braying.   [14] together.   [15] need.

Winner concludes his argument in this Fit, as Waster his, with a proverbial observation.

> *Better were meles many than a mery nyghte.*

In the third (and final) Fit, Waster opens the second (and final) bout of the flyting. Although an abundant harvest is a blessing from Heaven, Waster observes that it does not at all suit Winner. It brings down prices and reduces Winner to despair. Winner's private interests are in this respect counter to the common good; he is thus represented satirically as a character opposed to nature and providence.

> *Then the pure plente of corne that the peple sowes,*
> *That God will graunte, of his grace, to growe on the erthe,*
> *Ay to appaire[1] the pris, that it passe nott to hye,*
> *Schal make the to waxe wod for wanhope in erthe,*
> *To hope aftir an harde yere, to honge thi-selven.[2]*

Waster seeks to show further that Winner is liable to become a menace to social stability. He himself, it seems, is a staunch up-holder of the established feudal order.[3] In such an order the poor also should have their share.

> *Late lordes lyfe als tham liste, laddes as tham falles,—*
> *Thay the bacon and beefe, thay botours and swannes,[4]*
> *Thay the roughe of the rye, thay the rede whete,*
> *Thay the grewell gray, and thay the gude sewes;*
> *And then may the peple hafe parte in povert that standes,*
> *Sum gud morsell of mete to mend with thair chere.*

If hunting, hawking and fishing were neglected and birds, beasts

[1] impair.

[2] Gollancz, in a note in his edition of the poem, aptly quotes the Porter in *Macbeth*, 'Here's a farmer that hanged himself on the expectation of plenty.' He explains that 'wanhope in erthe' here means 'despair at plenty'. '*Erthe* is a different word from the ordinary *earth*. Its first sense is the act of earing or ploughing, tilling; produce of arable land; and so *crop*.'

[3] Though the greater merchants—'prowde marchandes of pris' (in contrast to 'pedders in towns')—have now evidently an acknowledged position in society with the lords and prelates.

[4] i.e. while lords can live as they please, can afford bitterns and swans and other delicacies, the common people have to put up with bacon and beef.

and fishes multiplied without depletion, degree itself would be overthrown; for (Waster argues) there would be such a state of abundance that necessity would no longer compel any man to serve a lord. 'Ane henne at ane halpeny' would thus monstrously disturb the whole established order of society.

> *If fewlis flye scholde forthe, and fongen[1] be never,*
> *And wild bestis in the wodde wone al thaire lyve,*
> *And fisches flete in the flode, and ichone frete[2] other,*
> *Ane henne at ane halpeny by halfe yeris ende,*
> *Schold not a ladde be in londe a lorde for to serve.[3]*

Waster concludes proverbially that a Winner must have a Waster.

> *Who so wele schal wyn, a wastour moste he fynde.*

But Winner replies that it is Waster himself who has departed from the wise traditional way of life. Waster has neglected his responsibilities as a landowner, his paternal woods are sold for the present satisfaction of the vanity of women, regardless of the future needs of his children. Winner begins on a note of irony.

> *. . . me wondirs in hert*
> *Of thies povre penyles men that peloure[4] will by,*
> *Sadills of sendale, with sercles[5] full riche.*
> *Lesse that ye wrethe your wifes, thaire willes to folowe,*

[1] captured.   [2] eat.

[3] This medieval English passage might well be compared with the Shakespearian passage in Milton's *Comus* discussed by Mr. Leavis in *Revaluation*—Comus's argument (addressed to 'the aidless innocent lady') about Nature

> *. . . quite surcharged with her own weight*
> *And strangled with her waste fertility*
> *Th' earth cumber'd and the wing'd air dark'd with plumes.*

The Garden of Eden is here out of hand, run wild, grown excessive as a consequence of Nature's not being controlled and disciplined by being used. Though Comus is tempting the Lady to laxity on the plea that it would be ungrateful to reject the gifts of the Giver, there is paradoxically a sound moral and utilitarian element in his argument; and in the Shakespearian concrete richness of the poetry, there is, at the same time, conveyed an impression of the fertility of nature.

> *And set to work millions of spinning worms*
> *That in their green shops weave the smooth-haired silk.*

[4] fur.   [5] rings.

Ye sellyn wodd aftir wodde in a wale tyme,[1]
Bothe the oke and the assche and all that ther growes;
The spyres[2] *and the yonge sprynge*[3] *ye spare to your children*
And sayne[4] *God wil grant it his grace to grow at the laste,*
For to schadewe your sones: bot the schame es your ownn.

In former times landowners took pleasure in showing their guests round their estates; Winner gives here a charming glimpse of the human ways of the old-fashioned type of landowner.

Your forfadirs were fayne, when any frende come,
For to schake to the schawe,[5] *and schewe hym the estres,*[6]
In iche holt that thay had ane hare for to fynde,
Bryng to the brode lande bukkes ynewe,
To lache[7] *and to late goo, to lightten thaire hertis.*

Winner returns to the theme of 'lordships sold to maintain lady-ships'; estates inherited from one's fathers to pass on to one's children are now converted into extravagant dresses of women in fantastic new fashions.

With side slabbande[8] *sleves, sleght to*[9] *the grounde,*
Ourlede all umbtourne[10] *with ermyn aboute,*
That as harde es, I hope, to handil in the derne,
Als a cely symple wenche that never silke wroghte.[11]

Winner finally reminds Waster that Mary, Queen of Heaven, was simply clothed on earth, as an example that one should forsake pomp and vanity.

Waster has, however, the last word, though I think we are not therefore to regard his argument as prevailing. As a chivalric lover (somewhat like Chaucer's young Squire) whose lady's part is to love him loyally, inspire him to be bold in battle and to shun dishonour, he expresses indignation at Winner's meanness.

[1] short time.   [2] sprouts.   [3] saplings.   [4] say.   [5] go to the woods.
[6] coverts.   [7] catch.   [8] trailing.   [9] hanging down.   [10] bordered all round.
[11] The sewing of silk embroidery was the occupation of high-born ladies.

And ye loveli ladies with youre longe fyngres
That habbeth selk and sendel, seweth when tyme is.
(*Piers Plowman*, Passus VI)

Wynnere and Wastoure

What hafe oure clothes coste the, caytef, to by,
That thou schal birdes up-brayd of thaire bright wedis,
Sythen that we vouche safe that the silver payen.
It lyes wele for a lede his leman to fynde.[1]

Certain features of this contest between an evidently youthful Waster and an elderly Winner appear to be new shoots from the old contest between Youth and Age—that variant of the contest between Summer and Winter. Waster sees Winner, with a new moral emphasis, as an avaricious old man. The Devil and the executors will divide Winner's goods at his death; he will have Hell in return for what he has saved on earth. Waster cuts a final figure as, once more, the Revellour who advocates a short life and a merry one. In so doing he places himself, at the same time as he places Winner, in the context of the traditional morality.

Take the coppe as it comes, the case as it falles;
For who-so lyfe may lengeste lympes[2] *to feche*
Woodd that he waste schall, to warmen his helys,
Ferrere than his fadir dide by fyvetene myle.[3]

Though the poem as we have it appears to break off before it is quite completed, the King's judgement seems to be substantially complete. We may take it that it is the judgement which the poet thought should be the King's, and which, by this means, he suggests to the King. The King is represented as looking benig-nantly upon both antagonists. His judgement indeed implies no condemnation of the one in favour of the other, but rather the maintenance of a balance between them in relation to the ever-changing economy of the kingdom. Winner is to go abroad, but only temporarily. He is to stay with those who love him most, the Pope and the Cardinals—a satiric reflection upon the Pope and the Cardinals as hoarders of wealth: but it is certainly no hardship for Winner to stay with his friends. He is, moreover, to return to the King whenever supplies of money are needed; he represents a reserve which can be drawn upon at need.

[1] to provide for his sweetheart.   [2] it befalls, i.e. is likely to.
[3] i.e. 'The longer you live, the more timber you will use up for fuel, and in your old age you will have to send a long way—fifteen miles farther than your father did—for the wood to be wasted in keeping yourself warm.' (Gollancz's paraphrase.)

Waster is required to dwell in London for the present, there to keep a look-out for anyone with a purse passing through town and make him spend his money in riotous waste. The poem as we have it concludes—or almost so—with a satiric impression of Waster's London life. Thus even in the judgement the satiric note persists.

> *Chese the[1] forthe in-to the Chepe, a chambre thou rere;*
> *Loke thi wyndowe be wyde, and wayte[2] the aboute,*
> *Where any berande potener[3] thurgh the burgh passe;*
> *Teche hym to the tonne till he tayte worthe;[4]*
> *Doo hym drynk al nyghte that he dry be at morow,*
> *Sythen ken hym[5] to the Crete to comforth his vaynes,*
> *Brynge hym to Bred Strete, bikken[6] with thi fynger,*
> *Schew hym of fatt shepe scholdirs ynewe,*
> *Hotte for the hungry, a hen other twayne,*
> *Sett hym softe one a sete, and sythen send after,[7]*
> *Bryng out of the burgh the best thou may fynde,*
> *And luke thi knave hafe a knoke bot he the clothe spred;*
> *Bot late hym paye or he passe, and pik hym so clene*
> *That fynd a peny[8] in his purse, and put owte his eghe.[9]*
> *When that es dronken and don, dwell ther no longer,*
> *Bot teche hym owt of the townn, to trotte aftir more.*

The birds make their final appearance, in plentiful waste, in Waster's larder.

> *The herons, the hasteletez,[10] the hennes wele served,*
> *The pertrikes, the plovers, the other pulled[11] byrddes,*
> *The albus, the osulles, the egretes[12] dere;*
> *The more thu wastis thi wele, the better the wynner lykes.*

Thus, on the one hand, Waster's London life promotes a necessary flow of wealth; on the other hand, the accumulation of wealth by Winner provides a reserve for which there may come a

---

[1] go (imper.).   [2] watch, wait.   [3] purse.   [4] become merry, tipsy.
[5] afterwards introduce him (to the wine of Crete *or* to a tavern of that name).
[6] beckon.   [7] send and fetch.   [8] devil a penny.   [9] i.e. hoodwink him.
[10] meat roasted on a spit.   [11] plucked.
[12] the bullfinches, the ouzels, the herons.

need. It seems at that moment to have been more expedient that spending rather than saving should be encouraged. But the two antagonists are found to be complementary. The accumulators of wealth and the dissipators are both necessary in the economy of a kingdom; the problem is to keep an appropriate balance between them. This economic problem is, however, as it is presented in the poem, also a moral problem. Winner and Waster could be aspects of the same person. The way of wisdom in the individual life, as in the life of a kingdom, would seem to be to keep a just balance between the two extremes represented by Winner and Waster.

§ 4

The Three Ages of *The Parlement of the Thre Ages* are the three ages of man, Youth, Middle-Age and Old Age; each age is either becoming or has been the other, yet in the flyting of this poem they compose the three antagonists. Youth is a Waster and Middle-Age a Winner; Old Age, who has successively been the other two, shows in himself the vanity of both. The dreamer thus contemplates the three successive ages of his own—and everyman's—life. As the lawless green hunter or poacher—the Robin Hood or Summer King—of the prologue he is himself evidently still identifiable with the first of the three Ages. The pageant he witnesses and the flyting he overhears in his dream produce a salutary recognition of his own mortality. The poem thus establishes a wise attitude to life—involving a recognition of death—by presenting an inclusive view of the human condition.

The man's delight in the exercise and skill of deer-stalking and in wild nature, which seems itself to share and utter his delight, conveys the 'Pride of Life' experience; and this is the cunning prelude to the debate of the Three Ages of Man and the contemplation of Life in its relation to ultimate Age and Death. It is sophisticated art indeed. There is a compelling emotional logic of events in this poem, as there is in *Sir Gawayne and the Grene Knight*.

The wild woodland landscape of the prologue in this Midland poem is again unlike the enclosed rose-garden or gentle flower-embroidered meadow of the tradition of *Le Roman de la Rose*, though it is a Maytime scene. There is again—by the side of a stream where fertilizing dews and mists fall—God's plenty of flowers and wild creatures, the birds and beasts of this moun-tainous forest of Kynd.

> *There the gryse[1] was grene growen with floures—*
> *The primrose, the pervynke, and piliole[2] the riche—*
> *The dewe appon dayses donkede full faire,*
> *Burgons[3] and blossoms and braunches full swete,*
> *And the mery mystes full myldely gane falle:*
> *The cukkowe, the cowschote,[4] kene were thay bothen,*
> *And the throstills full throly threpen[5] in the bankes,*
> *And iche foule in that frythe faynere than other*
> *That the derke was done and the daye lightenede:*
> *Hertys and hyndes one hillys thay goven,*
> *The foxe and the filmarte[6] thay flede to the erthe,*
> *The hare hurkles[7] by hawes, and harde thedir dryves,*
> *And ferkes faste to hir fourme[8] and fatills hir[9] to sitt.*

The poet represents himself as entering the woods, a lawless hun-ter, in all the pride of manhood—'my werdes to dreghe'.[10]

> *Als I stode in that stede[11] one stalkynge I thoghte;*
> *Both my body and my bowe I buskede with leves;*
> *And turnede to-wardes a tree and tariede there a while;*
> *And als I lokede to a launde a littill me be-syde,*
> *I seghe ane hert with ane hede,[12] ane heghe for the nones.*

He is 'buskede with leves' for camouflage on a realistic deer-stalking venture, but his being thus decked in green leaves in May unmistakably suggests, at the same time, a Jack-in-the-Green or May King.

A hunting episode is a recurrent feature of the poems in the Midland alliterative tradition. Hunting was a frequent and necessary pursuit in an England which was still largely wild and

---

[1] grass. [2] wild thyme. [3] buds. [4] wood-pigeon. [5] sharply disputed.
[6] polecat. [7] squats. [8] nest, lair. [9] prepares herself. [10] my fate to try.
[11] place. [12] head of horns.

untamed, in which the human communities were barely holding their own against the depredations of the multitudes of wild creatures, and in which the wild creatures were themselves a much-needed source of food. Nevertheless, these hunting episodes in the poetry, though they derive much in the way of realism from direct observation and participation in the craft of hunting, are another of the traditional features that may go back ultimately to the ancient rituals. If one examines their nature, the emphasis on spectacle and costume in the descriptions, and considers the frequency of their recurrence as a significant feature in the different poems, one cannot but feel reasonably convinced that they belong —as much as does the feast—to the traditional pattern. The kind of episode, frequent in the traditional literature of the Middle Ages, in which a hero or knight meets a hart or other animal that turns out to be a person or faery being metamorphosed, does not seem very far removed from the episode in the prologue of our poem. The hart in our poem is no longer a person disguised as a hart or (the myth derived from the ritual) a person metamorphosed; even so it was by no means so simply a hart as it is to us. We need only recall its place in medieval Christian symbolism. Hardin Craig in *The Enchanted Glass* instances among 'the losses in the field of the emotional appeal which Elizabethan literature has suffered' our loss of the emotional appeal of animals, except perhaps for the cat, owl and snake. The process of evolution by which we have arrived at a hunting episode of the particular nature and quality of the one in our poem may well be the process from ritual (or myth) towards naturalism.

The realistic communication of the experience and excitement of an actual deer-stalking is, if this theory is correct, a late sophistication in such a development.

> *I waitted[1] wiesly the wynde by waggynge of leves,*
> *Stalkede full stilly no stikkes to breke,*
> *And crepite to a crabtre and coverede me ther-undere:*
> *Then I bende up my bowe and bownede me[2] to schote.*

Not only is the excitement communicated but also sensations of

[1] observed.   [2] made ready.

discomfort, the annoyance from the gnats that is aggravated because the stalker may not make the least movement.

> *Then I moste stonde als I stode, and stirre no fote ferrere,*
> *For had I myntid¹ or movede or made any synys,*
> *Alle my layke² hade bene loste that I hade longe wayttede.*
> *Bot gnattes gretely me grevede and gnewen myn eghne.*

The cutting-up of the slain deer is realistically described in
technical detail³—'the breris and braken blody'. The slaying was
evidently a lawless act; the slayer must conceal the pieces until
nightfall in a hole under fern, heath and 'hore mosse' and the
horns and the head in a hollow oak, and must himself lurk near-
by to guard them from wild pigs that 'wyse bene of nesse'.

Most likely the slaying of the deer was the way to secure a vision
or dream-guidance. Alfred Nutt, the folklorist, noted instances
from Grail and Mabinogi legends of the hero hunting a stag, slaying it and falling under an 'illusion' in consequence; the stag was a
regular messenger from the faery world and thus passed into Christian hagiology.⁴ The poets of *The Parlement of the Thre Ages* and of
Sir Gawayne and the Grene Knight could rely on their audience's
knowing the Arthurian and folk-lore motifs and being familiar
with the Grail mythology. Further, there seems to be evidence that
a slain stag was then regarded as a trophy proving that the hero had
arrived at manhood. Both these significances appear to be relevant
to our poem. It may be that the hunts here and in *Sir Gawayne and
the Grene Knight* were introduced to interest the huntin'-and-
shootin' section of the audience in the great hall, as the descriptions
of costume and lovemaking may have been introduced to please
the ladies. This may explain why the poet should introduce these
subjects, but it does not explain the use he makes of them as an
artist. The initial deer-stalking episode and the later episode of
Youth hawking by a river have clearly the greatest relevance in
conveying the Pride of Life experience that is contrasted with Age.
The slaying of the deer may therefore be assumed to have had
both the meanings I have indicated.

¹ aimed.   ² sport.   ³ As in *Sir Gawayne and the Grene Knight*, Third Fit.
⁴ The general process is illustrated in great detail in Saintyves's *Les Saints
Successeurs des Dieux.*

The Parlement of the Thre Ages

Certainly the slaying of the deer is the preliminary or overture to the dramatic pageant which the slayer proceeds to witness and overhear in his dream-vision. The Three Ages are seen by him as the three figures of this pageant; the impression—the emphasis of the description being on their visual appearances and 'array'—is of the entrance of three costumed actors.

Youth is a spring-like figure in green, gaily and richly attired, with a profusion of embroidery and jewellery which, as in *Sir Gawayne and the Grene Knight*, is significant of life resurgent. He is a rider; standing up in the stirrups he rides hawk in hand, as do similar figures in the ballads and other traditional literature.

> *A hathelle on ane heghe horse with hauke appon hande, . . .*
> *He ne hade no hode ne no hatte bot his here one,*
> *A chaplet one his chefe-lere,*[1] *chosen for the nones,*
> *Raylede alle with rede rose, richeste of floures,*
> *With trayfoyles*[2] *and trewloves*[3] *of full triede perles,*
> *With a chefe charebocle chosen in the myddes.*
> *He was gerede alle in grene, alle with golde by-wevede,*
> *Embroddirde alle with besanttes*[4] *and beralles full riche:*
> *His colere with calsydoynnes*[5] *clustrede full thikke,*
> *With many dyamandes full dere dighte one his sleves.*
> *The semys with saphirs sett were full many,*
> *With emeraudes and amatistes appon iche syde,*
> *With full riche rubyes raylede by the hemmes;*
> *The price of that perry*[6] *were worthe powndes full many.*
> *His sadill was of sykamoure that he satt inn,*
> *His bridell alle of brente golde with silke brayden raynes,*
> *His trapoure*[7] *was of tartaryne,*[8] *that traylede to the erthe,*
> *And he throly was threven*[9] *of thritty yere of elde,*
> *And there-to yonge and yape,*[10] *and Youthe was his name.*

Middle-Age is soberly clad in autumnal russet with a grey tunic. He is a Winner, a man of property, preoccupied with worldly

---

[1] hair.   [2] i.e. three leaves or petals.   [3] true lovers' knots.
[4] round gold ornaments or coins (named after Byzantium).   [5] chalcedonies.
[6] outfit of precious stones.   [7] saddle-cloth.   [8] silk (of Tartary).
[9] vigorously grown.   [10] eager.

matters. As Youth has the aspect of Pride, Middle-Age with his money-bags has the aspect of Avarice. He is seen in a sitting posture; he sits pondering on his gold and the management of his estate, respectable, worldly Middle-Age. His worldly life is reproduced in his thoughts.

> *The seconde segge in his sete satte at his ese,*
> *A renke alle in rosette that rowmly[1] was schapyn;*
> *In a golyone[2] of graye girde in the myddes,*
> *And iche bagge in his bosome bettir than othere.*
> *One his golde and his gude gretly he mousede,*
> *His renttes and his reches rekened he full ofte,*
> *Of mukkyng, of marlelyng, and mendynge of howses,*
> *Of benes[3] of his bondemen, of benefetis many,*
> *Of presanttes of polayle,[4] of purfilis[5] als,*
> *Of purches of ploughe-londes, of parkes full faire,*
> *Of profettis of his pastours, that his purse mendis,*
> *Of stiewardes, of storrours,[6] stirkes to bye,*
> *Of clerkes of countours,[7] his courtes to holde,*
> *And alle his witt in this werlde was one his wele one.*

Elde (Old Age) is seen as a figure leaning on his side, clad in black, with beads in his hand. He cries 'kenely one Criste'; yet he is 'envyous and angrye'. If Youth is proud and Middle-Age avaricious, Elde has the aspects of Envy and Wrath among the Sins. His thoughts are turning to religion, he is sorry for his sins; but so, in *Piers Plowman*, are the Seven Deadly Sins themselves penitent and weep for what they know themselves to be. Elde is, then, the physical and mental condition of being old visualized as a *tableau* figure but, within that formality, presented with disturbing realism.

> *The thirde was a laythe[8] lede lenyde one his syde,*
> *A beryne bownn alle in blake, with bedis in his hande;*
> *Croked and courbede,[9] encrampeschett[10] for elde;*
> *Alle disfygured was his face, and fadit his hewe,*

---

[1] i.e. corpulently.   [2] tunic, gown.   [3] requests.   [4] poultry.
[5] trimmings of robes.   [6] storers.   [7] treasures.   [8] loathly.   [9] bent.   [10] cramped.

The Parlement of the Thre Ages

His berde and browes were blanchede full whitte,
And the hare one his hede hewede of the same,
He was ballede and blynde and alle babirlippede,[1]
Totheles and tenefull,[2] I tell yowe for sothe;
And ever he momelide and ment[3] and mercy he askede,
And cried kenely one Criste, and his crede sayde,
With sawtries full sere tymes, to sayntes in heven;
Envyous and angrye, and Elde was his name.
I helde hym be my hapynge[4] a hundrethe yeris of age,
And bot his cruche and his couche he carede for no more.

Elde is represented not only as physically repellent; there is no certainty that he is wiser, because of his years, than Youth or Middle-Age. He is simply there to be reckoned with in any complete view of a human life.

The flyting in which the Three engage starts out of the antipathy of Middle-Age to Youth. Youth ('this gome alle in grene'), hawk in hand on his high horse, is a courtly lover who sighs for love and vows to wear no hood or hat till he has jousted and performed feats of arms for his lady's sake. To Middle-Age ('this gome alle in graye') this is all folly in comparison with substantial things, by which he means property. For all Youth's fine array, which is vanity, he has no land. All his possessions glow and glitter on his back. With his horse and bridle he ought to buy cattle, with his jewels buy land; be a Winner instead of a Waster. ('Fantome and foly' here remind one of the value Chaucer's 'fantasye' often has.)

For alle fantome and foly that thou with faris.
Where es the londe and the lythe[5] that thou arte lorde over?
For alle thy ryalle arraye, renttis hase thou none;
Ne for thi pompe and thi pride, penyes bot fewe:
For alle thi golde and thi gude gloes[6] one thi clothes,
And thou hafe caughte thi kaple,[7] thou cares for no fothire.
Bye the stirkes with thi stede,[8] and stalles thaym make;

[1] big-lipped.   [2] full of vexation, peevish.   [3] moaned.   [4] conjecture.
[5] folk, tenants.   [6] glows.
[7] So long as you have your horse in hand (you care for nothing else).
[8] Buy bullocks with (the price of) your steed.

Thi brydell of brent golde wolde bullokes the gete;
The pryce of thi perrye wolde purches the londes.

The values of Youth may be all 'fantome and foly'; it remains to be seen, however, whether the values of Middle-Age, of worldly prudence, are any more real.

There may indeed be justice in Youth's rejoinder that Middle-Age has no god other than his goods. Youth, who does not fail to acknowledge God who gave him life, declares that he would rather be arrayed for battle and see a knight ride at him than possess all the gold, property and people that Middle-Age possesses; he would rather ride hawking by a river.

The impression of Youth hawking by a river is one of the most vivid things in English medieval poetry. It seems, through the Pride of Life experience, to relate Youth to the dreamer himself, who is also a hunter, with the difference that the dreamer is a lawless hunter, whereas Youth rides hawking with full assurance as to a knightly sport he is born to. The episode of a company of gaily clad, glittering personages—sometimes the 'fayerye'—who ride hawking by a river is yet another of those episodes recurrent in medieval romances and ballads and almost certainly mythological or ritualistic in origin. The hawking episode in our poem surely comes from the same source, though we may once again agree that it derives its realistic aspect from direct observation of the contemporary knightly sport. The hawks in their Pride that 'heghe willen flye . . . as it were heven aungelles' are at the same time, however, as much symbols as the Windhover in Hopkins's poem ('Brute beauty and valour and act, oh, air, pride, plume . . .')

> And ryde to a revere redily there-aftir,
> With haukes full hawtayne[1] that heghe willen flye;
> And when the fewlis bene founden, fawkoneres hyenn
> To lache oute[2] thaire lessches[3] and lowsen thaym sone,
> And keppyn of thaire caprons,[4] and casten fro honde,
> And than the hawteste[5] in haste hyghes to the towre,[6]

[1] proud. [2] take out. [3] leashes. [4] slip off their hoods. [5] proudest.
[6] A term of falconry meaning 'turn, wheel in flight' but associated with 'tower' in the usual sense. Cf. 'A falcon towering in her pride of place', *Macbeth*, II, iv.

The Parlement of the Thre Ages

With theire bellys so brighte blethely thay ryngen,
And there they hoven appon heghte, as it were heven angelles.
Then the fawkoners full fersely to floodes thay hyen,
To the revere with thaire roddes to rere up the fewles,
Sowssches thaym[1] full serely to serven thaire hawkes.

Than tercelettes full tayttely[2] telys[3] doun stryken,
Laners and lanerettis[4] lightten to thes endes
Metyn with the maulerdes and many doun striken;
Fawkons thay founden freely to lighte,
With hoo and howghe to the heron thay hitten hym full ofte,
Buffetyn hym, betyn hym, and brynges hym to sege,[5]
And saylen[6] hym full serely and sesyn hym there-aftire.

Then fawkoners full fersely founden tham aftire,
To helpen thaire hawkes thay hyen thaym full yerne,
For the bitt of his bill bitterly he strikes.
They knelyn doun on theire knees and krepyn full lowe . . .
Than henntis[7] thaym one honde and hodes thaym ther-aftire,
Cowples up theire cowers[8] thaire caprons to holde,
Lowppes in thaire lesses thorowe vertwells[9] of silvere;
Than he laches to his luyre, and lokes to his horse,
And lepis upe one the lefte syde, als the laghe askes[10] . . .
Spanyells full spedily thay spryngen abowte,
Be-dagged for dowkynge[11] when digges ben enewede.[12]

The poetry flowers on into a joyous and glowing impression of the courtly order of life as seen through the eyes of Youth—lovely ladies to make love to and dance with, romances to read, singing and carolling, playing at chess. It is a variation of the garden of the Rose—or, more exactly, in that other Midland alliterative poem, Arthur's Court as evoked in the opening of *Sir Gawayne and the Grene Knight.*

---

[1] stir, beat up. [2] joyously, nimbly. [3] teals. [4] male and female falcons.
[5] i.e. bring them to ground. [6] assail. [7] receives.
[8] draws or ties the leather straps (of the hood). [9] small rings.
[10] as is the custom. [11] muddied with diving.
[12] when ducklings are driven into the water. With this whole vivid episode compare the hunting episodes in Tolstoy and Turgenev.

And than kayre to the courte that I come fro,
With ladys full lovely to lappyn in myn armes,
And clyp thaym and kysse thaym and comforthe myn hert;
And than with damesels dere to daunsen in thaire chambirs;
Riche Romance to rede, and rekken¹ the sothe
Of kempes² and of conquerours, of kynges full noblee,
How thay wirchipe and welthe wanne in thaire lyves;
With renkes in ryotte to revelle in haulle,
With coundythes³ and carolles and compaynyes sere,
And chese me to the chesse that chefe es of gamnes;
And this es life for to lede while I schalle lyfe here.

It is the life of sensuous and imaginative delight as it might have been lived at a court by a young noble. Youth contrasts such a life with that of anxious, worried Middle-Age, preoccupied with perhaps equally vain things.

And thou with wandrynge and woo schalte wake for thi gudes,
And be thou dolven⁴ and dede, thi dole schall be schorte,⁵
And he that thou leste luffes schall layke⁶ hym there-with,
And spend that thou sparede, the devyll spede hym ells!

Middle-Age, in vexation, refuses to continue his debate with Youth.

Fole es that with foles delys: flyte we no lengare!

It is left to Elde to say the last word; from now on the poem becomes a *Gerontion*, a summing-up of human life as looked back upon by Elde. From his point of view who has been both Youth and Middle-Age, the 'wisdom' of Middle-Age is as foolish as the 'folly' of Youth. Elde is the only one of the three who has experienced all three conditions—'makes youre mirrours bi me, men'.

---

¹ recount. ² warriors. ³ O. Fr. *conduts*, songs.
⁴ buried. ⁵ i.e. your wealth will not last long. ⁶ play.

The Parlement of the Thre Ages

While I was yonge in my youthe and yape of my dedys,
I was als everrous[1] in armes as outher of youre-selven,
And as styffe in a stourre[2] one my stede bake,
And as gaye in my gere als any gome ells,
And as lelly by-luffede with ladyse and maydens.

My likame[3] was lovely as lothe nowe to schewe,
And as myche wirchip I wane i-wis as the bothen;
And aftir irkede me with this, and ese was me levere,
Als man in his medill elde his makande[4] wolde have.

Than I mukkede and marlede and made up my howses,
And purcheste me ploughe-londes and pastures full noble;
Gatte gude and golde full gaynly to honde;
Reches and renttes were ryfe to my-selven.

Bot elde undire-yode[5] me are I laste wiste,
And alle disfegurede my face and fadide my hewe,
Bothe my browes and my berde blawnchede full whitte,—
And when he sotted my syghte, than sowed[6] myn hert—
Croked me, cowrbed me, encrampeschet myn hondes,
That I ne may hefe tham to my hede, ne noghte helpe my-selven,
Ne stale[7] stonden one my fete, bot I my staffe have.
Makes youre mirrours bi me, men, bi youre trouthe;
This schadowe in my schewere[8] schunte[9] ye no while.
And now es dethe at my dore that I drede moste;
I ne wot wiche daye, ne when, ne whate tyme he comes.
Ne whedir-wardes, ne whare, ne whatte to do aftire.

Elde is the mirror which reflects, in this passage with such disturbing vividness, what Youth and Middle-Age will become.[10]

The disproportionately long account of each of the vanished

---

[1] eager.   [2] fight.   [3] body.   [4] comfort.
[5] undermined.   [6] it made sore.   [7] firmly.
[8] mirror.   [9] avoid.
[10] It is essentially the mirror—'ane poleist glass'—in which Cresseid looks in Henryson's *Testament*; the leprosy is surely but an added horror, a sense of pollution, that intensifies the withering of age that is suddenly there in the awful moment of recognition. Pandarus speaks to Criseyde of such a mirror in Book II of Chaucer's *Troilus*.

Nine Worthies[1] seems to me of decidedly less merit than the rest of the poem, and, even if it is not an interpolation by another hand than the original author's, it interferes with the symmetry of the poem. The Nine Worthies seem to have been popular figures in pageant plays up to Shakespeare's time. Nevertheless, they appear in our poem as if they had been lifted from one context into another in which they are not perfectly made to belong.

Elde's concluding note—it is not quite the note of the poem as a whole even in its conclusion—is the melancholy note of the preacher, *vanitas vanitatum*. Life so bright in Youth (and in the lawless hunter whose dream-vision the poem is), the worldly substance that Middle-Age so busily accumulates, indeed all earthly life and its accessories vanish in dust.

> *Ne dethe wondes[2] for no witt to wende where hym lykes,*
> *And thereto paramours and pride puttes he full lowe,*
> *Ne there es reches ne rent may rawnsone your lyves,*
> *Ne noghte es sekire to youre-selfe in certayne bot dethe,*
> *And he es so uncertayne that sodaynly he comes,*
> *Me thynke the wele of this werlde worthes to noghte . . .*
> *Vanitas vanitatum et omnia vanitas . . .*
> *For-thi amendes youre mysse whills ye are men here,*
> *Quia in inferno nulla est redempcio . . .*
> *Thou man in thi medill elde, hafe mynde whate I saye!*
> *I am thi sire and thou my sone, the sothe for to telle,*
> *And he the sone of thi-selfe, that sittis one the stede,*
> *For Elde es sire of Midill Elde, and Midill-elde of Youthe:*
> *And haves gud daye, for now I go; to grave moste me wende.*

[1] It is the theme of

> *Hwer is Paris and Heleyne,*
> *   That weren so bryht and feyre on bleo?**
> *Amadas and Ideyne;*
> *   Tristram, Yseude, and alle theo?*
> *Ector, with his scharpe meyne;†*
> *   And Caesar, riche of worldes feo?*
> *Heo beoth iglyden ut of the reyne,‡*
> *   So the schef§ is of the cleo.||*
>
> (From *A Luve Run*; probably early thirteenth century)

* face.   † company (strength?).   ‡ realm, world (rain?).
§ sheaf. || hillside? (hook?).   [2] turns aside.

The Parlement of the Thre Ages

There is a deep affinity between Elde here and the old man in Chaucer's *Pardoner's Tale*.[1]

The dreamer is awakened by the sound of a horn and finds the sun has set. But as he makes his way soberly to 'town' we are again reminded that it was May and that it was among the green leaves that 'thies mirthes me tydde'.

> Als I schurtted me[2] in a schelfe[3] in the schawes faire,
> And belde[4] me in the birches with bewes full smale,
> And lugede me in the leves that lighte were and grene:
> There, dere Drightyne, this daye dele us of thi blysse,
> And Marie, that es mylde qwene, amende us of synn!

The poem is thus, by its sharp recognition of mortality, a correction of Pride. The summer leaves with which the dreamer is environed will wither;[5] autumn and winter will follow: there is no permanence or trust in earthly things. Yet the total wisdom of the poem cannot be said to be exclusively that of Elde, though Elde sums up; for we remember that Elde is envious and wrathful, though rightly sorry for his sins, which include the sins of his Youth and his Middle-Age. We must continue duly to allow for the positive values of life in Youth (so unforgettably presented) and in Middle-Age. These values surely remain, not entirely invalidated, in the total inclusive poem co-present with Elde's last words.

---

[1] Cf. *Piers Plowman*, the opening of Passus XI (B-text), how the dreamer is warned by Elde. Cf. also how in the final Passus the dreamer is assailed by the ills of the flesh, old age and death. It is worth comparing these passages in the final Passus with the Duke's speech in *Measure for Measure* in his role of friar confessor preparing the condemned man for death. They have in common a use of homely English and a curious depression of tone. The Shakespearian passage is of course much more complex.

[2] amused myself.   [3] nook.   [4] built.

[5] Cf. Yeats:

> Though leaves are many, the root is one;
> Through all the lying days of my youth
> I swayed my leaves and flowers in the sun;
> Now I may wither into the truth.

§ 5

The neglect of our medieval non-Chaucerian poetry other than Langland's must at least partly be accounted for by the clichés that have reigned for so long in the textbooks and literary histories, in lecture-rooms and examination halls. There seem to be three main fallacies.

First, there is the dogma that the language of these poems is essentially inferior to Chaucer's—archaic, uncouth, rustic, harsh. But the vitality and richness of the English of these poems should be apparent; it is a live speech, a full-bodied idiom that far from being a handicap was the sheerest good luck for a skilled poet. It lent itself particularly to majestic, large-scale and dramatic undertakings. It may well be that Chaucer's innovations and improvements in the direction of courtly ease and urbane sophistication, which imply changes of attitude as well as differences of language, versification and verse-form, involved also the loss of some things of value—such as the extra-rational and pre-Christian and provincial elements which are implicit in the rich vocabularies of the non-Chaucerian poems. Chaucer was not cut off from the country though he was a townsman, a man of letters and consciously allying himself to the art-poets of France and Italy; but with his sceptical politeness he is, by comparison with the northern and western poets of his century, nearer Pope in some ways than he is to the fourteenth-century alliterative poets and romance makers. What his poetry had gained in concision, grace and urbanity must be set against a loss not so easy to specify.

But the accepted attitude to the non-Chaucerian poems remains much as it was in this innocent summing-up by Gosse on *Sir Gawayne*: 'Unfortunately the language of the poem is exceedingly crabbed and the difficulty of following it is increased by the alliterative metre.' This seems to be Sisam's assumption too in his introduction to *Fourteenth Century Verse and Prose* where he says, 'The author of *Sir Gawayne* is an artist who never ceases to struggle with a harsh medium'—as though it could have been *that* work of art in any other 'medium'. Even when these poets are praised, it is without recognition of their essential strength. Thus Sisam praises the author of *Sir Gawayne* for having 'the gift of the painter' and discusses the poem as a matter of visual imagery. But the best way to bring out the virtues of this poet would be to compare his poem with *The Faerie Queene*. Yeats's criticism of Spenser in his essay in *The Cutting of an Agate*, which ends, 'He seemed always to feel through the eyes', is very much to the point here. The language of *Sir Gawayne* uses all the kinds of imagery—tactual, muscular, kinaesthetic, as well as aural and visual, as Shakespeare's does and as Spenser's does not. Spenser's smoothness of movement, his 'musical' versification, exposes in the comparison with *Sir Gawayne* a loss of this kind of strength. In such observations as Gosse's and Sisam's we seem to be listening to an echo of the familiar contrast between 'Tennyson's fine ear' and Donne's 'harshness' and 'crabbed metres'. The value the alliterative metre can have seems never to have been justly considered, though there are excellent initial hints in *Edda and Saga*.

Secondly there is an assumption that these poems are deficient in 'art' and cannot be supposed to have a serious meaning. As the scientists say, That hypothesis is the soundest which accounts for the most facts. The hypothesis that these poems are works of art, and were shaped to communicate a by no means negligible meaning, is borne out at every turn in a critical analysis, once the intention and method of such poems has been apprehended. Then the patronizing attitude commonly adopted, with its suggestion that they are rather childish, naïve and irresponsible, valuable only for their 'freshness', will be felt to be as impertinent as it is unprofitable.

And thirdly, there is the general agreement that the non-Chaucerian poetry of the fourteenth century has no essential connexion with the tradition of modern English poetry, being either a dead end, or a series of 'sports', or (what amounts to the same thing) the products of an unaccountable 'revival'. Thus Mr. Christopher Dawson in *Mediaeval Religion* can write: 'Langland uses the old alliterative accentual measure which was the native speech of English and Teutonic poetry and which now *suddenly arose, as it were from the dead*, as a sign of the renaissance of the

English spirit. . . . Poetry such as this stands entirely outside con- temporary literary tradition.'[1] If it does, so much the worse for a 'contemporary literary tradition' that denies so much of its own past and of its own nature. But these alliterative poets were using the same language as Shakespeare and in essentially the same way; and it seems that anyone prepared to deny the connexion of these poems with the tradition of modern English poetry must be prepared to deny to modern English poetry itself the characteristic qualities of English.

[1] My italics.

V

THE MYSTERY CYCLE: CERTAIN TOWNELEY PLAYS

V. THE MYSTERY CYCLE: CERTAIN TOWNELEY PLAYS

§ 1

Towards the close of her book, *The Elder Edda and Ancient Scandinavian Drama*,[1] Miss Phillpotts observes:

'We must not forget that Church drama and folk-drama are but the two streams into which the ancient Teutonic ritual drama divided on encountering the medieval Church. They meet again in Elizabethan times, and through them there passed into the Shakespearian drama "a wealth of tradition and sentiment elsewhere intercepted by changes of language, religion and education".

. . . In England the common Teutonic stock of ritual drama was reinforced by the influx of Scandinavian customs. The influence of the folk-play and the Church drama converged at an auspicious moment, and the ancient tradition took hold on a surer immortality in Shakespeare.'

These observations have the weight of Miss Phillpotts's book behind them. We cannot do better than take them as our starting-point and inquire whether the convergence of which she speaks may not be observed to have taken place earlier—in at least a number of the plays of the English Mystery Cycle.

There will be no need to recapitulate here the familiar history of how drama issued from the liturgy of the medieval Christian Church; and how from the Latin Liturgical Drama there evolved gradually, through various stages, the whole vernacular Mystery Cycle as we have it in the three or four complete versions that have

[1] p. 211.

survived in English. That history, as it has been reconstructed in E. K. Chambers's *Mediaeval Stage*, is now well known. Latin Nativity and Easter Plays continued to have their places in the Church services throughout the Middle Ages. The vernacular Mystery Cycle may not, therefore, be said to have superseded the Latin Liturgical Drama from which it evolved; it simply became something separate, different and altogether bigger, the climax of the year in the community-life of the medieval towns. The Mystery Cycle cannot therefore be explained in terms of the Latin Liturgical Drama alone. The earliest vernacular Christian Mystery Plays were, almost certainly, simple redactions from the Latin plays (which must have been more like opera than spoken drama). Indeed, some of the plays even in the surviving English versions of the Mystery Cycle still read like such redactions. But in others, and perhaps in the Mystery Cycle as a whole, we may distinguish important elements which do not belong to the Latin Liturgical Drama, must have come from some other source and may, perhaps, only be accounted for by such a convergence as that of which Miss Phillpotts speaks.

The Christian Liturgy itself had its origins in an earlier ritual that was not Christian, and, as Hocart shows in detail in his book *Kingship*, 'The Mass is indeed a mystery play'.[1] But, even if we grant that the whole English Mystery Cycle had its immediate origin—as distinguished from its remoter origins—solely in the Christian Liturgy, we should still find it impossible to explain how such a development could have taken place spontaneously from that Liturgy without relation to external conditions. The Liturgy has itself a dramatic character and potentialities. But we have still to discover what force, as it were, drew the new drama out from the Liturgy and made of it a separate object that expanded to the size and significance of the Mystery Cycle.

We may begin to find the answer by returning to the fact that dramatic ritual always has been a feature—indeed the central and characteristic feature—of religion in all parts of the world, and is not an invention of Christianity. As Miss Phillpotts and as Grönbech (in his book *The Culture of the Teutons*) show, a religious

[1] Chap. VI, p. 65.

ritual drama had been the centre of life among the Scandinavian and Teutonic communities. As other scholars have shown (surely most relevantly for the history of drama in this island), the same was true of the Celts. It is reasonable to conjecture that people accustomed to a ritual drama not merely as an accessory of religion but as the essential of religion and indeed of life, would not cease to feel that it was essential after they had adopted Christianity. Without a ritual drama there could, for them, be no religion and no significant life.

Not only was the need for ritual drama still there, but the thing itself was still there; the pagan rituals were not simply or easily abolished by the new religion. We know how desperately, throughout the Middle Ages, people tried to keep up their ancient ritual dances and ceremonies even in the churchyards and church buildings themselves for the very reason that these were now re-garded as the sacred places. There is ample evidence in the records of ecclesiastical prohibitions and anathemas of the trouble these practices—often regarded as devilish practices—caused the Church. But this negative ecclesiastical policy of repression was complemented by the positive remedy provided by the emergence of a Christian ritual drama and its remarkable development, cor-responding to the size of the popular need, into the large-scale Mystery Cycle annually performed by the townspeople in their Craft Guilds at the height of the year (usually as an intrinsic part of the Corpus Christi ritual procession in June).

The plays of the Mystery Cycle—or some of them—can them-selves alone provide the conclusive answer to the question of whether we can properly speak of a convergence already taking place. We learn from other sources that there was a great deal in the nature of drama still being practised among the people outside the churches which the Christian Drama—the new drama which itself had roots in the old—might not only find propitious to its growth but with which it might converge. It would be an error to suppose that the only kind of dramatic performances in medieval England were the Christian Mysteries (or the Moralities which, though later in beginning than the Mystery Cycle, did not supersede it but were for long contemporary with it). On the contrary, there is evidence of a multiplicity of dramatic or near-dramatic performances—ritual dances, games and ceremonies—widespread throughout medieval Britain. There are numerous contemporary records and allusions, such as the allusions in *Sir Gawayne and the Grene Knight* to 'layking of interludes' and 'Christmas gomes'. The fact that the words for these performances have not been preserved—except for a few fragmentary pieces—has the obvious explanation that, when there were words, they were not written down. Modern literary people have been apt to neglect to take account of the great fact and importance of purely oral tradition.

Apart from the contemporary allusions to them, there is another reason why we can feel certain that there must have been such dramatic rituals: among country folk there have persisted almost to our own day what are evidently descendants of dramatic rituals, and numerous versions of them have been recorded. The Mummers' Play, the Wooing (or Plough) Play, the Morris Dance, the Sword Dance have been considered in detail, notably by R. J. E. Tiddy and E. K. Chambers,[1] and it is now generally agreed that they are not the blundering efforts of the folk at dramatic creation but are the degenerate and confused remnants of an ancient, pre-Christian ritual drama. If so, these dramatic rituals *must* have been kept up, with no break in continuity, right through the Christian Middle Ages. The evidence of the contemporary records is that the performers in the May rites and plays of Robin Hood and in Christmas games and plays were not only peasant folk but also nobles and kings and queens. It should be possible for us to observe in individual Cycle plays whether or not these dramatic rituals deriving from an ancient Nature religion had an effect on the Christian Mystery Cycle and may be responsible for certain of its features—features which must have been incorporated after the Christian drama moved outside the church buildings.

As for the view that the Christian drama was invented and devised by ecclesiastics to instruct an ignorant and illiterate populace in the facts of their religion, that it was intended as visual education for those who for the most part could not read, the Vulgate

[1] R. J. E. Tiddy, *The Mummers Play*; E. K. Chambers, *The English Folk Play*.

made visible as a sequence of *tableaux* for instructional purposes—the plays themselves do not seem to bear out such a view. The composition of the texts and the making and annual production of the Cycle as a whole no doubt involved a collaboration between clerks and the townspeople in their craft guilds. But it is evident from the nature of the drama itself that it was a collaboration and not merely the clerks instructing the people by the device of drama.

The historians of the drama have made much of the degradation and eclipse of drama in Rome during the decadence and of the lack of continuity between the ancient Classical Drama and the medieval Christian Drama. It would perhaps be more to the point to appreciate the parallel between the ritual origins of Greek drama and those of English drama. We should remember that even the Rome of the Empire was never quite the world. The ultimate origins of specifically English drama are to be sought at least partly in the customs and ceremonies of the Scandinavian, Teutonic and Celtic peoples. While the city of Rome was in its decadence there was still among the Northern peoples a professional class—a kind of priesthood—of poets, held in high honour and, indeed, veneration by kings and nobles. These 'makers' recited their poems before audiences in the great halls and must have also been a kind of noble actors. Whether or not the tradition originated, as the evidence indicates, in ritual drama, the poems which have survived have—some more than others—a dramatic character. It is scarcely stretching a point to say that the last of the minstrels (fallen on evil days as they had done by the end of the Middle Ages) are the first of the Tudor actors; that the Elizabethan dramatists, including Shakespeare himself, are in the succession from the minstrels of the earlier age. The verse—combining alliteration and rhyme—of several of the plays of the extant Northern versions of the Mystery Cycle itself suggests a relation between them and the tradition of alliterative poetry. These particular Cycle plays must be attributed to poets who, whether they were clerks or not, had close affinities with the makers in the alliterative tradition.

The Mystery Cycle: certain Towneley Plays

The Mystery Cycle is not a didactic drama; as a whole and for the greater part it is still a ritual drama—as we may observe it in the three or four versions preserved in English. Regarding it in retrospect from our modern viewpoint, we can see that it was in process of becoming what we should describe as the drama of art. A few of the Cycle plays indeed stand out from the others, as having passed beyond the purely ritual stage and become art. The term 'art' has unfortunately nowadays often a limiting, if not mis-leading, suggestion but it may serve here in making the necessary elementary distinction between art drama and ritual drama. Jane Harrison, in her book *Ancient Art and Ritual*, decides very clearly the point at which the one may be said to have become the other. It may be that it is not always possible or desirable in practice to make an absolutely sharp distinction, but that does not invalidate the general usefulness of the distinction. At the performance of a ritual there is no division into actors and audience. All present are, or are assumed to be, worshippers and therefore more or less active participants. But when part of the crowd—a part considerable enough to be felt as a distinct presence—has become separated onlookers or detached spectators the ritual drama begins to be-come art. There is now an audience; and as soon as there is an audience of whom the performers are conscious the performance itself will begin to change its nature in the direction of becoming a spectacle for spectators, a play presented to an audience. As the more inactive or contemplative among the worshippers have become spectators, so the active impersonators of gods or heroes in the ritual have become actors in a drama of art.

If the Mystery Cycle is a ritual drama we should not try to see it as if it were a chronicle play or episodic history of the world. Those concerned had evidently no idea of the kind of thing we think we mean by history, or no interest in it. Thus the anachronisms in the Mystery Cycle—as when Christ is spoken of as dead before he is born—have been assumed to be blunders by nineteenth-century scholars and historians and their twentieth-century successors. If we are to think of the Mystery Cycle as history at all we have to think of it as altogether a different kind of history from what we think history is. In his chapter on the Creative Festival (or *blot*) Grönbech assists his readers to glimpse the nature of the ancient Teutonic ritual, and what he says may assist us also in seeking to avoid initial misunderstanding of the nature of the medieval Mystery Cycle.

'Life and history start from the *blot*. Time is not experienced . . . in the way we feel it, as a stream running along from the origin of all things to the end of the universe. Time begins over and over again. The festival forms what we should call a stage above the flow of hours and years, a sort of condensed eternity. . . . And from this very beginning, time, that is the subsequent year or six months, will flow out, made pregnant with the power and the events of *blot* hours. Thus it is also literally true that the real deeds are done in the *blot* hall, the battles and the harvestings of the outer world being but the external fulfilment of actions done during feast time or the evolving of ritual acts. The field is actually ploughed when the priest or chieftain thrusts his ploughshare into the soil and lets the oxen draw some three ritual furrows with appropriate formulae and the recitation of the legend of the first ploughman. . . . The gods are present as power in the events and as persons in the sacrificers. . . . This view suggests another type of history and another kind of poetry than ours. In reality, ancient history cannot be translated into our terms because it is not a theory but an experience; by saying that it is the projection of the actual upon the screen of the past we do nothing but replace fact with a travesty, setting up our system as an exclusive pattern of history. . . . What we call poetry and myth is nothing but history. . . . The legends will not tell us what happened some year or other according to chronology; in our craving for a kernel of historical truth in the myths, we naïvely insinuate that the myth-makers ought to think in a system unknown to them, for the benefit of our annalistic studies.'

The texts of the Mystery Cycle themselves show that the annually performed events of the cycle were not thought of as having happened once for all at successive times in the past. In the

annual performance these events were not merely being com-
memorated. They were thought of as being done over again, as
having to be done over again; in the course of the annual re-doing,
indeed, they were probably experienced not so much even as events
being re-done but as if they were being done for the first time there
and then. Thus, even in the twentieth century when in a Greek
Orthodox church the crowd at Easter exclaim 'Christ is risen' at
midnight, they do not feel that Christ rose nearly 2,000 years ago
but that Christ has at that very moment risen; an event of fundamental importance in their lives has at that moment happened.
Jane Harrison (*Themis*, p. 202, f. 2) reports the gloom and anxiety
in a Greek village the day before Easter in the early years of this
century because, as one old peasant woman expressed it, 'If Christ
does not rise tomorrow we shall have no corn this year.'

If we are to think of the Mystery Cycle as history, therefore, it
should be as history that had to be annually re-made or renewed
for the well-being of each and all of the community. The past had
to be re-made in order that the future, for that year, might be made
propitious. Past and future are mutually present in the Mystery
Cycle; indeed, the Cycle regularly ends with what we regard as a
future event, the Last Judgement. The Cycle must have been experienced as an annual renewal in which once again, as in past
years and originally, the world is created, Lucifer (the light-
bearer, the sun) is created and falls, man is created and falls,
Christ (the true sun) is born, is put to death but victoriously
'harrows Hell' and rises again; finally, the world is judged; and
the next year again witnesses its creation and again the whole
cycle, a ritual of never-ending life from Creation to Judgement.
The crowd must have been essentially sharers or partakers with the
performers—who were themselves not actors in our sense but impersonators—in events which were to them the significant events
of the year. We may be sure that these events were more significant
to the participants, who were the whole community, than events
of the same year which we now call history; life itself, as they
understood it, must have been felt by them to originate in the
ritual, to depend upon it and to derive from it all its meaning.

We shall now find it easier to understand what Grönbech tries to explain earlier in the same chapter. 'In the ritual man assumes the power of creating life. . . . Not only the future needed creation, the past too had to be renewed in the *blot* to retain its reality. The eternity of life lay not in the fact that it had once begun, but solely in the fact that it was constantly being begun, so that the *blot*-man's sacrifice points back as well as forward . . . the *blot* . . . not only condenses and renews the past, but in true earnest creates it over and over again. This reiteration or renovation, as we should call it, is not a repetition of an act primarily and for all times created years or ages ago. The present re-acting is as primary, as original as the very first acting; and the participants are not witnesses to the deed of some hero or god, not reproducers who revive the deed, but simply and literally the original heroes who send fateful deeds into the world, whether it be battles long ago or the creation of Middle-garth'.

It is difficult for us to understand creation rites—and almost all rites turn out to be creation rites of one kind or another; thus, coronation rites make a king, initiation rites make a new man. It is especially difficult for us to understand how those concerned could ever have supposed that they were creating the world itself, and even the gods. But, as Hocart explains,[1] the idea was not of creating something out of nothing; but rather of treating or reno-vating the earth, for example, so as to make it fertile, useful and fit for human habitation, in that sense to inaugurate it, to bring it into being. Myths of creation are simply records of ancient creation rites if we may believe what now seems the most authoritative and credible view. The first chapter of Genesis itself, as Hocart ex-plains it, is a record of ancient Hebrew creation rites that lasted for six days. (This is not to deny the universal significance which the chapter has come to possess.) As Hocart further explains,[3] the Old Norse mythological description of the world is a fairly literal description of the circular mound surrounded by a ditch which, for ritual purposes, signified all things; the great ash, Yggdrasil, whose branches overspread the world, including the abode of the gods, and whose roots penetrate the underworld, is simply (he

---

[1] *Kingship*, Chap. XVI, 'The Creation'.
[2] Ibid., Chap. XV, 'Myths and Mounds', p. 188.

thinks) the sacred ash which surmounted the sacred mound sig-
nifying all things. Thus when, at the very beginning of the Mystery
Cycle, God creates the world—Heaven and Hell, the Earth,
angels and man—he creates what is visible and substantial before
the worshippers as the 'pageant' stage and all that is on it; he says
in effect to that simple wooden structure, 'Be Heaven and Hell and
Middle-earth', and behold, it is so.

If we agreed that the Mystery Cycle is for the most part not yet
art but is still as a whole in the ritual phase, we shall agree that it
does not present an 'action' so as to be fully intelligible to an
audience unfamiliar with it. The Mystery Cycle is not representational or fully self-explanatory of an action; it does not unfold or
expose an action as for an audience who expect to be shown, so as
to understand, what happened and how it happened, how it began, evolved and ended. The reason for this (to our minds)
deficiency is obvious enough if there was not, as yet, assumed to be
any audience. The impersonator, indeed, often proclaims who he
is, narrates his past acts or announces his future intentions. If the
purpose of such declarations is merely explanatory, we must ask
who requires such explanations. Those present certainly knew
beforehand all that they came to see, and knew what to expect
without having to be told. It is more likely that the impersonator
is not explaining to an audience but simply establishing his
identity with a ritual personage already well known whose acts are
equally foreknown and prearranged.

The modern reader, who would prefer to see the whole Mystery
Cycle as a drama according to his conception, is naturally baffled
by the gaps in what appears to him an imperfect sequence of
events. He is accustomed—no doubt rightly—to expect from a
drama the apprehensible detailed unity of structure of a complete
work of art. The Greek tragedies are such; and so are those of
Shakespeare. But we shall continue to misunderstand the Mystery
Cycle if we try to regard it as a blundering effort at art instead of
still being, as a whole, at the stage of ritual. We can see from our
historical viewpoint that it is in process of becoming art—comedy
or tragedy—and we can see that there are individual Cycle plays
which we may claim to have become art, to be genuine dramatic

poems. It is these few outstanding plays which are properly the object of literary criticism; and it is one or two of these on which I propose we should therefore concentrate our attention. But we should recognize that the Mystery Cycle is not intended to be art and that it is not, as a whole, art. We should recognize this fact specifically in relation to those few individual Cycle plays which we claim to be indeed dramatic poems; because their significance as dramatic poems may perhaps be shown as still rooted in their significance as ritual. In having become—or been made into—dramatic poems they should not be assumed to have lost or disowned their earlier purely ritual significance; it is, indeed, on their original ritual significance that the depth and complexity of their final significance as dramatic poems may be shown partly to depend.

The abruptness and incoherence of ritual texts, in contrast to the coherence and completeness of those of art, is remarked on by Grönbech in the chapter already quoted. 'For the participants themselves, the story was made up of acts complemented by *formaelis* and verses. This means that we shall not be able to gather the meaning either from the words only or from the action alone; both must be taken together to bring out the whole.' In a Shakespearian dramatic poem it is in and through the words of the poetry that the drama is created; the action springs from and corresponds to the words, so that the reader involuntarily imagines it even though he has never seen the play produced in a theatre. The words of the poetry compel the imagination to realize the developing action. Words and acts are fused expressions or aspects of one and the same creative or pattern-making energy of life. But in the case of the Mystery Cycle as a whole there is not this kind of completeness. The explanation seems to be, as Grönbech suggests, that words have a different function in ritual. They seem to be added to or to accompany the acts, to complement them, to lend them additional force or, often, to alternate with them, to *replace* acts altogether, themselves to assume the force of acts. In the ritual flytings the words appear to replace or be equivalent to blows or missiles hurled against the antagonist; they seem to belong to the phase when words were conceived as having magic powers. Consequently, there are gaps in a characteristic ritual text which, in a performance, would presumably have been filled with acts, just as there would have been gaps in the action filled with recited formulae. We can understand, therefore, why such texts are often awkward in places for a reader and why they sometimes leave him comparatively unmoved; the feelings and tensions of the worshippers surely did not arise from these words alone. The crowd of participants, caught up in the annual cycle of well-known significant events, had no need of a complete verbal rendering of these events. Nor should we assume that at the purely ritual stage of drama the impersonator had as yet any thought of interpreting an action to an audience or of impressing an audience. His intention of impressing, if he had any, would not have been directed at anyone outside the ritual—there *was* no one outside—but would have been directed, with singleness of purpose, at his antagonist or someone else *within* the ritual. Because the action of the Mystery Cycle is not yet, as a whole, turned outwards towards any audience, it is not as a whole turned outwards towards the modern reader. It is half-hidden, only intermittently imaginable by a reader of the texts.

§ 3

There must have been numerous local versions of the Mystery Cycle differing in dialect and in detail from one town to another. But only four complete—or nearly complete—versions still exist, the Chester, the York, the Towneley MS Cycle and the 'N-towne Cycle'. The last-named has often been known as the 'Ludus Coventriae', though its English seems to be that of East Anglia and not of the Coventry district; it appears to differ from the three Northern Cycles in not being processional. There are, in addition, a number of single plays which probably had their places in the now vanished Cycles of various towns.

The particular plays which I propose to consider have their places in the version of the Mystery Cycle preserved in the Towneley MS. This version of the Cycle is thought to have been the one performed at Wakefield in Yorkshire. There is evidence from the three Northern texts preserved that towns borrowed and worked on one another's texts in producing their local versions of the Cycle. Several of the plays in the Wakefield Cycle appear to have been borrowed from the York Cycle—unless (as has been suggested) both York and Wakefield derived them from some parent-cycle. Though the Towneley MS has been dated about the third quarter of the fifteenth century, it is generally thought that the version of the Cycle which it preserves had already more or less assumed the form in which we have it by the end of the first quarter of the century. Many different hands at different times appear to have worked on the making of the Wakefield Cycle, as in the making of a cathedral, adding to it and altering it; it appears to be more heterogeneous in this respect than the Chester and York Cycles. It is possible to distinguish different layers or strata, most likely chronological, older and more recent strata, as in a geological structure. Thus Pollard[1] distinguished broadly three different strata in the Towneley MS. Cycle; it is possible to distinguish more, as indeed scholars have since done without (I think) discrediting the rightness of Pollard's broad distinctions.

The plays which I propose chiefly to consider appear to belong to the latest stratum, which has been dated as early fifteenth century. These plays have so many characteristics in common and are so outstanding in similar ways that they have resulted in the hypothesis of a single dramatic poet of genius who composed them and who composed also parts of other plays in the Cycle—the so-called Wakefield Master. These short plays are (we may claim) dramatic poems and the proper objects of literary criticism. But their significance as dramatic poems—as art—cannot perhaps be dissociated from their origin in ritual. Further, it may be possible to observe in them to what extent their ritual origins may be described as pre-Christian, whether there may be already that convergence of traditions of which Miss Phillpotts speaks. If they are the work of a single poet, then that poet himself—as his verse shows—belonged in a tradition or school which may be claimed as at least related to that of the alliterative poetry of the fourteenth century.

[1] *The Towneley Plays* (E.E.T.S.), Introduction by A. W. Pollard.

Each individual play should of course be viewed in its place in the whole Cycle. I cannot do more here than indicate the place of each of the plays which I shall consider. The Cycle regularly begins with the Creation. Thus the Towneley version begins with a monologue spoken by God ('I am Alpha and Omega') in which he announces each act of Creation. The Towneley version of the Fall of Lucifer follows; it is less complete and impressive than the formally antiphonal York version (in which, however, the brief dialogue between the fallen angels has a grim humour resembling that of the dialogues between devils in the Towneley Play of the *Last Judgment*). Twelve pages of the Towneley MS are missing where we should expect the episode of the Fall of Man. Instead, we come to the Play of *Cain and Abel* (Towneley MS No. 2). Parts of this play have been attributed to the Wakefield Master; but we should be careful not to attribute every racily engaging or lively piece in the Cycle to a single master. We may, however, claim some of the dialogue (despite the grim theme of brother slaying brother) as already comedy or farce for an audience. Cain and his boy are vigorous farcical characters, the perennial pair of quarrelling clowns. Cain is a surly ill-tempered peasant farmer, with a grievance against everything, a grouser; he abuses his horses and his boy, and is familiarly disrespectful to God himself.

> *Whi, who is that hob-over-the-wall?*

The reader of Elizabethan plays might well find the series of asides in which the boy mocks his master already typically Elizabethan. It is not, however, this play which I propose first to consider in detail but the play which immediately follows it, the Play of *Noah* (Towneley MS No. 3).

§ 4

The Play of *Noah* (one of those attributed to the Wakefield Master) is a variation on the theme of the whole Cycle in which it is an episode. The Cycle begins with the Creation and ends with the destruction of what was created—except that (in this Christian cycle) there is a Last Judgement of mankind, who are conserved for Salvation or Damnation. The Play of *Noah* has a pattern of destruction and renewal for *its* theme, the destruction of what was created, because it has fallen or declined, and its subse-quent renewal or re-creation. The play moves throughout with a sure rhythm to the completion of its ordered and unified structure; it is a dramatic poem, complete in itself, yet a significant part of the larger whole.

The play begins with a monologue spoken by the ageing Noah —a recapitulation of the initial episodes of the whole Cycle. Noah speaks first of God the Creator and of the variety and abundance of His creatures.

> Myghtfull god veray   Maker of all that is,
> Thre persons withoutten nay   oone god in endles blis,
> Thou maide both nyght and day   beest, fowel, and fysh,
> All creatures that lif may   wroght thou at thi wish . . .

He recalls the creation of the angels, the fall of Lucifer and finally the creation and fall of Man. He meditates on man's sinfulness and reflects that he himself is growing old. This theme of Noah grow-ing old accords with that of the general decline.

> And now I wax old,
> seke, sory, and cold,
> As muk apon mold
> I widder away.

But Noah will yet 'wax and multiply' after the Flood—'at the next world, that is at the next spring'.[1]

Noah's monologue is succeeded by a monologue spoken by God in which He meditates on the failure of His created work, on Man's failure. God will therefore destroy his Creation. But He provides for a renewal of mankind and indeed of all life by the preservation of Noah and all who are to go with him into the Ark. The first dialogue in the play is between God and Noah; God instructs Noah to build a ship, and promises

> Ye shall wax and multiply,
> And fill the erth agane,
> When all thise floodis ar past . . .

[1] 'A Nocturnal upon St. Lucies Day' (Donne).

The second dialogue is a farcical contrast—a flyting between Noah and his wife, the forerunner of more flyting to come. She has some real cause for complaint; as in the winter of the Shepherds' Plays, there is lack of food. The flyting match precedes an actual exchange of blows. (The exchange between Alisoun and Clerk Jankyn in the Wife of Bath's monologue develops this familiar or stock pattern.)

NOE: We! hold thi tong, ram⁄skyt   or I shall the still.
VXOR: By my thryft, if thou smyte   I shal turne the untill.
NOE: We shall assay as tyte[1]   have at the, Gill!
    Apon the bone shal it byte.
VXOR: A, so, mary! thou smytis ill!

Surely this buffoonery is an example of that joking 'in the presence of death, real or mystical',[2] which we shall meet again in the Shepherds' Plays.

The building of the Ark was evidently an intrinsic part of the performance, expressing (at one level) pride of craft, the craft of carpentry or boat⁄building. But the boat⁄building episode is not introduced simply as realism. The ship that is being constructed is the very special ship that is to weather the Flood—between two worlds—with frail humanity, vulnerable life in its keeping; it is the life⁄bearing vessel or womb of life. Like the boat in *Marina* ('I made this, I have forgotten') it may be regarded as symbolical—as well as realistic. Noah, as he takes off his gown and labours at the making of the ship, is made very conscious by his aches and pains that he has grown old.

A! my bak, I traw, will brast!   this is a sory note![3]
hit is wonder that I last   sich an olde dote
    All dold,[4]
To begyn sich a wark!
My bonys ar so stark,[5]
No wonder if thay wark,[6]
    for I am full old.

As the storm gathers and breaks, increasing in violence, Noah's

---

[1] at once.   [2] Hocart, *Kingship*, VII, 74.   [3] business.
[4] dulled.   [5] stiff.   [6] ache.

wife has her second outbreak; once again, there is buffoonery in the presence of death. Impressions of the rising flood—halls, castles and towers falling beneath the force of the storm—combine with her rebelliousness. The comedy of this episode of the intran-sigent wife is the more piquant here as it is at just such a critical moment that she should choose to be awkward. She appears to be sublimely careless as the flood rises. She will not go into the Ark till she has done her spinning. It is as if there were some hidden fateful relation between her spinning and the brewing-up of the storm.

VXOR: Sir, for Jak nor for Gill   will I turne my face
    Till I have on this hill   spon a space
      on my rok;[1]
    Well were he myght get me,
    Now will I downe set me,
    Yit reede[2] I no man let[3] me,
      for drede of a knok.

NOE: Behold to the heven   the cateractes all,
    That are open full even   grete and small,
    And the planettis seven   left has thare stall;
    Thise thoners and levyn   downe gar fall
      full stout,
    Both halles and bowers,
    Castels and towres;
    full sharp ar thise showers,
      that renys aboute;
    Therfor, wife, have done   com into ship fast.

VXOR: Yei, Noe, go cloute[4] thi shone   the better will thai last.

PRIMA MULIER: Good moder, com in sone   for all is over cast,
    Both the son and the mone.

SECUNDA MULIER: and many wynd blast
      full sharp;
    Thise floodis so thay ryn,
    Therfor moder come in.

---

[1] distaff.   [2] counsel.   [3] prevent.
[4] patch.

Vxor: In fayth yit will I spyn;
     All in vayn ye carp.[1]
Tertia Mulier: If ye like ye may spyn   Moder, in the ship.

'Ye may spyn, Moder, in the ship' sounds reasonable enough. The climax of this second flyting is a second exchange between husband and wife as she enters the Ark precipitately, having at last apparently realized the danger. The children wish for a reconciliation, and this again has, perhaps, a significance in relation to what follows.

The final movement of the dramatic poem is on the theme of the subsidence of the Flood and the reappearance of the sun and the green earth. There is a spring impression and a joyful feeling of wonder and of reverent gratitude at the miracle—surely an annual miracle—of restoration and renewal.

> Now are the weders cest   and cateractes knyt,
> Both the most[2] and the leest.
> Vxor: Me thynk, bi my wit,
>   The son shynes in the eest   lo, is not yond it?
>   we shuld have a good feest   were thise floodis flyt
>   So spytus.

They have been in the Ark 350 days—that is, virtually, a year.

Vxor: Bot, husband,
     What grownd may this be?
Noe: The hyllys of armonye.[3]
Vxor: Now blissid be he
         That thus far us can ordand!
Noe: I see toppys of hyllys he   many at a syght,
     No thyng to let me[4]   the wedir is so bright.
Vxor: Thise ar of mercy   tokyns full right.
Noe: Dame, thi counsell me   what fowll best myght,
     And cowth,[5]
     with flight of wyng
     bryng, without taryying,
     Of mercy som tokynyng
         Ayther bi north or southe?

[1] talk.   [2] greatest.   [3] 'Armenia' has become 'armonye'.   [4] prevent me.   [5] could.

Husband and wife are now harmonious: Noah asks his wife which bird they might release from the Ark to bring a sign or token. The dove brings back the olive branch.

> The dowfe is more gentill her trust I untew,
> like unto the turtill for she is ay trew.
> VXOR: Hence bot a litill she commys, lew, lew!
> she bryngys in her bill some novels[1] new;
>   Behald!
> It is of an olif tre
> A branch, thynkys me.

Although the Noah Play is based on the Biblical narrative what has re⁄animated and re⁄created it in this version, working in and through the poetry, enriching its significance, is clearly the seasonal theme of the Nature rituals, the festivals of the Year. This, then, is the other source of life which the Christian drama found when it passed out of the church⁄buildings and among the people.

§ 5

The play which comes after that of *Noah* in the Cycle is the Play of *Abraham and Isaac* (Towneley MS No. 4). The signifi⁄ cance, in the Cycle, of the sacrifice of Isaac is as an analogue or foreshadowing of the sacrifice of Christ, the Son by the Father. But it happens to be one of the Cycle plays which is especially interesting to modern readers who are on the look⁄out for the emergence of drama in the usual sense—tragedy or comedy. The situation has not only the elements of tragedy in it—the tragedy of a father under an overriding obligation or doom to slay his own son —but to some extent this situation, the pity, the fear, the irony, the suspense and the element of unexpectedness, is realized in the play (as when the son asks, 'Where is the beest that shuld be brend?'). The situation in itself is as tragic as those situations of a son doomed to slay his father, or a brother his brother, which are among the themes of the Greek tragedies. Nearness of kinship

---

[1] news, tidings.

between the slayer and the slain (though in this case after pro-
longed suspense the slaying is prevented just in time) is peculiarly
tragic, as the Greeks and as Shakespeare knew. Several of the
sagas, too, are family tragedies. Such situations may perhaps be
traced back (as Miss Phillpotts does) to an original ritual situation
in which the king is doomed to be slain by his successor (he may
be his son or brother) who is doomed to marry the queen (she may
be his mother or sister). But the Play of *Abraham and Isaac* is not
one of the plays I intend to consider here. I intend to pass on to
certain of the plays in the sequence about Christ which forms the
larger part—and the climax—of the whole Mystery Cycle. The
Christ sequence, to which all the preceding plays of the Cycle
are preliminary, may be said to begin with the lovely Play of the
Annunciation (Towneley MS No. 10) and its companion play,
the *Salutation of Elizabeth* (No. 11) both of which Pollard
regarded as belonging to the earliest stratum of the Towneley MS
Cycle. It is immediately after them that the two Towneley Shepherds' Plays come (Nos. 12 and 13).

§ 6

What has happened in the Noah Play has happened again still
more interestingly in the two Towneley versions of the Shepherds'
Play. Both plays are among those attributed to a single Wakefield
Master; and if we are to have a Wakefield Master they are indeed
sufficiently similar in texture to each other and to different plays of
the group to justify their both being assigned to him. Though the
second is the better known, the first seems to me almost as interesting; both are significant dramatic poems.

The first play begins with a monologue spoken by a First
Shepherd (Gyb) on the theme of winter downfall and poverty—
the theme of 'Wynter wakneth al my care'. He envies the dead;
they are free from vicissitudes.

> Lord, what thay ar weyll   that hens ar past!
> for thay noght feyll   theym to downe cast.

here is mekyll unceyll[1]   and long has it last,
Now in hart, now in heyll[2]   now in weytt, now in blast,
   Now in care,
Now in comforth agane,
Now is fayre, now is rane,
Now in hart full fane,
   And after full sare.

Thus this Warld, as I say   farys on ylk syde,
for after oure play   com sorrows unryde;[3]
for he that most may[4]   when he syttys in pryde,
When it comys on assay[5]   is kesten downe wyde,
   This is seyn;
When ryches is he,
Then comys poverte,
hors-man Iak Cope
   Walkys then, I weyn.

All his sheep are gone, and his 'purs is bot wake'. The monologue is, however, not quite all a complaint; there is a more hopeful note in its ending. Gyb is on his way to the fair to buy more sheep. Once again, as in the Noah Play, there is promise of a new abun-dance—at the next spring.

To the fare will I me,
To by shepe, perde,
And yit may I multyple,
   for all this hard case.

On his way to the fair he meets the Second Shepherd (John Horne) who enters addressing the crowd at the play directly in a second monologue. 'May God save us all from the different kinds of evil men', who may have seemed to be multiplying in the con-temporary England of the play, as it was traditionally believed they would do towards the end of the world and as they appear to do with the failure of life energies in winter and as darkness mul-tiplies. Degree is overthrown in the increasing confusion that seems to attend the winter overthrow.

[1] unhappiness.   [2] health.   [3] bitter.   [4] can do.   [5] to the test.

Benste, benste[1]   be us emang,
And save all that I se   here in this thrang,
he save you and me   ouertwhart and endlang,[2]
That hang on a tre   I say you no wrang;
   Cryst save us
from all myschefys,
from robers and thefys,
from those mens grefys,
   That oft ar agans us.

Both bosters and bragers   god kepe us fro,
That with thare long dagers   dos mekyll wo;
from all byll hagers[3] with colknyfys[4] that go;
Sich wryers and wragers[5]   gose to and fro
   for to crak.
Who so says hym agane,
were better be slane;
Both ploghe and wane
   Amendys will not make.

He will make it as prowde   a lord as he were,
With a hede lyke a clowde   felterd[6] his here;
he spekys on lowde   with a grym bere,[7]
I wold not have trowde   so galy in gere
   As he glydys.
I wote not the better,
Nor wheder is gretter,
The lad or the master,
   So stowtly he strydys.

John Horne hails Gyb, who is apparently straying over the corn, and the two shepherds greet each other.

SECUNDUS PASTOR: How, Gyb, goode morne   wheder
                        goys thou?

   Thou goys over the corne   Gyb, I say, how!

---

[1] benedicite.   [2] crosswise and lengthwise.   [3] bill-hackers.
[4] cabbage-knives.   [5] twisters and wranglers.   [6] tangled.
[7] noise.

The Mystery Cycle: certain Towneley Plays

PRIMUS PASTOR: Who is that? John Horne   I make god a
                                                    vowe!
They agree that 'poore men ar in the dyke'.

The strange buffoonery of the dialogue that follows is surely no
more accidental than is that of the mock-nativity—the sheep in the
cradle—in the Second Towneley Shepherds' Play. It is in the unbroken tradition in which, all over the world almost, joking and
buffoonery have been associated with death; ceremonial joking
(as Hocart explains[1]) often indicates 'the presence of death, real or
mystical'. What gives rise to this buffoonery appears to be the
association of death and re-birth, the one presupposing the other
and setting up an endless cycle. We may recall, as one classic
example, the episode of the drunken Herakles in the *Alcestis* of
Euripides—the buffoonery which precedes the hero's wrestling-
match with Death and his restoration of Alcestis.

In our present play, Gyb tells John Horne he is going to the fair
to buy sheep (his sheep, as he supposes, have all died in the
winter). Thereupon the two shepherds quarrel about where he
shall feed them, since there is evidently not grass enough to go
round. Suddenly Gyb starts shouting like a madman at imaginary
sheep, the sheep he has not yet bought at the fair. Thus we have
a farcical fantasy. In the midst of the winter dearth when the
shepherds have no real sheep left, or only a few, there is suddenly
all round them an illusion of abundance, a multiplicity of phantas-
mal sheep. This make-believe abundance—their own make-
believe, it seems—is not there as a mockery of them in the season of
deprivation. The tone is rather one of jollity as if what is seen is a
promise of the abundance of spring. The buffoonery of the shepherds is, it seems, a significant Christmas game in this Christmas
play—a game intended perhaps magically to help to induce the
abundance it pre-figures. Gyb and John Horne shout contradictory orders at the (as yet) purely imaginary sheep and involve themselves in a wildly farcical medley.

PRIMUS PASTOR: I go to by shepe.
SECUNDUS PASTOR: nay, not so;

[1] *Kingship*, VII, 74.

329

What, dreme ye or slepe?   where shuld thay go?
here shall thou none kepe.

PRIMUS PASTOR: A, good sir, ho!
   Who am I?
   I wyll pasture my fe[1]
   where so ever lykys me,
   here shall thou theym se.

SECUNDUS PASTOR: Not so hardy!
   Not oone shepe tayll   shall thou bryng hedyr.

PRIMUS PASTOR: I shall bryng, no fayll   a hundreth togedyr.

SECUNDUS PASTOR: What, art thou in ayll   longys thou oght
                                    whedir?

PRIMUS PASTOR: Thay shall go, saunce fayll[2]   go now,
                                Bell Weder!

SECUNDUS PASTOR: I say, Tyr!

PRIMUS PASTOR: I say, Tyr, now agane!
   I say skyp over the plane.

SECUNDUS PASTOR: Wold thou never so fane,
   Tup, I say, whyr!

PRIMUS PASTOR: What, wyll thou not yit   I say, let the
                                  shepe go?

In the midst of the confusion the Third Shepherd, appropriately named Slaw-pace, arrives late—as the New Year itself seems to do in winter.

SECUNDUS PASTOR: Here comys Slaw-pase
   fro the myln whele.

TERTIUS PASTOR: What a do, what a do   is this you betweyn?

Like a chorus, he comments that here are two *old* knaves, fighting about nothing, and he compares them proverbially with Moll.

Ye brayde of[3] Mowll   that went by the way—
Many shepe can she poll[4]   bot oone had she ay—
Bot she happynyd full fowll   hyr pycher, I say,
   Was broken;

---

[1] flock.   [2] without fail.   [3] are like.   [4] count.

'Ho, god,' she sayde,
bot oone shepe yit she hade,
The mylk pycher was layde,
 The skarthis[1] was the tokyn.

Gyb and Horne are old in this play for the same symbolic reason, perhaps, as Noah.

Slaw⁄pace carries a bag on his back; but it is empty. He shakes it out in front of everyone—so that it can be seen to be quite empty—as a conjurer might do, because later out of the same (surely it is the same) empty sack will come food and drink in never⁄ending abundance. Meanwhile he compares the bag, empty of meal, to the wits of the old shepherds; but surely the empty sack is at the same time symbolical of the whole winter dearth.

Hold ye my mare   this sek thou thrawe
  On my bak,
Whylst I, with my hand,
lawse the sek band;
Com nar and by stand
  Both Gyb and Jak,
Is not all shakyn owte   and no meyll is therin?
PRIMUS PASTOR: Yey, that is no dowte.

A boy appears (Jak garcio) and the contrast of Youth and Age must have been visible. He reveals that Gyb's sheep are not, apparently, lost after all. On the contrary they are in grass to the knee. The wonder is whence comes this abundance of grass, this miracle of fertility on a midwinter night. We may associate it with such legends as that of the cherry tree that bore fruit on Christmas Eve (for it is, of course, Christmas Eve).[2]

Immediately following the good news that the sheep are found there is yet another apparent miracle. Although the shepherds have complained of winter and starvation they unexpectedly produce between them—and even out of Slaw⁄pace's empty bag—a sudden abundance of food and drink, a more than substantial Yule feast. This miraculous feast immediately preceding the birth of Christ

---

[1] broken fragments.   [2] See, for example, the medieval romance *Sir Cleges*.

reminds one of those windfalls of food and drink that regularly
accompany the appearances of the Grail. Appropriately for Yule,
it is a boar feast; Grönbech shows how the boar was the sacred
animal, indeed a divinity, among the ancient Scandinavian and
Teutonic peoples and how at the sacred boar feast the life and
strength of the boar entered into those who feasted upon it. Grönbech shows in the same context how the ale also was, among these
peoples, a divinity whose life they drank. In our present play,
Christian though it is, the ale of the shepherds' Yule feast is still
spoken of as holy and as 'boyte of oure bayll', a phrase commonly
used of Christ.

SECUNDUS PASTOR: Lay furth of oure store,
    lo, here! browne of a bore,
PRIMUS PASTOR: Set mustard afore,
     oure mete now begyns;
    here a foote of a cowe   well sawsed, I wene,
    The pestell of a sowe   that powderd has bene,
    Two blodyngis,[1] I trow   A leveryng[2] betwene;
    Do gladly, syrs, now   my breder bedene,[3]
     With more.
    Both befe, and moton
    Of an ewe that was roton,
    Good mete for a gloton;
     Ete of this store.
SECUNDUS PASTOR: I have here in my mayll[4]   sothen[5]
                                and rost,
    Even of an ox tayll   that wold not be lost;
    ha, ha, goderhayll!   I let for no cost,
    A good py or we fayll   this is good for the frost
     In a mornyng;
    And two swyne gronys,[6]
    All a hare bot the lonys,[7]
    we myster[8] no sponys
     here, at oure mangyng.[9]

---

[1] blood-puddings?   [2] liver-pudding?   [3] my two brothers.
[4] bag.   [5] boiled.   [6] snouts.   [7] loins.   [8] need.   [9] feasting.

TERTIUS PASTOR: Here is to recorde   the leg of a goys,
    with chekyns endorde[1]   pork, partryk, to roys;
    a tart for a lorde   how thynk ye this doys?
    A calf lyver skorde   with the verjose;
      Good sawse,
    This is a restorete
    To make a good appete.
PRIMUS PASTOR: Yee speke all by clergete,
      I here by your clause;
    Cowth ye by youre gramery[2]   reche us a drynk,
    I shuld be more mery   ye wote what I thynk.
SECUNDUS PASTOR: Have good ayll of hely[3]   bewar now,
                                  I wynk,
    for and thou drynk drely[4]   in thy poll wyll it synk.
PRIMUS PASTOR: A, so;
    This is boyte of oure bayll,
    good holsom ayll.
TERTIUS PASTOR: Ye hold long the skayll,
      Now lett me go to.

Yet another bottle is found—'yit a botell here is'.

Can we mistake that what has once again taken possession of the Christian cycle here, and re-created it, is the tradition of the pre-Christian dramatic rituals as they still flourished among the people? Shakespeare later is still drawing on the same source, as in the sheep-shearing festival in *A Winter's Tale*.[5] There is no loss of the new Christian significance by this enrichment from an older tradition; thus the shepherds agree, with Christian charity, that the food and drink left over from the abundance of the unexpected feast should be distributed among the poor.

[1] gilded with egg-yolk.   [2] learning.

[3] 'hely' is usually explained as 'Ely'. But surely the word is to be at least associated with 'hele' (Anglo-Saxon 'haelu'), 'healing, health' and also with 'haly' (Anglo-Saxon 'halig'), 'holy'.

[4] deeply.

[5] It seems perfectly possible that even if Shakespeare as a child did not see the Mystery Cycle himself he would have been told about the old performances by those who had seen them. This might help to account for the sheep-shearing scene in *A Winter's Tale* and indeed the whole symbolism and some of the details being traditional. In particular Act III Sc.3 is surely not by accident reminiscent of the Shepherds' Plays of the Nativity.

For oure saules lett us do
Poore men gyf it to.

Having first asked Christ's blessing, the shepherds sleep after
the feast and are wakened by the angel—'he spake of a barne'.
There is the same feeling of wonder again in *A Winter's Tale* when,
after the tempest and the shipwreck and the man eaten by the bear[1]
(images of death), the old shepherd (again a *shepherd*) finds on the
seashore a newborn child—'Mercy on's a barne; a very pretty
barne.' The star looks like the lightning to Slaw-pace as he leans
on a stone—an image that may well date back to the association of
the sun-god with the lightning; it is in the midwinter night that
the new sun is born.

The dramatic poem ends with the Adoration of the Shepherds.[2]
Each of the Three Shepherds, as he recites or sings (probably
sings) his part in what is in effect a dramatic Christmas carol,
presents a gift—a spruce coffer, a ball and a bottle—to the newborn divine child. It is perhaps not too fanciful to suppose that the
bottle is the very same as that out of which earlier in the play the
'holy ale'—'boyte of oure bayll'—was drunk by the shepherds. The
gifts of the Three Shepherds (as of the Three Kings) have surely
some relation to the magical or otherwise rich gifts which are
bestowed on a newborn child or found beside an exposed child
in so many folk-tales and which often have to do with the ultimate
recognition of his supernatural or royal origin and status.

[1] 'Exit pursued by a bear.' There is in this Shakespearian scene again the strange
mixture of buffoonery and horror of death. Cf. also the Porter of Hell-gate scene in
Macbeth and the element of the grotesque in *Lear*, and the 'rural fellow' with the
basket of figs in *Antony and Cleopatra*.

[2] The shepherds criticize, with evident knowledge of what they are talking about,
the technique and quality of the angels' singing. This accords with the evidence
(cf. the references throughout the *Canterbury Tales*) that music and singing were
accomplishments widespread among the people in the fourteenth century. But
when Gyb, the shepherd, quotes the Latin of Virgil's fourth *Eclogue*, John Horne
protests

Tell us no clerge   I hold you of the freres,
  ye preche;
It semys by youre laton
ye have lerd youre Caton.

The Mystery Cycle: certain Towneley Plays

§ 7

Because the Second Towneley Shepherds' Play includes the episode of the sheep-stealing, involving the characters Mak and his wife Gyll, it has been acclaimed the first English comedy; we should have to add 'the first that has chanced to be preserved'. The excellently stage-managed farce of the concealment and discovery of the stolen sheep in the cradle certainly implies an *audience*—an audience who are in the know that the sheep is in the cradle and who may be counted on to hold their breath in suspense when the shepherds unexpectedly turn back to Mak's cottage (having inopportunely recollected that they have given no gift to the new-born child) and so make the discovery that the supposed child is the sheep. Since in this way it assumes an audience to appreciate it, the episode is already (if we apply Jane Harrison's distinction between art and ritual) art drama; it is comedy presented to, and for, an audience.

But it is the more significant as art drama because it has so immediately grown out of ritual drama; and because it is a dramatic poem in which the Christian Mystery Cycle has, once again, been crossed and enriched by the other tradition, the tradition of all that has been grouped under the heading of the Folk Play. Less than justice has been done to it as significant art even by those who have praised it; they have praised it too simply as farce, light comic relief intruded into the old solemn Nativity Play. Instead, it needs to be insisted that the play *is* a poem. The ancient association in dramatic ritual between dance and drama is still immediate in the vigorous, dancing rhythm that carries right through to the play's end. The deliberately broken, realistic dialogue, diversifying without breaking the strict stanzaic and metrical form, is carried along—like eddies within a steadily flowing larger current—within the unbroken dance-like metrical movement.

The progression or whole movement of the play is again, as in the First Towneley Shepherds' Play, from winter sorrow and death to the joyful birth. The play is again realism and something

335

more, or other, than realism; if we regard it simply as realism emerging, as a dissociated element, from convention we shall miss a large and essential part of the meaning. The shepherds (as in the first play) certainly strike one as realistic reproductions of the folk, English peasant folk, like those who appear occasionally in Shakespeare's plays and quite unlike the shepherds of the Eliza-bethan pastoral convention. But (as in Shakespeare) they have their significant parts to play in a total poem.

The opening monologue spoken by the First Shepherd is a vigorous protest—no mere sorrowful musical complaint—against the winter distresses and oppressions suffered by the poor. The poor are oppressed not only by winter, which is bad enough, but in winter by the rich. Social grievances and vexations increase, once again not only because the social order seemed to be breaking up in the England contemporary with the play, but because it is winter, the season when the life energies that hold all things to-gether begin to fail; the winter world (it was traditionally be-lieved) prefigures the final end of all things when the world will fall into wrack and ruin. This note of vigorous protest against the oppression of powerful, rich and evil men is the more readily absorbed—because it *is* vigorous—in the jollity that strangely develops in the play; it seems, indeed, to reinforce the jollity which it is finally absorbed into. 'So feeling comes in aid of feeling.'[1]

PRIMUS PASTOR: Lord, what these weders ar cold!   and I
                                                am yll happyd;
    I am nere-hande dold[2]   so long have I nappyd;
    My legys thay fold   my fyngers ar chappyd,
    It is not as I wold   for I am all lappyd
      In sorow.
    In stormes and tempest,
    Now in the eest, now in the west,
    wo is hym has never rest
      Myd day nor morow!

Bot we sely shepardes   that walkys on the moore,

---

[1] Wordsworth's *Prelude*, Book XI.   [2] dulled, numbed.

In fayth we are nere-handys   outt of the doore;
No wonder as it standys   if we be poore,
for the tylthe of oure landys   lyys falow as the floore,

   As ye ken.
We ar so hamyd,[1]
for-taxed and ramyd,[2]
We ar mayde hand tamyd,
   with thyse gentlery men.

The Second Shepherd protests in his turn, as he enters, against
the winter.

   Lord, thyse weders ar spytus   and the weders full kene.
   And the frostys so hydus   thay water myn eeyne,
     No ly.
   Now in dry, now in wete,
   Now in snaw, now in slete,
   When my shone freys to my fete,
     It is not all esy.

His monologue as a whole is the protest of a husband against
wives, a variation on the theme of the antagonism between Noah
and his wife as the Flood rises.

   For, as ever red I pystyll   I have oone to my fere,[3]
   As sharp as a thystyll   as rugh as a brere;
   She is browyd lyke a brystyll   with a sowre loten chere;[4]
   Had she oones wett hyr whystyll   she couth syng full clere
     Hyr pater noster.
   She is as greatt as a whall,
   She has a galon of gall:
   By hym that dyed for us all,
     I wald I had ryn to[5] I had lost hir.

The Third Shepherd (Daw) enters, just as the first two are asking what could have happened to him, and he compares the winter

---

[1] hamstrung, crippled.   [2] oppressed.   [3] mate.
[4] sour-looking face.   [5] till.

floods with Noah's; they evidently have a corresponding signifi‑
cance in this play.

> Was never syn Noe floode   sich floodys seyn;
> Wyndys and ranys so rude   and stormes so keyn;
> Som stamerd, som stod   in dowte, as I weyn;
> Now God turne all to good   I say as I mene,
>   for ponder.
> These floodys so thay drowne,
> Both in feldys and in towne,
> And berys all downe,
>   And that is a wonder.

The note of seeing wonders, or at least of the unexpected, is present
in Daw's monologue, and prepares for the miraculous events of the
night of Christ's birth.

> We that walk on the nyghtys   oure catell to kepe,
> We se sodan syghtys   when othere men slepe.
> Yit me thynk my hart lyghtys   I se shrewys pepe.

Daw appears to be the servant of the other two shepherds; if they
are poor, he, it seems, is still poorer. Yet they themselves enact in
some measure the inhumanity which they have just complained
of; for when he begs for food and drink—he, too, is hungry in the
winter—they upbraid him, as his masters, for being late. Daw
then protests against the hard lot of servants.

> Sich servandys as I   that swettys and swynkys,
> Etys oure brede full dry   and that me forthynkys;[1]
> We ar oft weytt and wery   when master‑men wynkys,
> Yit commys full lately   both dyners and drynkys.
>   Bot nately[2]
> Both oure dame and oure syre,
> When we have ryn in the myre,
> Thay can nyp at oure hyre,
>   And pay us full lately.

---

[1] grieves me.   [2] to some purpose.

When the first two shepherds ask him where their sheep are, Daw answers that he has left them in the corn; though everything is topsy-turvy, the beginning of the reversal to better fortune is indicated by Daw's news that the sheep have 'pasture good'.

SECUNDUS PASTOR: Wher ar oure shepe, boy, we skorne?
TERTIUS PASTOR: Sir, this same day at morne
   I thaym left in the corne,
      When thay rang lawdys;
   Thay have pasture good   thay can not go wrong.

The Three Shepherds join in a mirthful part-song because their sheep appear to be well provided for after all; Mak enters to the accompaniment of their singing, and the Mak farce commences.

The central episode of the farce, the Three Shepherds' discovery of the stolen sheep in the cradle, is clearly a kind of parody of the serious subject of the whole Nativity Play, a mock-nativity. In the final episode of the whole play the newborn Christ, Agnus Dei, in the cradle—probably, in the performance, the same cradle—is adored by the same shepherds. In the farcical episode (the spirit of which is similar to that of the popular beast fables) a beast is found in the cradle.

   What the dewill is this?   he has a long snowte . . .
   Sagh I never in a credyll
   A hornyd lad or now.

Finally, the infant God is found in the cradle between two beasts.

   In a cryb full poorely,
      Betwyx two bestys.

The phrase 'little day starne' is first used by one of the shepherds of what he supposes to be Mak's child and the audience knows to be the sheep; the same phrase is later in the play used of the Christ child (as, indeed, it is commonly used in the carols of the Christ child).

The 'hornyd lad' in the cradle has perhaps a still more particular significance. He may be none other than the 'horned god'—the God incarnated as goat or sheep, bull or stag—whose worship continued throughout medieval Britain as the evidence assembled in Margaret Murray's *God of the Witches* seems to show. To quote but one instance, together with her own comments, from her chapter, 'The Horned God': 'In 1303, the Bishop of Coventry was accused before the Pope of doing homage to the Devil in the form of a sheep. The fact that a man in so high a position as a bishop could be accused of practising the Old Religion shows that the cult of the Horned God was far from being dead, and that it was in all probability still the chief worship of the bulk of the people. It should be also noticed that this is one of the first British records in which the old God is called the Devil by the Christian writers of the Middle Ages.' If so, the point about the 'hornyd lad' in the Christ-child's cradle could not have been missed by the crowd at the Mystery Cycle; though whether the joke was at the expense of the New Religion or the Old might depend on whether one chose to regard the 'hornyd lad' as displacing the Christ-child in the cradle or the other way round. It is difficult to suppose that the joke could have been much relished by clerics. The attempts of the Church authorities to suppress the Mystery Cycle can be accounted for if it seemed to them that within the Christian Cycle itself the Old Religion was rearing its head as a dangerous rival.

'So frequently is joking and buffoonery associated in various parts of the world with death that when we come across ceremonial joking it is advisable to consider whether we are not in the presence of death, real or mystical.'[1] The buffoonery in this play once again (as in the First Towneley Shepherds' Play) indicates the presence of death and birth in their age-old association. The mock-nativity does not appear to be introduced in the mocking spirit of scepticism. There is probably no irreverence to the Christian religion intended. The boisterousness of the Mak farce as a whole, culminating in the tossing of Mak in a blanket, may rather be interpreted as an expression of the jollity of the folk as the re-birth significance of the midwinter festival overcomes the death significance. As the consciousness of the distress of winter is absorbed into the boisterousness of the farce, so the latter in its turn is finally absorbed into the joyous wonder of the Adoration of the Shepherds. The move-

[1] See before (Hocart, *Kingship*, VII, 74).

ment of the dramatic poem is from the winter sorrow of the opening monologue, through the jollity of the Mak farce, into this final reverent joy and wonder. The Mak farce, including the mock-nativity, is thus not finally incongruous with the whole play as a Nativity Play, but indeed contributes to a total complex harmony. The boisterous jollity is resolved or transmuted into more complete joy as the *Gloria in excelsis* is sung. We who read are apt not to allow for what would have been the effect of the singing.

Though Mak[1] first enters to the accompaniment of the mirthful singing of the shepherds, the farce commences, on the part of Mak himself, on a note of distress that corresponds with that of the opening of the play. He enters as a cloaked figure.[2]

---

[1] Who is Mak, the sheep-stealer? Was he invented for this play, or did he have a previous existence in tradition? Is he more than he seems? There is a resemblance between Mak and that other rogue, Autolycus, in *A Winter's Tale* (allowing, of course, that the Shakespearian character is much more various). We can, perhaps, find a clue to the underlying significance of the one by pondering the significance of the other in his context. Autolycus (like Mak) is a thief. At his first entrance he alludes to Mercury: 'My father named me Autolycus; who being, as I am, litter'd under Mercury, was likewise a snapper-up of unconsider'd trifles.' But Mercury, besides being the patron of thieves, was also the go-between to and from the lower and upper worlds. As such, he conducts Proserpina, the spring-goddess, back to the upper world. Now it is precisely Autolycus who introduces the spring note into *A Winter's Tale* in the song which he enters singing—and he snatches away the linen bleaching on the hedges (surely the snow). He heralds or prepares the way for Perdita whose role in the shepherds' spring festival is that of the flower-girl or spring-goddess (it is no accident that she alludes to Proserpina). He is also, we may note, a shape-shifter; at least he is continually disguising himself or assuming deceptive appearances for his professional purposes. If we agree that this Shakespearian character has a tradition behind him, he is likely as an English character to have descended from a tradition other than the Greek or Roman, most probably the Celtic or Norse. Among the Norse gods, Loki was not only a shape-shifter (like the Celtic sun-god Curoi) but dishonest, a ne'er-do-well and a thief. It is a fair guess that the grand original of Mak and of his wonderful Shakespearian counterpart, Autolycus, is none other than Loki. Loki is believed to have been fire and an associate (perhaps aspect) of the sun-god. But whoever was their original (or originals) it is improbable that either Mak or Autolycus was invented to meet the exigency of providing light comic relief; they have every appearance of being traditional figures which, in the case of Autolycus at least, a great poet has known how to make the most of in a specific dramatic-poetic context. 'The poets', says Hocart again, 'do not invent half so much as they are supposed to do, but rather turn ancient facts to poetic uses' (*Kingship*, Chap. VIII, p. 101).

[2] MS: Tunc intrat Mak, in clamide se super togam vestitus.

MAK: Now wold God I were in heven   for there wepe no barnes
   So styll.
PRIMUS PASTOR: Who is that pypys so poore?
MAK: Wold God ye wyst how I foore!
   Lo, a man that walkys on the moore.

Then he pretends not to be Mak and breaks into a fit of boasting and flyting, like the antagonists in the Mummers' Play or like Herod or Pilate elsewhere in the Mystery Cycle; he declares that he is a yeoman of the king and 'sond from a greatt lordyng'; but the shep-herds recognize him and suspect him of being a thief. He is the wild man of the moor—'a man that walkys on the moore'. He would cheat his neighbours for the sake of a dinner for himself, his wife and his too numerous progeny. But he also suffers the common lot of poor men in winter, he also is hungry; he is as much the oppressed as he is the oppressor. Though he is a rogue, he is (like Autolycus) a merry rogue. He risks hanging; yet, perhaps because he provides merriment, the worst that actually happens in the end, when he is exposed, is that he is tossed in a blanket, as if it were a Christmas game—as indeed it *is*. Thus there is no tragedy to mar the good-humoured mirth of Christmas, and the element of jollity achieves a boisterous victory in the play. At the same time, though Mak is not actually hanged he *is* essentially the 'hanged man'; for Mak in being tossed in the air undergoes what is essentially a mock death.

What drives Mak to sheep-stealing is, then, the hunger which he and his family suffer in the winter in common with the shep-herds.

    Bot a sekenes I feyll   that haldys me full haytt,[1]
    My belly farys not weyll   it is out of astate.

He has more children than he can feed—though it seems that there is a fire in his hut.

PRIMUS PASTOR: How farys thi wyff? by my hoode   how farys
                                   sho?
MAK: Lyys walteryng,[2] by the roode   by the fyere, lo!

[1] hot.   [2] wallowing.

And a howse full of brude   she drynkys well to . . .
And ilk yere that comys to man
She bryngys furth a lakan,[1]
    And som yeres two.
The shepherds are ill-clad and without a fire
   I am cold and nakyd   and wold have a fyere.

Mak is something of a magician, for he pronounces a spell over them, when they lie down to sleep, in order to put them into a deeper sleep. There is an element of comic melodrama in his monologue as he draws a circle round them—a circle 'as rownde as a moyn'—and, while they are snoring, steals a fat sheep. There is a suggestion of Mak as the wolf stealing into the fold; later, indeed, it appears that one of the shepherds has dreamt that he saw him clad in wolf-skin.[2] There is rather more action and movement in this play than is usual in a Cycle play.

The monologue is followed by a dialogue between Mak and his wife, Gyll, as he arrives at the hut where (like Noah's wife and like the fairy women) she sits spinning. She is glad to see him but she fears that he will be hanged for the sheep.

---

[1] child.

[2] 'The strange kinship between sun and wolf', union and conflict, association and opposition, is examined by H. Flanders Dunbar in *Symbolism in Mediaeval Thought*, in which she provides proof of Dante's use of ancient symbolism and imagery. 'Although there have been many guesses, no one knows exactly when or how there was established the strange kinship between sun and wolf, yet in regard to Zeus himself it has been argued as to whether in reality he was wolf-god or light-god. The very words are related etymologically, the word "wolf" with "light", and the word "wolf-skin" with "darkness". Firmly established as are the light associations of Zeus, Sir J. G. Frazer has said: "The connexion of Lycaean Zeus with wolves is too firmly established to allow us seriously to doubt that he is the wolf-god." Moreover, Zeus is not the only "Shining One" with whom there exists this close association with the wolf. Osiris, god of the sun, whose sign was Sirius the dogstar, was represented clad in a wolf-skin. It is unnecessary to give more examples, since the symbolisms of these two were fundamental in the forming of Dante's tradition; and whether or not he was aware of the facts, they had shaped the symbolisms that he found at hand. The wolf for Dante was in manifold association with the sun.'

One may have less hesitation in connecting Mak with Loki and the wolf when one reflects that Loki appears in the myths as a mischief-making *servant*, that the Norse end of the world begins with a wolf devouring the Sun, and that the monster Fenris-wolf who is then to vanquish Odin was conceived by Loki.

MAK: Good wyff, open the hek![1]   seys thou not what I bryng?
VXOR: I may thole the dray the snek[2]   A, com in, my swetyng!
MAK: Yee, thou thar not rek   of my long standyng.
VXOR: By the nakyd nek   art thou lyke for to hyng.
MAK: Do way:
    I am worthy my mete,
    For in a strate can I gett
    More then thay that swynke and swette
        All the long day.
VXOR: It were a fowll blott   to be hanged for the case.
MAK: I have skapyd, Jelott   oft as hard a glase.[3]
VXOR: Bot so long goys the pott   to the water, men says,
    At last
    Comys it home broken.
    Com thay or he be slayn   and here the shepe blete!

MAK: Then myght I be tane,   that were a cold swette!
    Go spar
    The gaytt doore.

It is she who devises the ruse of swaddling the stolen sheep and
putting it in the cradle. Mak has already returned to his place
between the sleepers when they wake ('*Resurrex a mortuis!*' exclaims the First Shepherd awaking). Almost their first concern is
as to the whereabouts of Mak whom, it is clear, they do not trust.
Mak pretends to waken after having dreamt that his wife has
given birth to yet another boy.

    Wo is hym has many barnes,
        And thereto lytyll brede!

On Mak's second return to his hut there is first a brief flyting
outbreak between him and his wife.

VXOR: Why, who wanders, who wakys   who commys, who
                                                                    gose?
    Who brewys, who bakys?   What makys me thus hose?[4]
    And than,

---

[1] door.   [2] draw the latch.   [3] blow? slippery place?   [4] hose? hoarse?

It is rewthe to beholde,
Now in hote, now in colde,
Full wofull is the housholde
    That wantys a woman.

They anticipate an awkward visit from the shepherds, who are meanwhile counting their sheep. Gyll swaddles the sheep and hides it in the cradle. In the subsequent developments of the farce there are two 'discoveries' made by the shepherds, first the loss of a sheep, then the sheep in the cradle. The buffoonery of the sheep lost and found—found in a cradle—corresponds, at the farcical level, to the death⁄and⁄birth theme of the play as a whole.[1]

To the accompaniment of Mak singing a lullaby and Gyll groaning, the Three Shepherds arrive to seek their lost sheep.

TERTIUS PASTOR: Will ye here how thay hak?   oure syre lyst croyne.[2]

PRIMUS PASTOR: Hard I never none crak   so clere out of toyne;
    Call on hym.

SECUNDUS PASTOR: Mak!   undo youre doore soyne.

MAK: Who is that spak,   as it were noyne,
    On loft?
    Who is that I say?

TERTIUS PASTOR: Goode felowse, were it day.

MAK: As far as ye may,
    Good, spekys soft,
    Over a seke woman's heede   that is at mayll easse.

Mak welcomes them.

MAK: Ye have run in the myre   and ar weytt yit:
    I shall make you a fyre   if ye will syt . . .
    I have barnes, if ye knew,
    Well mo then enewe,
    Bot we must drynk as we brew,
        And that is bot reson. . . .

TERTIUS PASTOR: Yee, oure shepe that we gett,
    Ar stollyn as thay yode   oure los is grette.

[1] At the highest and most serious level, the daughter lost and found in *A Winter's Tale*, *Pericles* and *Lear* has a corresponding symbolical meaning.
[2] feels like crooning.

MAK: Syrs, drynkys!
   Had I bene thore,
   Som shuld have boght it full sore.
PRIMUS PASTOR: Mary, som men trowes that ye wore
   And that us forthynkys.

The irony throughout this scene—Gyll accusing the shepherds themselves of being thieves and protesting she will eat the child in the cradle if ever she cheated them—clearly assumes an audience to appreciate it.

VXOR: I swelt![1]
   Outt, thefys, fro my wonys!
   Ye com to rob us for the nonys.
MAK: Here ye not how she gronys?
   Youre hartys shuld melt.
VXOR: Outt, thefys, fro my barne!

All that the shepherds can find in Mak's cottage are 'bot two tome platers' that plainly signify the winter lack of food as, in the First Towneley Shepherds' Play, Slaw-pace's empty bag at first does.

   Just when, at the departure of the shepherds, the suspense has relaxed and the audience has begun to draw breath again the shepherds return—a well-managed dramatic surprise—and make the discovery of the sheep in the cradle.

PRIMUS PASTOR: Gaf ye the chyld any thyng?
SECUNDUS PASTOR: I trow not oone farthyng.
TERTIUS PASTOR: Fast agane will I flyng,
   Abyde ye me there.
   Mak, take it to no grefe   if I com to thi barne.
MAK: Nay, thou dos me greatt reprefe[2]   and fowll has thou
                            farne.

TERTIUS PASTOR: The child will it not grefe   that lytyll day
                            starne.

   Mak, with youre leyfe   let me gyf youre barne,
   Bot sex pence.
MAK: Nay, do way: he slepys.

---

[1] faint.   [2] reproach.

TERTIUS PASTOR: Me thynk he pepys.
MAK: When he wakyns he wepys.
    I pray you go hence.
TERTIUS PASTOR: Gyf me lefe hym to kys   and lyft up the
                                                        clowtt.

    What the dewill is this?   He has a long snowte.

Yet Gyll persists in maintaining that the sheep is not a sheep but
her child—'A pratty child is he as syttys on a woman's kne'. In
this mock nativity in which Gyll comically corresponds to, or pre-
figures, Mary there is the suggestion, if not of a miraculous birth,
at least of a supernatural occurrence; her child (Gyll claims) has
been metamorphosed by an elf.

> He was takyn with an elfe,
> I saw it myself.
> When the clok stroke twelf
>   Was he forshapyn.

The farce attains its climax with the tossing of Mak in the air—
buffoonery instead of a death.[1] The change or transformation in
the play thereupon happens with the Angels' singing of the *Gloria
in excelsis* and the Shepherds' wondering recognition that 'He
spake of a barne'. They marvel that the newborn Saviour is
'poorly arayd' and comes 'to so poore as we ar'. He is the Saviour
of all mankind—of the poor above all. Thus the note of the distresses of the poor in the opening of the play finds its response
towards the close. The play concludes, as does the First Play, with
the Adoration of the Shepherds. The natural human tenderness
towards a child is expressed and is at the same time hallowed by
the recognition that this child is God. The Three Shepherds
approach each with a gift—a 'bob of cherys', a bird and a ball.

> Lo, he merys;
> Lo, he laghys, my swetyng,
> A welfare metyng,

---

[1] TERTIUS PASTOR: Syn thay manteyn thare theft   let do thaym to dede.
MAK: If I trespas eft   gyrd of my heede.

I have holden my hetyng;[1]
　Have a bob of cherys. . . .
Hayll! I kneyll and I cowre.　　A byrd have I broght
　To my barne.
Hayll, lytyll tyne mop!
Of oure crede thou art crop:
I wold drynk on thy cop,
　Lytyll day starne. . . .
Hayll! put furth thy dall![2]
I bryng the bot a ball:
Have and play the with all,
　And go to the tenys.

We should not jump to the conclusion that 'go to the tenys' is naïvety on the part of the shepherd, that he is unconscious of such a remark being incongruous to a newborn infant. On the contrary, it is surely intended as this shepherd's conscious humour. It is too easily assumed that everything in these plays is naïve.

§ 8

Between the Creation and the Judgement the central events of the Mystery Cycle—as of the Christian year—are the birth, death and resurrection of Christ; in relation to these events the Old Testament episodes in the early part of the Cycle are in the nature of a prologue. In the sequences of the Nativity, Passion and Resurrection Christ has to contend with a succession of antagonists who are yet essentially one and the same. Thus the principal antagonist of the newborn god in the Nativity sequence is Herod. He is succeeded as principal antagonist by Pilate in the Passion sequence. Yet the Herod and the Pilate of the Mystery Cycle are both much of a piece, boasters and ranters, half villains and half clowns. In these respects we may note that they bear a resemblance not only to each other but also (for example) to the Turkish Knight of the Mummers' Play. This would not be surprising if all

---

[1] promise.　　　　　　　　[2] hand, fist.

three represent a character type which has a common origin—an origin as one of the combatants in the ritual flyting and combat between the old god (or king) and the new. The consistency of the character of the Towneley Pilate through the various plays of the Passion sequence has recently been demonstrated by an American scholar, Arnold Williams, in a detailed study.[1] But it is less certain whether or not this consistency was produced by the texts having been worked over by the Wakefield Master or by any individual dramatist. Herod exhibits in different plays a similar consistency which cannot, in his case, be attributed to a single dramatist. If we ask why the Pilate of the Mystery Cycle should have developed, or been developed, into a character type different from the Pilate of the New Testament and very like the type to which the Herod of the Mystery Cycle and the Turkish Knight of the Mummers' Play also belong, the explanation may well be that a ritual dramatic antagonist of the Christ in the Mystery Cycle was needed who would fit the old traditional pattern. If the Herod and the Pilate are in this way a traditional ritual type, we meet once again in the new Christian drama a feature that belonged originally to the old pre-Christian ritual drama.

In the Towneley Plays of the *Magi* (No. 14) and of *Herod the Great* (No. 16)—plays in which the Nativity sequence continues after the Shepherds' Plays—Herod is the old king who, as in so many folk-tales, is afraid of the newborn child and tries to do away with him because of prophecies and rumours that the child will grow up to challenge and overthrow him as king. Though menacing and dangerous, the Herod of the Mystery Cycle is at the same time a kind of clown, a *sinister* clown. Perhaps the imagination has here distorted him into a grotesque caricature because he is really feared, as a type of the powerful oppressor such as the Shepherds complain of in the Shepherds' Plays and who exists in fact in the world; but if he was originally the impersonator of the old god he could never have been quite human and may always have been more or less grotesque. The Towneley Play in which the ranting Herod is most given his head in masterly dramatic verse is the play of *Herod the Great* (the only play of the Nativity

[1] *The Characterisation of Pilate in the Towneley Plays.*

sequence other than the Shepherds' Plays which has been found attributable to the Wakefield Master). But though the Herod rant is more developed in this play than in the *Magi*, he is essentially the same Herod in both, a character type that had not needed to be specially invented.

The Play of the *Magi* is not the equal of the Shepherds' Plays in variety and complexity as a dramatic poem, though it is good workmanship in stanzaic verse, a self-consistent and worthy rendering of its traditional subject. It appears to be more directly and simply in the line of descent from a Latin original in the Liturgical Drama. In the Towneley Play of the *Magi* the star[1] is described as brighter than sun and moon, and clearly signifies the newly risen *sol verus* who is Christ. The play combines in a well-knit unity of opposites the Journey and Adoration of the Magi set over against the hostile rages and menaces of the Herod. The gifts of gold, incense and myrrh betoken the kingship, godhead and destined death of the infant whose birth has wonderfully happened.

The subject of the Play of *Herod the Great* is the forbidding and indeed revolting one of the Massacre of the Innocents. Strangely enough, this theme of the persecution of the innocent (who may be a being about whom there is at least the suggestion of supernatural origin) runs through a number of the old traditional tales that in various versions continued to be popular throughout the Middle Ages—the tales, for example, of Patient Griselda, Constance and Emare. In this Towneley Play of Herod the abhorrent episode is presented in so stylized a manner as to suggest, at once, that the art here has not departed far from its ritual origin, and is here more complete art for that very reason. Only as ritual rather than life could such an episode have been made into dramatic art. Had the play been more naturalistic than it is, the balance between realism and ritual would have been upset, and the play would surely have been merely revolting. An element of humour—a kind of ceremonial clowning as an aspect even of the slayings—is again strangely present.

The play begins with a ranting monologue spoken by Herod's

---

[1] In the performances of the Latin Nativity plays the *Stella* suspended in the church appears to have been, like the cradle itself, a central sacred object or symbol.

Messenger and ends with a ranting monologue spoken by Herod himself. They evidently address the crowd at the performance directly (as still in some Elizabethan plays). In the opening monologue Herod's Messenger, who boasts and rants only less than his master himself, declares Herod to be sole king of all the kingdoms of the world and demands the undivided allegiance of everyone to him. Such violence of assertion, however, itself suggests that Herod's kingship has been seriously shaken by the birth.

> Thay carp of a kyng,
> Thay seasse not sich chateryng.

The Messenger's monologue heralds the entrance of Herod himself raging and, like the ogre of folk-tales, threatening to break everyone's bones. Herod is angry more particularly because the Three Kings have not returned. His Three Soldiers or Knights (*milites*) announce that the Three Kings have gone home by another way; and this announcement starts off a flyting between Herod and his Knights as a consequence of which the latter temporarily retire. Herod then calls for his Counsellors or Clerks who consult their books and quote the prophecies about Christ, thus aggravating the storm of Herod's ragings.

> Fy, dotty-pols, with youre bookys!
> Go kast thaym in the brookys!

They appease him by suggesting a Massacre of the Innocents. Herod's Messenger instructs the Three Knights to execute this plan and to array themselves for the purpose in bright armour (as for some ceremony).

> In all the hast that ye may   in armowre full bright,
> In youre best aray   looke that ye be dight.

(The bright armour fits in well with the view that the originals of Herod's Three Knights were the attendants and supporters of the old sun god in his ritual contest with the young sun god.) Each of the Three Knights is in turn opposed by a woman and her child; each mother in turn calls for vengeance for the innocent whose blood is shed. This pattern is accordingly repeated three times; and is characteristic of the formal patterning of the play as a whole. The Three Knights boast to Herod of what they have done, and claim a reward. In the ranting monologue which rounds off the play Herod again boasts and triumphs and promises extravagant rewards to his Three Knights—next time ('when I com agayn').

In these plays Herod and Pilate are thus served by lesser Herods and Pilates who evoke (in Yeats's phrase) the 'emotion of multitude'. Though often rebellious and continually brawling, they do their master's bidding, cowed by his more powerful rant. Themselves oppressed they are themselves oppressors and—even when only three in number—*seem* to be a multitude. The recurrence of three figures, Three Shepherds, Three Kings, Three Marys and (of the opposite party) Three Soldiers, Three Devils, is characteristic of the Mystery Cycle—as of mythology.

§ 9

What happens in Christ's life in between the two great events, his birth and his death, is somewhat sketchily represented in the Mystery Cycle and is indeed mostly not there. As Raglan remarks (in *The Hero*[1]) there is characteristically something of a gap between the birth of the hero (or god) and his *agon* and death; and this would not be surprising if the gap corresponds to the interval between two ritual ceremonies. We must, of course, distinguish between the Christ of the Mystery Cycle, a ritual dramatic figure, and Christ (of the New Testament).

In the Towneley plays of the Passion the opening rant of Pilate in the *Conspiracy* (No. 20), the whole of the *Buffeting* (No. 21) and of the *Scourging* (No. 22) and the greater part of the Play of the *Talents* (No. 24) have been attributed to the Wakefield Master and are of such a texture as to justify the attribution. On the other hand, the *Crucifixion* (No. 23), which shows signs of various revisions, appears to belong on the whole to an earlier stratum.

In this great sequence of the Passion we are close to the origins

[1] Chap. XVII.

of Tragedy in ritual drama—in the dethronement and sacrificial death of the king or god. The role of Christ here is that of the dying or sacrificed god preliminary to his resurrection and final victory over the demons of darkness. Pilate presides over Christ's death and is, as Herod is, something of a terrible clown who at his first entrance (in the *Conspiracy*) brandishes a sword, rages and rants. But he is a rather more multifold villain than Herod, a fearsome oppressor and at the same time, as he describes himself, a politic double-dealer (in both respects a prototype of some of the villains of the Elizabethan stage).

> For I am he that may   make or mar a man;
> My self if I it say   as men of cowrte now can;
> Supporte a man to day   to-morn agans hym than,
> On both parties thus I play   and fenys me to ordan
>   The right.

Pilate's instruments—and in the Play of the *Buffeting* the instruments of Cayphas and Anna—are the knights or soldiers, grumbling, brawling ruffians, humorous savages like the devils of the *Last Judgment*. Christ speaks only once, and only a line or two, in the Play of the *Buffeting* and similarly in the Play of the *Scourging*. His silence is of course in the New Testament account morally most impressive. But in these episodes of the Mystery Cycle Christ has something of the mysterious impersonal or non-human quality of the sacrificial victim, something even of the passivity or immobility of a masked figure or of a sacred doll or puppet, image of a god. Thus the *Buffeting* is, it seems, essentially a rite. Christ is placed on a stool blindfold and mockingly required to say who struck him last.

> We shall teche hym, I wote   a new play of Yoyll.

The resemblance to those rough medieval games, Hot-cockles and Hoodman-blind, is surely not accidental. (In Hot-cockles the blindfolded man had to guess the name of his buffeter; in Hoodman-blind—from which our Blind Man's Buff is derived—the victim who wore his hood over his face had to try to catch one of his unseen buffeters.) We may remember also the farcical episode in the *Frogs* of Aristophanes in which Dionysos and his servant are beaten in order to establish which is the true god.

This sequence of episodes must seem painfully brutal and primitive to us. There *may* have been a grim recognition that the savagely humorous, mocking soldiers do not know whom thay are maltreating. But this sense of irony may be a modern interpretation; the crowd at the Mystery Cycle are unlikely to have been so detached. The likelihood is that the soldiers know well enough—as well as do all the participants. The underlying dilemma was perhaps that the god had to be sacrificed, and at the same time those who actively sacrificed him had to be condemned. Neverthe less, there seems at this point to be at least a partial identification of the worshippers with the soldiers rather than with the god. This savage clowning becomes more understandable once we recognize some connexion between it and the ancient frenzied or orgiastic rites of mutilating or tearing to pieces the god,[1] preparatory to his triumphant reappearance or resurrection in renewed power and glory like the sun scattering his enemies, the demons of darkness.

> For after this shall thou se   when that I do com downe
> In brightnes on he   in clowdys from abone.

The strange savagery—strange because humorous, and again buffoonery in the presence of death—that breaks out again in the Passion sequence of the Christian Mystery Cycle only becomes intelligible by means of some such explanation.

So Mary, too, by her lament at the foot of the Cross (in the Play of the *Crucifixion*) takes her place in the succession of the wailing women of the ancient rituals weeping for Adonis or for Baldur.

In the Play of the *Talents* (the immediate sequel to the *Crucifixion* in the Towneley Cycle) Pilate and the Three Soldiers cast dice to decide who shall have Christ's coat. There is again New Testament authority for this episode in the mention of the drawing of lots for Christ's garments. But it is clear from what is said about the coat that in the play it is regarded as in itself a very special coat

---

[1] We need scarcely remind ourselves that in some primitive rites the sacrificed god—often an animal—was of course also devoured, not in order to destroy him but to possess him completely, that his life and power might enter into his people.

coveted for very special reasons; it is supposed to possess magical properties. (This is as we might expect if we remember that the kingship or godhead was regarded as itself inhering magically in the robe donned or doffed in ceremonial rites by a king or human representative of a god.[1]) It is his own title to the kingship that Pilate is concerned to establish or usurp immediately upon Christ's death, as is shown by his rant at the opening of the Play of the *Talents*. Of course, the game between Pilate and the Three Soldiers is quite irregular—a mere buffoonery of a solemn rite. Though Pilate walks off with the coat, he has not in fact won it. He proves himself once again a double-dealer and a bully, the arch-rogue; although he loses in the dice throwing he insists on keeping the coat. The scene is, at the same time, a realistic representation of a scene in a contemporary ale-house where dice were cast or games played for someone's hood as prize. As such it is excellent farce. At first Pilate, having thrown a high figure, thinks he is winning; but when he unexpectedly loses to the Third Soldier, he first asks the winner for the coat as a gift, and, when he is not given it, he impudently takes it. Then the Three Soldiers forswear dice and (surprisingly as coming from them) express vigorous moralist sentiments that seem to have flowered out from the medieval vernacular sermons.

FIRST SOLDIER: Now thise dyse that ar undughty[2]   for los
                                                of this good,
  Here I forswere hertely   by Mahownes blood;
  For was I never so happy[3]   by mayn nor by mode,
  To wyn with sich sotelty   to my lyfys fode,
    As ye ken;

[1] In Hocart's *Kingship*, Chap. VII, p. 79, we read, for example: 'The garments with which the Indian king is invested . . . represent the various membranes of the womb into which the king is supposed to enter in order to be born again. They are termed the cauls and the womb of dominion or sovereignty. After putting on the womb the priest hands to the king five dice, saying, "Thou art the master; may these five regions of thine (i.e. the four points of the compass and the zenith) fall to thy lot." Sovereignty is thus acquired by decision of the dice, and this reminds us of the game played for supremacy between the Dalai Lama and the King of the Demons in Tibet; this leads us back to the idea of victory.'

[2] unprofitable.   [3] lucky.

Thise dysars and thise hullars,[1]
Thise cokkers[2] and thise bollars,[3]
And all purs-cuttars,
    Bese well war of thise men.

SECOND SOLDIER: Fy, fy, on thise dyse   the devill I theym
                                                            take![4]

Unwytty, unwyse   with thaym that wold lake;[5]
As fortune assyse[6]   men wyll she make;
Hir manners ar nyse[7]   she can downe and uptake;
    And rych
She turnes up-so-downe,
And under abone,
Most chefe of renowne
    She castys in the dyche.
By hir meanes she makys   dysers to sell,
As thay sytt and lakys,[8]   thare corne and thare catell.

§ 10

We might well ask why the episode of the Harrowing of Hell
(from the Apocryphal Gospel of Nicodemus) should have assumed
such significance for medieval people that it forms one of the outstanding and apparently indispensable episodes in the Mystery
Cycle. If a text of it was lacking locally it had at least to be borrowed, as the Towneley play (No. 25) appears to have been
borrowed from the York Cycle. Surely the answer may have to do
with the fact that in the mythologies the descent of the hero or god
into the underworld is one of the regular, if not essential, episodes
in his career. More specifically what we find enacted once again in
the Play of the *Harrowing of Hell*, in a new form and with a new
significance, is the age-old contest between light and darkness, the
triumph of the sun-god over the demons of darkness. The association of Christ with the sun and with light is unmistakable even in
the sequence of the Passion. Thus the soldiers remark of Christ's

---

[1] lechers.   [2] fighters.   [3] drunkards.   [4] give to.   [5] play.
[6] appoints.   [7] foolish.   [8] play.

face that it is 'fare shynyng' and that, on the cross, 'it shoyn as any glas'; and Mary exclaims at the moment of his death:

> Alas! thyn een as cristall clere   that shoyn as son in sight,
> That lufly were in lyere[1]   lost thay have thare light,
> And wax all faed in fere[2]   all dym then ar thay dight!

The Play of the *Harrowing of Hell* enacts the victory that follows this temporary eclipse. The approach of Christ is experienced by the imprisoned souls as the approach of light dispelling the darkness in which they sit. It is one more proof of the accuracy of Hocart's observation: 'Thus the old beliefs which began before our earliest written records continue to supply Christianity with its imagery'.[3] The identification of Christ as the true sun-god (*Sol Verus*) appears to have been deliberately made by St. Patrick and other early missionaries as a means of appealing to the pagans. Thus, having been given a new spiritual-symbolic meaning, this important centre of the pagan mythology could be incorporated into Christianity. The episode of the Play appears to correspond to the ceremony of re-lighting the candles in the night before Easter, and, perhaps more fundamentally, to the first breaking of light on Easter morning. The plays of the Passion and the Resurrection correspond, in general, to the ceremonies of Holy Week.

Christ himself, in the opening monologue or prologue of the play, proclaims—'A light I will thay have.' There follows a dialogue between the souls in which their mounting excitement is felt, and it is on the theme of the dawning of light. Adams begins:

> Fower thowsand and sex hundreth yere
> Have we bene here in darknes stad;[4]
> Now se I tokyns of solace sere,[5]
> A gloryous gleme to make us glad.

Eve responds:

> This menys solace certain;
> Sich light can on us leynd[6]
> In paradyse full playn.

[1] face.   [2] power? (Icelandic, *faeri*).   [3] See also *Kingship*, XVIII, 'The Gods'.
[4] placed.   [5] manifold.   [6] fall.

Isaiah recognizes that his prophecy is about to be fulfilled:

> I spake of folke in darknes walkand
> I said a light shuld on theym lende.[1]

John the Baptist joins his testimony to theirs:

> His light is on us layde,
> And commys oure karys to kele.[2]

Moses describes the nature of the light as he experienced it on the occasion of the Transfiguration. ('Of that same light lernyng have I', as it is in the York Play, has been altered here in the Towneley Play to 'Now this same nyght lernyng had I'.)

> As whyte as snaw was his body,
> His face was like the son for bright,
> No man on mold was so myghty
> Grathly[3] durst loke agans that light;
> And that same light here se I now
> Shynyng on us, certayn . . .

The triumph of light over darkness, and generally of life over death, which is the sublime theme of the *Harrowing of Hell*, is thus the climax of the contest on the Cross in which Christ had only appeared to be the loser. The First Soldier in the Play of the *Crucifixion* had said, 'Ye just in tournament'. Christ is thus conceived, on the analogy of the romances, as the knightly champion whose opponent in the first joust in the Play of the *Harrowing of Hell* is Satan. He lays siege to his opponent's castle, symbolically breaks open the gates—they burst open at his command—and liberates the imprisoned souls within, releases imprisoned life, as victor over death.

JESUS: Attollite portas, principes . . .
RYBALD: Out, harro, out! what devill is he
  That callys hym kyng over us all?
BELZABUB: Go, spar the yates, yll mot thou the![4]
  And set the waches on the wall . . .

---

[1] fall. [2] cool, i.e. assuage. [3] directly. [4] fare.

DAVID: Nay, with hym may ye not fyght,
>   For he is kyng and conqueroure,
>   And of so mekill myght
>   And styf in every stoure;[1]
>   Of hym commys all this light
>   That shynys in this bowre . . .

The play preludes the triumphant Easter morning theme of the Play of the *Resurrection* (No. 26).[2]

The Towneley Play of the *Harrowing of Hell* may be compared (as may also the Play of the *Fall of Lucifer*) with what appears to be its earlier and more complete form in the York Cycle. The elaborate, formal stanzaic verse of the York Play—alliterative and rhymed and not unlike the stanzas of *Pearl*—has not been very successfully kept up in the Towneley Play. The balanced, formal structure of the play, as it is in the York version, has correspond-ingly been disturbed by displacements and by some expansion and diffusion as well as simplification. Nevertheless the general arrangement, and much of the detail, remains substantially the same in both versions. A prologue spoken by Jesus is followed by a dialogue between the souls who sit in darkness. This dialogue is formal, antiphonal, yet expresses an excited sense of light ap-proaching, an expectancy of deliverance at hand. The devils or demons notice the commotion, and it communicates itself to them; they themselves in turn become disturbed—there is an element of farce here.

RYBALD: How, Belzabub! bynde thise boyes,   sich harow was
>   never hard in hell.

BELZABUB: Out, Rybald! thou rores;   what is betyd? Can
>   thou oght tell?

RYBALD: Whi, herys thou not this ugly noyse?
>   Thise lurdans[3] that in lymbo dwell . . .

---

[1] battle.

[2] The inspiration of Passus XVIII of the B-text of *Piers Plowman* could well have come from the witnessing of the Plays of the *Crucifixion* and of the *Harrowing of Hell*. Certain passages in this Passus, notably ll. 57–67, 259–69, 304–5, 313–23, 362–70 and 409 to the end, witness how sublimity of effect may be attained in homely phrases and diction.

[3] lazy louts.

BELZABUB: They shall never pas out of this place.
　　Call up Astarot and Anaball
　　　To gyb us counsell in this case;
　　Bell, Berith, and Bellyall . . .

The devils are only less sturdy than those of the Play of the *Last Judgment* and certainly appear to have come from the same mythological source, the demons of darkness whom light quells. It is at this point in the play that the voice of Jesus is heard for the first time commanding:

　　　　　　Attollite portas, principes . . .

The Latin words are those heard during the services of Holy Week and used also in such ceremonies as the consecration of churches, the opening of the barred door and the expulsion of the demons from the building (they must have accumulated solemnity through the centuries from such uses). The devils make ready to defend the castle of darkness; Belzabub calls up Satan himself, who appears grumbling and demanding what is the matter.

SATAN: The devill you all to har![1]
　　What ales the so to showte?

For the second time in the play, the voice of Jesus is heard:

　　　　　　Attollite portas, principes . . .
　　　　　　Ye prynces of hell open yowre yate
　　　　　　And let my folk furth gone . . .

The final stage of the contest is then entered upon, a dialogue exchange (or flyting) between Jesus and Satan at the end of which Satan sinks vanquished into the pit—a second fall of Lucifer.

§ 11

The Play of the *Harrowing of Hell* thus seems to correspond to the restoring of light in the night of vigil before Easter—in the Holy Week services—the relighting of the candles that had been

---

[1] harry.

put out and the first breaking of light on Easter morning. It is therefore immediately followed by the Easter play, the Play of the *Resurrection* (No. 26). This Towneley Resurrection play appears to be based, like the *Harrowing of Hell*, on the York version. We may regard it as, in a sense, the oldest play in the Cycle, if we regard the Liturgical Resurrection play as having been the earliest of the Liturgical plays and these plays as the ancestors of all the plays that were gradually put together to form the Mystery Cycle. In the course of about two centuries, even after the change-over from Latin to English, the pattern of the Resurrection play appears to have been little altered. The soldiers on watch sleep, Christ rises, the Three Marys advance towards the vacant sepulchre, the Angel asks whom they seek, they answer, and so on, much as the New Testament episode had been performed by priestly actors in the church services. But though the pattern of the play itself has been little changed, the triumph of the occasion must have been somewhat anticipated in the Cycle, by the triumph-of-light theme in the preceding *Harrowing of Hell*. The pattern of the Cycle as a whole must necessarily have been altered by the introduction of the Harrowing of Hell episode, which now receives stronger emphasis than the Resurrection; the Harrowing of Hell, as it were, steals the thunder from the Resurrection.

The reappearances of Christ after his Resurrection are shown in a play called the *Peregrini* (No. 27) which represents the events on the road to Emmaus, and a play first entitled *Resurreccio Domini* on the MS and later altered to *Thomas Indie* (No. 28). These re-appearances are typical of the slain hero or god in that (as is emphasized in the plays) it is not a mere ghost who appears but Christ himself in the body. No one in the plays denies the appearances. But the sceptics such as Thomas (Doubting Thomas) insist that it was a mere ghost who was reputed to have appeared.

Ye segh hym not bodily   his gost it myght well be.

Jesus himself then reappears to Thomas and convinces him—and no doubt the crowd at the play—that he is no ghost but actually himself again in the body. He can be touched, and he sits down and eats with his Apostles once more as at the Last Supper; there could be no stronger proofs of his substantiality. The Play of the *Ascension* (No. 29)—a patchwork of various metres that may indi-cate the work of various hands over a number of years—is far from a triumphant episode, because Christ, of whose bodily substance and actual restoration we have become convinced, is rapt away again through the clouds, and his people on earth are left mourn-ing his absence from sight and touch. In the next and final play of the Cycle, however, the Play of the *Last Judgment* (No. 30), he comes again in power and majesty to judge the world.

§ 12

The greater part of the Towneley Play of the *Last Judgment* (No. 30) consists, as it now stands, of two dialogues between devils. It is not surprising that these two dialogues have been attributed to the Wakefield Master; they are dramatic poetry of a higher order than the rest of the play and indeed than most of the Towneley Cycle, and are similar in texture—allowing for the difference of their grim theme—with the two Shepherds' Plays. The devils (or demons) are again traditional types in the sense that they have almost certainly not been invented for the Mystery Cycle but have descended from some ancient or pre-Christian mythology; they appear to be of the nature more particularly of earth-demons who live underground and are antagonists of the light, the ancient demons of darkness. They are typical of the devils of other episodes of the Towneley and other versions of the Mystery Cycle, grimly humorous savages. The difference is simply that, as re-created in these two dialogues by a master poet, they are more alive and real than they commonly are. When the uncommon energy they here have as dramatic characters is analysed, it will be found once again to be identical with the uncommon satiric verve and raciness of the language in which they talk and flyte and in which a poet has re-created them. The colloquial language of the dialogue is heightened into remarkable alliterative-and-rhyming verse; and the traditional satiric flyting mode has here achieved perhaps its most vigorous renewal in the whole Towneley Cycle.

At the beginning of the first dialogue two demons have heard the trumpet of the Judgement. They express amazed bewilderment; they are badly shaken and cannot make out what has happened. They, too, have suffered a resurrection. The chains that had bound them have been shattered by the blast. It may have been that in the original mythology these chains were of ice—ice shackles—and the type of experience here expressed is of the sudden thaw in which the ice world breaks up, as happens with violence in the Scandinavian North (after all, the earlier home of such at least of the British people as were of Norse descent). At any rate, whether or not it was originally the hard, icebound earth in which the demons were fettered, the effect here is not only of their having been rudely wakened and shaken up but of their being benumbed and aware throughout their bodies of aches, pains and cramps. There are noticeable parallels between this episode and (as described in the Eddic visionpoem *Völuspa*) the Old Norse end of the world when the dreadful Gjallahorn makes a roaring sound through all the worlds and the dwarfs are groaning. (It may not be fanciful to see in these traditional demons, earth spirits, of the Mystery Cycle, at least as much as in the 'salvages' of the newly discovered lands, the ancestry of Caliban). The condition of the demons, as described by themselves, is principally a state of body, and the trumpet blast has also had a physical effect, as of an earthquake, upon their habitat, the region of darkness, in which they appear to have been hibernating.

PRIMUS DEMON: Oute, haro, out, out!   harkyn to this

horne . . .

I was bonde full fast
In yrens for to last,
Bot my bandys thai brast
    And shoke all in sonder.

SECUNDUS DEMON: I shoterd[1] and shoke   I herd sich a rerd,[2]
When I harde it I qwoke   for all that I lerd,
Bot to swere on a boke   I durst not aperd;[3]
I durst not loke   for all medillerd,
    Full payll;

[1] shuddered.   [2] roar.   [3] show myself.

363

Bot gyrned and gnast,[1]
My force did I frast,[2]
Bot I wroght all wast,[3]
  It myght not avayll.

PRIMUS DEMON: It was like to a trumpe   it had sich a sowned;
  I fell on a lumpe   for ferd that I swonde.
SECUNDUS DEMON: There I stode on my stumpe   I stakerd
                                              that stownde,[4]
  There cachid I the crumpe   yet held I my grounde
  Halfe nome.
PRIMUS DEMON: Make redy oure gere,
  We ar like to have were,
  For now dar I swere
    That domysday is comme.

It has slowly penetrated to them that it is Doomsday and that
'we are like to have war'.[5] Hell is by then vacant because the souls
—whom they regard as their property—have already answered the
dreadful summons. The demons recognize that their interests and
their property are at stake. They must prepare to defend their legal
rights and claims. It is necessary that, although they are afraid of
the great Judge, they should themselves attend the Judgement—
conceived as a great parliament—and make their way there up
Watling Street (a familiar name for the Milky Way); these
demons have a local habitation. Like the dwarfs of folk-tales, who
carry bags on their backs, the demons of this play also have bags.
These they declare to be stuffed full of sins and sinners—or of rolls
which are the records of sins and sinners.

Here is a bag full, lokys,
  Of pride and of lust,
Of wraggers and wrears[6]   a bag full of brefes,
Of carpars and cryars   of mychers[7] and thefes,
Of lurdans[8] and lyars   that no man lefys,

---

[1] gnashed (teeth).   [2] try.   [3] in vain.   [4] instant (pang?).
[5] As described in *Völuspá*, too, there is a last universal war in which the gods
perish.
[6] twisters and wranglers.   [7] pilferers.   [8] lazy louts.

364

Of flytars, of flyars[1]   and renderars of reffys;[2]
   This can I,
Of alkyn astates
That go bi the gatys,
Of poore pride,[3] that god hatys,
   Twenty so many.

Here the first demon laughs till (as he says) he ties himself in a knot, and he offers his companion a drink. The demons with their rolls have now assumed the aspect of lawyers—or of clowns burlesquing lawyers—and the episode thus evolves into a parody of the Judgement. We do not know—we can only guess—what clowning there may have been in the performances in addition to that explicitly suggested in the text. Their rolls, judging from the multitudinous recordings referred to, were surely too big and too many for them; we have probably here something of that type of clowning in which little fellows are overwhelmed by objects too large and too many for them, and continually dropped. But the demons are gleeful because they have accumulated such a superfluity of evidence in favour of their claims; it is an ill wind that blows nobody good, and Doomsday is likely to increase their wealth. But had Doomsday been delayed much longer they would have had (the Second Demon says) to build Hell bigger; with the approach of Doomsday, evil has been multiplying in the world as darkness in winter.[4]

As in the Shepherds' plays a Third Shepherd appears on the scene later than the other two, here a Third Demon (named Tutivillus) makes his appearance late. All three demons are, of course, late for the Judgement itself, and now and then express dread of the consequences. Tutivillus is recognized as his servant by the First Demon—again the figure of the mischievous servant—and is even more of a clown than the other two; he acts the clever and learned lawyer, quoting bits of Latin, and is complimented for his cleverness and learning by the other two. He boasts that he has sometimes fetched more than ten thousand souls in an hour to Hell, something of a conjuring feat.

---

[1] fugitives from justice?   [2] plunder?   [3] i.e. penniless pride.
[4] In *Völuspa*, too, there is brother against brother as the world nears its end. With the whole episode compare the case in Chancery in *Bleak House* (Chapter 64).

Mo than ten thowsand   in an howre of a day;
Som at ayll-howse I fande   and som of ferray.[1]

The resemblance between Tutivillus's 'ranting rhyming' and
that of Burns and the other Scots satiric and comic verse-makers
may not be accidental, since both belong to the province of
Northern verse.

Here a roll of ragman[2]   of the rownde tabill,
Of breffes in my bag, man   of synnes dampnabill;
Unethes[3] may I wag,[4] man   for wery in youre stabill
Whils I set my stag, man.

Tutivillus's rant occasionally passes into resounding Latin
gibberish, like Herod's and Pilate's.

Mi name is Tutivillus,
  My horne is blawen;
Fragmina verborum   Tutivillus colligit horum,
Belzabub algorum   Belial belium doliorum.

He, too, has a horn which surely parodies the terrible horn of the
Judgement. Thus the whole solemn and terrible occasion is to
some extent parodied.

Tutivillus proceeds to enumerate the wealth of sins and sinners
who have been accumulated for the aggrandisement of Hell. In
particular he has collected records of the proud and vain sinners
who dress extravagantly while their children go without bread.

Gay gere and witles   his hode set on koket,[5]
As prowde as pennyles   his slefe has no poket,
  Full redles;[6]
With thare hemmyd shoyn,
All this must be done,
Bot syre is out at hye noyn
  And his barnes bredeles.

The Otherworld—and its multitude of faery women—has been
annexed to the Devil's kingdom, its nature hideously changed and

---

[1] plundering.   [2] document with seals.   [3] scarcely.
[4] move?   [5] cocked.   [6] without counsel.

distorted. Among the multitude of women consigned to Hell are sinful hags whose ugliness is disguised by finery.

> So joly
> Ilka las in a lande
> Like a lady nerehande,
> So fresh and so plesande,
>   Makys men to foly.
> If she be never so fowl a dowde   with hir kelles[1] and hir
>   pynnes,
> The shrew hir self can shrowde   both hir chekys and hir
>   chynnes;
> She can make it full prowde   with japes and with gynnes,[2]
> Hir hede as hy as a clowde   bot no shame of hir synnes
>   Thai fele;
> When she is thus paynt,[3]
> She makys it so quaynte,
> She lookys like a saynt,
>   And wars then the Deyle.
> She is hornyd like a kowe . . .
> The cuker[4] hyngys so side now   furrid with a cat skyn.

Though 'hornyd like a kowe' describes head-dresses actually fashionable and 'furrid with a cat skyn' actual footwear, the phrases introduce also suggestions of animal characteristics and affinities, if not of animal disguises actually worn in festival ceremonies and dances. Satiric mockery of fantastic new fashions in dress keeps recurring.[5]

> Yit a poynte of the new gett[6]   to tell will I not blyn,[7]
> Of prankyd gownes and shulders up set   mos and flokkys
>   sewyd wyth in.[8]

An impression of an immense diversity of sins and sinners is built

---

[1] cauls, ornamental hairnets.   [2] jests and tricks.   [3] painted.
[4] a kind of half-boot or gaiter.
[5] There is a very similar poem on the Follies of Fashion in the Harley 2253 manuscript of the beginning of the fourteenth century.
[6] fashion.   [7] stop.   [8] i.e. for padding.

up—a diversity of perverted life that corresponds, perhaps, to the original diversity of created life.

> Yit of thise kyrk⸗chaterars   here ar a menee,[1]
> Of barganars and okerars[2]   and lufars of symonee,
> Of runkers[3] and rowners   god castys thaym out, trulee.

But the proudest of all in this phantasmagoria of perverted life are the Seven Deadly Sins.

> Thise laddys thai leven   as lordys riall.[4]

It may be that it was through the vernacular sermons that the Seven Deadly Sins passed into the poetry and drama of the Middle Ages. But we must ask exactly how these monstrous caricatures could have been created out of abstract moral classifications. The possible explanation is that they are—at least in part—moralized reincarnations of older mythical or ritual beings as these had per⸗sisted in the traditions and imagination and perhaps actual cere⸗monies[5] of the people. They appear to have lived on as a power in the vernacular itself; for, if we examine the passages in which they occur we see that it is a tendency in the vernacular itself that seems to create or re⸗create them. It is a tendency to magnify or distort certain elementary aspects of human nature and, occasion⸗ally, also to metamorphose the human form into the likeness of some animal. Tutivillus's descriptions of Drunkenness and Sloth are realistic enough; but, as a whole, the Deadly Sins here as else⸗where are caricatures of isolated aspects or elements of human life. They certainly seem no less real than the ordinary human life they spectacularly illustrate; they are imbued with a terrible farcical intensity as if, indeed, they moved in some primitive ritual dance. The Seven Deadly Sins may, therefore, again be regarded as essen⸗tially traditional figures, not invented for this or for any other play of the Mystery Cycle but incorporated into it. Moreover they represent an important element—as in the comedy of Ben Jonson

---

[1] company.   [2] usurers.   [3] whisperers.   [4] royal.
[5] Dunbar's *Dance of the Seven Deidly Sins* and the scene in Alloway Kirk in Burns's *Tam o' Shanter* could almost be eyewitness descriptions of actual assemblies and dances of the witch cult.

and of Dickens—of what became the English comic tradition.
The description of the Deadly Sins in the final flyting monologue
spoken by Tutivillus forms the grand climax of the first dialogue
of demons. (The passage, as it has survived, is unfortunately very
corrupt.)

His luddokkys[1] thai lowke   like walk-mylne cloggys,
His hede is like a stowke   hurlyd[2] as hoggys,
A woll blawen bowke[3]   thise fryggys[4] as froggys,
This Jelian Jowke   dryfys he no doggys
    To felter;[5]
Bot with youre yolow lokkys,
For all youre many mokkys,
Ye shall clym on hell crokkys
    With a halpeny heltere.

And Nell with hir nyfyls[6]   of crisp and of sylke,
Tent well youre twyfyls[7]   youre nek abowte as mylke;
With youre bendys and youre bridyls   of Sathan, the
                                                whilke
Sir Sathanas Idyls   you for tha ilke
    This Gill knaue;[8]
It is open behynde,
Before is it pynde,
Bewar of the West wynde
    Youre smok lest it wafe.

Of Ire and of Enuy   fynde I herto,
Of Covetyse and Glotony   and many other mo;
Thai call and thai cry   'go we now, go!
I dy nere for dry'   and ther syt thai so
    All nyght;
With hawvell and jawvell,
Syngyng of lawvell,[9]

---

[1] buttocks.   [2] covered with bristles.   [3] belly.   [4] creatures.   [5] tangle?
[6] trifles, frills.   [7] twirls, curls.   [8] knave.   [9] 'hawvell', 'jawvell' (cf. 'jawing'),
'lawvell'; i.e. gabbling and jabbering and blasphemous singing.

Thise ar howndys of hell,
  That is thare right.

In Slewthe then thai syn   goddys warkys thai not wyrke;
To belke[1] thai begyn   and spew that is irke;
His hede must be holdyn   ther in the myrke,
Then deffys hym with dyn   the bellys of the kyrke,
  When thai clatter;
He wishys the clerke hanged
For that he rang it,
Bot thar hym[2] not lang[3] it,
  What commys ther after.

And ye Janettys of the stewys   and lychoures on lofte,
Youre baill now brewys   avowtrees[4] full ofte,
Youre gam now grewys[5]   I shall you set softe,
Youre sorow enewes[6]   com to my crofte[7]
  All ye;
All harlottys and horres,
And bawdys that procures,
To bryng thaym to lures,
  Welcom to my see!

Ye lurdans and lyars   mychers and thefes,[8]
Flytars and flyars   that all men reprefes,
Spolars, extorcyonars   welcom, my lefes![9]
Fals jurars and usurars   to symony that clevys,
  To tell;
Hasardars and dysars,
Fals dedys forgars,
Slanderars, bakbytars,
  All unto hell.

Such multitudes of souls are now crowding into Hell that the
Porter at the gate—like the Porter in *Macbeth*—is overworked.

    Saules cam so thyk   now late unto hell
      As ever;

[1] belch.   [2] he need.   [3] wish.   [4] adulteries.   [5] turns to horror.
[6] renews.   [7] enclosure.   [8] Cf. p. 364 (notes 7 and 8).   [9] dears.

> Oure porter at hell yate
> Is haldyn so strate,
> Up erly and downe late,
> He rystys never.

Obviously the author of Act II, Sc. 3 of *Macbeth* knew of the Mystery Cycle and moreover expected his audience to take the reference to the 'porter at hell yate' in the sacred drama, with all its implications for the Shakespearian tragedy.

The second of the two dialogues between demons in the Play of the *Last Judgment* may be regarded as the sequel to the first; it is spoken between the demons as they are driving the flocks of the damned into Hell. Their attitude towards the damned souls is, of course, quite unsympathetic. The latter should have known better. Where are now their gold, their retinues and their finery? They were once sturdy and proud, finding fault with others. The view-point is the opposite of that of the final monologue spoken by Doctor Faustus.

§ 13

Two additional pieces follow the Play of the *Last Judgment* in the Towneley MS, a Play of *Lazarus* (No. 31) and of the *Hanging of Judus* (No. 32). It may be assumed that they have been displaced from earlier in the Cycle. But one can well see how the episode of Lazarus might have gravitated towards the Last Judgement—the occasion of the general Resurrection of the Dead. In the play, Lazarus newly risen from the dead (to say 'I am Lazarus come from the dead') speaks a grim monologue—and, if it really did in some performance come at the end of the play of the Judgement, an epilogue on the theme of vanity and death.

> Ilkon in sich aray   with dede thai shall be dight,
> And closid colde in clay   wheder he be kyng or knyght
> For all his garmentes gay   that semely were in sight,
> His flesh shall frete[1] away   with many a wofull wight.
> Then wofully sich wightys[2]

[1] eat.   [2] creatures.

Shall gnawe thise gay knyghtys,
Thare lunges and thare lightys,[1]
  Thare harte shall frete in sonder;
Thise masters most of myghtys
  Thus shall thai be broght under.

Under the erthe ye shall   thus carefully then cowche;
The royfe of youre hall   youre nakyd nose shall towche;
Nawther great ne small   to you will knele ne crowche;
A shete shall be youre pall   sich todys shall be youre
                                         nowche;[2]
Todys shall you dere,[3]
Feyndys will you fere,
Youre flesh that fare was here
  Thus rufully shall rote;
In stede of fare colore
  Sich bandys shall bynde youre throte.

Youre rud[4] that was so red   youre lyre[5] the lylly lyke,
Then shall be wan as led   and stynke as dog in dyke;
Wormes shall in you brede   as bees dos in the byke,[6]
And ees out of your hede   thus-gate shall paddokys pyke;
To pike you ar preste[7]
Many uncomly beest,
Thus thai shall make a feste
  Of youre flesh and of youre blode.

Even here, macabre as it is, the poetry is perhaps to some extent lifted out of morbidity or mere horror by the element of vigorous farce. The references to the activities of toads, dogs, bees and frogs, and the incongruities and indignities—

Shall gnawe thise gay knyghtys . . .
The royfe of youre hall   youre nakyd nose shall towche . . .

render the horrors of physical death vigorously and produce an effect of grim farce.

---

[1] eyes   [2] brooch.   [3] hurt.   [4] complexion.   [5] face.
[6] bees-nest, hive.   [7] ready, quick.

§ 14

It may now be evident, from certain of the Towneley plays we have considered, that the Mystery Cycle is by no means a straight development or expansion from the Liturgical plays. There are things in the Cycle plays about which it is not surprising that the Church was more than doubtful; indeed, it is not surprising that the whole Cycle came to be regarded, from the Church's official point of view, as something which had got out of hand. Was it merely the tendency in unregenerate human nature to turn sacred things to buffoonery and farce which was responsible for the transformation? There is surely a profounder explanation. The Mystery Cycle was for the people, organized in their medieval town-communities, deeply important and not merely an opportunity for irresponsible releases of rowdiness. The new Christian drama was adopted by the townspeople and kept up by them for the same kinds of reason that old pagan ceremonies and dances continued to be kept up, in some cases almost desperately, in defiance of the prohibitions of the Church—because they were still, though perhaps obscurely, felt to be sacred and fundamental to life. How long such a feeling, once sanctioned by religion, can persist after the religion has been lost is suggested by what Dr. Marett (as quoted by E. K. Chambers in *The English Folk-Play*) reports of an Oxfordshire participant in the now degraded and ludicrous Mummers' Play who, at a suggestion of his, protested: 'Oh, you wouldn't have women in that; *it's more like being in church.*'[1]

The classic Greek drama was evolved, we know, out of earlier dramatic rituals. The evolution of the English drama—the drama of Shakespeare—was perhaps in some respects more complex. In its case it is necessary to take account, for example, of the influence of Classical models at the time of the Renaissance. Nevertheless, the only truly national (and communal) English drama before the Shakespearian is the Mystery Cycle; and it is already the outcome

---

[1] In the Cycle plays, Noah's wife and Mak's wife, Gyll, would have been played by men-actors.

of a union, a unique combination of the dramatic rituals of the old religion and the new, such as the priestly class could not by itself have accomplished even supposing it had wanted to do so. Thus we have noted that the Herod and the Pilate of the Mystery Cycle bear an unmistakable resemblance to the Turkish Knight of the Mummers' Play. But do we not see them again also on the Eliza-bethan stage itself as the prototypes of some of the villains and of the clowns or farcical characters? Do we not see them as an element occasionally even in certain of the Elizabethan 'tragic heroes'—in Lear or Macbeth in certain of the phases of their moral pro-gressions? The Elizabethan dramatists did not need to borrow the stage type of the ranter or boaster from the Latin comedy or the Senecan tragedy—though, of course, the more scholarly of them were quick to find a Classical sanction for their own creations or re-creations. These types (they exist of course in life) were there already in the native English dramatic tradition as Herod and Pilate and generally as the antagonists in the flytings that are a regular feature of the pattern of the Cycle plays. The association of buffoonery with death, which is another characteristic feature of the plays of the Mystery Cycle, has again its counterpart later in that mixture of comedy and tragedy which is so characteristic of Elizabethan English drama and which so distressed neo-classic critics. Furthermore, certain themes and symbolisms in the Shake-spearian drama (such as some of the symbolical significances of storms and disorders both social and natural, of winter and spring, youth and age, death and birth, the lost and the found one, dis-guises and metamorphoses, recognitions and restorations) are there already in the Mystery Cycle; as they were there, perhaps, in the dramatic rituals with which the Mystery Cycle appears to have had connexions.

Thus, from his own point of view, Frazer in his *Folk-lore of the Old Testament* perhaps hints at what should be our approach to this drama when he says, 'Far-fetched as this idea may appear to us, it may seem natural enough to the folk and to their best interpreters the poets. . . . In investigating every branch of folk-lore, the student may learn much from the poets, who perceive by intuition what most of us have to learn by a laborious collection of facts. Indeed, without some touch of poetic fancy, it is hardly possible to enter into the heart of the people. A frigid rationalist will knock in vain. . . . The porter will not open to Mr. Gradgrind.' The best of the Cycle plays yield their fuller meaning when they are recognized as poetic drama rooted in ritual drama. They have to be responded to fully as *poems*. The formula that drama is 'character in action' will only tend to inhibit this complete response, just as it does our response to Shakespeare. It will not be of use always to be looking in these plays for something in the character of any of the *dramatis personae* to explain what happens. The *dramatis personae* are often vivid enough as presences created out of the poetry of the dialogues and monologues; but what happens can never in these plays be explained simply in terms of characterization. Impersonal forces, forces outside personality, have as much or more to do with the shaping of events; and these impersonal elements and conditions are what the poetry makes us apprehend at least as much as it makes us apprehend persons.

The traditional art which shows itself successfully at intervals throughout the Mystery Cycle has perhaps had less acknowledgement as being an element in the Elizabethan drama than has Morality art (at any rate recently). The latter appears now to be recognized as at least as important an element as the more famous Senecan influence, important though the latter was stylistically and in other ways. Yet, when taken together with the dramatic games, ceremonies and dances widespread among the people—and which Shakespeare may have had opportunities of being familiar with in his youth at Stratford—the traditional art of the Mystery Cycle may prove to be even more deeply implanted in the Elizabethan dramatic tradition, subtler in its shaping influence and certainly not less important. The drama of the Elizabethan London theatres was rooted in the traditional civilization of England as a whole, though in touch with the new Renaissance culture of the scholars and courtly poets; it was conscious of Classical and Italian models, but not subservient to them.

VI

THE RELATION BETWEEN THE LITERATURE AND THE PAINTING AND SCULPTURE IN MEDIEVAL ENGLAND

VI. THE RELATION BETWEEN THE LITERATURE AND THE PAINTING AND SCULPTURE IN MEDIEVAL ENGLAND

§ 1

Little has been done to correlate the imagery and symbolism of medieval art with those of the poetry and drama, though there is clearly the closest, most intimate relation between them. A great deal that is obscure in the literature might be made less so if literary students were to pay more attention to the art. What concerns us here is not how these images originated but what was there, particularly in the churches and cathedrals, to be seen by the people and the poets. We may conclude that what was there to be seen by them almost daily must have secured a permanent lodgement in their minds, whenever or however these images originated. What was there to be seen would not, of course, consist only of the work of the sculptors and painters who were contemporary with the poets of any one generation. There were also the sculptures and paintings from the previous century and still earlier. (Indeed, we have the evidence before us that the sculptors of the fourteenth century did not invent the greater part of these images, because most of these images are there also in what remains of the sculpture of the preceding centuries.) We may dispute about what we suppose was in the conscious minds of medieval people. But we can at least still see with our eyes some of the same things that they saw with their eyes, the things that their artists made and that they daily looked upon. Although we are told[1] that 90 per cent of the

[1] According to Lawrence Stone in his *Sculpture in Britain in the Middle Ages* Introduction, p. 2.

sculpture there was in the medieval English cathedrals and churches was destroyed, we may well be astonished by the wealth of what still remains.

The wall-paintings and sculptures in the cathedrals and churches, the drama, the sermons, the religious poetry (notably *Piers Plowman* and the religious lyrics) render the same great religious subjects, the Annunciation, the Nativity, the Passion, the Resurrection, the Judgement or Doom. In the churches we find the pictorial and sculptural equivalents of the scenes and episodes of the religious literature. Itinerant craftsmen and artists[1] had more than a mode of life in common with itinerant minstrels and makers. They had minds stored with the same images, and they were certainly aware of each other's work. The audiences for the poems and the Miracle Plays must also have been taught to *see* and, by way of the symbolism, to think and feel largely by means of the paintings and sculptures in the churches. These images in colour, stone and wood were an essential part of their visible and imaginative world, and are mostly allegorical or symbolical, multiplex in meaning. The symbols are often highly sophisticated and elaborate, some in forms (such as the Tree and the Wheel) of ancient types, having a long and involved cultural history. By means of these symbols, and with the aid of the preachers who expounded them, the audiences of the poets must have been made accustomed to symbolism and expert at symbolical, not merely literal, interpretation. The medieval mind must have been filled by these images and symbols, and shaped by them; and therefore the conclusions for the poetry should be of interest. The symbolism of the one art may provide the modern reader with a clue to that of the other. It seems we cannot be on the wrong track if we expect to find symbolical meanings in medieval poetry.

It may be that at some stage in the evolution of sculptural art or painting linear designs sprouted into leaves or burst into animal or human shapes. But such a theory does not really account for the origins of these images. We would have to ask why the lines burst

[1] E. W. Tristram quotes records which show that craftsmen were brought from fourteen different counties for work on St. Stephen's Chapel from 1350 onwards. *English Wall-Painting of the Fourteenth Century*, II, pp. 30 *et seq.*

into these particular shapes and not others. Further—perhaps a more pertinent question—why do certain images persist? Why do certain images possess more vitality than others? The images of medieval art do not simply correspond to 'ideas' as the rationalists of the seventeenth- and eighteenth-century enlightenment understood the word. They are not simply formulations of the rationalistic mind, each image neatly equated to an idea. On the other hand, they are not simply linear patterns having no meaning, not 'pure art' as understood by nineteenth- and twentieth-century aesthetes. The most likely conclusion is that certain images persisted because successive generations felt that, for some reason, these images exerted some kind of power over them. It must be supposed that those images in particular which persisted for centuries responded to some continuing need or demand of the mind or nature of man.

§ 2

The enthusiasm of the late eighteenth and the nineteenth century for Gothic may sometimes strike us as an enthusiasm for ruins and melancholy darkness. We ourselves, however, can form but a poor idea from the medieval cathedrals and churches as they now are of the splendour, indeed gaiety of colour, they once displayed. It is surely not fanciful to recognize what corresponds to it, a feeling for distinct shapes and clear colours, not only in the passages in the *Romaunt of the Rose*, the *Book of the Duchess* and wherever Chaucer is describing decorated and painted walls and chambers but throughout his poetry—and throughout medieval poetry. In *Pearl*, for example, we find a splendour of colour—including the non-natural colours that distinguish the paradisaical garden from a garden in nature—associated with jewel-imagery and a quality of light; and in this respect the poem seems to correspond to the cathedrals and churches in their original glory of wall-paintings, painted sculptures and stained glass (with its unique combination of colour and light).

The wall-paintings and the sculptures in the churches are, of course, more especially relevant to the religious literature, the plays and carols, the sermons, *Piers Plowman* (aptly described by Dr. Owst[1] as the 'quintessence' of the vernacular sermons). But much of the detail, particularly of the sculptures and wood-carvings, may be found to have some relevance also to the alliterative poetry as a whole and to the romances.

Castles and manor houses, too, appear to have been decorated with wall-painting. While much of it also was probably on religious subjects, such remnants as have survived, if put together with the descriptions of decorated chambers in Chaucer and elsewhere, indicate that some of it illustrated subjects from the romances. Other illustrations of the romances have survived throughout Europe, in France, Germany and elsewhere, illuminated books, tapestries, embroideries, ivories. The archivolt of Modena Cathedral, which shows the sculptured figures of Arthur, Gawain and other knights rescuing 'Winlogee' (Arthur's Queen) from the castle of her abductor, has been dated as being of the early twelfth century. This is very early indeed if one remembers that Geoffrey of Monmouth's *Historia* was composed about 1137. Another of the earliest pictorial records of Arthur is also Italian. The mosaic pavement (dated *c.* 1165) of Otranto Cathredal shows Arthur—'Rex Arturus'—riding a goat. The popularity with sculptors and painters of the image of Tristram and Iseult under the tree, among whose branches King Mark is perched, is another indication of the fascination of the tree-symbol for the medieval mind and of the tree-subject for the artists.

Certain of the illustrations in the wonderful French illuminated books might surely have relevance to our appreciation of *Sir Gawayne and the Grene Knight* and of the other English alliterative poems and romances which we may associate with it. There is the picture of *Mai* in the fifteenth-century *Calendrier de Charles D'Angoulême* which seems to show that the story of the Gawain and the Green Knight contest *was* based on some kind of ritual contest; for here is evidently an episode from the regular French May-day rites in which two Green Knights, dressed in leaves and with tree lances and saplings for clubs, engage in a ritual jousting. The Green Knight's green horse may also be explained by the

[1] *Preaching in Mediaeval England*, VII, 295.

horses in the picture being decked, indeed draped and masked, in greenery. This is surely evidence to support the view that the story of the poem was founded on ritual and myth which were so generally known that the knowledge of them could be taken for granted by the poet. The evidence is not invalidated by the fact that, in the poem, the May rite has become associated with the Christmas or New Year play or ritual game.

Another French fifteenth-century illuminated book, *Les Chasses a Chantilly*, provides the modern reader of *Sir Gawayne and the Grene Knight, The Awntyrs of Arthure* and other romances with splendid pictorial equivalents of the hunting episodes which are such a spectacular feature of these poems. The gay picture of a cart decked in greenery for camouflage, in *Les Chasses*, may appro-priately come to the mind of the reader of the initial episode of *The Parlement of the Thre Ages* in which the youthful deer-stalker's camouflage of greenery makes him look like what he feels, a sum-mer king. The illustration of the month of May in *Les Très Riches Heures du duc de Berry* shows a May-day cavalcade of knights and ladies and their horses all decked in green garlands, three ladies entirely in green being especially prominent. This is a type of theme that is frequently represented also in the English poetry, no doubt taken by the poets directly from the life, but perhaps also from pictures illustrating the life, of courtly folk. In the same book the illustration for the month of December shows a subject that appears also in that midwinter poem, *Sir Gawayne and the Grene Knight*—a boar hunt.

The boar's head of the Christmas or Yule feast is, of course, as prominent throughout the art as it is throughout the poetry of the Middle Ages. Lawrence Stone[1] draws attention to 'the dramatic and powerful head of a boar set over the tower doorway in the little Saxon church of Deerhurst in Gloucestershire'. Five cen-turies later (in the fifteenth) our versions of the Boar's Head Carol were written down. In the sculptures and wall-paintings that illustrate the seasons or the Labours of the Months, December is regularly represented by a peasant killing a pig with an axe, the domestic or farmyard equivalent of the midwinter boar hunt.

[1] Op. cit., Chap. III, p. 34.

There is a fifteenth-century Swiss tapestry[1] picture of 'wild men' and animals in a wood. The humans are unmistakably wearing animal skins which terminate at the ankles, wrists and necks; the 'wild man' is distinguished by a shaggy beard and a club.[2] Whether they are simply intended to represent savage inhabitants of the forest or, as seems more likely, performers in some ritual, they help the modern reader of the alliterative poems and romances to visualize, if not to understand, this strange subject of the 'wild man'.

§ 3

The medieval English sculptors and painters were, like the poets, working very largely with imagery and themes inherited from the pre-Christian past even when dedicated and devoted to the rendering, through the same imagery, of Christian religious subjects and symbolism. One of the ever-recurring and most pro-nounced features of the art, particularly of the sculpture, through-out several centuries, is a decorative wealth of flora and fauna, animal and half-animal, half-human forms, bipeds and quad-rupeds, entwined and interlocked, their own tails or limbs often forming the interlacing pattern, heads frequently peering from among interlacing foliage, twisting, turning, struggling, 'up-coiling and inveterately convolved'.[3] This feature can be traced right back through the sculpture of several centuries, without a break in continuity, to pre-Christian Scandinavian, Teutonic and Celtic art. These sometimes fantastic, sometimes realistic figures are frequently conceived as locked in deadly combat, human forms in combat with animal or bird forms or enveloped by coiling vegetation, animals in combat with animals, birds with birds, the biting beak, the gripping claw. Even the foliage interlacings are hardly restful but seem one continual movement. In the work of the sculptors in particular (to a lesser extent the painters) these

---

[1] Victoria and Albert Museum.

[2] Cf. the annual procession of masks and wild men in certain Swiss valleys to his day.

[3] Wordsworth, *Yew-trees.*

images are, in effect, disciplined, controlled, firmly held in place in highly decorative formal patterns which yet powerfully suggest a concentrated dynamic energy and movement. They are both highly stylized—bodies and limbs often elongated to form or to conform to the overruling pattern—and at the same time often astonishingly realistic as well as forceful.

Whatever the symbolic meanings—such as the struggle between Good and Evil—which in the later centuries were imposed on these often fantastic shapes, the power rising from beneath the level of consciousness remains. It does not help us much to say that images of coiling foliage or struggling or agonized bodies provided—at a certain early 'baroque' stage in a developing sculptural art—a rewarding subject, opportunities for displaying sculptural skill. We should once again still be confronted with the unanswered, perhaps unanswerable, question where these images came from in the first instance. But whether these images of combats were memories of the forest life and struggle of earlier pioneering men, or whether they were representations of the experiences of contemporary huntsmen or representations of ritual combats, they are for some reason peculiarly persistent. There is, for example, the recurrent image of the backward⁄turning stag involved with the clawing, biting dragon or of hero engaged with monster or, simply, knight with knight. As Stone remarks, the popularity of 'the theme of the human being struggling amid enveloping coils of foliage containing monstrous beasts is surely of more than purely stylistic significance'. This theme of contest and of physical combat, often of an unorthodox kind, is as pronounced in the alliterative poems and romances as it is in the art.

The English art of the thirteenth and fourteenth centuries—the sculpture, the wood⁄carvings (notably those on the misericords), the illuminated margins of MSS, the stained glass and the wall⁄painting—is particularly rich in 'babewyns' or grotesques: jesters, jugglers, contortionists, beasts, birds and fishes, animals behaving like humans or riding on the backs of other animals, goats playing musical instruments, composite monsters, the Signs of the Zodiac, the Seven Deadly Sins, satiric caricatures of humans each distorted to resemble the particular sin he indulges, faces that look like grotesque actors' masks (reproduced perhaps from those of the demons or Herods and Pilates of the Mystery Plays), and, frequently, the face among the oak-leaves with leaves sprouting from its mouth. By no means all of the 'babewyns' are hideous grotesques; many, on the contrary, seem to express a loveliness and gaiety of fancy, though the craftsman's fancy may be playing on a traditional subject, and though there *may* be an overruling intention of symbolism. Many of the subjects appear to come directly from the bestiaries and fables. But, as one traces the sculptures and paintings back to early Scandinavian, Anglo-Saxon and Celtic art, one can see in these natural or fantastic creatures, monsters and caricatures essentially a persistence, in the mind and visual imagination, of the imagery of the pre-Christian art long after the images have been given Christian moral and religious meanings and have even been incorporated into an elaborate Christian symbolic system or iconography. The marginal things, such as the 'babewyns', are most likely to have been, and most apparently are, survivals from the earlier art. A revealing paragraph in Lawrence's chapter about the cathedral in *The Rainbow* describes Anna as feeling that the grotesques suggest the 'many things that had been left out of the great concept of the church'. This element in the art is present also in the poetry as the 'wild men', monsters and related figures who, together with frequent congregations of forest beasts and birds, feature in the alliterative poems and romances, the demons of the Mystery Cycle, the Seven Deadly Sins and the satiric moral caricatures. Though themes and images in art may be 'explained' in terms of the evolution of technique—lines sprouting into foliage or bursting into animal shapes—they do come, the foliage and the animals, from human experience, from observation, and still relate to observed facts, otherwise they could have no meaning. Why otherwise did the lines assume these particular shapes and why did these shapes persist in the art of successive centuries? The ancient forest is still present in modern literature, though it may have become an interior one of the mind.

> . . . *how entangled he was,*
> *with ever-extending tendrils of inner event*

interlaced to patterns already, to strangling growth,
to forms that were chasing like beasts. How he gave himself—.

Loved.

Loved his innermost being, its wilderness, this
primeval forest within him on whose silent downfall
his heart stood, light-green.[1]

In his consideration of the sculpture throughout several centuries, Stone remarks on the persistence of pagan elements in an
art which is Christian, in which Christian meanings have become the predominant ones. He remarks, for example, of an
eleventh-century sculpture in Dorset: 'There is no surviving piece
of sculpture extant which better typifies the demonic element that
was still a latent influence in eleventh-century England than this
sinister totem image. Taken together with the dozens of fertility
carvings built into village churches, particularly in the West Midlands, in the late eleventh and early twelfth centuries (of which one
even represents a grotesque phallic parody of the Deerhurst angel)
it is not unreasonable to suggest that this carving is an expression
of a paganism that lingered on below the outward Christianity
of eleventh-century England.'[2] Speaking of some post-Conquest
subjects, he says: 'Commoner still are combats of animals or of
animals and men. Sometimes the scene can be explained as
representing the triumph of Christianity over the forces of evil,
but . . . many of the uncouth animals seem more like propitiatory
representations of pagan demons, a reversion both to the old
religion and to a persistent barbaric taste for savage dragons.'[3]
Passing to twelfth-century sculpture and referring particularly to
Canterbury Cathedral, he has this to say: 'Not a single one of the
themes chosen for illustration on the capitals bears the slightest
relation to any religious or moral purpose. Jugglers and contortionists, fabulous animals playing musical instruments, combat
scenes of monsters and dragons, such are the themes, pagan or
secular, that are illustrated. This is a feature that was to persist
throughout the twelfth century, for England never succumbed to the

---

[1] Rilke, *Duineser Elegien*, III, translated by Ruth Speirs.
[2] *Sculpture in Britain in the Middle Ages*, III, 37.   [3] Ibid., IV, 54.

orthodoxy of Christian iconography which imposed itself in such a large measure upon Continental art. A very high proportion of rural tympanum carvings in England continued to display scenes of fierce human and dragon combat rather than incidents from the Bible. Didactic, strictly Christian sculpture is in fact not very common in twelfth-century England, the bulk being purely decorative in purpose, and much of the rest concerned with scenes such as would find favour among a still latently pagan population.'[1] He quotes the famous protest of St. Bernard of Clairvaux (as translated by Coulton):[2] 'What profit is there in those ridiculous monsters, in that marvellous and deformed comeliness, that comely deformity? To what purpose are those unclean apes, those fierce lions, those monstrous centaurs, those half-men, those striped tigers, those fighting knights, those hunters winding their horns? Many bodies are there seen under one head, or again, many heads to a single body. Here is a four-footed beast with a serpent's tail; there a fish with a beast's head. . . . We are more tempted to read in the marble than in our service books and to spend the whole day in wondering at these things than in meditating the law of God. For God's sake, if men are not ashamed of these follies, why at least do they not shrink from the expense?' There could indeed be no clearer testimony that the inherited pagan imagery could by no means easily or completely be assimilated, as symbolism, into Christian conceptions and that there were Christian ascetics who felt it must be rejected altogether.

§ 4

The greater part of the sculptural and pictorial art of the Middle Ages is symbolical and not, or not simply, representation; it should therefore not surprise us if we have to take account of symbolism, sometimes more concealed than allegory, throughout the poetry. Stone speaks of the Northern peoples having been 'unaccustomed to representational art'. In the service of Christian religious and moral meanings, symbolism and allegory were the

[1] *Sculpture in Britain in the Middle Ages*, V, 57.   [2] Ibid., VII, 77.

peculiarly appropriate expressions. The combat, for example, readily became symbolical of the conflict between moral good and evil. Thus not only are the great religious subjects, the Annuncia/ tion, the Nativity, the Passion, the Resurrection, the Doom—the events celebrated in the feasts and ceremonies of the Christian year and in the Mystery Cycle—represented in paintings and sculp/ tures, but also many religious allegories and moralities such as those of *Les Trois Vifs et les Trois Morts*, The Seven Works of Mercy and the Seven Deadly Sins. Readers of *The Parlement of the Thre Ages* or the first episode of *The Awntyrs of Arthur* may well feel that there is a close relation between these poems and the Morality of *Les Trois Vifs*, as correctives of pride. For, as Tristram remarks of this Morality (the popularity of which in the fourteenth century may have been partly an effect of the Black Death), it is 'not, primarily, a warning that all must die, as it has often been interpreted, but one against Pride, the head and fountain of the Deadly Sins; it therefore includes by inference an insistence upon the virtue of Humility, Pride's opposite or remedy'.[1] The three living men who are confronted by the three corpses are usually hunting kings. The Seven Deadly Sins and their opposite, the Seven Works of Mercy, often appear as the fruit of a Tree or within a Wheel. But these ancient symbols mean very different things in the various wall/paintings and sculptures. There is the Wheel of Fortune, the Wheel of Heaven and its music, the Wheel of Life or of the Seven Ages of Man, the Wheel of the Senses, and so on. The Tree is a symbol even more rich and multifarious in meaning; and it, too, figures both in the art and in the poetry, notably in *Piers Plowman* (B/text, Passus XVI)[2] and in the religious lyrics. After noting that in certain wall/paintings the Tree of the Virtues is Christ and that the boughs are, in one sense, the virtues and, in another, all the elect; that it is also in one of its aspects the Tree of Life and again—an obvious association—the Tree of Jesse; that the boughs also symbolize the Seven Beatitudes,

---

[1] *English Wall/Painting of the Fourteenth Century*, V, 'The Allegories and Moralities'.

[2] In this Passus grave religious and moral meanings are closely associated with familiar experience of English orchards, the troubles that afflict apple/trees and the struggles involved in the care of them.

Tristram concludes:[1] 'In fact, every part of the Tree, even the leaves and fruit, incorporates a double or triple symbolism. The fruit, by contrast with the Tree of Evil, consists in The Seven Corporal Works of Mercy.' Tristram goes on to consider 'the Tree of the Sins, the contrasted counterpart of the Tree of Virtue'; he says: 'Some features of the Tree of Evil, just as those of the Tree of Jesse, seem to have been inspired by Seth's vision of a Tree of Paradise in the Legend of the Cross; for the roots of the last were in Hell, entwined with the body of Cain, and the Tree of Evil usually rises from the gaping jaws of Leviathan. . . . The figure of Satan often forms the trunk.' It need hardly be added that the Tree of Evil is a frequent feature also in the sculptures and wood-carvings, sometimes with animals or birds pecking at the fruit. Evidence that the holly and the ivy of the Holly and the Ivy Carols were sometimes regarded as evil (presumably because associated with what had been pagan rites) is provided by a fact which Tristram notes: 'As well as the fruit, there are leaves, often so conventionalized in treatment as to be unrecognizable but now and then identifiable as those of the holly and the ivy.'

It is clearly unwise for us to be dogmatic as to what any one symbol means, whether in the painting, the sculpture or the poetry. The same image may mean different things in different contexts, and it may mean several things at one and the same time in the same context. Our interpretation must take account always of the particular context, for its particular meaning at any one time must finally depend upon that. An image was evidently always a potential symbol to the medieval mind. What the modern reader can expect, therefore, is often to find that an image in the poetry, as in the art, is principally a symbol rather than simply a representation or copy. Further, as Stone notes,[2] 'comprehension has been made yet more difficult by the habit of the English romanesque artist[3] of reverting to his barbaric traditions and mixing with his esoteric Christian symbolism a range of subjects of animal combat or pure fantasy'. The creative energy, the fertile inventiveness particularly of the sculptors and wood-carvers, has not been entirely

---

[1] Op. cit., V.   [2] *Sculpture in Britain in the Middle Ages*, VII, 92.
[3] And, we might add, many of his fourteenth-century successors.

absorbed by the conscious religious intention—and the same may be said of the poets.

§ 5

'A strong sense of dynamism and of movement, poses and ges' tures abrupt and often distorted' is, according to Stone, more characteristic of English medieval sculpture than of Continental. Whether this is so or not, the same characteristic is to some extent to be observed in the English wall-paintings. The many lovely and gay fourteenth-century wall-paintings of dancing angels, whether or not modelled on or at least reminiscent of actual 'carollers', wonderfully suggest the movement of the dance and may well seem to the modern reader of the carols their linear equivalents. One of the features which the alliterative poetry, in its different medium, has in common with the sculpture and wall' painting is a strong suggestion of physical movement and action, conveyed in the case of the poetry by means of its rhythm and imagery. Related to this power of expressing movement and suggesting actions that are frequently violent there is, in the sculpture particularly, a tendency to distortion and caricature and occasionally to satire and burlesque in the work of these medieval English predecessors of Hogarth and Rowlandson. The paintings of Bruegel and Bosch, too, may well strike one as pictorial equivalents for some of the characters and episodes in *Piers Plow' man*. Hell with its scowling, grimacing devils and the Sins or types of wicked men and women (the glutton with his protuberant belly, the drunkard vomiting into the bowl, the wrestlers who signify anger), bulk large in English medieval art, perhaps because these subjects afforded greater opportunity for the kind of thing that it could do well. In the literature and the drama the same tendency shows itself in the character types and caricatures, the devils, the Herods and Pilates, the Seven Deadly Sins and types related (as are Winner and Waster) to the Sins. But in the art this dynamism is disciplined, concentrated or reorganized into formal patterns. A corresponding tendency, occasionally triumphant, shows itself in the poetry—in the stylization and formal arrange' ment of *Winnere and Wastoure* and *The Parlement of the Thre Ages* and in the structural balance of *Sir Gawayne and the Grene Knight* and, generally, throughout the alliterative poetry in the combination of clarity with vigour and in the bold handling of large masses.

VII
CONCLUSION

VII. CONCLUSION

§ I

If we take the whole of this medieval English poetry together, what does its meaning amount to? What does it all mean? The only answer is that it means nothing less than *all* that it does or is in every detail; its meaning in the fullest sense is being given only in the actual process of reading the poetry. But we may, perhaps, legitimately ask what image of human life the poetry leaves most persistently with the mind of one who has been perusing it. Among the images which haunted the medieval mind, if we may judge from the literature, two of the most persistent were the image of human life in its earthly state as a castle besieged and that other, perhaps still more persistent image of it as a journey or pilgrimage.

It is not difficult to see a correspondence between the monk behind the walls of his monastery, outside of which was 'the wilderness of this world' full of hostile powers, and the knight besieged in his castle. The religious and moral allegorists saw a further correspondence, that of the soul besieged by its enemies, the World, the Flesh and the Devil.[1]

But more frequent, at least in the poetry with which this book has been concerned, is the image of life as a journey or pilgrimage —in the romances frequently a quest. Sometimes the image is of a procession of folk, more often the journey is a solitary one. The idea of having lost the way in a wilderness, waste or wood is frequent, and is common to the romances and to the allegories of the soul's progress, as in the opening of the *Divine Comedy* itself. In romance after romance a knight rides on a solitary journey

[1] Cf. *Piers Plowman*, Passus IX (B-text).

through a forest or waste, engaged in a quest, seeking to find someone or something that is lost. In the wilderness which he traverses the knight is surrounded by perils, many of which are not at the time to be understood, and has to contend with hostile powers, antagonists who appear unexpectedly, who assume various shapes and disguises and are often monstrous or magical. The romances are not themselves allegories. But the audiences for the medieval allegories and the romances were contemporaneous and must often have consisted of the same persons. In any case, these journeys and quests of the romances may reasonably be taken by the reader as essentially, though not ostensibly, a kind of allegory of human life. There is surely a correspondence between them and the religious and moral allegories in which the soul journeys through the world—its earthly condition—a region of deceiving appearances, in which things and people are often not what they seem, in which it is hard to distinguish the true from the false, a region of perils and enchantments.

> *In the middle, not only in the middle of the way*
> *But all the way, in a dark wood, in a bramble,*
> *On the edge of a grimpen, where is no secure foothold,*
> *And menaced by monsters, fancy lights,*
> *Risking enchantment.*[1]

This, or something like this, appears not to be an uncommon experience and such as may be expressed in the poetry of any age. It may suddenly flash upon one that this apparently so familiar, accustomed world is a strange, unexplained place. One is liable at any moment to be subject to

> *Fallings from us, vanishings;*
> *Blank misgivings of a Creature*
> *Moving about in worlds not realised.*[2]

In the poet's recollection, the boy in Book I of the *Prelude* has such an experience.

> *. . . for many days, my brain*
> *Worked with a dim and undetermined sense*

[1] T. S. Eliot, *East Coker.*   [2] Wordsworth, *Ode on Intimations of Immortality.*

Conclusion

Of unknown modes of being; o'er my thoughts
There hung a darkness, call it solitude
Or blank desertion. No familiar shapes
Remained, no pleasant images of trees,
Of sea or sky, no colours of green fields;
But huge and mighty forms, that do not live
Like living men, moved slowly through the mind
By day, and were a trouble to my dreams.

But this sense of being a stranger is counterbalanced, in Words-worth's poetry, by its opposite—a sense of belonging, of being connected, of being planted in the universe.

No outcast he, bewildered and depressed:
Along his infant veins are interfused
The gravitation and the filial bond
Of nature that connect him with the world.[1]

I think we find the equivalent of this latter feeling also, the medieval equivalent of it, deeply present in medieval English poetry.

§ 2

It may not have been accidental that the friars and the Arthurian romances—the earliest Arthurian romances we have being those of Chrétien de Troyes—made their appearance in history at about the same time (*c.* 1200). The itinerant knight of the romances and the itinerant friar represent a not dissimilar ideal of life in the world—an ideal which, if not entirely new, seems at any rate to have gathered renewed power about this time. This is one among the many interesting suggestions in R. W. Southern's *The Making of the Middle Ages*[2] where the changes in the outlook of Europe are described. The change from the static life of the monk, in a state of siege behind his monastery walls, to the war of movement of the friars, a change from the defensive to the offensive and from a local life, life in one place, to a journeying through the world—still,

[1] *Prelude*, Book II.   [2] Chap. V, 'From Epic to Romance'.

however, conceived as largely a hostile and perilous place for the soul—was indeed a spectacular one. The emergence of the orders of friars may be regarded as one of the signs (along with the crusades and pilgrimages, often to far-distant shrines) of that increasing restlessness of spirit which has been noted as characteristic of the Middle Ages as they ran their course. It may not be fanciful to see a connexion between the wanderings and journeyings of the crusading knights, the friars and the pilgrims and those of the knights in the romances. The latter may well be significant of more than a taste for tales of adventure. The makers of the romances and the alliterative poems no doubt inherited their tales of journeyings and voyagings from earlier times. But the new emphasis on journeyings, the renewed popularity of such tales associates them perhaps with a changed attitude to life. These medieval poets have inherited also from the heroic poetry a conception of the world as a battleground, a place of contention and testing, of combats and flytings, strife and debate. This conception also assumed a new, more inward meaning in the moral allegories which represent a war in the soul, as well as throughout the world, between good and evil.

§ 3

But, side by side with this melancholy, or bracing, conception of earthly life as a journeying and a contending, there is in medieval English poetry a gladder or (shall we say) a merrier conception of life on earth—this 'merry middle-earth'. In *Sir Gawayne and the Grene Knight* both attitudes or visions are present and to some extent reconciled. But, throughout a great part of medieval English poetry as well as in this poem,[1] there is expressed a glad sense of man as not altogether forlorn in this earth and as having a place in the scheme of the universe. At least, it is alternately a sad and a merry thing that man's earthly life forms part of the natural pattern or rhythm, shares in the alternation of day and night, in the revolution of the year, winter and spring, sowing-time and harvest,

[1] Cf. also the passages on Nature and its wonders in Passus XI and XII of *Piers Plowman* (B-text).

in the cycle of youth and age, death and birth, destruction and renewal. At the basis of much of the poetry there is a sense of the unity, the indivisibility of the whole diversity of things and creatures, and of an intimate connexion between them and man. The nearest and the farthest things—from the influences and potencies of the stars, the sun and moon, rainfall, to the properties and qualities of the plants at his feet—are felt to bear directly on his life. At his happiest, if not also perhaps his clearest, the medieval poet, as medieval man, feels this. He is sustained by a sense of the universe—the king of which *is* his friend—and of a relation be-tween each particular in the divinely made whole. Earth and water and fire, birds, beasts and fishes, trees, flowers, crops and fruits are conceived to be a single divine creation, interfused and interconnected. Yet there are times when it seems that all earthly things are appearance only and that reality is not here but some-where behind and beyond this shadowy realm of temporal appearance. There are other moments, however, when it seems that appearance itself is the closest we can come to reality, is itself a *degree* of reality or a stage towards it—continuous with an ultimate or divine reality—and that the natural is after all planted in the supernatural, the temporal in the eternal, that the here and now blossoms out of ultimate reality or divinity.

'The old Church knew that life is here our portion, to be lived, to be lived in fulfilment. The stern rule of Benedict, the wild flights of Francis of Assisi, these were coruscations in the steady heaven of the Church. The rhythm of life itself was preserved by the Church hour by hour, day by day, season by season, year by year, epoch by epoch, down among the people, and the wild coruscations were accommodated to this permanent rhythm. We feel it, in the south, in the country, when we hear the jangle of the bells at dawn, at noon, at sunset, marking the hours with the sound of mass or prayers. It is the rhythm of the daily sun. We feel it in the festivals, the processions, Christmas, the Three Kings, Easter, Pentecost, St. John's Day, All Saints, All Souls. This is the wheeling of the year, the movement of the sun through solstice and equinox, the coming of the seasons, the going of the seasons. And it is the inward rhythm of man and woman, too, the sadness of Lent, the delight of Easter, the wonder of Pentecost, the fires of St. John, the candles on the graves of All Souls, the lit-up tree of Christmas . . .

'The Early Christians tried to kill the old pagan rhythm of cosmic ritual, and to some extent succeeded. They killed the planets and the zodiac, perhaps because astrology had already become debased to fortune-telling. They wanted to kill the festivals of the year. But the Church, which knows that man doth not live by man alone, but by the sun and moon and earth in their revolutions, restored the sacred days and feasts almost as the pagans had them, and the Christian peasants went on very much as the pagan peasants had gone, with the sunrise pause for worship, and the sunset, and noon, the three great daily moments of the sun: then the new holy-day, one in the ancient seven-cycle: then Easter and the dying and rising of God, Pentecost, Midsummer Fire, the November dead and the spirits of the grave, then Christmas, then Three Kings. For centuries the mass of people lived in this rhythm, under the Church. . . . Now you have a poor, blind, disconnected people with nothing but politics and bank-holidays to satisfy the eternal human need of living in ritual adjustment to the cosmos in its revolutions, in eternal submission to the greater laws. . . . Vitally, the human race is dying. It is like a great up-rooted tree, with its roots in the air. We must plant ourselves again in the universe.'[1]

[1] D. H. Lawrence, *Apropos of Lady Chatterley's Lover.*

INDEX

Index

Index

Index